CREATING THE NORTH AMERICAN LANDSCAPE

Consulting Editors

Gregory Conniff

Bonnie Loyd

David Schuyler

The City Beautiful Movement

The City Beautiful Movement

WILLIAM H. WILSON

The Johns Hopkins University Press
Baltimore and London

This book has been brought to publication with the generous assistance of the National Endowment for the Humanities.

48496

The Johns Hopkins University Press, 701 West 40th Street, Baltimore, Maryland 21211
The Johns Hopkins Press Ltd., London

The paper used in this publication meets the minimum requirements of American National Standard for Information Sciences—Permanence of Paper for Printed Library Materials, ANSI Z39.48-1984.

Library of Congress Cataloging-in-Publication Data

Wilson, William H. (William Henry), 1935–
    The City Beautiful movement / William H. Wilson
        p.   cm.   — (Creating the North American landscape)
    Bibliography: p.
    Includes index.
    ISBN 0-8018-3758-8 (alk. paper)
    1. Urban beautification—United States—History—20th century. 2. City planning—United States—History—20th century. I. Title. II. Series.
HT164.U6W55 1989
307.1'2'0973—dc19   88-28244
                                                                            CIP

For Katharine Cousley Lehr

and

To the memory of James Wesley Lehr

Contents

Introduction   1

PART I. ORIGINS AND IDEOLOGY

  1. Frederick Law Olmsted and the City Beautiful
     Movement   9

  2. Municipal Improvement and Beautifying the
     Entire Community   35

  3. The Columbian Exposition and the City Beautiful
     Movement   53

  4. The Ideology and Aesthetics of the City
     Beautiful Movement   75

PART II. THE EARLY CITY BEAUTIFUL

  5. The Struggle for an Urban Park and Boulevard System
     in Kansas City   99

  6. An Elite Campaign for Beauty and Utility in
     Harrisburg   126

  7. John C. Olmsted's Plan for Seattle   147

  8. Bossism as Civic Idealism, Planning, and Reform
     in Denver   168

PART III. THE LATER CITY BEAUTIFUL

  9. The Kansas City UnionStation and the City
     Beautiful Ideal   193

  10. The Collapse of the Civic Center Dream in Seattle   213

11. The Realization of the Civic Center Ideal in Denver   234

12. The Survival of the City Beautiful Technique in Dallas   254

PART IV. THE NATIONAL LEVEL

13. The Glory, Destruction, and Meaning of the City
    Beautiful Movement   281

      Notes   307

      Note on Sources   351

      Acknowledgments   353

      Index   357

The City Beautiful Movement

Introduction

The heyday of the City Beautiful movement, from about 1900 to 1910, saw middle- and upper-middle-class Americans attempt to refashion their cities into beautiful, functional entities. Their effort involved a cultural agenda, a middle-class environmentalism, and aesthetics expressed as beauty, order, system, and harmony. The ideal found physical realization in urban design. Public and semipublic buildings, civic centers, park and boulevard systems, or extensions and embellishments of them, were the tokens of the improved environment. So were ordinary street improvements, including good paving, attractive furniture such as lampposts, and carefully selected and maintained trees. The goal beyond the tangibles was to influence the heart, mind, and purse of the citizen. Physical change and institutional reformation would persuade urban dwellers to become more imbued with civic patriotism and better disposed toward community needs. Beautiful surroundings would enhance worker productivity and urban economics.

In the broadest sense, then, the City Beautiful movement was a political movement, for it demanded a reorientation of public thought and action toward urban beauty. The environmental reorganization necessary to the City Beautiful and its immediate forebears required an altered political structure, including state enabling legislation, new public institutions such as park boards, and grants of power to private entities to build railroad stations and other semipublic buildings. The reorganized urban politics was remarkably flexible, encompassing both new or vitalized administrative agencies and expanded popular participation. Improvements of the City Beautiful type often required voter approval through bond issues, election campaigns, or other devices of participatory politics. The movement involved, too, a politics of accommodation between the expert planning professional and the enlightened citizens on the board or commission that set the basic planning goals and oversaw their construction. The political dimension of the City Beautiful went beyond structure and process to an element underlying much of the surface change: citizen agitation and activism on behalf of beautification.

Within its large political context, the City Beautiful movement was, of course, a planning movement. Comprehensive planning was introduced to cities by Olmstedian landscape architecture, a City Beautiful antecedent. Comprehensive planning considered the city as a whole, sought to direct its often almost violent growth, dealt with its major problems as the activist middle class defined them, and tempered solutions to the expressed or perceived needs of particular neighborhoods. After 1900 the City Beautiful retained some diversity of thought and practice, but the movement's leadership asked citizens to think of each victory for beautification as an incremental gain for a broadly conceived vision. Thus an embowered dooryard, a restrained and tidy billboard, monumental public buildings surrounding a plaza, all were valuable for themselves and as contributions to the ensemble of urban beauty.

From such examples of beauty and utility the City Beautiful movement edged into more functional concerns such as sewerage and water supply, refuse collection, active recreation, and public transportation. But usually not too far. Planners grounded in landscape architecture and architecture, and citizen activists, mentioned those issues, often in connection with improved designs for items such as trash receptacles or trolley poles. The need for specialized expertise in these areas limited their effectiveness, however. The distinction by no means precluded parallel political campaigns for a wide range of functional-aesthetic improvements.

So the movement continued through the first decade of the twentieth century. From 1909 architects, engineers, housing experts, and city planners with a more rigorously defined "city practical" agenda attacked the City Beautiful's supposedly superficial, costly concern for urban embellishment. They were mistaken, mostly, but they largely succeeded in discrediting the movement's activity and ideals, for it was true that the City Beautiful movement failed to realize all of its aspirations. Many sections of American cities remained ugly and squalid. Worse, the City Beautiful's hoped for control and direction of rampant urban growth never materialized. These shortcomings were well cataloged. Less often remarked were the movement's successes: emerald parks, sinuous parkways, graceful trees flanking parked boulevards, stately public buildings of surpassing workmanship and decoration, magnificent monuments, and even a few civic centers.[1]

All these public works were, and are, important because they were the physical expression of an ideal, because they functioned in a limited way as their proponents claimed that they would, and because they still provide recreation, relaxation, and repose. The public buildings symbolized a coherent architecture, an ideal comprehended if not always achieved.

This book focuses on the growth of the City Beautiful idea and its development into a cultural, aesthetic, political, and environmental movement. Some recent studies of urban politics and planning reverse this emphasis, locating the City Beautiful in the context of municipal politics. Their approach is a welcome advance over earlier political studies that ignored the

City Beautiful, save for repeating an occasional cliché about its ineffectiveness. It is a gratifying rejection of the assumption of planning historians that the City Beautiful was a species of art history unconnected with politics or, at least, with any effective politics.

The newer approach is better, but it is not the entire answer, for placing the City Beautiful in a political context risks making the movement a prisoner of three invalid assumptions. The first is that the City Beautiful was merely a planning movement. The second is that the movement was simply another Progressive Era reform like restructuring city government, expanding the urban bureaucracy to include a health department and inspection services, or crusading for the short ballot. The third assumption is that the planning theme may be subordinated to what is known about the politics of, usually, one case study city. In fact, City Beautiful activity, though complementing other reforms, possessed its own ideology, purpose, and mode of operation. It partook of political and bureaucratic reform but was separate from both, a reality the strictly political approach obscures. Subordinating the City Beautiful to politics devalues its distinctiveness and encourages the description of city plans and planning instead of their analysis. The concentration on urban politics tells us more about a subject on which we are relatively well informed but throws little light on the City Beautiful movement, about which we know much less. This study keeps the focus on the varied City Beautiful activities, with the hope of illuminating them in fresh ways on both local and national levels.

Although histories of urban planning have not ignored the City Beautiful movement, traditional planning history has well-established heroes and villains, winners and losers, patrons and audience. The writers and readers of planning history are, mostly, the professional and intellectual heirs of the city practical, the city scientific, and the city functional. The city practical long ago prevailed over the City Beautiful in a fight that was less over two distinct approaches to planning—the aesthetic and the practical—and more about vocational and professional dominance, appeals to the taxpayer's pocketbook, and bureaucratic control. To oversimplify somewhat, the architects, engineers, and others fighting for the city practical beat the landscape architects and architects representing the City Beautiful. And in planning no less than in other activities, history belongs to the winners. The city practical hung on the City Beautiful the labels aesthetics-obsessed, socially primitive, and inutilitarian, and made them stick. The upshot is that even treatments sympathetic to the City Beautiful are infected by the city practical. In these accounts the City Beautiful makes its modest contributions before yielding to a more advanced, higher, or more inclusive planning mode.[2]

The results of these two approaches, the planning, with its overtones of art criticism, and the political, with its inclusion of the City Beautiful in the progressive homogeneity, are remarkably similar. Reviews of Daniel H. Burnham's plan for San Francisco, and of the city's Civic Center, from the perspectives of planning, art criticism, and politics reinforce a conclusion drawn from each and all. It is that Burnham's plan represented a vision that if realized, would have improved San Francisco in some respects but on the whole it is just as well that such an expensive, disruptive plan was ignored in the city's rapid rebuilding from the 1906 earthquake and fire. Thomas S. Hines, Burnham's most recent biographer, refutes this conclusion.

Hines claimed too much for Burnham, however, when he awarded his subject the paternity of the City Beautiful movement. A similar assertion has been advanced on behalf of Charles Mulford Robinson, the planner-publicist. Both Burnham and Robinson were distinguished men who greatly enriched the City Beautiful, but neither founded the diverse, complex movement. Both men drew outstanding plans, but neither achieved much City Beautiful construction through the urban political process.[3]

Besides being a revisionist planning history in which several planners and politicians share the stage, this book advances a set of arguments about the City Beautiful movement. The movement's concerns for converting ugliness to beauty and for controlling and enhancing economic and physical growth were compelling. Equally powerful were its desires for comprehensiveness, utility, and functionalism. Its partisans upheld expertise and interclass obligation in an atmosphere of optimism about the future of the American city. They were committed environmentalists, but to make them advocates of social control through design or seekers after mere order is unfair. The City Beautiful movement was too hopeful, too uplifting to be very cynical or manipulative. Aesthetically, it blended naturalistic and classic forms, an important European legacy. The City Beautiful architectural style was almost always neoclassic, a circumstance productive of much fatuous criticism, founded on the alleged artificiality, pomposity, and reactionary nature of neoclassicism. The neoclassic was in fact an effective design, whether standing by itself or enhanced by naturalistic landscaping.

Beyond all these considerations is the daunting reality of the City Beautiful movement. It has roots in the midnineteenth century, yet its influence extends into the late twentieth. It was a nationwide movement led by prominent planners and lay organizations, yet scores of cities witnessed highly individual battles over City Beautiful issues. Obviously a careful examination of a movement with hundreds of local examples is beyond the strength of an author, not to mention the patience of a reader. The solution is a mix of nationally focused definitive chapters and case studies illustrating the issues involved in the movement.

The case studies range in time from a late-nineteenth century, premovement campaign for an Olmstedian park and boulevard system to efforts in the second decade of the twentieth, years of the movement's decline. The choice of case-study cities rests upon the illustrative value of each; thus the availability of letters and other papers written by planners and citizen activists was critical. Because success is more pleasant to write and read about, a chosen city had to exhibit at least the partial realization of City Beautiful goals. And there was little point in replicating studies already undertaken.

The last two considerations ruled out such places as New York, much examined and an example of, at best, limited success. There the City Beautiful was confined to magnificent isolated artifacts such as the now-demolished Pennsylvania Station. The considerations required the exclusion of Washington, D.C., Chicago, and San Francisco, cities already extensively studied, if not precisely from the perspective presented here. The autocratic government of Washington decreed its physical transformation; thus the process bore little or no relation to the usual City Beautiful politics. The national chapters do of course consider Chicago, Washington, and other cities important from the national perspective.

The cities that most often met the criteria for case study were of two types. One group consisted of smaller cities outside the South, places not too large to inhibit comprehensive replanning. Harrisburg, Pennsylvania, is the example from this group. The other selections are from among the relatively young, western, rapidly growing but still plastic cities having significant commercial and transportation activity. They are Denver, Seattle, Dallas, and Kansas City.

The book is divided into four sections. The first examines the movement's origins in the late nineteenth century to its consolidation at the dawn of the twentieth. The first chapter pays particular attention to Frederick Law Olmsted, whose thought and example underlay much of the City Beautiful. Examination of the movement's municipal improvement and civic design origins follows. Chapter 4 analyzes the ideology and aesthetics of the emergent City Beautiful. The second section sees the movement through the lenses of four cities: Kansas City, where a successful park and boulevard movement utilized an ideology, rhetoric, and technique absorbed wholesale into the City Beautiful; Harrisburg, where the business elite pushed through a City Beautiful program combining aesthetic and utilitarian elements; Seattle, where John C. Olmsted designed and advised on the construction of a traditional park and boulevard system for a western port city; and Denver, where a boss politician sensitive to civic needs produced magnificent City Beautiful improvements.

The third section is devoted to the later City Beautiful. It begins with an analysis of Kansas City's reorganization of its rail traffic and achievement of a union station, an attractive complement to its park and boulevard system. Chapter 10 discusses Seattle, where the City Beautiful was repudiated when the Bogue plan failed at the polls. The plan was expensive and primitive by the standards of housing reformers, settlement house workers, and socialists. It was not, however, defeated for those reasons, although they often are cited as explanations for the failure of the City Beautiful. Neither Kansas City nor Seattle secured a civic center, but Denver's civic center movement triumphed. In Dallas, planning began in the late City Beautiful era and continued with loss of purpose but with remarkable consistency of technique into the 1940s.

The fourth section returns to the national level to examine the fading City Beautiful and assess the movement's contributions. All together this book is an analysis and appreciation of the principles, the conflicts, and the achievements of the City Beautiful movement. The men and women of the movement based their dreams, not on escapist alternatives to the city, but on urban reality. They took the world as found and tried to make it better. Sometimes their aspirations were frustrated, but they succeeded well enough to allow their heirs to go on living and dreaming.

I ◆

Origins and Ideology

1 ◆ Frederick Law Olmsted and the City Beautiful Movement

FREDERICK LAW OLMSTED AND THE ANTECEDENTS OF THE CITY BEAUTIFUL MOVEMENT

The taproot of the City Beautiful movement lies in nineteenth-century landscape architecture, personified by Frederick Law Olmsted. Some historians of urban design and planning argue the opposite, that Olmsted and his fellow landscape architects created natural, humane environments in contrast to the overblown formalism and fake grandeur of City Beautiful. That interpretation rests upon an exaggeration of differences in design rather than on an examination of similarities of approach.

The search for differences hinges on certain presumptions. Olmsted has been elevated to secular sainthood in the planning pantheon, where he deserves to be. Olmsted, in a word, was good. Olmsted's successor chronologically, the City Beautiful movement, was not exactly bad but was a much less effective response to American urban problems. When Americans abandoned the City Beautiful, they embraced the city practical, and what is more American, or better, than practicality? Although most writers do not state things so baldly, they do exalt Olmstedian constructions and the city practical over that less fortunate interlude, the City Beautiful. One of their techniques for reinforcing their positive assessment of Olmsted is to emphasize his differences with the City Beautiful.[1]

The great landscape architect was emphatically not a City Beautiful figure. Although he lived into the City Beautiful era, he existed by then in a twilight world of confused old age. Furthermore, he opposed City Beautiful design insofar as he understood it, which was not very far. He did not accept the progressive values—for example, a belief in urban plasticity—that underlay the City Beautiful movement. Vital points of continuity nevertheless existed between the movement and Olmstedian thought and practice.

The concentration on Olmsted, Olympian figure that he was, is not intended to slight other landscape designers, including Andrew Jackson Downing, Horace W. S. Cleveland, Charles Eliot, and Olmsted's erstwhile partner

Calvert Vaux.[2] The adjective *Olmstedian* is intended to embrace ideas and activities not exclusively Olmsted's. Nor is what follows merely another biographical summary of Olmsted or a review of all the aspects of what David Schuyler has termed the "ideology of the park movement."[3] Concentration on one powerful figure is the most direct and simplest way to present the nineteenth century's cultural and intellectual antecedents of the City Beautiful movement. The following excursions into nineteenth-century cultural and intellectual life, Olmsted biography, and influences on Olmsted are intended to demonstrate Olmsted's impact. They are the foundation of an explanation of how Olmsted came to contribute to the City Beautiful and what he contributed, as well as what he and the Olmstedian approach did not contribute.

Olmsted made three fundamental contributions to the City Beautiful movement. First, he moved from the designing of single, although multifunctional, parks to the planning of comprehensive, multiple-purpose park and boulevard systems. Olmsted's systems became increasingly varied internally, while they interacted with the city's inhabitants and its other systems.

While he was developing the park and boulevard system, the design mainstay of the City Beautiful, Olmsted was also formulating part of the movement's ideology. He argued that parks (and by later extension, all aesthetic improvements) raised surrounding land values, contributing to private enterprise and returning their costs through increased municipal real estate taxation. More fundamental to him, however, were the restorative, recreative influences of natural landscape on city-bound people. The park was a magnet for all urbanites and a benign instrument of class reconciliation and democratization. Olmsted's conception of the landscape park antedated the organicism and environmentalism of the City Beautiful era, but his conclusions were quite congenial to City Beautiful enthusiasts. They would replace his rationales with their own, yet their justifications would undergird the very same Olmstedian arguments.

Olmsted's third contribution to the City Beautiful was the flourishing consulting practice he developed and bequeathed to his son and stepson. The practice of hiring an outside consultant to solve urban problems preceded Olmsted, the City Beautiful movement, and the Progressive Era's enthusiasm for the expert. Later consulting landscape architects nevertheless depended upon the tradition Olmsted established for their profession. The consultant's relationship with a city or with the economic and cultural elites who had commissioned his work often ended with the submission of a plan and the tendering of a fee. Less frequently the consulting relationship continued, with the designer paid a retainer from a park board or similar body. The experts attached to city engineers' offices eventually undermined this Olmstedian legacy, but it dominated the era of the City Beautiful.

The man who bequeathed so much to the City Beautiful movement was born on 26 April 1822 in Hartford, Connecticut. His well-to-do, indulgent father underwrote a lengthy, diverse, yet ultimately apposite career. Not until 1857 did he discover his eventual life's work and gain some measure of financial independence. In that year he became superintendent of New York's Central Park and in 1858 submitted, with Calvert Vaux, the winning design for the park's development. With the outbreak of the Civil War, he became secretary of the U.S. Sanitary Commission, but he then quit the commission to become the resident manager of the Mariposa Mining Company in California. The Central Park commissioners and Vaux lured him back to Central Park in late 1865. From then on, Olmsted settled into his career, first in partnership with Vaux and then under a variety of office arrangements. In 1877 he was removed for the last time from his job of landscape architect at Central Park and became a professional consultant. In 1881 he left New York for the Boston suburb of Brookline and remained at the head of his firm until he lost his mental lucidity in 1895. He died in 1903. Throughout, Olmsted remained a man of extraordinary ambition, with a keen intellect less original than it was absorptive and integrative.

The influences on Olmsted are so transparently evident because they are always seen in the light of his ultimate career choice. Yet it is possible, without dropping through the post hoc trap, to examine the components of Olmsted's integrative intellect irrespective of his pursuit of landscape architecture. Those elements were secularization, urbanization, the despoliation of the natural landscape, and the special appreciation for landscape that Olmsted received from his family, contacts, and experiences. The impact of each element save the last was becoming obvious to thoughtful people, and the effects became more pronounced as the nineteenth century advanced.

Olmsted accepted the secularizing world, but not to the point of rejecting all Christian thought. His was a nonsectarian ethical Protestantism emphasizing duty, obligation, and the piety of good work. Conscientious social effort, Olmsted believed, would achieve the redemption of humanity on earth. His secular vision was of a perfect democracy, with the poor and deprived raised to a cultural level of gentility and refined comprehension. "There's a great *work* wants doing in this our generation, Charley, let us off jacket and go about it," he wrote when he was twenty-five and still searching for vocational expression. The object of his exhortation, his close friend Charles Loring Brace, hardly needed the advice. Brace would found, in 1853, the New York Children's Aid Society, designed to rescue the young from their harsh, depersonalizing urban slum environment. Eventually Olmsted would find an outlet for his social consciousness in landscape architecture.[4]

After secularization, urbanization influenced Olmsted, and not only because he sought opportunity in New York. Urbanization was a complex process, but it certainly included the expansion and severe congestion of America's urban centers. Epidemics rioted through these densely compacted places without halting their galloping growth. Their crowding, noise, and stench contrasted with the spacious suburbs and farms beyond, where nature had been subdued in the service of humanity but had not yet given way to artificial constructions.[5]

Farm abandonment, rural depopulation, and the relative decline of secondary centers such as Olmsted's Hartford were also consequences of urbanization. The deterioration of rural-village life by westering or a move cityward was especially noticeable in New England. Olmsted came to blame urbanization for the destruction of community values expressed in such traits as mutual regard and spontaneous assistance to the afflicted. He was aware of the American tradition of veneration of rural life and concern about any threat to it. Urban expansion and rural contraction were, to him, portents of trouble for American civilization.[6]

Concurrently with the increase in secularization and urbanization, Olmsted witnessed the destruction or the radical alteration of large areas of natural landscape. This experience reinforced his skepticism about the advantages of urbanization, because the phenomenon was both a direct and an indirect cause of the destruction of the natural landscape. Urbanization's accompanying industrialization and commercialization occupied increasing space within, and on the periphery of, large cities. The resulting death of attractive natural areas in and near cities had frightening social consequences because, Olmsted believed, spaciousness and naturalness fostered the caring gregariousness of the village community. In 1853 he argued for public maintenance "at points so frequent and convenient that they would exert an elevating influence upon all the people, public parks and gardens, galleries of art and instruction in art, music, athletic sports and healthful recreations, and other means of cultivating taste and lessening that excessive materialism of purpose in which we are, as a people so cursedly absorbed." If parks and other public areas were not provided, Olmsted warned, "the employment of simple and sensible social life in our community, seems likely to be entirely destroyed."[7]

Industrialization and urbanization were also invading some rural-village areas of the sort familiar to Olmsted during his childhood. The industrialization and urbanization of the river falls areas around Boston supply an example. Thomas Bender has analyzed the transition of Lowell, Massachusetts, from an agricultural settlement, to a veritable factory set in a garden, to a big city with its panoply of urban problems, including pauperism and class divisions. During this transition Lowell's relationship with the surrounding countryside underwent a radical transformation. The easy relation of village and farm gave way to a reciprocity typified by the temporary residence in Lowell of young female mill hands from nearby farms. They and other Lowellians often traveled to the farmlands to visit family or friends or to get away from the town. By the depression of 1837 Lowell's labor demography had tilted toward immigrant males, strangers to the Massachusetts countryside. The visual and psychic separation between city and country was complete when, in 1845, the mayor complained of being "hemmed in by walls of brick and mortar." He sought a city park to substitute for the "green shady fields on our outskirts," where No Trespassing signs were appearing. The chronology of the birth and maturation of Olmsted and of Lowell were remarkably similar.[8]

What united the big cities and the smaller, more specialized Lowell is the radical change in land uses at their interiors and at their peripheries. Brick and mortar sprang up in both large and small cities, and the countryside fell before both, but the big cities had long given lessons in depravity. The destruction of nature and the concession to antinature were, therefore, more poignant at Lowell. The Lowell "experiment" in fact combined great material success and, in terms of its expectations, staggering social failure. The compatibility between manufacturing and natural landscape, the industrialization-and-nature continuum, proved to be as fleeting as the span of human childhood and adolescence.

Landscape despoliation was not confined to cities; rural destruction was an indirect result of urbanization. Man mutilated the landscape in a mighty but apparently hopeless effort to appease the ravenous material appetites of an urbanizing population. This type of destruction occurred wherever exploitable resources existed; scenic values received no consideration. So it was that the natural landscape was altered by clearing for large farms, for mining, and, most violently, for lumbering.

The fourth general influence on Olmsted was an appreciation of scenery. Olmsted's parents deliberately introduced him to landscape scenes; though the deepest impressions may have come from his casual boyhood rambles through the woods and meadows of Connecticut. The parental role, in any case, was important. Olmsted remembered those early family scenic drives when he wrote of recalling "less of any enjoyment I may then have had than of my impression of the enjoyment my father & mother constantly found in scenery." Writing of his father, he declared that the "influence which came to me from him was probably the strongest element in my training."[9]

Another person influencing Olmsted's landscape vision was Andrew Jackson Downing, a horticulturist and landscape architect. His design discussions emphasized the botanic aspect, interspersed with how-to advice. His landscape layouts surrounded rural dwellings, a vanishing alternative for growing numbers of urbanizing Americans. Downing's landscapes, moreover, tended to the bowers, bedding, and tightly looping lanes of the Reptonian style.[10]

Olmsted nevertheless felt Downing's influence. Downing's writing argued, directly and simply, for the landscape gardener to be considered an artist who created a "middle" landscape, a scenic delight shorn of the gross, ugly, or fetid elements sometimes found in nature. The landscaper created "not only an imitation . . . of the agreeable forms of nature, but *an expressive, harmonious, and refined imitation.*" Except for special effects or circumstances, Downing dismissed the "Geometric," or "ancient," style with its patterns, rectilinear walks, axial effects, and topiaries. Instead he defined and applied the categories of the beautiful and the picturesque, well known to Olmsted, to the

American landscape problem. Downing served, too, as a conduit of European romantic ideas.[11]

Downing agitated for urban parks, especially in New York City. In 1848 he began advocating "salubrious and wholesome breathing places," parks "open to all classes of people, provided at public cost, maintained at public expense, and enjoyed daily and hourly, by all classes of persons." Parks, together with libraries and galleries, "would soften and humanize the rude, educate and enlighten the ignorant, and give continual enjoyment to the educated." In the campaign for Central Park he again emphasized the role of the park in encouraging democracy and promoting class reconciliation. "It is republican in its very idea and tendency . . . and raises up the man of the working men to the same level of enjoyment with the man of leisure and accomplishment."[12]

Downing also influenced Olmsted in more personal ways. They corresponded, Olmsted visited Downing at his home, and Downing wrote letters of introduction for use during Olmsted's first (1850) trip to England. His magazine, *The Horticulturist and Journal of Rural Art and Rural Taste*, published several Olmsted contributions. During his own trip to England Downing persuaded the architect Calvert Vaux to emigrate and become his assistant. Five years after Downing's death in 1852, Olmsted and Vaux began their long and fruitful collaboration.[13]

Downing and others prepared Olmsted intellectually for his trip to the British Isles and Europe, conditioning him to comprehend the social significance of landscape. Among the landscape constructions Olmsted admired was the public park at Birkenhead, a suburb of Liverpool. In admiration and dismay he exclaimed over "the manner in which art had been employed to obtain from nature so much beauty, and I was ready to admit that in democratic America there was nothing to be thought of as comparable with this People's Garden." He was much impressed by the English countryside, by large private estates, and by formal gardens, although he had reservations about each of them.[14] The unrecorded Continental portion of his trip centered on France and Germany. Olmsted's Continental rambling probably followed the pattern set in England. If so, he saw a great many more pastoral and agricultural scenes, romantic landscapes, and formal gardens of Renaissance inspiration. The romantic and the classic were never so separated in landscape practice as the scholarly division of styles and schools suggests.

Travels through the landscapes of the American South followed the European tour. As did others of his generation, Olmsted neglected the unifying elements of culture and aspiration to search out the differences between North and South. The presence of a gentlemanly class and the relative absence of free poor masses in the South caused him to reflect on the possible use of landscape parks, other institutional art, and uplift organizations to "elevate" the mass of poor northerners.[15]

In a return visit to Europe in 1856 Olmsted saw for himself the Roman-Italian landscape of formal, axial elements. He observed the uses of Mediterranean foliage and of fountains in a climate sunnier and drier than England's. Even in the cradle of the Renaissance, however, Olmsted's integrative vision operated through the lens of romanticism. Landscape was most expressive when it followed, not human designs, but nature, which was God's creation. Geometry in landscape was all very well, but only if subordinated to naturalistic construction.[16]

Olmsted's conviction can be related to the revolution in the American attitude toward natural scenery. This shift in values involved most spectacularly a modification of the belief in the transformation or "improvement" of wilderness for productive uses. At least some wilderness preservation was encouraged because of the sublime beauty of wild places and because they harbored animals and "primitive" humans who would be destroyed by the complete conversion of all landscape to civilized uses. Besides, civilization itself required the uncivilized as a living museum, a benchmark of its own progress.[17]

Two interacting developments usually are credited with bringing about this aesthetic revolution. The first was the near-obliteration of nature to satisfy the demands of civilization or to introduce a civilized scene. Exploitation to the point of destruction, however, violated the long-held American belief in the New World mission to attain spiritual perfection. Spiritual perfection implied, and was partly dependent upon, purposeful improvement through environmental reshaping, but not destruction. The second development was the rise of the romantic aesthetic. The romantic view triumphed over neoclassicism and associational psychology during Olmsted's maturation. The ascendancy of the romantic resulted partly from the writings of men who profoundly influenced Olmsted, including Emerson, Carlyle, Ruskin, and the landscape writers Sir Uvedale Price and William Gilpin. Landscape painting also fueled romanticism. Painting probably affected Olmsted little, certainly less than writing. Yet it attracted many admirers, spread the idea that it was respectable for an artist to create or imitate landscape, and gave expression to the romantics' aesthetic divisions of the sublime, the picturesque, and the beautiful. The paintings of Claude Lorrain and Salvator Rosa and, in the United States, those of Thomas Cole, Asher B. Durand, and the Hudson River school were influential representatives of romanticism.[18]

Commentaries on the triumph of romanticism focus on the new American admiration of the sublime, which replaced aversion to the overwhelming wilderness of jagged mountains, crashing waterfalls, and the deep, dark woods where enemies once lurked. Less noticed is the fresh aesthetic appreciation of pastoral and agricultural landscape. Formerly praised because they represented radical modification of wilderness for productive purposes, they were in the romantic age invested with "natural" qualities. They were no less the domain of man, but nature throve there, too, displaying her picturesqueness and beauty in a middle landscape poised between wilderness and town.[19]

The sublimity of wilderness was not reproducible, except at unwarranted expense or by some absurd contrivance such as a miniature. Human artistry was fully capable, however, of creating the middle landscape. One could create or enhance the picturesque, which Downing defined as "a certain spiritual irregularity, surfaces comparatively abrupt and broken, and growth of a somewhat wild and bold character." One could equally well bring into full being the beautiful, described by Downing as "outlines whose curves are flowing and gradual. . . . In the shape of the ground, it is evinced by easy undulations. . . . In the form of trees, by smooth stems, full, round, or symmetrical heads of foliage. . . . In walks and roads, by easy flowing curves, following natural shapes of the surface, with no sharp angles or abrupt turns. In water, by the smooth lake with curved margin." The picturesque and the beautiful, moreover, could be introduced in a brick-and-mortar urban setting, in a public park.[20]

All these influences—secularization, urbanization, the decline of the natural landscape, and landscape appreciation—made specific contributions to Olmsted's career in landscape architecture: his sense of a secular mission applied to parks; his work in America's burgeoning cities; his calls for preservation of the Yosemite, Big Tree Grove, and Niagara Falls; and his employment of art in enhancing a natural landscape.

Beyond these specifics, Olmsted at the outset of his landscape practice was directly influenced by the existing relationships among public parks, cities, and society. These relationships involved, first, the public's use of parks and squares and the theories about the beneficence of such use and, second, the park designs intended to promote and enhance human enjoyment. To Olmsted the parks of London and its environs were the most striking examples of the sharing of urban pleasure grounds by the aristocrats and the masses. Though some were once royal by ownership, they had long since been dedicated to the public formally or through uncontested occupation. Popular use—100,000 in one day at Victoria Park; 130,000 one day in Hyde Park—did not deter the wealthy. Hyde Park contained "the fashionable riding course of London" and carriage drives passed in or along the periphery of four other parks. The London parks realized Olmsted's social ideal, the democratic intermingling of all classes. The display of riding horses and luxurious carriages moving among throngs of ordinary citizens was a visual affirmation of an interdependent, organic society. Promenades in parks also encouraged the members of "the largest classes of the people" to make "their best presentation of themselves."[21]

In the early nineteenth century the rural cemetery movement provided one alternative to the urban enclosure. Rural in design only, the cemeteries were really suburban burial grounds romantically landscaped to provide inviting interment sites as well as areas for strolling and picnicking. Mount Auburn in Cambridge, Massachusetts, opened in 1831. The movement spread throughout New England in the following fifteen years. As Downing and later Olmsted pointed out, however, they were not true parks. They were privately owned, socially stratified, accessible only to those with the time and means to reach them, and dedicated to potentially incompatible functions.[22]

Urban parks became more environmentally important as cities grew. They were referred to as the "lungs" of the city and its "breathing places" years before Olmsted became involved with Central Park. These references did not spring from an organic theory of the city. In the United States especially, the city was regarded as an artificial construction, hardly to be confused with a living being. The references were to the lungs and breathing of the city's inhabitants, who were unable to draw a breath of air uncontaminated by the dirt and odors of city life, except in parks. Man-made poisons increased while God's handiwork withered. As private land was subdivided, trees, with their pleasant oases of shade and their shapes contrasting with buildings, retreated to the parks.[23]

What all this meant in practical terms, if not in aesthetic theory, was a close identification between beauty and utility: open ground, plantings, natural scenery, the contrast between the natural and the artificial, and delightful views effectively elevated the human spirit. A New Yorker in 1855 lamented the destruction of a mid-Manhattan lake, stream, and nearby hill with "a natural and abundant fountain." If these had been preserved, "how charming that portion of the city would have been." Downing, although declining to "enumerate the great usefulness of trees," did exactly that when he discussed their visual impact. "To a pile of buildings, . . . they communicate new life and spirit by their irregular outlines, which . . . contribute greatly to produce intricacy and variety. . . . Buildings which are tame, insipid, or even mean in appearance, may be made interesting, and often picturesque, by a proper disposition of trees. Edifices, or parts of them that are unsightly, or which it is desirable partly or wholly to conceal, can readily be hidden or improved by [trees]."[24]

The author of these romantic sentiments may have been unaware of their full meaning. Natural scenery, Downing was writing, had the eminently practical effect of softening and screening man's artificial constructions. He implied a great deal more: cities were artificial. With the best will in the world men were bound to build them by replacing natural scenes with tight, rectilinear buildings and streets drawn up in rigid ranks. At best their efforts would introduce some homely, graceless effects. Lacking the best will, they would produce worse. There was little theory of the city in these statements, beyond an implied condemnation of it as nothing but a commercial necessity. Olmsted would at first accept the implication, and though he later mitigated his antiurban sentiment, he never abandoned the core of it.

The design theory accompanying these attitudes toward parks, societies, and cities was, in a phrase, that parks should be in cities but not of them. The English landscape design, reinforced by romantic aesthetics, perfectly suited the purpose. In refined rural-pastoral surroundings of the English style, urban denizens could escape the unyielding city. They could drink their fill of soft, irregular scenes while they reaffirmed their social unity and, especially in the case of the lower economic classes, developed their sensibilities. English landscape design, however, was no tidy transatlantic cultural inheritance. The works of William Kent, Lancelot "Capability" Brown, Humphry Repton, and others formed a gallery of styles. The gallery contained florid wild patches, axial lanes bounded by close-cropped hedges, elaborate geometric designs, and white pantheons. The landscape practice that accepted all this variation within a loose pastoralism could hardly give rise to an explicit theory of public park design. Nor was it necessary to do so. English practice provided Olmsted with a rich, complex rural design heritage. He would use it to counter the atmosphere of urban artificiality.[25]

Olmsted's contributions to the City Beautiful movement arise from his creative assimilation of secularization, urbanization, landscape despoliation, landscape appreciation, ideas about the role of parks in cities and society, and of park design. But Olmsted's link with the City Beautiful movement was not apparent. His own urban theory seemed unreconcilable with the later, hopeful view of cities developed by Charles Mulford Robinson and others associated with the City Beautiful. The aged Olmsted's ascerbic comments about neoclassical architecture reinforced the idea that he rejected the movement's civic grandeur. It would be better to say that Olmsted never tried to understand the movement's origins and development. City Beautiful adherents, on the other hand, often adopted Olmsted's rhetoric and designs while rejecting some of his premises and modifying others.[26]

Olmsted's theory of the city developed during his off-and-on residence in New York and was influenced by its sights, sounds, and smells. The early influence of New York may be inferred from his and Vaux's *Greensward* plan of 1858. This sensitive, sophisticated design offers the romantically landscaped park as anodyne for the moral, mental, and nervous afflictions of the city. The overall scheme was a brilliant adaptation of existing landscape elements and as such has been analyzed many times. What matters here is Olmsted's view of the city so far as it may be recovered from his and Vaux's collaborative statements.[27]

Concerning the famed transverse roads, slicing through the park on depressed roadways, the designers emphasized the incompatibility of their urban traffic. "Inevitably they will be crowded thoroughfares, having nothing in common with the park proper, but every thing at variance with those agreeable sentiments which we should wish the park to inspire. . . . They must be constantly open to all the legitimate traffic of the city, to coal carts and butcher's carts, dust carts and dung carts . . . a turbid stream of coarse traffic." It is clear that the transverse roads represented a cacophony and hurly-burly utterly opposed to the idea of a park. Indeed the city was to be walled out whenever possible. Olmsted and Vaux proposed a "line of trees all around the outer edge of the park," to hide "the houses on the opposite side of the street from the park, and to insure an umbrageous horizon line." The park was to be the antithesis of the city, "a beautiful open green space, in which quiet drives, rides, and strolls may be had." The thrust of the *Greensward* language strongly suggests that Olmsted accepted the thinking of the day about cities. However necessary, they were aesthetically unappealing places of din and tumult, producing anxiety and exhaustion.[28]

By early 1870, when Olmsted delivered his major theoretical statement on cities, his inquiring, assimilative mind had absorbed many new experiences, forcing his partial reappraisal of the urban environment. He had traveled to Europe again, seeing its cities and their pleasure grounds through professional eyes. In Central Park he had worked with George E. Waring, Jr., the great sanitary engineer, and applied advanced health and sanitation concepts during his tenure with the U.S. Sanitary Commission. He had prepared a park and boulevard report for San Francisco. His and Vaux's essay of 1868 ascribing the growth of cities to their deconcentration and their improved public health reflected Olmsted's increased knowledge.[29] His Mariposa, California, experiences had reminded him of the deprivations of remote country. He had noted, too, how some people remained stubbornly mundane, uninfluenced by wild grandeur. Finally, he had lived, worked, and observed for several more years in New York, watching the great city grow.

Olmsted conceded much to cities when he delivered his paper "Public Parks and the Enlargement of Towns" to the Social Science Association in Boston, 25 February 1870. From experience and reading he knew of the headlong urbanization in Europe and the United States. People of all ages and classes were leaving the rich lands in California and had abandoned "old agricultural neighborhoods, such as fifty years ago were the glory of New England," to decadence. Those who remained were in thrall to "town" for fashion, furnishings, food, education, and health care. If people had not taken leave of their senses—and Olmsted could never assume that creatures made in God's image could be utterly depraved—then there must be some bright, beckoning quality to cities.[30]

Olmsted discovered cities' attractions in a close connection between urbanization and "civilized progress," which he identified with the rise of institutionalized culture, organized and commercial recreation, the division of labor, rapid advances in transportation, communication, utilities and public health, and the mechanization of agriculture. All these developments except the last were unfolding in the booming cities and were synonymous with "the emancipation of both men and women from petty, confining, and narrowing cares." He predicted that the exodus from country to city would accelerate, that cities "are likely to be still more attractive to population in the future; that there will in consequence soon be larger towns than any the world has yet known, and that the further progress of civilization is to depend mainly upon the influences by which men's minds and characters will be affected while living in large towns."[31]

Olmsted had not yet finished his encomium to cities. Against the aesthetic norms of his day, he proclaimed the potential beauty of cities and appropriated the word *picturesque* to describe it. He declared to the assembled Bostonians: "Picturesqueness you can get. Let your buildings be as picturesque as your artists can make them. This is the beauty of a town." In the next sentence Olmsted declared for pastoral beauty in urban parks, and so returned to safe ground.[32] Even so, he may have left a few old romantic transcendentalists wondering whether they had heard aright. Had someone said that cities could be beautiful?

As much as he welcomed urbanism for its fostering of progress, however, Olmsted never abandoned his prejudice against cities. Their public health could be increased, their streets widened and better lighted, their institutions improved, and all that, but cities they remained. They were still crowded, dirty, inhospitable, and unyielding. If there is a word for Olmsted's city, it is intractable. Humans, unfortunately, were more malleable than bricks and mortar. In Olmsted's sociology the cities forged unnatural men. In "the interior parts of large and closely built towns," pollution "carries into the lungs highly corrupt and irritating matters. . . . The irritation and waste of the physical powers . . . very seriously affect the mind and the moral strength." Worse, secondary relationships and impersonality flourished in the city, where men every day "have seen thousands of their fellow-men, . . . and yet have had no experience of anything in common with them." Urban congestion contributed to this alienation, for in the jostle of sidewalk crowds "we have constantly to watch, to foresee, and to guard against" other pedestrians. "This involves a consideration of their intentions, a calculation of their strength and weakness, which is not so much for their benefit as our own." Commercial transactions, the life's blood of cities, exhibited "the same tendency—a tendency to regard others in a hard if not always hardening way." Thus it was that the man urban born and bred displayed, "along with a remarkable quickness of apprehension, a peculiarly hard sort of selfishness." In this proto-progressive passage Olmsted came close to abandoning his Christian belief in man's inherent goodness for the secular view of man as merely the creature of his environment and experiences.[33]

Be that as it may, Olmsted's statements about cities and their implications for humanity are scarcely optimistic. Three other phases of his thought and work further dimmed his hopes for the city. First, Olmsted had already opted for the politically independent suburb as the ideal "combination" of "urban conveniences" and "the special charms and substantial advantages of rural conditions of life." In suburbs, freestanding houses would be arranged to encourage both community and private domesticity. Spacious house lots, large public parks, and first-rate utilities systems would enhance the rural aspects of suburbs, while easy access to the city would bring its business buildings, shopping, entertainment, and cultural institutions within reach.[34] Second, Olmsted doubted that the crowded, emotionally restrictive "interior parts" of large cities could be changed for the better. The crime, disease, and low life expectancy of crowded areas could be improved by their destruction and redevelopment but "these means are made use of only with great difficulty." Conventional rebuilding after fires in London and New York were proofs in point.[35]

Worse yet for a humane view of cities was Olmsted's apparent belief that a substantial number of urban residents would remain in the crowded inner areas. True, he spoke of the increasing separation between home and work, one in a spacious setting, the other in a congested area. At other times he suggested an open arrangement in all noncommercial parts of town, but was on record about the near impossibility of achieving it. Moreover he urged his listeners to go themselves to see "the ordinary state of things to many" Bostonians. "Oftentimes you will see half a dozen sitting together on the door-steps, or, all in a row, on the curbstones, with their feet in the gutter, driven out of doors by the closeness within." Not only the poor lived in close quarters. Six years later Olmsted would criticize the New York grid and lot arrangement for imposing long, narrow, poorly lighted, and ill-ventilated houses on the middle class. Far from improving, the New York situation was deteriorating as backyards were built over to accommodate the growing population.[36]

Finally, Olmsted predicted rapid urban growth and proposed an elaborate park and boulevard system to disperse it. Superficially his solution was optimistic, but he did not suggest how to prevent concentrated or reconcentrated growth. Here and elsewhere he advanced the attractive image of urbanites strolling and riding over verdant thoroughfares, escaping commercial areas. But how were cities to expand at the rate Olmsted projected without a commensurate growth in their business districts? In the absence of land use controls, how would a boulevard intersection be preserved from retail uses or from closely built houses? Perhaps Olmsted's hearers and readers were swept along by his vision and did not reflect on such problems. But could they have been entirely accepting of his heady vision? It is unlikely. Olmsted proposed an urban morphology radically different from that of his own time, and even while proclaiming the transformation, he doubted its possibility.[37]

In sum, Olmsted had on intellectual seven-league boots in the years between 1857 and 1870. He leapt from accepting the city as commercially necessary but humanly destructive to acknowledging the city's role as the carrier of culture. He traveled a great distance, but he stopped short of embracing the city. Cities, for all their advantages, distorted human nature, were best enjoyed in suburbs, trapped inner city residents in practically hopeless confinement, and could resist his plans for restructuring them.

Intellectually and emotionally Olmsted never made it to the civic idealism of the City Beautiful movement. He remained unreconciled to the neoclassicism that was its hallmark. This is not surprising considering his already substantial concessions to the city and his relatively late age—almost forty-eight—at the time he articulated a theory of urbanism. Too, Olmsted considered himself an artist whose creations were as delicately wrought, as personal, and yet as universal as those of any painter or poet. What he considered tampering with his designs could drive him into depression or a state approaching frenzy. He was capable of displaying "artistic" temperament when he perceived threats to the integrity of his parks—that is, any building, planting, or public use not designed or approved by himself. The great landscape architect's pride and acerbity are forgivable. They prohibited him, however, from understanding that he could not always be consulted and did not permit sensitivity to the schemes of others.[38]

His ambivalence about the World's Columbian Exposition is a case in point. Olmsted was the landscape architect of the Chicago fair and a major consultant, but there was no doubt of his subordination to the much younger chief of construction, the neoclassical architect Daniel H. Burnham. Olmsted fought to keep his precious Wooded Island free of exhibit buildings but finally capitulated to minor, harmonious construction. He found the completed exposition too starkly white, too cluttered with small buildings, and insufficiently inviting. Two years later, he was denouncing Stanford White and his associates, the designers of a neoclassical entrance to his Prospect Park in Brooklyn. He called them "doctrinaires and fanatics and essentially cockneys" (*cockneys* being his term for ignorant despoilers of natural landscape).[39]

Olmsted's acerbic rhetoric threatens to sweep the reader into anti-neoclassicism. But a caution is in order, for his attack on City Beautiful formalism was inconsistent with his own use of formal, axial, and monumental effects. In 1893 Olmsted was an old man. His critical letters about the Chicago fair were later, crotchety renditions of his earlier attacks on design situations that he could not control. He wrote his bitter "cockneys" letter of 1895 during his sad descent into dotage. Only two months afterward, befuddlement prevented his taking alone a simple train trip from North Carolina to Washington, D.C. Olmsted, his injury-wracked body given up to chronic insomnia and his brain dimming, could do no more than register a complaint against a new generation of determined and hopeful designers who saw visions not his own. He cannot be taken seriously as the author of a consistent, rounded anti-neoclassic aesthetic.[40]

Strands of nineteenth-century culture and the traditionalist's reaction to radical changes incident to urbanism shaped Olmsted's thinking about cities and design. This heritage forms the context of Olmsted's profound, if unintended, contributions to the City Beautiful.[41]

OLMSTED'S FIRST LEGACY TO THE CITY BEAUTIFUL

Olmsted's first great legacy to the City Beautiful consisted of his parks and, later, his park and boulevard systems. His parks were massive public works projects designed to reshape the land in basic ways. Olmsted created ideal scenery from suggestions in the existing landforms and from his imagination, in proportions dependent upon the circumstances. He was no respecter of existing natural features unless they could be subordinated to his plan. This deliberate re-formation of the land did no violence to Olmsted's theory of art, whatever it might do to the original landscape. Olmsted believed in the artist's obligation to create beauty from natural materials and to make art apparent to the observer. His finished scenes were artifices, built in the romantic or pastoral mode. They were inventions and constructions just as surely as was an Asher Durand painting or the Court of Honor at the World's Columbian Exposition. They were not natural but were the products of naturalistic construction.

Olmsted and Vaux took only the barest suggestions from the site when fashioning Central Park. Olmsted's estimate of 4,825,000 cubic yards of earth and rock moved is amazing when the era's limited equipment is considered. The vast volume equaled "nearly ten millions of ordinary city one-horse cartloads, which, in single file, would make a procession thirty thousand . . . miles in length." Blasting in the park required 260 tons of gunpowder. The engraving *Constructing Prospect Park in 1867* depicts the laborious pick and shovel work, the cart teams, and the more than two dozen huge earthen berms of a vast works project. Boston's Franklin Park required relatively little change, but even that modest alteration involved extensive grading.[42]

Olmsted did not hesitate to convert virtually featureless terrain into a pastoral-romantic landscape. His naturalistic constructivism stood forth most dramatically in two lakefront designs, for Buffalo's proposed South Park along Lake Erie and for the World's Columbian Exposition on the shore of Lake Michigan. South Park, bounded on two sides by railroad tracks impossible to move and difficult to screen, was mostly low and swampy. The higher ground was largely level and undistinguished. Olmsted's 1888 plan called for a pastoral green on the lakefront, girt by trees and a carriage drive. Elsewhere he planned a series of lagoons with picturesque borders and islands built up by dredging. Elaborate electric lighting, painted and gilded lagoon boats, and other appurtenances would be frankly artificial and so would "a symmetrical flower garden, which may have some seats and architectural decoration."[43]

Olmsted's landscape work for the World's Columbian Exposition was as consciously a creature of the imagination as any other feature of that dominantly neoclassical exhibition. The marshy Jackson Park site along Lake Michigan was distinctly unpromising, a series of ridges and troughs paralleling the lake, spotted with scrub oak. To call Jackson Park unimproved or neglected might not be fair to the Chicago park authorities, but they had not built the elaborate lagoon that Olmsted and Vaux had suggested in an 1871 report. For the exposition, Olmsted proposed naturalistic waterways. When completed, they and the Wooded Island in the main lagoon were the product of dredging, earth moving, and elaborate planting, the epitome of naturalistic constructivism. The City Beautiful's fearless reorganization of urban scenes for the sake of civic art had precedent in these calculated, radical disruptions of the landscape.[44]

The City Beautiful, sometimes criticized for the cost of its projects, continued a well-established tradition of heavy municipal expenses. The costs of Olmsted's park projects for the most part lie buried in archives and annual reports. There is no doubt, however, that they were expensive. Through 1873 Central Park had cost almost $14 million, of which nearly $9 million was for improvement, an enormous sum for the day. Part of the expense was for a labor force as large as 3,800 men. If one city could shoulder such a burden successfully, then so could others, so long as the public project returned a civic benefit. [45]

Artistic collaboration characterized the City Beautiful, but the collaboration of architects, sculptors, mural painters, and, sometimes, landscape architects found precedent in Olmsted's activities. His collaboration with Vaux in Central Park produced a complex, integrated design, including Vaux's masterful Terrace at the north end of the Mall. Jacob Wrey Mould, whose reputation as a bohemian dandy rivaled his architectural talents, designed the Bethesda Fountain and other accents. Olmsted worked closely with two horticulturists, Ignaz Pilat, who died in 1870, and William L. Fischer. The great sanitary engineer, George E. Waring, Jr., built the park's drainage system. Olmsted learned a great deal from Waring and other members of his engineering staff. It was not until after the engineering collaboration that Olmsted's reports stressed the public health significance of parks, such as the role of trees in soil drainage and air purification. [46]

The collaborations continued. Olmsted worked with Vaux for many years, with Fischer on the Boston parks and parkway system, and with Waring on the Riverside, Illinois, suburban project, the Stanford University campus, and other commissions. Other members of the engineering staff were associated with him in California, on Prospect Park and various New York City projects; and during his great rural undertaking, the William Vanderbilt estate, Biltmore. The World's Columbian Exposition was his final and most spectacular collaboration. Such shared efforts looked to European inspirations and precedents, especially to the tradition of the Ecole des Beaux-Arts in Paris. Beaux-Arts-style collaboration, however, was only part of the story. Collaboration was an accepted practice with Olmsted and his associates long before the neoclassical revival of the 1890s. [47]

Olmsted's cosmopolitanism suffused all of his design work, including his park planning. It is easy to forget, while borne aloft by Olmsted's pastoral-rural reminiscences and rhetoric, that he was a man who sailed before the mast to China, toured his own country in peace and war, studied the tropical horticulture of Panama, lived in remote California, and traveled to Europe several times. His 1859 visit to England and France while superintendent of Central Park was perhaps the most important. He saw the developing parks and broad, formal boulevards of Paris and conferred with their designer, Jean Alphand. His design inheritance was a rich one, for although the nineteenth-century English landscape and landscape parks were of primary importance to his plans, the English style was itself a complex development that had absorbed significant Continental and classical influences. His use of a wide variety of plants, formal elements, vistas, spaces, and crowd control techniques in parks reveals his sophistication and cosmopolitanism.

Olmsted was not, and did not pretend to be, an expert horticulturist. He made plant selections extremely carefully, however, with a critical eye for light, shade, contrast, color, and, occasionally, the unexpected. He was undogmatic in his choices, displaying no preferences for native species simply because they were American or familiar to a region. A hardy plant that complemented a developing landscape composition was what he wanted. His approach revealed a man sensitive to the lessons of faraway Panama and of Alphand, who showed him thrifty subtropical plants growing in the Parisian climate. The "tropical island" in the lake at Central Park and the original dense plantings along the watercourses of the Boston parkway system are artistically wild and picturesque scenes made up of the most suitable materials available. They had nothing in common with New England pastoral scenery or with an English sheep meadow. They were living examples of Olmsted's denigration of purists who insisted on native plants only or on the separation of domestic and foreign species. They were proof of his studied eclecticism and of his striving for effect, characteristics he shared with the practitioners of the City Beautiful.[48]

Olmsted used formal vistas and neoclassical structures in his parks. Central Park abounds in them. The Mall in its glory days was a series of parallel ribbons below arching elms. The Terrace and several bridges are neoclassical; the Terrace and the adjacent Bethesda Fountain are powerful organizational features. Long, short, closed, and open vistas greeted the Central Park visitor. Olmsted also used formal design features in Prospect Park's Plaza and concert grove, in Franklin Park's mall, the Greeting, and in later parks. Although he subordinated these designs to the prevailing naturalistic constructivism, the elements of the City Beautiful—vista, formality, and neoclassicism—were nevertheless present.[49]

Despite his rhetorical opposition to intrusions into his landscape parks, Olmsted planned to accommodate large crowds engaged in diverse activities. His deft direction of park visitors and his careful placement of the growing collection of park attractions anticipated the urbanism of the City Beautiful and the multiuse city park of more recent times. The separated roads and paths in Central Park provided four distinct circulatory systems for carriages, equestrians, pedestrians, and through traffic. They curved and looped (except for the transverse roads for through traffic) to provide delight in a rapid succession of new scenes or of familiar scenes from new perspectives, to suggest a more spacious amd open ground than really existed, and to create "a sense of enlarged freedom." These arrangements have often been remarked upon. What is less noticed is the crowd control feature of these pathways. Curves, loops, inviting nooks, and planted screens visually separated strollers and riders from one another and from others in their own category. They enforced slower travel through the park, thereby promoting its recreational and restorative functions. The formal, architectonic Mall, on the other hand, invited civic gregariousness among those strollers and loungers who wished to see and be seen.[50]

The long, narrow Central Park rectangle, the park commissioner's design requirements, and Olmsted's relative inexperience limited his ability to arrange park features for the maximum introduction and separation of main elements and for the greatest possible direction and control of the varied human mass pouring into the park. He did better with Prospect Park, where he located "not quite compatible" uses catering to urban diversity at or near the park's periphery or adjacent to it, across a tree-lined boulevard. These elements included a formal entrance, concert grove, baseball field, zoo, museum, and parade ground. Within two years he had added an elaborate children's playground. Olmsted dispersed the park roads and walks to concentrate people at a lookout, a restaurant, and the concert grove, where they would enjoy the landscape and the "attractive and diverting spectacle" of massed, moving humanity.[51]

Olmsted refined his crowd control techniques in later designs, as in those for the Chicago parks. The Chicago park plans of 1871 included open play areas and formal watercourses. In the Boston system he introduced play areas for children, a further differentiation of function in the landscape park. This was another of his concessions to the growing, diverse demands of cosmopolitan park use. His reports reveal that his concessions were not always grudgingly made. Crowds, design variety, foreign plants, formalism, and professional collaboration appealed to his personal cosmopolitanism. The naturalistic constructions of his huge, expensive park undertakings reflected his artistic ideals and commitment to a democratic social policy.[52]

The parkway system, or park and boulevard system, extended Olmsted's great park legacy. He suggested how a park and boulevard system could direct the growth of newer residential areas while it relieved traffic, provided carriage drives, and permitted diverse, specialized parks. He showed how such a system could stifle urban sectional jealousies by introducing some green space into all residential areas.

Olmsted developed his boulevards from mere park connectors to the sinews of a city-girdling system in his plans of the 1860s and 1870s. His plan for San Francisco published in 1866 featured a remarkable diversity of park elements tied together by boulevards. Given some City Beautiful designers' penchant for water gates, it is intriguing to find Olmsted proposing a verdantly framed "sea-gate" on San Francisco Bay, a "suitable landing quay and plaza," "where foreign dignitaries and our own national representatives will land and embark." He advised against a "very large" entrance, but the entrance he proposed could hardly have been a modest bit of naturalistic landscape. He advised that it "be open and large enough to be used for a drill ground by a battery of artillery or a regiment of infantry." He also urged that "an elegant pavilion" for a band and a reception committee be gaudily "decorated with flagstaffs, marine trophies, and eventually with monuments to naval heroes, discoverers and explorers."[53]

Olmsted next outlined his plans for a close-in, small "rural ground," or landscape park, juxtaposed to a modest parade ground. The parade ground clearly was designed to serve the civic, as opposed to the governmental, functions of a civic center, with space "for music, for fireworks, and for public speaking," where "a crowd of many thousand persons might be assembled." Finally, he proposed a European-style boulevard, a promenade, connecting the existing Yerba Buena Park, his park and parade ground complex, and the water gate. Though European in inspiration, it would be tailored to local conditions by depressing it at least 20 feet below grade and planting evergreens atop the banks to break the prevailing wind. Olmsted projected a grand concourse 280 feet wide at street level, 152 feet at grade between flowered and shrubbed banks. He designed separate roadways for carriages, equestrians, and pedestrians, and limited access for carriages from the streets above. This regal concourse would have no other function than to provide San Francisco's carriage-and-horseflesh society with pleasurable movement to the rest of Olmsted's creation, unless one includes those on foot or hoi polloi gawking down at the spectacle from the commercial streets and overpass bridges. The promenade was primitive by Olmsted's later standards, for it did not encircle the city or attempt to influence its growth. But this unbuilt vision was an Olmsted design for the "imperial San Francisco" that Daniel Burnham and Edward Bennett imagined forty years later when they gazed upon the city from their shack on Twin Peaks.[54]

By the time Olmsted's San Francisco report appeared, he was back in the familiar New York environment, where he and Vaux were at work on their preliminary report to the commissioners of Brooklyn's Prospect Park. Olmsted and Vaux suggested, almost as an afterthought, a boulevard looping through the rural districts beyond Brooklyn, crossing the East River, and connecting with Central Park in New York. They suggested further that such a boulevard would connect with the proposed drives north from Central Park. Together the boulevards would expose the carriage traveler to a variety of urban, rus-urban, and rural scenery. Though Olmsted and Vaux asserted that the boulevard "forms no part of our plan and may seem premature," they had advanced beyond Olmsted's plan for a park-connecting, formal promenade in San Francisco. They now saw a boulevard as an "extension" of a park drive. The "extension" would provide the pleasure driver with a panorama of views unavailable in a park, while serving him with a smooth carriage road equal in quality to a park road.[55]

From this liberation of the boulevard from its connector role, it was a short intellectual step to the parkway Olmsted and his partner proposed two years later, again to the Prospect Park commissioners. Their parkway program, a plan for a park and boulevard system, appeared at the end of a lengthy historical review of street development. After acknowledging the role of the European connector boulevard, they moved beyond it with a 260-foot-wide avenue combining elements of the park, park drive, park footpath, and residential-commercial street. More, they designed the parkway to influence the character and direction of urban growth, one of the fundamental aims of the City Beautiful movement.[56]

In the center of the road they placed the pleasure drive, next pedestrian walks and seats, and then the regular roads flanking the houses on either side of the drive. Six rows of trees were to be interspersed with the walks and drives. Except for the addition of park benches for those wishing to rest or to observe the passing scene, the parkway appeared indistinguishable from the connector boulevard. It varied significantly, however, in three ways. First, Olmsted and Vaux proposed boulevard branches "to the ocean beach at Coney Island" and to a bridge that would connect with a street to Central Park. Thus they reaffirmed their recognition of the metropolitan character of New York and Brooklyn even though the two were then separate cities. Second, they suggested that the Prospect Park commissioners assume a new, far-reaching responsibility through the medium of the parkway by extending boulevards "to any points at which it should appear that large dwelling quarters were likely to be formed." They may not have grasped all the implications of their statement, for they were proposing that a commission charged with the development of a precisely limited plot of ground would in the future predict and shape residential growth by thrusting parkways into the city's penumbra.[57]

The first and second departures from the connector boulevard, however significant, would have had relatively little impact without the designers' third suggestion. This was an elaborate plan for a huge residential development, "a series of lots adapted to be occupied by detached villas each in the midst of a small private garden," flanking the parkway along its entire platted length. On either side of the parkway Olmsted and Vaux planned lots 100 feet wide and a block deep, with a street at the rear of the lots giving access to stables. They proposed to protect the opposite side of the stable street from "houses of inferior class" by drawing a smaller boulevard a block beyond, "widened to 100 feet and sidewalks shaded by double rows of trees." The houses fronting on the narrower parallel parkway would also rest on 100-foot-wide, block-deep lots and back up on the stable street.[58]

The situation on either side of the parkway would then be expensive houses fronting upon the parkway, with stables at their rear looking out upon the stable street. The stables across the stable street would belong to the houses facing the smaller boulevard. All together, Olmsted and Vaux proposed a four-block-wide strip of upper-middle-class homes, a verdant ribbon influencing both the nature and the direction of growth. They would create a suburban-style swath running through the developing areas, establishing a building style for an indefinite distance on either side of the parkway. Olmsted and Vaux did not suggest the source of authority or funds for their radical scheme, nor was it built. It was, however, an inspiration for later park and boulevard systems by Olmsted and Vaux and by their followers.

The partners reiterated their views in their 1871 Chicago report. They criticized the system of separate Chicago park districts for thwarting the development of a unified park and boulevard system, and they recommended widening a parkway to better absorb the heavy traffic that improved parks would generate. In 1881 Olmsted and his stepson, John, proposed a comprehensive park and boulevard system for Buffalo. This system was comprehensive because it was pervasive, reaching almost all areas of the city save its commercial core; multifunctional, with separate parks designed to meet distinct civic and recreational needs; and formative, designed to direct and harmonize the city's future growth.[59]

OLMSTED'S INTELLECTUAL LEGACY

Olmsted's second legacy to the City Beautiful was intellectual. His ideological bequest cannot be fully appreciated in advance of an examination of City Beautiful thought, but it is possible to outline five contributions. First, Olmsted upheld the environmental value of naturalistic beauty over urban forms, which could, at best, be merely picturesque. Partisans of the City Beautiful went beyond Olmsted to argue for a generalized civic beauty, but they accepted his belief that beauty created a positive environment capable of influencing human thought and behavior.

Second, Olmsted advanced many of the arguments associated with the City Beautiful conviction of the inseparability of beauty and utility. Burnham encapsulated the conviction for the twentieth century when he declared that "beauty has always paid better than any other commodity and always will."[60] Olmsted rejected such limited functionalism but he did insist that naturalistic beauty paid off in the areas of competition among cities, behavior modification and psychic restoration of the workforce, a rise in property values beyond the cost of improvements, and increased emphasis on recreational activity.

In his epochal 1866 San Francisco report Olmsted asked San Franciscans to consider New York's "libraries, museums, galleries of fine art, and more than anything else, . . . its Park," all of which explained "the extraordinary attraction it has for people who are not deeply absorbed in the mere *pursuit* of wealth." Worse for San Francisco, and New York for that matter, was the cultural eminence of London and Paris, great cities beckoning men "by the advantages which are offered them—not for making money, but for enjoying the use of it. . . . There are hundreds of men of large fortune, born in the United States, who are now, with their families, permanent residents of Paris and London, for this reason." San Francisco's competitive response should be to equip itself with public improvements matching its future as "one of the largest, if not the largest city in the world." Olmsted and Vaux's 1868 report on the Brooklyn park contained a similar, if more localized, suggestion: parkways would draw residents from New York City to Brooklyn, which could "soon be made to offer some special advantages as a place of residence to that portion of our more wealthy and influential citizens, whose temperament, taste or education leads them to seek for a certain amount of rural satisfaction in connection with their city homes."[61]

Beautiful parks also benefited resident businessmen who needed an escape from the unceasing care and anxiety of business. If restored by naturalistic scenes once or twice a week, they would bring greater productivity to their work and avoid an early retirement. The economic gains were by no means limited to the white-collar workforce. Olmsted expected blue-collar "tired workers" to flock to Central Park, and not surprisingly, he discovered what he expected. In his 1870 Boston address he asserted that the working class was most susceptible to the positive influences of the park, which filled a void in lives untouched by institutional religion. He recounted the story of a saloon keeper who visited the park soon after its opening and declared, "I came to see what the devil you'd got here that took off so many of my Sunday customers." The park evidently was "in competition with grog-shops and worse places." Park visitors increased when the police closed the "grog-shops" on Sunday, but "there was no similar increase at the churches."[62]

The restorative effects of park beauty embraced the worker's family. Children benefited from play, exercise, and natural scenery. Working-class mothers seemed to draw a special strength from their cavorting offspring. "I have, in fact," Olmsted intoned, "more than once observed tears of gratitude in the eyes of poor women, as they watched their children enjoying themselves." Olmsted's poor mothers would become rhetorical fixtures of the City Beautiful, but of greater importance to him was "neighborly" recreation, families and friends together amidst the beauties of the landscape park. Family ties were strengthened while each member relaxed and was refreshed. No wonder that Olmsted claimed that parks paid by attracting visitors and permanent residents who considered urban cultural conditions when making their travel and living arrangements. Parks paid, then, by retaining and restoring the city's resident population while they helped the city win the competition for tourists and for new residents of quality.[63]

Landscape beauty paid enterprising cities directly, by raising property values and swelling tax revenues. Olmsted declared that "the cost of forming parks has been more than met by the increased taxable valuation of real estate benefited by them." The Olmsted and Vaux 1868 Brooklyn report noted how Prospect Park had increased nearby property more than four times in value, testimony to the desirability "of convenient access from a residence to a public pleasure-ground. . . . The advance in value, in this case, is quite marked at a distance of a mile." A parkway acting as a park extension would transform a wide area potentially the locale of "shanties, stables, breweries, distilleries, and swineyards" into valuable residence property, where nearby "driving, riding, and walking can be conveniently pursued in association with pleasant people, and without the liability of encountering the unpleasant sights and sounds . . . in the common streets." In his Boston address Olmsted spoke of the opponents of Central Park who assumed that the park would attract undesirable uses on its periphery. They were confounded instead when property "immediately about the Park . . . advanced in value at the rate of two hundred per cent. per annum."[64]

Olmsted's argument soon became a cliché. The 1874 report of the Boston park commission included a table demonstrating how "land adjacent to parks" had risen far beyond the "average increase" in New York and other cities. Olmsted feared the dangers of urban sectionalism in such comparisons, for not everyone could live near a park or a parkway. He had to remind the public how beauty benefited each and all. In his 1886 report to the Boston commissioners he described how Brooklyn property owners the "most remote" from Prospect Park received a "special exemption" from park taxes. "Nevertheless, long before the plan of the park had been fully carried out, the people of this very district began to resort to it in such numbers that two lines of street cars were established, and on holidays these are now found insufficient. . . . There is no doubt that the health, strength, and earning capacity of these people is increased by the park; that the value of life in their quarter of the town is increased; that the intrinsic value, as well as the market rating, of its real estate is increased."[65]

Park beauty paid as well because it encouraged spending on recreational equipment and activities. Olmsted reported to his 1870 Boston audience how in twelve years the number of pleasure horses in New York had increased from practically none to ten thousand. In the 1886 report to the Boston commission he pointed to the enormous impact of Central Park on spending and leisure habits. For the sake of using the park, he maintained, "the dinner hour of thousands of families was permanently changed, the number of private carriages kept in the city was increased tenfold, the number of saddle horses a hundredfold, the business of livery stables more than doubled, the investment of many millions of private capital in public conveyances made profitable." Olmsted implied that, without the park, "habit and fashions, customs and manners" would be less socially constructive than with the park in place. Behavior modification was, for Olmsted, the outward sign of the restorative power of naturalistic beauty.[66]

Though Olmsted argued for the tangible monetary returns from beauty, social utility was a higher priority with him. In this third area of identification with the City Beautiful, he stressed the park's role as a meeting and greeting area, the locale of class reconciliation. If the heterogeneous, cosmopolitan population of New York could find a common ground, there was hope for cheerful, democratic, interclass gregariousness in urbanizing America. In Central Park, he told his Boston audience, "you will find . . . all classes largely represented, with a common purpose, . . . each individual adding by his mere presence to the pleasure of all others. . . . You may thus often see . . . poor and rich, young and old, Jew and Gentile." After sixteen years he remained convinced that class lines dissolved in the presence of beauty. "The poor and the rich come together in [Central Park] in larger numbers than anywhere else, and enjoy what they find in it in more complete sympathy than they enjoy anything else together."[67]

Fourth, Olmsted conveyed to the future a conviction about the inevitability, if not the desirability, of urban growth. He spoke with authority on city growth, for he had marked New York's headlong expansion through the years before and after the Civil War. The cities he planned for, he asserted, were bound to emulate New York's metropolitanism. Environmental planning should, therefore, begin at once, with parks and parkways projected on the basis of a population several times greater than the present. An early beginning meant buying park property and land for other improvements before urbanization drove up prices. It meant influencing future high-quality private development adjacent to the improvements rather than permitting miscellaneous, disorderly growth at the whim of the landowners. A park designer's problem, Olmsted informed San Franciscans in 1866, was "to consider how the convenience and pleasure of future generations are to be affected," a number "two or three times" the present population and eventually "many millions of people." In 1888 he predicted that within a generation "Buffalo will be not only a city of much larger trade, . . . wealth and . . . population, but it will be a city of much more metropolitan character." Therefore, if decisions are "put off, the more difficult it will be to plan them, the more difficult to secure the adoption of a plan, and the greater the cost to both the citizens personally and to the city as a whole."[68]

Finally, from his concern for immediate beginnings came Olmsted's insistence on the value of expert planning by a specialist capable of designing for large civic purposes as well as for delightful detail. The full flowering of professional self-definition and self-consciousness came after Olmsted's time, when architects and engineers seized the leadership in city planning. Olmsted, nevertheless, stated the core of the case for professional over laymen's design decisions. He welcomed public discussion, Olmsted told his 1870 Boston audience, but public, or political, involvement in design was something else. What he called "even the most elementary park questions, questions of site and outlines and approaches," were not the sort of issues lending themselves to individual or group pressures. They were not, in other words, "questions to which the rule applies, that every man should look after his own interests, judge for himself what will favor his own interests, and exert his influence so as to favor them." Instead, such matters should be placed in charge of the expert, "somebody who is able to take hold of them comprehensively as a matter of direct, grave, business responsibility."[69]

The expert should be alive to the potential of the site, creative, and

innovative. His plan, once prepared, should not be changed unless the alterations were consistent with the overall scheme or "with the purpose intended
to rule in that locality." Olmsted's legacy to the City Beautiful included his
popularization of romantic insights about the positive influence on humans of
natural scenery. He continually urged the value of European precedent, citing
the excellence of English parks and Continental boulevards. Lastly, he understood his work to be comprehensive in meanings and relationships beyond the
usual identification of "comprehensive" with city plans. Planning, to be fully
effective in altering the urban landscape and improving the quality of human
life, had to advance in relation to political and administrative improvements,
the growth of public education, the development of public comprehension of
artistic effort, and the rise of institutionalized culture.[70]

Consulting: Olmsted's Third Legacy

Olmsted's third major contribution to the City Beautiful was his development of a large consulting practice. The demands on his time forced him to
develop his business into a kind of atelier, where Charles Eliot, Henry Sargent
Codman, Warren H. Manning, his stepson, son, and others gained professional knowledge and stature. His fame brought other landscape architects,
including the young George Kessler, into his orbit. Many of these younger
men became planning consultants during the City Beautiful era, producing
City Beautiful plans under arrangements similar to Olmsted's. In 1890
Olmsted proudly counted as an enduring achievement helping "to educate in
a good American school a capital body of young men for my profession."[71] He
wrote only part of the truth. Olmsted helped to educate a group of young men
in the business of consulting, as well as in city planning.

Olmsted's most important nontechnical lesson to his young charges was the
importance of judicious and responsible planning. He told San Franciscans in
1866 that parks should be located so as to be easily policed, displace few
existing buildings or utilities, little impede normal traffic flows, "or otherwise
cause heavy losses or depreciation of value to the existing property of the city,
or that of corporations or private citizens." In 1888 he urgently advised the
Buffalo park commission against extravagance. He may have had in mind the
remarkable but impractical plans for Boston of Robert Fleming Gourlay and
Robert Morris Copeland when he told Bostonians that "cities grow in a
manner not to be accurately foreseen." He advocated, therefore, both recreational specialization and flexibility of location within the context of overall
design principles. Olmsted's recognition of political and schematic realities
exemplified a career in which his famous tiffs over the development of Central
and Prospect parks were exceptions. City Beautiful professionals similarly
stressed economy, flexibility, and adaptability of design.[72]

Summary

The nineteenth-century realities expressed as secularization, urbanization, the decline of natural landscape, and growing landscape appreciation operated on Olmsted to produce a distinctive career in city planning. Though he did not refer to planning in its twentieth-century intellectual dimensions, he prepared the path of the City Beautiful movement in significant ways. He developed the landscape park and later the park and boulevard system, both of which are basic to City Beautiful design. He worked out an elaborate rationale for planning, a rationale that City Beautiful advocates accepted and extended. And, though he did not originate consulting, he promoted the role of the expert consultant and the consultant firm. A profound expression of Olmsted's significance for the future came from none other than Daniel Burnham. Burnham—frequently forced in planning history to play the role of antithesis to geniuses such as Olmsted, Louis H. Sullivan, and Frank Lloyd Wright—delivered a moving tribute to the absent Olmsted during an 1893 World's Columbian Exposition dinner. "In the highest sense he is the planner of the Exposition," Burnham declared. Olmsted, he asserted, deserved the honor "not for his deeds of later years alone, but for what his brain has wrought and his pen has taught for half a century."[73] In 1893 it was too early for Burnham or his audience to grasp the full truth of those words. As the years unfolded Burnham and other City Beautiful practitioners would consciously or unconsciously claim Olmsted's precepts for their own.

2 ◆ Municipal Improvement and Beautifying the Entire Community

Frederick Law Olmsted left the City Beautiful movement a great legacy of ideology, inspiration, and action, but he would never move into the late-nineteenth-century world of professional and civic organization. He did cast about for a means for landscape architects to link with others of similar interests. Magazine publication was the vehicle he chose, but the authors and audience remained too loosely bound. His successors turned, in the fashion of the day, to a formal organization. Soon they reached out to others interested in *outdoor art,* a term originally encompassing landscaping, architecture, and similar interests. The organization steadily moved away from traditional Olmstedian interests to embrace the comprehensive political and beautification concerns of municipal improvement. Municipal improvement, in turn, identified with the City Beautiful movement when it incorporated newly developed ideas of civic design.[1]

In 1888 Olmsted joined with Charles S. Sargent, director of the Arnold Arboretum, and others to found the weekly magazine *Garden and Forest.* Landscape enthusiasts, forest preservationists, and art critics such as Mrs. Schuyler (Marianna Griswold) Van Rensselaer and Mira Lloyd Dock published in its pages. Olmsted himself used it as a vehicle for his strictures against a speedway racetrack in New York and the emerging architecture of the City Beautiful. Neither *Garden and Forest* nor *Park and Cemetery and Landscape Gardening,* established in 1890, achieved any real cohesion among landscape practitioners. The need for a formal organization became more apparent in the closing years of the nineteenth century, when professionals across the spectrum of specialization were organizing to advance the application of new knowledge and technology to social problems, to create a sense of identity and pride among themselves, and to further their particular goals through legislation and public education. National organizations representing urban experts or the rising concern for the urban environment were less common, though the National Municipal League, founded in 1894, well represented both. The

American Society of Municipal Improvements, also founded in 1894, brought together civil engineers specializing in urban questions.[2]

Early in 1897 Warren H. Manning, an Olmsted alumnus, wrote to a number of landscape architects, park superintendents, and sympathetic laymen suggesting an association of "landscape gardeners" organized into a hierarchy with landscape architects at the summit. He received twenty-nine replies, most in some degree favorable, but two heavily qualified responses shaped the sort of general organization that would result. John C. Olmsted, stepson of the great Olmsted, argued that because the few landscape architects had diverse backgrounds, a professional organization would be an arena of debate rather than a spearhead of propaganda for landscape architecture. Olmsted's partner, Charles Eliot, urged "a general association, to be made up of all who desire the advancement of landscape art." Eliot's pertinent advice continued with the suggestion of a committee organization, including a committee on membership to "drum up new members among village improvement societies and elsewhere." Landscape architects who made their living solely from their profession were few, perhaps fewer than a dozen. They needed all the allies they could muster.[3]

Manning took the advice to heart. He worked with the Louisville, Kentucky, park commission and its staff, which issued a 22 April 1897 call for a 20–21 May meeting of "Park Commissioners, Park Architects, and Park Engineers," baiting them with a postconference trip to Nashville and the Tennessee Centennial Exposition. Twenty-seven men, plus the nine-man Louisville delegation, responded despite the short notice. They included park board presidents and park superintendents but also some of the younger landscape architects who would become major figures in City Beautiful planning: John Olmsted, Manning, and Kessler.[4]

Three themes dominated the resulting organization's seven-year existence. The first was to move beyond the concept of the original call, "a wider influence . . . throughout the country in the line of park work and in proper construction of pleasure grounds for the people," to Eliot's idea of appeals to "all who desire the advancement of landscape art." The group reflected this broader quest in the cumbersome name it chose, the American Park and Outdoor Art Association (APOAA). Marianna Griswold Van Rensselaer's *Art Out-of-Doors* (1893) supplied both the name and the idea of inclusiveness, suggesting the "advancement of landscape art" in varied settings, often in tandem with architecture and sculpture. Despite rearguard action in favor of a professional group, the APOAA emphasized from the first its national and inclusive character.[5]

Second, the APOAA affirmed what were by then traditional Olmstedian ideals. John Olmsted in a paper "The True Purpose of a Large Public Park," delivered at the first meeting, spoke against the rising demands for active recreational and institutional space in landscape parks. The purpose of parks, he declared, was to enable large numbers of people to "enjoy beautiful natural scenery and to obtain occasional relief from the nervous strain due to the excessive artificiality of city life." Park commissions should not cater to demands for cheap thrills of the "Coney Island" type from those who "do not know what is good for them when they go to a park to look for more exciting pleasures. They should be gradually and unconsciously educated to better uses of large public parks and not have their crude demands alone catered to." Olmsted urged a decades-old solution, reserving "suitable lands adjoining a large public park which can be held in reserve, as sites for public museums, grounds for parades, fireworks, public speaking, baseball . . . skating, . . . zoological collections, for a public conservatory, and so on." If pressures for building in landscape parks were not resisted, "a large public park is little more than a tract of beautiful vacant building lots, which the public is temporarily enjoying as a playground, until it shall be gradually required for one public or semi-public building after another."[6]

Other papers called for apolitical park management, for subordinating fountains and statuary to landscape effects, and for subjecting park development to a preconceived design, all respectable Olmstedian principles. Another extolled public investment in parks and hailed the rise in real estate values presumably attributable to parks, a faithful echo of Olmsted's earlier assertions.[7]

The rhetorical commitment to the old values, though present to the end, steadily weakened. The change made sense in the context of rapidly changing definitions of urban beauty. When the APOAA organized in 1897, declaring "the times are ripe for action," the times had passed for seeing or shaping the city exclusively in Olmstedian terms. The World's Columbian Exposition, that enormous cultural influence, amazed the public during the summer and early autumn of 1893. The same year saw the publication of the plans for the Boston metropolitan park system and for the park system of Kansas City, Missouri, both examples of advanced Olmstedian practice that left much of the old rhetoric behind. In 1893 Richard M. Hunt founded the neoclassically oriented Municipal Art Society in New York, and in 1899 the organized municipal art movement held a convention. The latter year saw the first use of the phrase *City Beautiful* in something like its mature meaning. By then the village improvement movement—with citizen activism and the recapture of a sense of community at its core—was assuming an urban dimension. The antibillboard fight was under way. Engineers were solidly entrenched in appointive municipal offices. From these bastions they made a daily impress on the city's physical form that the landscape architects would never match. Though they made some contributions to comprehensive planning, engineers more often won civic admiration for solving specific, immediate problems of drainage, water supply, and traffic. Engineers and political scientists were proponents of cost-conscious, efficient, technologically proficient conduct of urban government.[8]

Early in 1902 the Senate Park Commission formally unveiled its stunning, neoclassical scheme for the revitalization of Washington, D.C. The next year Charles M. Robinson published his epochal *Modern Civic Art, or the City Made Beautiful*, a systematic advocacy of urban beauty. The organized playground movement was rapidly growing. By then a myriad of civic organizations had developed on local and national levels, shared overlapping memberships, and were actively exchanging information related to common goals in an atmosphere of infectious optimism about the urban future. These activities and events had left traditional, narrow park concerns behind, even as Olmsted himself had done. In the course of doing so, however, they had invested planning with values that Olmsted did not share. Olmsted's legatees had to accommodate themselves to the new values and groups or suffer a loss of influence.

The third theme of the APOAA meetings and publications grew from this reality. That theme was the acceptance of newer trends and events, the incorporation of the new ideas into park-related matters and outdoor art, and alliance with like-minded groups. The APOAA's moves were evident at its 1898 meeting at Minneapolis, where Olmstedian sentiments from H. W. S. Cleveland and others competed with rising concerns for active recreation (sports and the like) and urban beauty. Speakers who urged getting the poor to the parks, restricting the use of Keep Off the Grass signs in parks, and enhancing the childhood environment presaged the organized playground and adult recreation movements. Other papers revealed how quickly the village improvement movement was spreading to cities. Edwin L. Shuey of the National Cash Register Company in Dayton, Ohio, detailed his firm's efforts to spruce up its grounds, plant flowers and shrubs, and spread the gospel of cleanliness and beauty. Its influence had resulted in an improvement association and improvement sessions in children's Sunday school.[9]

Mrs. Robert Pratt of the Minneapolis Improvement League announced that the purpose of her organization was to create "one of the most healthful and beautiful cities in the world." The league was agitating against overflowing garbage, billowing smoke, the male habit of spitting on the sidewalk, obstreperous billboards, and ugly vacant lots. The organization favored leashing dogs, hitching horses, and removing board fences, all worthy goals, even if none of them had much to do with outdoor art.[10]

The pure Olmstedian flame flickered in the midst of its keepers. During his banquet remarks, L. E. Holden, the editor of the *Cleveland Plain Dealer*, declared that Minneapolis was a "beautiful city" because of its parks and boulevards. Olmsted could not have imagined anything more farfetched. The grand old man of landscape architecture believed in the benign influence of parks on all urban residents, and he believed in creating fine residence districts and linear park extensions by building boulevards. He never hoped to beautify the entire city through some aesthetic ripple effect. The city was harsh and hard, and parks and boulevards were alternatives to it. Yet there was Holden, announcing that parks and boulevards had the power to beautify a city. But

Holden's statement was another instance of rhetoric pulling abreast of reality. City plans from the hands of Olmsted and others had for several years assumed the aesthetic infiltration of parks and boulevards into the urban fabric.[11]

The broadening movement within the APOAA continued. At its 1900 meeting in Chicago the group received Frederick Law Olmsted, Jr.'s major report on outdoor advertising and heard George Kriehn's withering denunciation of the billboards. "The ancients' guardian of hell was a huge dog with three heads, called Cerberus," Kriehn declared. "Chicago's Cerberus is negligence, and the three heads are dirt, smoke, and billboards." The billboard concern became a crusade, part of the continuing interest in municipal improvement.

In 1903 George A. Parker, the park superintendent of Hartford, declared in the traditional vein, "I believe with all my heart and soul in the naturalistic park, and in its beauty, restfulness and in the inspiration which it gives to everyone who passes within its borders." In the next breath he descended to heresy. "I do not believe it is much help to the workman and his family. They seldom go there, and many of them never go." So much for the landscape park as the site of friendly interclass mingling. Parker's solution for the industrial city was "a system of parks, one of which should be a large country park but I would not build it first." Parker would build three- to ten-acre parks in working-class neighborhoods. Each small park would be a community center with children's playgrounds, a sports stadium, well-lighted outdoor tables, and a roomy shelter. Here the city would hold band concerts and the workingman would "arrange for himself lecture courses, debating clubs, theatricals, concerts and parties." The workingman, Parker concluded, had no use for "paternalism, but he does need and is willing to pay for communityism if the city will provide the way in which it can be brought about."[12]

Olmsted had recommended neighborhood parks, of course, partly to supplement the landscape park and partly to accommodate working-class activities incompatible with a naturalistic park. However, bright lights, parties, and concerts appealing to, rather than elevating, working-class taste were outgrowths of the cacophonous, nerve-wracking city and emphatically not part of Olmsted's design world. Parker had stood Olmsted on his head. Not only had he carried Olmsted's evolving designs to a point where they embraced the city's active life rather than rejecting it, he had boldly advocated the revolution within a context of Olmstedian rhetoric. And the entire apostasy appeared in a report signed by John Olmsted![13]

By 1903, too, the idea of landscape design had stretched to include the aesthetic development of ordinary residential streets, of home grounds as modest as a cottage plot, and of public buildings. *Outdoor art*—a phrase once restricted to architecture, landscape design, sculpture, and horticulture—had expanded nearly to meaninglessness. It included the beautification of school grounds, the school garden movement, forestry, scenic preservation, and all the miscellaneous efforts to control urban ugliness.[14]

Despite its intellectual and ideological development, the APOAA had succeeded merely in reaching out to embrace a movement. It had not directed or captured it. Its small size was symptomatic of its limitations, although at first the members could take heart from a rapid increase. The thirty-six founders soon brought ten others into the committee structure, including Marianna Van Rensselaer, Liberty Hyde Bailey of Cornell University, and August R. Meyer, a wealthy Kansas City businessman and park commissioner. In 1899 there were 252 members. Four years later the APOAA could boast 413 individual members, ten auxiliary local and regional societies, and 373 individual members in its women's auxiliary, formed to press for aesthetic and sanitary reform on the local level. The auxiliary also listed fourteen affiliated societies and nine local branches. The gain was stunning if expressed as a percentage increase over the original membership but hardly remarkable for a seven-year-old nationwide organization. Worse, growth was slowing. Secretary Robinson complained in 1903 of but twenty new members during the past year.[15]

Moreover, the character of the APOAA membership was changing, even as its objectives reached beyond the promotion of outdoor art narrowly defined. The occasional struggles of park designers and officials to gain control of the organization were desperate responses to the change. So was the complaint of Edward C. Van Leyen, a Detroit park commissioner, in 1900 that while park commissions paid the way of several members to the annual meetings and while the papers were good, the sessions were "mostly foreign to park work." The formation in 1899 of the American Society of Landscape Architects and of various park superintendents' organizations at about the same time helped to decrease the demands for professional control. The sheer weight of numbers of citizen activists as opposed to professionals clinched the issue. "Less than one-sixth of our members are park commissioners and less than one-third are directly connected with the management of parks so far as I can determine," wrote Manning, then the secretary, in 1901. "The majority of our members represent the unofficial general public who believe that the *beauty and healthfulness of communities* [italics added] depend not alone upon their parks, but upon the efforts of individuals and organizations to raise the standard of the community by working to improve the surroundings of factories, business establishments, churches, schools, and homes."[16]

The APOAA confirmed its direction in 1902 with two moves. The first followed an "Experience Meeting," when about a dozen representatives of national civic groups met at the APOAA convention to exchange information and ideas. The upshot was an APOAA resolution to name a representative to a committee on a proposed federation of civic societies, tentatively named the Civic Alliance. The representative, Robinson, and the new president of the APOAA, Clinton Rogers Woodruff, personified the increased number and activity of organizations striving for civic improvement. Robinson was active in the City Beautiful movement as a member of organizations, a writer, and a planner. Woodruff's election to the presidency of the APOAA affirmed its abandonment of narrow professional concerns, for Woodruff was also the secretary of the National Municipal League. Together Robinson and Woodruff wrote most of the proposed Civic Alliance charter, which provided for the some forty organizations involved in one phase or another of civic work to have a common clearinghouse of information "to eliminate duplication of effort, and to secure a greater efficiency than is now possible." Each group would maintain its identity but the unwritten assumption of the Civic Alliance was its operation as an umbrella organization that would encourage the merger of its smaller, weaker constituents.[17]

The Civic Alliance never matured, despite endorsements from the APOAA, the National Municipal League, the Architectural League of America, and other organizations. The APOAA had more success with its second initiative: to study the possibility of merging with an organization sharing its goals, the American League for Civic Improvement. The ALCI was younger and smaller but active in municipal improvement from its beginnings in 1900. Moreover, its involvement with municipal improvement immersed the ALCI in the larger urban progressive movement.[18]

Middle-class and upper-middle-class people inspired and staffed the widely ranging progressive movement. Their aims included the spreading of middle-class values through the uplift of unfortunates and the establishment of their own cultural hegemony. They promoted the adoption of business efficiency in government and in private, nonbusiness realms such as reform and philanthropic organizations. They wished to tame the apparently disorganized, wildly growing city and to establish or restore a sense of community—that is, feelings of civic responsibility, of commitment to a common purpose, and of municipal patriotism. The progressives exuded hope, optimism, and a conviction of their own rightness. They believed that they could reform through successive approximations of their urban ideal—a clean, beautiful, well-governed city—and eventually achieve a heaven on earth, secular in form though imbued with Christian principles. They called their movement the "civic renaissance," the "civic awakening," and "the uplift in American cities," terms indicative of their lofty aspirations.[19]

Municipal improvement, despite its later link with progressivism, traced its origins to the pre–Civil War village improvement movement. Village improvement from its formal beginnings in the 1850s shared some of the impulses in nineteenth-century American life eventually subsumed under progressivism, such as community pride. Its ultimate value for progressive city planning was, however, its comprehensive vision of the village. All parts of the village, in this view, could be made beautiful or at least be beautified. This distinctly non-Olmstedian outlook gained ground through the nineteenth century until, in 1898, the editor of the *Cleveland Plain Dealer* applied it to Minneapolis, a city of 200,000. The elements of the ideal vision included well-drained soil, up-to-date sanitation, tree-lined streets and walks, promenades, open ground, an attractive railroad station, presentable shops, trim front lawns with fences removed, flowers, and freshly painted houses bespeaking a satisfying home life and an active community involvement.[20]

This comprehensive view of the village was not comprehensive planning or planning of any sort, if planning is the conscious effort to direct population growth by shaping the community's form. For one thing, village improvement began in New England, where arresting town decline was the issue, not controlling growth. For another, the advocates of village improvement thought of discrete projects resulting collectively in physical attractiveness and community betterment. Their concerns did not revolve around one fulcrum for development, such as a park and boulevard system.

The village improvement movement was portentous, nevertheless, and not the least because the idea of the whole community as a potentially beautiful place moved from the village to embrace the small and medium-sized city. Before the turn of the century this idea had merged with park and boulevard system planning to produce a new notion of civic beauty. This was a vision of aesthetically powerful parks and boulevards quickening beautification in all urban areas. The improvement movement also had hit upon a descriptive yet marvelously elastic word. *Improvement* referred to the entire movement, its ultimate goal of community attractiveness, and each of the activities involved, whether they were strictly utilitarian, entirely aesthetic, or combined beauty and use, like a street macadamized to provide improved driving while reducing dust film on houses and plants. *Improvement* was much better for these purposes than *outdoor art*, a phrase limited to aesthetic connotations. Village improvement demonstrated the inseparability or at least the effective combination of beauty and utility. The paved street or walkway was one example. A tree planted to grace a street or yard while it helped to drain the soil through transpiration was another. Finally, village improvement presumed active citizen involvement—a vital feature of municipal improvement and of the City Beautiful movement.

The tradition of village improvement has it that summer visitors to New England villages insisted on urban amenities such as porches and bay windows. The founder of the first improvement society, Mary Hopkins of Stockbridge, Massachusetts, supposedly was shamed into organizing the Laurel Hill Association (1853) when she "overheard some of the visitors commenting on the intelligence of a population willing to live in" a town "devoid of any attempt at sanitation or adornment." The visitors and Hopkins herself may not have given enough credit to the town's trees, which Downing remembered as helping to create "long and pleasant avenues . . . refreshing and beautiful to look upon." However that may be, local activists wished to combat a selective draining away of population to cities, leaving behind a contented, uncaring residue. Added impetus for the movement came from the example of the cities' suburbs, which offered spacious yards, trees, sanitation, and other amenities without urban heat, noise, and crowding. Greater village health and beauty would arrest the stagnation or decline in town property values. "Every acre of land and every homestead in Stockbridge has appreciated in value by reason of this society," wrote Birdsey Grant Northrup, an early advocate of village improvement. In New Milford, Connecticut, a refurbished main street, resuscitated green, and other changes begun in 1897 had "attracted wealth and culture from abroad and enhanced the value of property."[21]

Village improvement muted elite concern over the influx of immigrant or other strange populations and over the loss of homogeneity and spontaneity. A villagewide improvement campaign focused on one large, simple, surmountable problem that united the town in the face of its physical decline. "Indeed among the best services of an efficient local improvement society," Northrup declared, "is the solvent it provides for the animosities of politics and religion in furnishing a safe common ground for the display of mutually beneficial activity. A society engaging all classes instead of one or two is bound to be more immediately successful than one that includes only one class or 'set.'"[22]

Village improvement provided a major outlet for the talent and energy of summer residents and, especially, of middle-class women. "Many efficient associations have been formed by women, and of nearly all at least a part of the officers are women," Northrup wrote. "Women succeed better in getting money and in securing the cooperation of all classes." The Honesdale, Pennsylvania, association limited full membership to women, admitting men only as honorary members. The proponents of village improvement also urged a children's auxiliary to interest the young in community activity at an impressionable age. Improvement activities included prizes for tree planting or brightened dooryards. In Stockbridge the famed financier Cyrus W. Field, who was born in the town, and others donated prizes. These led in turn to more substantial donations including an improved railroad station and grounds, a library, and a mountain park.[23]

From Massachusetts the movement quickly spread through New England and the Middle Atlantic states. In 1880 a vigorous association organized in Wyoming, Ohio. The next year the concerned citizens of Pasadena, California, formed the Village-Improvement and Library Association. Aiken, South Carolina, acquired a Village Improvement Society in 1895. In the closing years of the nineteenth century, the improvement impulse moved upward on the population scale to cities and large towns. Some citizens of Springfield, Massachusetts, a city of 44,000, formed the Springfield Improvement Society in 1889. Its statement of purpose demonstrated how the comprehensive ideas of village improvement were migrating. The society proposed "to cultivate public sentiment in beautifying the homes, streets, and surroundings of Springfield and to promote in every legitimate manner the best development of the whole city." The society encouraged such disparate activities as wintertime indoor flower growing, street improvement, and the acquisition of 340-acre Forest Park, all but 93 acres of which was donated.[24]

As village improvement matured into municipal improvement, it pointed the way to identification with the national progressive goals of civic responsibility, efficiency in government, and nonpartisanship. One student of the phenomenon, Mary Caroline Robbins, discerned a connection between a village population "niggardly with their money for sanitary and aesthetic purposes" and a village "extravagant with franchises to all sorts of companies, to which they give permission to hack trees, to tear up roads, and to disfigure streets with unsightly poles and wires, regardless of the added expense they bring upon the town." Obviously, the civic response to the ravages of utilities companies lay in a thoroughgoing program of civic aesthetics. Northrup claimed that efficient urban road systems would be built when the effective administration of road building lifted "the roads, as we do the schools, out of politics." The trees, flowers, street sprinkling, and town hall at Wyoming, Ohio, demonstrated not only "town pride and civic patriotism" but "the wisdom of excluding National politics from local elections."[25]

National magazines carried articles on the growth of village improvement, but the journal *Home and Flowers* (originally called *Home Florist*) gave exceptional space to town beautification associations. "These articles were fully illustrated, showing the beauty in plaza, street and yard and the improved sanitary conditions." The mail response to the series overwhelmed the writer, Jessie M. Good, who responded to several correspondents' suggestions about the need for a national organization to act as a clearinghouse of improvement information and advice. The improvement proponents who gathered in 1900 at Springfield, Ohio, the headquarters of *Home and Flowers*, organized the National League of Improvement Associations. During the next two years the organization became closely identified with the influential Chautauqua movement and renamed itself the American League for Civic Improvement (ALCI). The new name indicated a shift from an emphasis on the organizational clearinghouse function to, first, individual and corporate memberships (as the APOAA had done from its beginning) and, second, an aggressive dispensation of information and propaganda on behalf of civic beauty. The ALCI moved its headquarters from Springfield to Chicago, a change calculated to "give to the propaganda of the League a metropolitan tone and a wider appeal."[26]

The ALCI maintained its contacts with village improvement. It also strove to become the national organizational spokesman for municipal improvement. The majority of papers and reports at its August 1901 meeting involved urban organizations (such as the Woman's Civic League of St. Paul and the dynamic Harrisburg, Pennsylvania, Civic Club) and urban improvement concerns (including the school garden movement and smoke abatement). Mira Lloyd Dock, a Harrisburg City Beautiful activist, spoke about her recent forestry study trip to Europe. Dock's prominence on the program symbolized the central role of women in the emerging City Beautiful movement and the movement's indivisible concern for the preservation or re-creation of natural beauty, whether urban or rural.[27]

Another indication of the ALCI's cityward orientation was the election to its presidency of Charles Zueblin, a University of Chicago sociologist with a reputation as a dynamic speaker. The ALCI held part of its convention at Buffalo during the Pan-American Exposition, an action bespeaking the presumed identity between expositions and municipal improvement. Sessions at Lake Chautauqua symbolized the ALCI's propaganda and educational role. The appointment of a committee to study the possibility of federation with the APOAA revealed how the comprehensive planning of the landscape architects and the comprehensive view of village improvement had merged in municipal improvement. This merger was also evidenced by the growing number of experts and citizen activists taking membership in the ALCI while playing active roles in the APOAA.[28]

A resolution to the president of the Louisiana Purchase Exposition, scheduled to be held in St. Louis in 1904, lent support to a movement, already under way, for a municipal improvement exhibit. The resolution expressed the ALCI's enthusiasm for education and publicity and its acceptance of newer ideas of civic design, including grouped buildings and well-designed street fixtures such as lamps and trash receptacles. The resolution hoped for "an exhibit of Municipal Art and Science" to include, significantly, "a small group of buildings, located, if possible about a plaza. The site should be isolated to insure the illustration of certain outdoor principles of city making," an early use of the term. "The buildings," the resolution continued, "should contain exhibits of maps, plans, photographs and projections of the leading municipal improvements of the world, as well as plaster casts of public buildings, bridges and statuary, with representations of artistic and scientific street fixtures."[29]

Significant as the resolution was, the codification of the municipal improvement movement occurred a few months before the August 1901 ALCI meeting with the publication of Charles Mulford Robinson's *The Improvement of Towns and Cities; or, the Practical Basis of Civic Aesthetics*. The book soon sold out its first printing. Before 1901 ended it was in the first of many reprintings or revisions. It was a remarkable achievement for a man who was neither architect, landscape architect, nor engineer and who for many years lacked formal technical training in any related field such as urban horticulture or drafting. Robinson was a journalist, publicist, and poet, who nevertheless wrote twenty-five published planning reports noted for their insightful analysis and careful recommendations. In addition he wrote other reports, scores of magazine articles, and seven other books. He held the first appointment to the Chair of Civic Design at the University of Illinois in 1913. Despite this record, a sympathetic critic doubted whether any other of his achievements "actually made a greater contribution to the betterment of cities than" *The Improvement of Towns and Cities*.[30]

Superficially Robinson seemed an unlikely man to wield influence over a nationwide movement or to deal effectively with the politicians, official boards, private civic groups, and commercial bodies involved with planning in the age of the City Beautiful. Born in 1869 in Ramapo, New York, he was taken to Rochester while an infant and grew up there. The University of Rochester awarded him the A.B. degree in 1891. After graduation he plunged into newspaper editing and article writing and published two limited-edition books about Rochester. In maturity Robinson dressed neatly to the point of nattiness and wore a moustache and a trim, short Vandyke on his heart-shaped face. He parted his hair down the middle. His broad, high forehead rose above large, luminous eyes. However much he appeared to be an aesthete, Robinson presented his judgments firmly and clearly. As did many another shrewd planning consultant, he deferred to local expectations by incorporating existing or desired improvements in his plans. His optimistic outlook on the American city and its future dovetailed nicely with the prevailing progressive reform sentiments.[31]

In 1899 Robinson laid the base for *The Improvement of Towns and Cities* when he published a three-part series "Improvement in City Life" in the *Atlantic Monthly.* The third article, "Aesthetic Progress," forecast much of the book and used the phrase *City Beautiful* to describe the growing movement. The editors of *Harper's Magazine*, impressed by the *Atlantic* articles, asked him to go to Europe to investigate and write for *Harper's* a series on municipal improvement in Europe. Thus Robinson deepened the already sizable knowledge of European civic art he displayed in "Aesthetic Progress." The *Harper's* series duly appeared, but Robinson's abundant material and the rising interest in municipal improvement suggested a book-length treatment.[32]

The Improvement of Towns and Cities was an elaborate municipal improvement tract, as its title suggested. Robinson's foreword included a "partial list" of seventy-five local, state, and national improvement societies in the United States alone, excluding settlement houses, cultural institutions, village improvement societies, state federations of women's clubs, state municipal leagues, park commissions, and other organizations involved in improvement work. Robinson adopted the comprehensive view of the city implied by his use of "city building." He exempted no urban area from beautification effort, even if limited to street cleaning, screening of unpalatable scenes, or nuisance abatement. He insisted upon ensuring "that civic art's transforming touch is carried into every portion of the community." He refused to follow "the custom for municipal art to avert its face from tenement districts," arguing instead for the constructive exploitation of potential ethnic and "scenic picturesqueness" in slum areas. He tied this comprehensive view to the idea of a park and boulevard system articulating the city and controlling its growth. Again and again he stressed the inseparability of beauty and utility. "The best planned city," he asserted, "would be hideous if the care stopped with the planning." A bridge, for example, was so "monumental a structure that we should not be satisfied merely with durability and strength, but should demand that to these be added fitness, grace, and beauty." Of overhead wires, he wrote that "clear as is the menace of their web in case of fire, or the danger of electric shock . . . these real perils are referred to no more commonly than is the detraction of their mesh to city beauty."[33]

Robinson also recognized the citizen activist, whose work, however limited or narrow, created a piece of the comprehensive improvement mosaic. He termed his study a "handbook" highlighting the "co-ordination of the efforts, the dependence of each upon all the others, in order to secure a logical, harmonious result; the place and duty of each regiment of fighters in the battle for urban beauty. . . . There is no one panacea for the ugliness, dreariness, or monotony of towns and cities; there is no one road to victory." By using such terms as "city beauty," "urban beauty," and "city beautiful" Robinson welcomed the civic design concepts centering on grouped public buildings, formal spatial arrangements, murals, statuary, and graceful street furniture and integrated them with existing ideas of municipal improvement.[34]

The Improvement of Towns and Cities revealed the rich texture of the City Beautiful movement, although Robinson as yet focused on municipal improvement. He dealt with virtually all aesthetic and practical urban developments, historic and recent, except for subsurface drainage and transportation. Urban sites, watercourses, playgrounds, street patterns, paving, lighting, and sanitation, as well as the aesthetic possibilities of street furniture and utilities, passed under review. He addressed the need for controlling urban smoke, noise, and billboards. He underscored the value of natural beauty by advocating street trees, flower gardens, parks, and drives, but was equally concerned with the sculptural, mural, and architectural arts. He stressed the urgency of the need for popular education in the arts of civic design, because the ultimate success of art rested on public opinion. He pointed to valuable European examples such as Scottish and English cities' regulations of advertising signs, the work of the Society for Checking the Abuses of Public Advertising in England, and the Belgian civic art organization L'œuvre nationale belge. American cities furnished him with practical examples of all the concerns, from street sweeping in New York to the creation of a Municipal Art League to promote the group plan of Cleveland's public buildings.[35]

Robinson frankly accepted the city, artificial though it might be, as an aesthetic object. He urged cities and towns to reserve the "dominating height" for the public, both because it would be a commanding overlook "whence the city may be mastered at a glance," and because the citizen could gaze upon the common property. He held out for naturalistic treatment of harbors and river courses, but "if commerce must rule" he urged "that the shore line be made richly urban" instead of degenerating into "degraded nature." Adroitly, he brought in Olmstedian arguments to bolster his progressiveness: one vital reason for smoke abatement was that uncontrolled smoke drove the wealthy and their vulnerable art collections to cities with cleaner atmospheres. Also, he asserted that parks were the mingling places of the rich and the poor and improved the areas adjacent to them, and their "pastoral scenes" possessed "nerve-soothing power." However, his discussions of municipal art societies, art commissions, and the neoclassical architecture of grouped public buildings revealed the impact of the civic design movement. So too did his acknowledgment of the premier position of the architect, who "far more easily than his *conferes*, can offer . . . a new and tangible civic ideal. He can lead the citizen of to-day to compare his city . . . with the city that might be . . . ten, twenty, or thirty years hence."[36]

Robinson found the solution to a dilemma troubling to City Beautiful advocates although they rarely faced it directly. When they suggested the possibility of beauty in all parts of the city, they denied the Olmstedian view of the immutable city. Yet they knew very well that the city was not supple. It yielded, to be sure, but only to forms more urbanistic, as when residential districts retreated before commercial or industrial encroachments. The advancing commercial and industrial areas, as well as many residential tracts, were neither natural nor friendly to humans. Could something so natural, so filled with life as a park, be sutured into such an unreceptive environment? The solution, Robinson wrote, was tenaciously to blend the beauty of a park and boulevard system into the city. Beauty could not be "superimposed" or "added on." A park, he wrote, almost backing into his resolution of the dilemma, "remains a separate entity until it becomes an essential feature of the city's plan, grows into a seemingly natural part of its organism." In a sentence Robinson had endowed the city with life and negated the problem by offering a different way of viewing the city. The city was an "organism" conducive to shaping, molding, and directed growth.[37]

The municipal improvement movement reached maturity at the 1902 meeting of the ALCI. President Charles Zueblin's address, "A Decade of Civic Improvement," provided a fully developed, if too historically tidy, rationale for the movement. Though its lineage could be traced to the Stockbridge improvement, Zueblin declared that 1893 was really the pivotal year. In 1893 and after, most park and boulevard systems were established or grew. Before then there was little civic spirit, little conscious effort to shape cities, and little training of the citizen in urban necessities. Above all, the fabulous World's Columbian Exposition of 1893 provided "for the first time in the history of universal expositions, a comprehensive plan for buildings and grounds on a single scale . . . happily accomplished by the cooperative effort of the chief architects, landscape architects, and sculptors of America." Zueblin's enlisting the stunning Chicago fair in the service of municipal improvement was adroit, for he could then relate later urban improvements to the exposition's order, symmetry, neoclassical beauty, and landscape effects. Recent plans for Harrisburg, Pennsylvania, and Washington, D.C., and other developments had "brought us to the point where no city should be content with anything less than a comprehensive plan incorporating the best accomplishments of the last ten years." The municipal improvement movement would have been "sadly premature" in 1893 but had progressed in ten years to a condition requiring the "unification of improvement forces."[38]

The ALCI's actions paralleled Zueblin's words. It moved beyond the previous year's decision to seek "close affiliation" with the APOAA and chose a committee to study federation with the APOAA. The ALCI selected as its new president J. Horace McFarland, a prosperous businessman, APOAA member, and citizen activist who had labored for the Harrisburg plan. McFarland delivered, in absentia, a major address to the convention, "Harrisburg's Advance," which stressed the role of the layman in defining and promoting the essentials of the plan. His election emphasized the ascendancy of the informed, involved citizen in the municipal improvement movement. Clinton Rogers Woodruff's election to the presidency of the APOAA responded to the same circumstance. By then the two organizations had all but formally merged. The expert's eclipse in the APOAA meant that the two lay-dominated groups shared common ideas and purposes and advocated the identical improvement methods. Virtually their only difference was size, the APOAA's 819 members of 1903 comparing with the ALCI's 1902 membership of 517, a membership partly overlapping that of the older, larger organization.[39]

McFarland's was one among many citizen voices raised at the ALCI convention. Jane Addams spoke on the "Artistic Possibilities in European Immigrants," a caution against destroying the entire immigrant heritage during the Americanization process. Justus Ohage, speaking on "The Smoke Nuisance in St. Paul," attacked the equation of dense smoke with municipal prosperity. Mrs. Louis Marion McCall, a vice-president of the Civic League of St. Louis, traced the origins of the league to the influence of the forthcoming Louisiana Purchase Exposition and the desire of some St. Louisians to present a clean urban face to exposition visitors. Some talks strayed from matters of immediate citizen concern, as in Albert Kelsey's "Architecture, Signs and Fixtures."[40]

Laymen were ascendant in the APOAA and the ALCI but they never doubted the planning expert's central role. They marked out a division of labor between layman and expert. Laymen might presume to make general recommendations, such as the parking of a certain bluff or ravine or the general sweep of a boulevard along a riverbank, but their major function was to deliver the public support and funds for improvements. The planning expert or team of experts made specific recommendations about park boundaries, paving, or public building groups, and about how individual projects should be integrated with the whole. The APOAA membership did not forget its origins in park professionalism, and the citizen activists of the ALCI upheld the expert against the well-meaning incompetent. "Experience prompts me to suggest," said Kelsey of the ALCI and the Architectural League of America, "that the [1902] convention should recommend all improvement societies to avoid costly blunders by including an expert advisor as a paid member of the executive board." Kelsey added an organic metaphor: "The anatomy of a city is too complex to be trifled with." The expert bore the same relation to the urban "anatomy" as a physician to a patient. "Municipal art is never the result of amateurish experiment, and an expert adviser is as essential upon an improvement board as a doctor on a hospital staff."[41]

During the later nineteenth century, landscape designers consciously united with the broader municipal improvement movement. In 1903 their APOAA and the improvement-oriented ALCI agreed to merge. In doing so the landscape designers modified Olmstedian verities such as the preeminent role of the large landscape park as the scene of class mingling and passive recreation, and the city's inorganicism and immutability. Municipal improvement absorbed a sizable conceptual cluster from village improvement, but three contributions from the earlier movement to the larger City Beautiful stand out. They are (1) the belief in the potential beauty of the whole community, not just new or favored portions of it; (2) the inclusiveness of the idea of "improvement," comprehending all physical developments whether utilitarian, aesthetic, or some combination of the two; and (3) the inseparability of beauty and utility. Municipal improvement encouraged citizen activists, male and female, to preempt a large planning domain, an attitude congruent with the progressive reform impulse.

The American Civic Association (ACA) gave organizational expression to the struggle for the City Beautiful, uniting citizen activists and professionals in the fight for civic perfection. It resulted from the merger negotiations of the APOAA and the ALCI, consummated in 1904 at the Louisiana Purchase Exposition. The ALCI president, McFarland, presided over the ACA and would for twenty years. The new organization's structure and function reflected his influence. McFarland was a firm feminist who had no use for organizational distinctions between men and women. He abandoned the women's auxiliary of the APOAA, although women's groups lingered for a few years in the ACA committee structure. The ACA retained the clearing-house function of the ALCI, informing its members of techniques and advances in civic improvement through articles, press releases, letters, and lectures. McFarland dropped the annual reports of the parent organizations to concentrate on another ALCI feature, a series of how-to pamphlets, in a $5\frac{1}{4}$- by 8-inch format, eight to forty-eight pages long, written by specialists. These bulletins covered beautification of the home and yard, billboard regulation, mosquito control, and village improvement. Frederick Law Olmsted, Jr., coauthored the authoritative pamphlet on smoke abatement. Joseph Lee, the recreation expert, produced a playground pamphlet that went into a second edition and, McFarland proudly noted, was pirated by the National Playground Association of America. In all, from October 1904 to November 1905, McFarland claimed that "207,641 pieces of printed matter were distributed." Despite pressure to publish annual reports, McFarland stayed with the bulletins, "invariably read and digested," in contrast to "fat but useless" annuals designed "to give temporary satisfaction and gather permanent dust on the shelves."[42]

After his organization's earliest years, McFarland in effect *was* the ACA. Until December 1908, Clinton Rogers Woodruff, former president of the APOAA, served as first vice-president and, after Robinson's brief tenure, as secretary. Woodruff, a Philadelphian, was also the secretary of the National Municipal League and at least as bright a star as McFarland in the firmament of civic activity. He probably restrained and directed his friend McFarland to a degree. Soon after Woodruff's resignation, the new secretary moved from Harrisburg to Washington, D.C., while McFarland operated the president's office from his Harrisburg printing plant. McFarland admitted that he treated his board members as rubber stamps much of the time, even though they enjoyed some independent power under the ACA constitution. He gave about half his time to the organization and to civic improvement generally, controlled the ACA's fund raising drives, and in 1914 personally made up half its four-thousand-dollar deficit.[43]

McFarland pointed the ACA toward smaller cities, explaining that two-thirds of the urban population lived in cities of 2,500 to 250,000. Most city planning dealt with the smaller places, too, yet they carried little weight in Washington or the state capitals. McFarland lectured mostly in smaller eastern cities roughly analogous to Harrisburg in population and problems or in larger but less formed communities farther west, such as Lincoln, Nebraska, and Houston and Dallas in Texas. Large cities occupied some of his thought and took some of his time, because the "big nineteen"—with 1910 populations exceeding 250,000—shared some concerns with the smaller places. For instance, no official servant intervened for any of them as the Department of Agriculture did for the rural population. The civic hopes of cities large and small fused in Washington, where City Beautiful planning had created "a permanent civic exhibit" and "the model community of America." McFarland praised the nation's capital for the work of its Fine Arts Commission, its street lighting, its "vista making," and its street tree preservation. Its government was undemocratic, but that circumstance allowed the national capital to experiment more freely with improvement ideas.[44]

Through the ACA, McFarland became the national spokesman for the City Beautiful. He wrote hundreds of letters of advice and exhortation to individuals and groups across the country. His printing company maintained 2,000 slides that were organized into several City Beautiful topics and were available to the ACA's members for a nominal fee. The company printed the ACA pamphlets, on all of which McFarland probably did some editorial work. He was in such demand for speeches that he charged fifty dollars (raised to seventy-five dollars in 1916) plus expenses and the cost of a lantern slide projector for each appearance, though he occasionally remitted his fee. Despite charges that were fairly substantial sums for the citizen groups before which he appeared, he had delivered his "Crusade against Ugliness" lecture or a similar speech in more than 250 cities and towns by 1911. In addition, he addressed Theodore Roosevelt's conservation conference in 1908, the annual conventions of the ACA, and other meetings. He had written *The Awakening of Harrisburg* and at least thirteen articles on Harrisburg or civic improvement by 1913. His "Beautiful America" series appeared in the *Ladies' Home Journal* from January 1904 through April 1907.[45]

The doughty printer's schedule of thirty-five or forty speeches a year made him something of a fixture at the meetings of local improvement groups and at the quasi-revivalistic City Beautiful mass meetings so popular in the early twentieth century. He carried his determination and zeal to the point of abrasiveness, but this negative personal quality was less distracting at long distance or in a brief acquaintance. His letters and speeches bluntly and crisply described unkempt urban scenes or the organizational inadequacies of citizen reform. Then his optimism and encouragement would override the hard-hitting negatives. "Your criticism of Trenton stung like sixty but was the best thing that could have happened," wrote a hearer.[46]

In the early years of McFarland's speaking and writing, the ACA grew from 1,552 members at its founding in 1904 to 2,215 two years later. Afterward, it grew more slowly, a symptom of difficulties inherent in the ACA's structure and policies and in changes in city planning. McFarland's continuing personal domination of the ACA distanced the other members from decision-making involvement. The ACA's constituent organizations were a grab bag of citizen groups having an independent, often prior local existence. They could enjoy certain ACA services through affiliation but terminating that affiliation did not affect their local status or their ACA privileges so long as one member retained an individual ACA membership. McFarland's tight administrative control did not extend to the functions of the constituent organizations and individuals and so allowed for spontaneity at the local level. His policy of nonduplication, on the other hand, restricted the role of the ACA as new citizen and professional groups emerged. But that was for the future. In its early years the ACA typified the merger of municipal improvement and landscape architecture with fresh ideas of civic design.[47]

3 ◆ The Columbian Exposition and the City Beautiful Movement

From its opening in Chicago in May 1893, the World's Columbian Exposition has exerted a major cultural influence. After its closing in October, the demolition or removal of almost all its buildings and the reconstruction of its site only heightened the poignant memory of this transient yet eternally enthralling vision of huge, white neoclassic buildings, blue lagoons, and green naturalistic landscaping. So great was its visual power that contemporaries and later critics may be forgiven for finding in the Chicago fair the source for one of the twentieth century's great historiographical clichés. It is that the exposition was the inspiration for the City Beautiful movement and the beginning of comprehensive city planning in the United States.[1] This oft-repeated, if sometimes challenged, assumption is plausible though mostly mistaken. The first objection to the prevailing interpretation is chronological. The fair closed in 1893, but the City Beautiful movement was not named until 1899 and did not mature until 1902 and after. Evidently a connection had to rely on some relationship other than a direct temporal link. Elite authors discovered visual, technical, and organizational connections and exploited them shrewdly. The second objection is cultural and rejects the idea that the exposition was a stylistic imposition on the United States. In fact, it was the fair's vivid American qualities that endeared it to the public and opened the door to acceptance of the elite argument.

Understanding this myth of the world's fair begins with a rapid overview of the exposition itself. A clamor rose in the 1880s for holding an exposition to commemorate Columbus's discovery of America. The exposition would be one more, albeit the most spectacular, of a series of international expositions celebrating progress in human endeavor while inculcating nationalism. Groups in Chicago, Washington, D.C., New York City, and St. Louis put in bids. Congress awarded the site to upstart Chicago. In 1890 Olmsted and his associate Henry Sargent Codman journeyed to the booming city and, working with Daniel Hudson Burnham and his partner John Wellborn Root, settled on the marshy, largely unimproved site at Jackson Park. Olmsted is generally credited with the site selection and landscape layout; Root, with developing the idea of a water basin surrounded by the major exhibition buildings. The finished design consisted of two juxtaposed elements. A large, naturalistic lagoon containing a "wooded island" paralleled Lake Michigan. At right angles to the lagoon, an esplanade featuring a water basin and main buildings thrust eastward to the lake. The arrangement owed much to the collaboration of Burnham, Root, Olmsted, and Codman and to the precedent of the Paris Universal Exposition of 1889. The Paris exposition revivified, on a grand scale, the practice of combining naturalistic and formal landscape elements with neoclassical design.[2]

Burnham rose to national prominence through his direction of the Chicago fair. His presence ensured that the exposition would be derivative in only the most general sense and an American original in every way that mattered. Burnham was an impressive man. Tall, with a broad-shouldered, athletic frame beginning to yield to his appetite for good food and wines, he turned forty-four in 1890. Thick, dark brown hair and a flourishing moustache set off his handsome face. His deep voice, charm, courtly manner, and erect posture were important business assets. After a series of false starts reminiscent of Olmsted's fumblings for a career, Burnham settled for good on architecture. He was then twenty-six. A year later, in 1873, he and Root left the Chicago office that employed them and formed their own firm. Root was genial, humorous, and more talented and intellectual than Burnham, but he lacked Burnham's business savvy. Burnham got the clients, established high standards of interior design, and restrained some of Root's flights of architectural fancy. It was a storybook partnership.[3]

By 1890 Burnham and Root were at the top of the pathbreaking Chicago architectural profession. The local corporation formed to deal with exposition matters on the ground retained them as consulting architects. Burnham quickly ingratiated himself with this group and with its powerful board of directors. Though a national committee supposedly exercised ultimate control, he regarded it as a remote, ineffectual nuisance and increasingly ignored it. The local directors, composed of such heavyweight Chicago businessmen as Lyman J. Gage, Cyrus J. McCormick, and Charles H. Schwab, filled the vacuum. Late in 1890 the board created the job of chief of construction and called Burnham to fill it. From that time forward he displayed an almost magisterial executive ability while consolidating his position as the undisputed manager of the exposition. He was aggressive and ambitious, persuasive and manipulative, and the beneficiary of adventitious circumstances.

One of Burnham's early requests was for the release and reappointment of everyone serving in a supervisory or consulting capacity, including Root and the Olmsted firm. All were reappointed, but they were no longer on an equal footing with Burnham. That done, Burnham next confronted a quadrilateral difficulty compounded from limited time and funds, the need to affirm a truly national exposition by inviting architects from outside Chicago to participate in building design, the jealousy of Chicago architects, who already chafed under the favored treatment shown to Burnham and Root, and the resentment of Chicagoans who would rebel against outsiders if they were allowed to pick all of the design plums. In December Burnham cited temporal and monetary constraints when requesting the local committee on grounds and buildings to eschew a single architectural firm or a competition, and instead empower him to select leading architects. The committee granted his wish. Burnham had already felt out the non-Chicagoans he wanted and thought he had them lined up. Only Van Brunt and Howe of Kansas City, formerly a Boston firm, responded favorably. The others expressed reservations. Burnham cleared this hurdle in a quick trip to New York to visit the holdouts. He was both persuasive and conciliatory. It is probable that he cut a deal with the easterners: they would come in if he would agree to their informal decision favoring a neoclassical motif and a uniform cornice line. The deal confirmed the unified grouping already planned. More importantly, Richard M. Hunt, the dean of the profession, and the firms of McKim, Mead & White, George B. Post, and Peabody and Stearns of Boston were in the bag.

Burnham had in two strokes consolidated his position as general manager and acquired the power to withstand any future challenge to his preeminence. He had selected the architects in a manner confirming his own position while meeting the immediate problems of time and money. His official letter of invitation, issued before his quick trip east, affirmed that this would be no ordinary commission. Burnham's office would "supply you with all data about materials, sizes, general disposition, and cost of building" and supervise construction. Root, he assured the easterners, "would act as your interpreter" while preserving the aesthetic integrity of their work. The easterners accepted the arrangement when they came in; Burnham had given up nothing that mattered to him, had subordinated the easterners, and had certified the national character of the fair. Further, it was now clear that Burnham and Root would design no buildings themselves, thus appeasing the envy of other Chicago architects insofar as it was possible to do so.[4]

Successful as he was, Burnham had yet to cover the fourth side of his problem, to mollify those powerful Chicagoans who wondered why a Chicago-financed exposition would not be at least partly Chicago-designed. This he did by appointing Adler and Sullivan, Solon S. Beman, Burling and Whitehouse, Henry Ives Cobb, and Jenny and Mundie. Soon Burnham's dominion would benefit from a fortuitous development.

In January 1891, while all of the architects were meeting in Chicago, John Root died. Root's death from pneumonia was a cruel blow to Burnham, and there is no doubt of the profound loss to American architecture. Root was a master of the Romanesque, was fluid and undogmatic of mind, and was concerned about developing a sense of urban ensemble. He might have objected to the exposition's neoclassical cast and its monumental uniformity. Organizationally his objections would have presented no problem, for Burnham had carefully defined and limited his authority. But Root was persuasive and respected. Then again, Root might have gone along, devoting his talents to reinforcing the neoclassical effect. What can be asserted is that Root's death removed a potential challenge to Burnham's preeminence.

The architects' conversations continued in the midst of the mourning for Root. They affirmed the exposition's neoclassicism and the uniform cornice line of the buildings. Burnham insisted upon the greatest possible individuality for each building within the confines of the neoclassic. The choice of style is scarcely surprising, considering the resurgence of the neoclassical on the East Coast and the Beaux-Arts associations or allegiances of the easterners. Given the range of building uses and sizes, Burnham's plea for diversity-in-unity made sense. All these decisions were confirmed and refined in a famous February 1891 meeting of the grounds and buildings committee with the architects, who were organized into a board of architects with Hunt as chairman. Augustus Saint-Gaudens was there to advise on sculpture.

From then until opening day Burnham oversaw the myriad of tasks involved in completing the exposition. He moved to the site and stayed there most of the time. He was by turns demanding, peremptory, patient, and humane. When architects were late with plans or renderings, or when the local staff disagreed with him or performed inadequately, he could be merciless. He exploited two local instances to tighten his administrative grip. While the exposition's director of color was out of town, Burnham approved a suggestion, popular among the architects, to paint most of the major buildings white. The director of color, William Pretyman, was properly enraged when he returned and told Burnham not to interfere in his domain. Burnham replied that the decision was his. Pretyman resigned. Burnham replaced him with Francis D. Millet, an inspired appointment. Burnham argued with Abram Gottlieb, the consulting engineer, over wind bracing for the huge but temporary buildings. Gottlieb reminded Burnham that he, not Burnham, was the engineer. Burnham responded that he knew more about wind bracing than Gottlieb, and Gottlieb quit. His replacement, a man from Burnham's firm, caused no such problems.

Burnham was apparently everywhere at once, driving everyone hard, and driving himself harder. All issues causing construction trouble or reflecting upon the exposition came to his attention. He responded by trying to extend his control over them (the pass policy and press relations, for example). If the matter were beyond his control, such as policing Jackson Park to keep out labor agitators, he insisted upon a satisfactory solution from those responsible. At the fair's end the board of directors hailed his essential contribution. Louis Sullivan, whose autobiography depreciates Burnham and denounces the neoclassical style, admitted that he demonstrated "remarkable executive capacity. He became open-minded, just, magnanimous. He did his great share." Truly Burnham had found his métier, not in neoclassicism but in the organization and administration of a great, carefully wrought enterprise.[5]

Almost all the later analyses of the exposition suggest a kind of inexorable development from Burnham's "White City" to the City Beautiful movement and city planning. The argument is pictorially plausible. Many later civic center proposals resembled the exposition's Court of Honor, substituting a rectangular turf or a paved esplanade for the water basin. *White City,* the popular phrase for the exposition, was more than descriptive. It made a linguistic connection between the "mirage" on Lake Michigan and the reformation of urban reality. A few shrewd critics warned against producing permanent civic copies of the plaster-coated fair buildings, warnings avidly seized upon by later foes of the neoclassical as prophecies of architectural atavism.

There is no question about the exposition's enormous influence. It is possible that Burnham, absorbed in the struggles of completing and staging the gargantuan undertaking, was unaware of the range and depth of that influence until the contemporary written commentaries were published. Once he grasped the implications—and in any event his understanding came early— he strove to relate his professional life and work to the great fair. In doing so he helped to converge the diverse streams of exposition influence upon the thought and aesthetic expression of the City Beautiful movement.[6]

None of this means that Burnham or the White City founded the City Beautiful; indeed, the exposition was itself an effect as well as a source. It was both a consummation and a cause. Thomas Adams's insight that "the Fair represented the culmination of a period of over twenty years' activity in the sanitary and aesthetic improvement of cities" is compelling. Adams understood that the fair was an amalgam of artistic, architectural, and engineering practices already applied in the United States.[7]

To begin with the prosaic, the fair was a sanitary wonder. The paving, nightly sweeping and cleaning, many water closets, filtered drinking water, and sewage treatment at the exposition were the apotheosis of nineteenth-century urban sanitary engineering. The functional-aesthetic segregation of commercial deliveries from daytime exposition activities, elimination of billboards, and strict control of signs and pamphlets suggested how a benevolent reform might reshape cities based on existing possibilities rather than utopian formulas. Nor were the applications of accumulated knowledge limited to sanitation and aesthetics. The generally effective Columbian Guard demonstrated how contemporary urban police techniques could maintain public safety, once freed from corruption and political interference. Transportation included the convenient but underused railroad spurs and station, an elevated intramural railway, and a moving sidewalk. The vivid nighttime strands of alternating-current light bulbs foretold the urban illumination possible with a present, if pioneering, electrical system.[8]

The women's movement, closely related in some of its phases to urban aesthetics, was well represented at the Chicago fair. The growing role of women in the spreading village improvement movement, in municipal reform, and in the cultural life of the nation was reflected in the exposition's Women's Department and in the Woman's Building, designed by a woman (winner of the only architectural competition for a national building) and embellished by the murals of Mary MacMonnies and Mary Cassatt.[9]

Adams's remark about the Chicago fair as "culmination" applies equally well to the aesthetic motifs considered to be the legacies of the exposition: building design, building grouping, landscaping, and artistic collaboration among architects, sculptors, and mural painters. The neoclassicism of the fair, though new to Chicago, was scarcely new to the Western world or the United States. American neoclassicism prospered during the early nineteenth century, to be shouldered aside by the vernacular and by other styles, notably, near century's end, the Romanesque. Neoclassicism was in eclipse but not abandoned. Architects repeated versions of the nation's Capitol with its Roman dome in statehouses across the country; other neoclassical buildings were built or survived in Washington, Boston, and Philadelphia. The resurgence of neoclassicism came first on the eastern seaboard. The design for the new Library of Congress—from the first prize in the architectural competition of 1873, through the accepted plans of 1886, to alterations before and after construction began in 1888—was modified Italian Renaissance. Its light-colored stone, rustication, classical window shapes, horizontal emphasis, and achievement of symmetry and harmony through the repetition of forms bore a strong resemblance to the neoclassic. Charles F. McKim's more graceful, sophisticated Boston Public Library (1888–95) also was Renaissance in spirit. McKim's flamboyant partner Stanford White designed the neoclassical Washington Memorial Arch (temporary version, 1889) and several other structures that imparted the neoclassical spirit through the use of light colors, arches, horizontality, and the rhythmic repetition of elements. The colonial revival, an essentially domestic design but related to the neoclassical, had begun its long run of popularity.[10]

Eastern architects had not just revived a building style, they had rediscovered the ancient tradition of the square as space defined by complementary buildings. The Chicago exposition was a dramatic showcase of neoclassicism and grouped buildings but it had a domestic precedent in Copley Square in Boston. In designing the Boston Public Library to close the west end of Copley Square, McKim treated the space as a developing Renaissance piazza. He adjusted the library's facade elements to harmonize with existing structures, including Trinity Church across the square, the Museum of Fine Arts to the south, and the S. S. Pierce Building at the southwest corner. McKim or someone else at McKim, Mead & White drew a perspective of a fountain embellishing the square, a proposal for a formal focus to augment or replace the nondescript grass plot in its middle. McKim's sense of clarity, definition, and convergence, displayed in the library and the proposed fountain, was a remarkable application to a late-nineteenth century public area.[11]

Sculptors and mural painters cooperated with the architects at the Chicago fair. Such collaboration was a hallmark of the famed Parisian Ecole des Beaux-Arts. The Beaux-Arts architectural section attracted so many Americans that it became synonymous with foreign architectural training. The Ecole emphasized the student's discovery of the logically correct solution to the architectural problem confronting him. When the student accurately applied the principles of proportion, scale, balanced arrangement of forms, and unity, he would solve the problem. The Ecole advocated no particular style, but its emphasis on logic, vigor, and the fine arts favored the classic. In 1846 the Ecole admitted Richard Morris Hunt, its first American student. Two Americans were admitted during the 1850s, ten in the 1860s, thirty-three in the 1870s, and twenty-nine through the 1880s. Organizational activity accented the growing professional numbers and rising disciplinary self-awareness. The American Institute of Architects dated from 1857, and the Architectural League of New York from 1881.[12]

The awakening American interest in patriotic embellishment influenced domestic artistic collaboration, for it brought Hunt some commissions for outdoor sculpture bases, notably the base for the Statue of Liberty. But this was not Beaux-Arts-style collaboration, for the size and shape of the statue influenced the form and volume of its base. Architect Henry Hobson Richardson, a Beaux-Arts student, produced truly collaborative works designed by the architect, embellished by the sculptor: the Brattle Square Church (competition won in 1870) and his magnificent Trinity Church (consecrated in 1877). McKim, himself a student of the Ecole and of Richardson, brought artistic collaboration to new levels with the Boston Public Library. It was not only because of the library's decorative sumptuousness that this was so, for McKim had anticipated the Chicago fair in another major respect. As David F. Burg wrote of the fair's amenities: "Within the White City every person was sovereign. Therein all could experience the rights and privileges which belonged to citizens but which they were denied by the facts of urban life." The library was but one building. McKim's intention, nevertheless, was to bring to the public the sort of glory otherwise available only to the wealthy. The building itself, the seals by Augustus Saint-Gaudens, his brother Louis's Siena marble lions flanking the main stairway, the murals by Puvis de Chavannes, John Singer Sargent, and Edwin Austin Abbey, and all the other decorations were a rich, permanent civic celebration. So were the interior and exterior sculptures originally planned for the Library of Congress.[13]

Before the exposition, then, there were definite moves toward artistic collaboration under the direction of architects, who had three goals. They wanted to impart respectability and standing to municipal art, so that public officials would no longer think in terms of construction merely, but rather of fully embellished municipal buildings. They wanted architecture to dominate the process of artistic collaboration, to advance their own profession in the eyes of their patrons, and to assert hegemony over the often complex questions of site and design. Finally, they desired to create civic monuments expressing the city's governmental and cultural functions while conducing the individual citizen to embrace higher ideals through a new artistic environment.[14]

The last consideration of the Chicago fair's antecedents involves a concern critical to the later City Beautiful—civic spirit. Nonpartisan devotion to community welfare received its highest praise during the Progressive Era of the twentieth century, but it was practiced in Chicago before the fair. The exposition, indeed, owed its Chicago location to the ability of the city's businessmen to submerge whatever political, partisan, economic, or cultural antagonisms divided them and to unite in pursuing specific goals. Chicago's businessmen were not selfless, for the exposition paid dividends to its shareholders; the fair created a brisk trade. They were capable, nevertheless, of taking risks in the name of a collective, enlightened self-interest. They were proud of Chicago's rapid development, its recovery from the fire of 1871, its park and boulevard system, and its developing cultural institutions. While New Yorkers squandered time and energy attempting to harness their world's fair bid to one or another political faction, Chicagoans organized a corporation to raise capital, developed an elaborate committee structure, and lobbied effectively for the measure that President Harrison signed in 1890. The exposition in its very existence was therefore an expression of civic pride, cooperation, and patronage of the arts.[15]

It is now evident that the White City was the focus of a wide variety of nineteenth-century advances related to the City Beautiful: sanitation; aesthetics; rationalized urban functions; women's involvement in culture, civic improvement, and urban reform; building design; artistic collaboration; architectural professionalism; and civic spirit. It has long been supposed that the World's Columbian Exposition was the origin of many of these impulses, and while this supposition is mistaken, nonetheless the 1893 fair enjoyed an enormous influence. Sorting out its impact on City Beautiful–related activities is now the task at hand. Thomas Adams's statement is once more pertinent, for after declaring the fair to be a "culmination," he wrote that it was a realization "rather than the beginning of a new period of effort." The statement is true if it is applied to Adams's larger concern, city planning, but the Adams statement must be modified to include Robinson's earlier observation about the fair. In his 1899 article on "Aesthetic Progress" he found "false" the claim "that the world's fair created the subsequent aesthetic effort in municipal life," but "to say that it immensely strengthened, quickened, and encouraged it would be true."[16]

The exposition's effects may best be considered as a dualism operating within American culture, as interacting but separable impacts on the elite and on the masses of visitors. The effect on professional artists was immediate and immense. This was because leading architects, sculptors, and muralists lent their prestige to the undertaking, demonstrating the unity of the decorative arts on an unprecedented scale. Any project that could claim the talents of

Hunt, Post, the McKim, Mead & White firm, Adler and Sullivan, and William LeBaron Jenny was certified. Among sculptors, Daniel Chester French, the rising young Frederick MacMonnies, Karl Bitter, and Lorado Taft participated. The dean of them all, Saint-Gaudens, preferred his advisory role, though his previously sculpted *Diana* flashed above McKim's Agriculture Building. Edwin H. Blashfield, Will H. Low, Kenyon Cox, and others painted murals on the plaster coves of building interiors.[17]

Their unified approach soon appeared in different guise when, in 1892 Hunt helped to found the Municipal Art Society. This collaborative artistic organization, if not born of the fair, was stimulated by it. The society's aim was nothing less than to extend the collaborative design ideal expressed in the fair to a living city, "to provide adequate sculptural and pictorial decorations for the public buildings and parks in the City of New York and to promote in every way the beautifying of its streets and public places." The society donated two allegorical murals by Edward Simmons in the Supreme Court room of the new Criminal Courts Building. For a time afterward it foundered until it hit upon holding competitions for street furniture designs. Meanwhile, the idea took hold in other cities: Cincinnati in 1894 and in Cleveland, Chicago, and Baltimore in 1899. In December of 1899 the Baltimore group held an extensively publicized Municipal Art Conference. The New York society went on to press for an official art commission and for city planning activity. National painters' and sculptors' societies also were founded in the 1890s.[18]

The fair's stunning collaborative effects probably resulted in the enriched sculptural and mural program for the Library of Congress. Sculptors French and MacMonnies and painters Blashfield, Cox, and Edward G. Simmons among others moved mallet or palette from Chicago to Washington. The fair probably also stimulated the growth of formal professional canons, such as the acquisition of an architectural degree, and the decline of the apprenticeships that Hunt had done so much to raise to respectability. Thomas E. Tallmadge found a dramatic change in illustrations in architectural journals. Up to the time of the fair two-thirds or more of contemporary American architectural scenes were in the Romanesque or similar styles. The fair produced an "immediate change" to neoclassical domination. Carroll L. V. Meeks, instead, viewed the exposition as a further incident in a gradual evolution to "Renaissance" forms. Nevertheless he ascribed great design influence to the graceful Terminal Station, with soaring arched windows above its three portals, its flanking wings, and its quiet, recessive Renaissance motifs. As Meeks put it, "this temporary station engendered a whole family of permanent stations which includes Washington, Kansas City, New York, New Orleans, Chattanooga, Detroit, and Toronto." Regional expositions copied at least some aspects of the Chicago fair, reaching a climax of sorts in the mimicry of Omaha's 1898 Trans-Mississippi and International Exposition. Lastly, the fair probably encouraged local architectural clubs to continue and extend their competitions. In 1895 the Cleveland Architectural Club held a competition for a grouping of the city's public buildings similar to the grouping of buildings around the Court of Honor.[19]

None of these professional artistic activities resulted in anything like the comprehensive, pervasive, multiple-purpose schemes that had been on the drawing boards of Olmsted and other landscape architects for a generation. An enlarged comprehensive planning emerged from the fair, first, because of the exposition's peculiarly American characteristics; second, because of their impact upon professional artists and nonprofessionals alike; and third, because Burnham and his associates projected these impressions in the stunning visual representations of the McMillan Plan for Washington, D.C. The fair's special nature grew out of its very Americanness, its size, beauty, celebration, and organization.

The exposition not only reflected American developments, it projected America. It was immense, as were the country's continental dimensions. The Jackson Park site alone comprised 686 acres, compared with the 72 of the 1889 Paris exhibition, the design model for the Chicago fair. The main fair buildings and other constructions were breathtakingly huge, a fact that may escape the viewer of their photographs in ensemble. In closeups, however, the tiny figures strolling about their bases reveal the gigantic proportions. The dome of Hunt's Administration Building soared 277 feet, 6 inches above the paving of the Court of Honor, topping the national Capitol by 57 feet. The Manufacturer's and Liberal Arts Building, the largest roofed structure in the world, measured 787 by 1,687 feet. The sculpture was in proportion, for the smallest of the figures in Frederick MacMonnies' busy Grand Columbian Fountain was a twelve-footer.[20]

Sheer dimension was, of course, not the only impressive feature. The Pyramids are big, too. But the vast complex in Chicago was created, comparatively, in a breath. The period from planning to designing, to construction, to operation and maintenance occupied less than three years. Steel, iron, and wood framing techniques, the exterior plaster called "staff," spray painting, the spirit of dedication and cooperation, not to mention Burnham's hard driving, had wrought a splendor truly urban in its scale. The White City, or Dream City, was emphatically a city, one built in a whirlwind, yet fit for royalty to gambol in. The possibility of quickly making or remaking other cities on a vast scale was present from the birth of the World's Columbian Exposition.[21]

Another American quality of the fair was the particular form of its beauty. Contemporary commentators often described the fair as the epitome of "unity," but the exposition's unity should be viewed in terms of civic design, as one component of beauty. The architects established unity through the device of the uniform cornice line and the decree that the structures around the Court of Honor should be neoclassical. They achieved harmony by a series of careful adjustments and compromises on sites and facades. Skillful siting and Burnham's stern warnings against bizarre design proposals for state buildings helped maintain the harmony of the Court of Honor throughout the grounds. The gigantic proportions of the fair's other components were so well harmonized that they, too, contributed to its beauty.[22]

The unity, harmony, and proportion of the Court of Honor have been emphasized again and again, but equal attention should be paid to the fair's controlled diversity of form and color. The landscaping combined the graceful formalism of the Great Basin with the naturalistic constructivism of the Lagoon. The architecture embraced an amazing variety of form and color from the white neoclassicism of the Court of Honor, through the highly individual, if reasonably restrained, state and national buildings, through Henry Ives Cobb's white but richly Romanesque Fisheries Building, to Louis Sullivan's polychromatic Transportation Building, with its Golden Doorway offsetting its spare, shedlike outlines. On the Court of Honor itself there was no stark contrast of white buildings and blue basin, but instead a richness of color including French's gilded *Statue of the Republic* rising 100 feet above the Great Basin. There were areas of turf and flowers. Robinson remembered, "as a half-hidden beauty of the Columbian Exposition at Chicago, beds of pansies nestled against the facade of one of the largest buildings." Nor was every building all white. The Administration Building's huge black dome sported gilded ribs. Unfortunately, the monochrome photographs and chiaroscuro engravings of the fair conceal rather than reveal its multihued diversity. The spectacular night lighting that outlined the buildings around the Court of Honor opened up new visions of urban display.[23]

The exposition's beauty was American in its architectural adaptation of neoclassicism. The architecture was not copied from Rome, Renaissance Venice, contemporary Europe, or mad interior visions of an imperial America. Christopher Tunnard's spirited defense of the White City notes that though some of the fair's "designers had been trained in France, the architecture was not the same thing being built in any European country." The buildings and their setting were designed to produce beautiful scenes on a magnificent scale. As the scale was urban, so was its beauty. The exposition affirmed the possibility of making cities beautiful.[24]

The architecture also affirmed the fair's festive purpose, as McKim's biographer remarked. The fair was, in the largest sense, a festival of international culture. In a more tangible way, every day at the fair was a festival. Again, prints and photographs fail to convey the quality of the exposition experience. Diversity of shapes and colors contributed to the festive air, but so did the playing bands, surging crowds, snapping flags, and brilliant garlands of electric light. Here was the interclass mingling and celebration so essential to Frederick Law Olmsted's vision of a successful public park. It was not, however, taking place in a park but in a showcase of American urban possibilities.[25]

Another important aspect of the fair was the organization involved in its creation. The organizational scheme was not in itself original, having developed from the Paris exposition, business precedent, and necessary improvisation. It was significant as the distillation of Chicago's civic pride. It was also a convincing demonstration of the power of organization to effect a rapid altera‐ tion of a semideveloped parkland to a splendid civic ornament. It impressed thoughtful commentators with the need to organize in order to advance change. Further, the organization included experts in landscape architecture, sculpture, painting, and architecture, with Burnham's role being that of the expert in ensemble, the coordinator and arbiter of overall effect. "A Board of Beauty made the White City the glory and the marvel that it was," Mrs. Edwin D. Mead told the 1900 meeting of the APOAA.[26]

In sum, the World's Columbian Exposition was an immediate stimulant to professional artistic activity. To professionals and nonprofessionals alike it was a powerful statement of American scale, beauty, festival, and organiza‐ tion. The fair's direct effects were enormous. Reid Badger's estimate that 5 to 10 percent of the United States population saw the fair is based on the 21,500,000 paid admissions, less multiple visits and foreign visitors, plus free admissions.[27] Badger's estimate is probably conservative and does not intend to account for the exposition's indirect influence through the descriptions of relatives and friends, articles, and illustrations. In the minds of the cultural elite and in the mass mind, the fair was linked with American progress in the urban arts and sciences. The fair was also an expression of the best features of the United States. It was in the highest sense a patriotic exercise. Burnham learned much about management and fundamental problems of visual unity and harmony during the fair's planning and construction. Nevertheless, the rich vision and demonstration that was the World's Columbian Exposition was not translated into urban planning for several years.

Consider the chronology. The fair's undoubted influence over millions of people contrasts with the delay in the widespread use of the term City Beautiful until 1899. The general adoption of Chicago exposition features such as architectural neoclassicism, spatial formality, public building groups, and axiality waited until 1902 and after. The lag dooms the argument that the City Beautiful movement sprang from the world's fair. This would be so even if the multiple origins of the movement were not considered, for by itself, the fair could be no more than a major event in the development of civic design. There simply was no demonstrable linear development from the fair through the turn of the century's rebirth of interest in civic design and the rise of national improvement organizations. The fair had an immediate effect on artistic thought and practice, but artistic collaboration and public building design are not city planning.[28]

Furthermore, when nonprofessional interest in civic design and municipal improvement grew in the late 1890s, it did not look to the fair. Interest focused instead on European cities' achievements in aesthetic and functional matters, on potentialities and missed opportunities in American cities, or on obtaining or developing park and boulevard systems. New York City's Reform Club began publishing its short-lived but influential Municipal Affairs in 1897.

Its bellwether articles on urban needs often looked to European practice and, in the tradition of American landscape architecture, held up European cities as guides and inspirations, not as models to be copied. In any case, the earliest years of the nationwide civic design and municipal improvement movements did not hark back to the White City by Lake Michigan.[29]

If it is conceded that the City Beautiful and its neoclassical city planning did not spring from the fair, then the next issue is, how and why did the fair come to be associated with the City Beautiful? We have only exchanged one historiographical problem for another if that question remains unanswered. The answer lies in the elite's realization that such a vital event could be turned to the service of urban planning. As we have seen, in his 1902 address to the ALCI, Charles Zueblin found it useful to tie the fair to the mature municipal improvement movement. Burnham's insight and activity within the context of architects' drive for dominion over urban improvement were equally critical. Other explanations, which do not ignore Burnham, should first be acknowledged and considered. One is that the terrible depression of 1893 inhibited aesthetic development, and only when economic conditions improved in the late 1890s were citizens again able to consider long-range urban goals. This explanation notes Burnham's failed attempt, despite his reputation, ingratiating manner, and careful preparation, to have a lakeshore improvement scheme accepted in Chicago during 1895–96. Similarly frustrating were the stillborn schemes for a group plan of public buildings in Cleveland. The difficulty with the "depression explanation" is dual. First, elaborate, comprehensive park and boulevard plans were drawn up, partially constructed, or expanded during the depression, perhaps partly to alleviate unemployment. Second, village improvement forged ahead with its tradition of specific betterments.[30]

Another explanation is that only after the creation of complex city plans such as Washington's McMillan Plan (1901–2) did the lessons of the fair stand forth in clear relief. But this explanation begs the question of why the Chicago fair should suddenly loom so large after the passing of more than eight years. There was never a mystery about the possible applications of the fair's elements to real cities. Besides, references to the fair in municipal improvement and civic design literature appeared in 1899, 1900, and 1901, well before the diffusion of the new plan for Washington.[31]

A third explanation of the fair's impact on city planning, combining some assertions of the first two while adding others, is necessary to a generalization fitting what is known about planning developments from 1893 to 1902. The depression certainly inhibited some planning activities. Elaborate collaborative efforts already underway, such as the Library of Congress and the Boston Public Library, continued to completion, but the later 1890s were not the time for fresh public essays in the combined arts, witness the struggles of the New York Municipal Art Society and the slow spread of the municipal art movement. Otherwise, as already noted, other aspects of urban planning continued apace. The revival of civic design—if it may be dated arbitrarily from the launching of *Municipal Affairs* in 1897—accompanied the first signs of an economic upturn and rising interest in municipal political reform. In 1897 the APOAA organized. Some APOAA members were aware from the beginning of the organizational strength of the village improvement movement. Three years later village improvement graduated to municipal improvement and became nationalized with the founding of the National League of Improvement Associations.

It was at this time that the references to the Chicago fair appeared. The question is, why did the improvement groups and the professional organizations turn to the fair for specific examples? The answers differ with each, but they have a point of intersection. The nonprofessionals recognized that the beauty of the fair was the result of the efforts of two groups: the nonprofessional elite who mobilized Chicago's civic spirit and wealth to secure the fair and the professional experts who carried the project through. The experience of proplanning citizen groups in towns and cities demonstrated a need for organizations to mobilize public opinion and generate funds through bond issues or other means. The fair was one of the few spectacular, large-scale, readily comprehensible projects that such techniques had brought to a conclusion. Moreover, the exposition was a showcase for the brilliant work of expert professionals and was a compelling contrast to the results of old, slipshod "political" methods. The professionals enjoyed wide latitude in all aesthetic matters but were subject to the ultimate control of a citizen board. Such an example was invaluable in an era when citizen elites staffed new or revitalized park boards or boards of public works charged with supervising the era's aesthetic and utilitarian improvements.[32]

As for the professionals, the architects were the first legatees of the fair. The exposition stimulated their artistic vision to be sure. It also inspired them to seek a far grander goal, which was nothing less than the design control of urban improvement. The vision wavered in the 1890s, but the growth of professional schooling and organizations and the revival of interest early in 1900 of the Fairmount (later Franklin) Parkway in Philadelphia were reaffirmations of the dream. The Philadelphia project was especially significant because it revived, under the auspices of the Art Federation, the ideal of cooperation between lay civic leaders and experts. The proposal for a formal diagonal line some fifteen blocks from Fairmount Park to City Hall, slicing through Logan Square, was urban in scale and architectonic in scope. Most important of all, however, was the American Institute of Architects' (AIA) decision to hold its December 1900 convention in Washington to celebrate the centennial of the city's founding.[33]

Celebration, however, was the last thing on the minds of the conference leaders. They were determined to wrest the design future of Washington from the hands of the Corps of Engineers and commit the federal government to developing the capital Mall area on lines laid down by architects. The architects' concern also originated in the travesties visited upon the sophisticated and sensitive plan of Pierre L'Enfant drawn up in 1791. There were many well-known desecrations. The Treasury blocked the view from the Capitol end of ceremonial Pennsylvania Avenue to the White House, which was in any case too modest a structure to close the vista. The Washington Monument at the west end of the Mall had been placed off line from the Executive Mansion and from the center of the Mall, skewing the vista from the Capitol. Then there was the Mall itself, disfigured by the ungainly, outmoded Baltimore and Potomac railroad terminal and its tracks athwart the green space near the foot of Capitol Hill. The Mall west of the depot had been made over into naturalistically landscaped parks, indifferently maintained.[34]

Various individuals and groups had been at work on their own improvement schemes. One involved a memorial, or centennial, bridge across the Potomac River to Virginia, near the site of the present Memorial Bridge adjacent to the Lincoln Memorial. Another conceived the replanning of the present Federal Triangle south of Pennsylvania Avenue between Fifth and Fifteenth streets, backed on the south by the present Constitution Avenue. The proposal called for converting a scruffy, mixed-use area into a site for federal office buildings. Still another urged a magnificent park and boulevard system uniting the Capitol-Mall area, the river parks, Rock Creek Park, and the various heights in the District. The bridge and Federal Triangle proposals involved some city site planning, and the park and boulevard system was as comprehensive as any other urban system of the day. The architects' conference papers did no more than mention the park system, concentrating instead on the Mall, Federal Triangle, and memorial bridge. Some papers evoked the order, unity, dimension, and spacing of the Court of Honor at the Chicago fair and proposed similar arrangements for new federal buildings. The spacious plazas and boulevards of European capitals provided other inspirations.[35]

The next step was to create a commission to recommend some partial rescue of the L'Enfant idea. Jon A. Peterson's analysis of the "politics of architectural intervention" can only be summarized here. Key AIA members allied with Senator James McMillan, chairman of the Senate Committee on the District of Columbia. McMillan was intensely interested in the Centennial and was in charge of park legislation. Amid much difficulty McMillan secured, on 8 March 1901, a Senate resolution for his committee to report on "the development and improvement" of the District park system. The AIA accepted the idea of a park system report in order to obtain action on the Mall improvement. The AIA representative and members of McMillan's committee selected Burnham amd Frederick Law Olmsted, Jr., as commissioners and empowered them to pick a third. Burnham and Olmsted chose Burnham's world's fair associate McKim. The three later added Saint-Gaudens, but illness limited his participation. Burnham's appointment was both natural and supremely significant. Burnham had proved himself the consummate architect-administrator at the Chicago fair and, as president of the AIA in 1893 and 1894 had battled fiercely, if unsuccessfully, for the full implementation of the Tarsney Act. That act authorized the supervising architect of the United States to hold competitions for federal building designs, a clear expression of the professional architects' thrust for control.[36]

The Senate committee had given Burnham a dream commission, which was the opportunity to replicate the World's Columbian Exposition in a real city while serving larger goals of national patriotism and local civic pride. But Washington was not just any city, it was then an autocracy as complete as the administration of the world's fair. Several Senate and House committees, the Corps of Engineers, the District of Columbia commissioners, and, ultimately, Congress itself controlled the District's political and administrative life. Once these bodies reached a decision, it was carried out in Washington as resolutely and with as little regard for public opinion as any undertaking at the Chicago fair. While Burnham lacked the ultimate power of implementation in Washington, he controlled the visualization of its future. His early proposal to consider such matters as the details of transportation and residential land use demonstrate his understanding of his great, if limited, influence. Burnham behaved as he had a decade earlier in Chicago: overriding timid counsels of economy, committing his supervisors to cost overruns, and producing, in the end, a stunning result.[37]

The result of Burnham's and his fellow commissioner's efforts was a bold redefinition of the Mall area and a masterfully integrated park and boulevard system tied to the Mall. The Mall area became not only distinctive by itself but also an important component of the entire plan. The evocative illustrations of his plan and the large, well-crafted, three-dimensional models of, first, existing Washington and, second, the Washington that was to be created a sensation when the commission displayed them at Washington's Corcoran Gallery in January 1902. Sensation notwithstanding, the McMillan Plan deserves some of the criticism leveled at it then and since. It is correct to criticize Burnham and his colleagues for their scheme, happily unrealized, to load up Lafayette Square across from the White House with large government buildings. The extreme concentration of federal offices was a bad idea given Washington's lack, at the time, of a subway system. The buildings would have overpowered the White House. Their construction would have involved demolition of historic buildings: none of Robinson's preservationist concern intruded here. Also, the placing of a north-facing monument on the White House axis and the dearth of terminal vistas were departures from the accepted canons of civic design. The elaborate design for the base of the Washington Monument was ineffective and impractical.[38]

These and other criticisms pale before the grand visual and public relations triumph of the McMillan Plan. The centerpiece was the redeveloped Mall and Federal Triangle with neoclassical buildings along the Mall, the terminal memorial (now the Lincoln Memorial) beyond the Washington Monument, and the proposed pantheon (now the Jefferson Memorial), the Memorial

Bridge, and the water basin between the Washington and Lincoln memorials. The commission recognized, either subconsciously or consciously, that the long vistas of Pennsylvania Avenue and the then "B" Streets flanking the Mall precluded vistas closed by any but the most gargantuan buildings. Such structures would have rivaled the Capitol in size, overwhelmed their surroundings, and cost appalling sums. When an opportunity for vista presented itself, however, the commissioners seized it. Their adroit canting of the Mall roads brought the complementary vistas between the Capitol and the Washington Monument into line. Finally, there was Burnham's coup, persuading the Pennsylvania Railroad to locate a monumental passenger station facing a grand plaza three blocks northeast of the Capitol grounds. The Pennsylvania's move vacated the Mall of the shambling depot of its subsidiary, the Baltimore and Potomac.[39]

What was the contribution of the McMillan Plan to the City Beautiful movement? Its impact was palpable and immediate, in both the architectural and popular press. Montgomery Schuyler, the most incisive architecture critic of the day, praised the McMillan commission for reminding the public of "the all-importance to a city of having a plan." The plan for the Mall area made a profound impression, with its bold execution, fine detail, and evocation of patriotism and unity through the articulation of national monuments, public buildings, umbrageous and verdant vistas. City Beautiful advocates of all backgrounds saw for the first time a group plan of public buildings united with an advanced park and boulevard system. The Mall area, with its limited scope and precise definition, was readily illustrated and so dominated the visual representations of the plan. What observers saw was a grand architectonic production, a confirmation of the role of civic design in city planning.[40]

The incorporation of landscape architecture and municipal improvement into civic design also was significant for professional control. Architects had pressed for the improvement of Washington and dominated the Senate Park Commission. They were in charge of, or important to, new or revived planning efforts in New York, Philadelphia, Baltimore, Cleveland, and Denver. This activity was the context for Burnham's next coup—the identification of all contemporary city planning with his architectural-administrative triumphs, the Chicago fair and the McMillan Plan. Burnham did so in his "White City and Capital City," in the February 1902 Century Magazine. There he wrote of the "great truth" revealed to the public in 1893, "the supreme one of the need of design and plan for whole cities." At the White City, he declared, "every one saw plainly that, though a pond be beautiful, a grassy lawn or bank beautiful, a building beautiful, all of these elements wrought into a harmonious design attain another and greater beauty, and that the beauty of the whole is superior to that of each of the several parts of the composition exploited separately." Citizens who reflected on their own cities through the lens of the Chicago fair made the "vital discovery . . . that they had built great public works in piecemeal, unrelated and without the unity of a comprehensive general plan." In New York, San Francisco, Cleveland, Chicago, and, later, elsewhere, citizens inspired by the new revelation organized movements "to obtain and officially adopt a plan for all future public improvements." The fair, to Burnham, was a crystallization "of dumb desire already strong in all American hearts."[41]

This was virtually manufactured history. The statement is not intended to discredit Burnham, who was a sincere man, writing in an age when elites routinely identified their sociopolitical activities with popular ground swells. The truth was, as the previous discussion has shown, that the public enthusiasm for planning arose from the movements for municipal improvement and comprehensive park and boulevard systems and not from the World's Fair. The exposition may have, as Robinson observed three years earlier, "immensely" advanced popular aesthetics, although concrete evidence is lacking. Its immediate inspiration was limited to the few professionals who offered group plans and other systematic improvements. Burnham's concern was therefore to claim for the Chicago fair what Robinson denied it was, the source of the public's enlightenment about planning. He wished to ensure that those who dominated the design of the exposition, the architects, would also dominate the design of cities. He wanted those citizens who yearned for comprehensive planning to turn to architects, not to city engineers or landscape architects, for expert guidance.

Burnham's ambition and will were limited only by his gentlemanly sensibilities. He was determined to expand the architect's traditional domain to embrace all the visual, recreational, transit, and circulatory aspects of urban planning. He would realize in the broadest scope Robinson's vision of the architect who would, "in the popular mind, . . . make aspiration, desire, endeavor, take the place of satisfaction, with the result that the city will march surely toward an aesthetic ideal."[42]

But it was Burnham's view of the fair's catalytic and linear influence, not Robinson's richer, more complex tapestry of aesthetic advance, that carried the day. Burnham's and Olmsted Jr.'s aggressive publicity of the plan for Washington helped to reinforce Burnham's theme. Charles Zueblin, the dynamic president of the ALCI, persuasively elaborated it before his organization's annual meeting in 1902. Zueblin, indeed, went beyond Burnham when he tied the White City to the City Beautiful in his presentation "A Decade of Civic Improvement." Zueblin had to acknowledge the municipal improvement tradition, of course, but he relegated it to a less significant role. More germane to him were the Boston metropolitan park system and, especially, the plans for Harrisburg and Washington. Most important, however, was the current need for the "unification of improvement forces"—not merely municipal improvement organizations but all the elements of the City Beautiful—under the standard raised at Chicago in 1893.[43]

In a related article Zueblin strengthened the ties between the Chicago fair, the development of city planning, and the growth of a sense of community in the diverse and complex city. Zueblin's "'The White City' and After" appeared in the December 1903 *Chautauquan* in its "Civic Renascence" series and reached a vastly larger audience than his address of the year before. His purpose remained the same, to advance and expand the cause of municipal improvement. Zueblin stressed the uniqueness of "the White City itself." Other expositions had featured discovery and invention, displayed art collections, introduced architectural wonders, and paraded advanced academic and intellectual achievements before the world. The feats of engineering, landscape architecture, architecture, and mural decoration had been achieved elsewhere, individually. The fair, then, was a triumph of ensemble, "a miniature of the ideal city." To Zueblin, "the great triumph of the White City was the Court of Honor, where the greatest ideal of modern city making received its unrivaled demonstration." In contrast to Chicago, the "White City was a symbol of regeneration." The city of Chicago was "slow to learn" the lessons of the fair but was at last doing so. Thus the fire that destroyed the Court of Honor was "a purifying fire" revealing the "foundations" of "the art of permanent city making."[44]

Lastly, the Chicago fair and subsequent expositions had demonstrated the need for a "background" for the "fuller," cooperative, more leisurely urban life of the twentieth century. "We are tired of polluted air and water, dirty streets, grimy buildings and disordered cities. From the 'White City' to the 'Ivory City' [the St. Louis fair] the lesson has been impressed that ugliness and inconvenience for the present and the future, will yield to the magic power of the comprehensive plan." Through the talisman of comprehensive planning the "individual gains comfort and the community beauty by uninterrupted cooperation."[45] Zueblin's writing established the World's Columbian Exposition's supposed relation to other planning activities and to city planning generally. He lightly passed over the inadequacies of the other origins of city planning: municipal improvement's influence was episodic and its projects piecemeal, while landscape architects had failed to engender mass enthusiasm. Only civic design, from the unified expression at Chicago to the comprehensive plan at Washington, successfully blended all the elements of efforts past into the City Beautiful.

Burnham's and Zueblin's writings and other publicity efforts succeeded because the Chicago fair displayed so many potential applications to American cities. The public accepted the connection because it was thematically and visually plausible even if chronologically false, and it supplied the City Beautiful movement with a unified, vivid, and highly regarded origin. Ambiguity and complexity, always troublesome, were banished in a brilliant manipulation of public opinion and replaced with a simple explanation for the rising City Beautiful.

The redoubtable Robinson made the strongest statement for the ascendancy of the City Beautiful in his *Modern Civic Art, or, The City Made Beautiful*. First published in 1903 and republished three times during the next fifteen years, the book was significant for two reasons. First, it revealed Robinson's intellectual journey from municipal improvement to civic design, or "civic art" as his more restrictive phrase ran. Second, it demonstrated how Robinson's flexible mind had reflected on the urban problem literature of the day and on his independent observations to produce a rich and refined study. [46]

Taking the transition to civic design first, it is remarkable how quickly Robinson moved away from municipal improvement, with its reliance on the citizen activist. To be sure, he was writing for the layman committed to the City Beautiful, but *Modern Civic Art* was more a textbook of aesthetic-utilitarian taste than it was a call to battle for municipal improvement. Robinson welcomed the growth of civic organizations but paid them little heed in his text. The notable exception was a portion of his chapter on "minor residential streets," scarcely a significant topic in comparison with civic centers, the overall street pattern, the tenement question, and comprehensive planning. The message of *Modern Civic Art* was that, while the layman could grasp the principles of good street design and organization, of statuary's contribution to civic amenity, of comprehensive planning, and of park design, he was to assign such problems to the expert and trust to the expert's judgment so long as the expert upheld the established principles. Civic art, he wrote, depended upon the combined talents of "sculptors, painters, artists, and landscape designers," working to "glorify the city" through art. Within the new context Robinson expounded upon familiar themes: the need for proper approaches to the city, for a railroad station adequate to its role of urban gateway, for a civic center or centers, for a vital street system, for building height limits, and for a park and parkway system, preserved from incompatible encroachments. [47]

Robinson's intelligent application of studies in reform Darwinism, urban geography, environmental psychology, urban sociology, and housing were as astounding as his shift to civic design. Optimistically, he believed the city to be within sight of its ultimate development. Then "there dawns a day of civic art" supervised, he hoped, by "administrative officers of the city . . . whose education, refinement, and culture—as well as executive ability and business sagacity—are a guarantee that the right things will be done and done well." Robinson argued that the American urban citizenry arrived at comprehensive planning through a series of evolutionary steps. First came demands for outwardly attractive buildings. Next appeared the recognized need for mural paintings and other interior decoration. Third came the realization of requirements for harmoniously grouped buildings, the "idea of gaining an aggregate effect that should be more impressive than any series of individual results could be." Colleges and universities showed the most advanced results of the drive for unified building groups, "but its beginnings as a factor in modern civic art reached back at least to the Columbian Exposition at Chicago. That (1893) was the great popular object lesson in the value of extensive cooperation, in the placing of buildings and their landscape development as strictly as in their architectural elevation." Here as elsewhere in *Modern Civic Art*

Robinson dropped his earlier, subtler appreciation of the Chicago fair and endorsed the prevailing wisdom about the relationship between the fair and the City Beautiful movement. [48]

Robinson's next development was "the grouping of the public buildings of town and city and the development of a civic centre." Then "came the appointment of an expert commission" the McMillan commission of Washington, D.C. Finally, emerging from the Washington experience, came "a widespread demand for expert advice." Robinson suggested the ideal commission makeup: a sculptor, an architect, a landscape designer, an engineer, and one additional member standing "for all of these together and comprehensively, as one who has made a special study of the general science and art of city-building." He would have precisely filled his own bill for the fifth commissioner. [49]

Robinson was not content to find merely, or only, a Darwinian development in cities culminating in civic art and the comprehensive plan. He was a keen student of urban geography, which led him to propose a sophisticated street system. He advocated the selective widening of streets in the business district and the development of radial or diagonal streets to residential areas. Business expansion, he argued, would creep along the radials, sparing residential neighborhoods from commercial encroachment. Robinson's proposal for a civic center did not blind him to the centrifugal tendencies of the contemporary city. Therefore he proposed neighborhood foci, centered on schools or other public buildings, or on play areas. However, deconcentration should recognize functional compatibility; it might not be best to place a school next to city hall, given the low level of much urban politics. "In the physiology of cities," Robinson concluded, "it is not accurate to-day to speak of 'the heart' of the town; but, rather, of a series of nerve centres." [50]

Robinson shared a devout environmentalism with his fellow enthusiasts of the City Beautiful. "Social problems are to a large degree problems of environment," he declared. One of his justifications for fountains in cities was their unusual "power to charm" based, possibly, on a racial memory of free-running water in woodlands. He advocated the curvilinear street partly because of the visual delight to the traveler or outward-looking resident. He believed that civic art had no "higher call" than to "make beautiful the surroundings of the homes of men," where the first and most lasting impressions were gained. [51]

His understanding of geography, environmentalism, and of sociological and housing problems enabled him to propose an answer to the plight of the slum or tenement district, descriptions he used interchangeably. He was also influenced by planned industrial suburbs and the Garden City movement, although he rejected the radical utopianism of the Garden City idea in favor of the drastic improvement of existing cities. Robinson posited a solution to the tenement problem that he admitted was severe. He proposed deconcentration into industrial suburbs, where cheap, decent housing would be available amid green fields. The reduced population remaining could then be wholesomely housed within walking distance of work through tenement law enforcement; the creation of neighborhood centers, recreation areas, and squares; and the careful handling of converging streets. Though he likened a major street cut through a slum area to "a stream of pure water cleansing what it touches," he was unwilling to recommend such a solution in his chapter on the tenement problem. Instead he urged that the streets in the slum district be left off the main lines of travel to avoid reintroducing noise and congestion to the recently depopulated areas. He was optimistic about improving the slum conditions but tempered his optimism with a shrewd understanding of the high mobility in slum districts. The slum "population is really of as many gradations as that in the other residential areas," thus the "upper stratum" is the one moving out, while the "influx is at the bottom," a situation requiring unremitting struggle to improve conditions in the poorest areas.[52]

Robinson's individuality surfaced in still other statements. He refused to accept all of the statistical measurements and regulatory ordinances so dear to some progressive reformers. In "the tenement district mere density of population is not a sure indication of overcrowding." Indeed, more density per acre in higher buildings could be tolerated if the buildings themselves were safe and commodious and their surroundings pleasant. The authorities could inculcate civic patriotism, he wrote, if they relaxed a few regulations and catered to the ethnic distinctness of each tenement area. Finally, he discounted the idea of a fixed ratio of park land to population. Population density, park distribution, the topography and apparent spaciousness of the parks themselves, all counted for more than a mere ratio.[53]

Robinson produced by far the most richly textured and astute statement of the City Beautiful. He was at one with Burnham, Zueblin, and other City Beautiful advocates in enunciating its widely ranging concerns, including a utilitarian but aesthetically graceful handling of the problems of traffic circulation, utilities, recreation, general cleanliness, park and parkway development, and comprehensive planning. In the year or two after the publication of *Modern Civic Art*, the movement reached its maturity. By then its supporters had developed a serviceable aesthetics, as well as an ideology and program of political action.

4 ◆ The Ideology and Aesthetics of the City Beautiful Movement

CITY BEAUTIFUL ADVOCATES: AN INTERPRETATION

The City Beautiful movement worked through politics to achieve a congeries of socioenvironmental reforms related to urban design. By 1903–4 an ideology in support of the movement emerged. It was compounded from several sources, including nineteenth-century sociology, psychology, and biology, plus several planning reports. What follows is an examination of that ideology, beginning with a look at its advocates. City Beautiful advocates were mostly male and members of the urban middle class or upper middle class. They were often the owners or managers of businesses large by community standards, for example, newspaper editors, managers of manufacturing plants, or owners of sizable retail establishments. There was some representation from smaller businesses and, rarely, skilled labor. Other prominent City Beautiful supporters included professional people: attorneys, bankers, physicians, and real estate specialists and investors. These elites worked to achieve citywide, unifying planning schemes. They articulated the purposes of planning in intensive publicity campaigns conducted through boards of trade, chambers of commerce, or various ad hoc groups.

The women involved were usually from the same middle and upper classes and were often the wives of business leaders. The women were active in organizations of the municipal improvement type. They allied with the men in the same or parallel campaigns, though they tended to form separate organizations and promote more specialized causes, such as street sanitation.[1]

Finally, there were the experts themselves, who belonged to the same class background as the City Beautiful activists, who worked well with local elites, and who sometimes participated in planning publicity.

All this is scarcely news. City Beautiful activists were similar in class, education, and general background to other reformers of the Progressive Era. The problem is, how should the motives of such people be interpreted? The usual reply is based on a sort of sociopolitical determinism. Its burden is that, as soon as we know who the reformers and their groups were, then an analysis free of old-fashioned normative categories will reveal what it was they really wanted. What they wanted turns out to be the centralization of urban functions and politics, the protection of property and property values, and the exercise of class and social control over the (to them) dangerous urban masses. Other goals included the development of a city bureaucracy dedicated to municipal cleanliness, order, and the pursuit of legitimate business goals, and the recruitment of the experts to deal with large-scale problems of public health, transportation, and the like. Some arrangements had to be sacrificed to achieve these ends, including the relatively intimate politics of the ward-based system of representation, neighborhood influence over schooling and recreation, and community-based intervention in urban politics.[2]

There are problems with this interpretation. For one thing, the normative attitudes tossed out the front door have a way of sneaking around back. Implicit in the deterministic view is that centralization that does not allow for considerable local autonomy is wrong, that bureaucracy and expertise are antithetical to democracy, that social control is of little or no merit, and that class control is bad unless it is the working class that is asserting its privileges over those of the others. Also involved is a conviction that small-scale democracy and neighborhood control are creatable or preservable values in the era of the metropolis. The issue is not the validity of the ethical positions described, but their latent presence in the interpretation.

The determinist approach assumes that the reformers involved in a citywide activity opposed any significant concession to democracy, neighborhoods, or ideas of community. Roy Rosenzweig and Stephen Hardy have attacked determinism, arguing that working- and middle-class people were not passive but battled urban elites over questions of park design, equipment, and recreational programs, and won often enough to make the struggle worthwhile. Their observations are insightful. Most City Beautiful programs necessitated an initial democratic ratification, such as a bond issue, for implementation. Therefore, the proponents could not afford to ignore the democratic process or neighborhood or community concerns. Too many other people had to be persuaded. After a program successfully ran the democratic gauntlet, it could be removed to the realms of expertise and bureaucracy, but the experts and the bureaucrats had to produce publicly acceptable work. This need for popularly approved results remained because a park and boulevard system, a street beautification-improvement program, or a civic center was practically never complete with one bond issue. Popular approval of the next phase of land acquisition or construction depended upon citizen acceptance of what was created before. So the relationship between public and expert or citizen board was not authoritarian or undemocratic but reciprocal. Therefore, the interclass arguments over park facilities should be viewed partly as elite capitulations to the necessity of continued popular support. They might also be seen to be the neighborhood or community struggle against central control that is familiar to observers of the urban scene. On the other hand, when workers won and elites lost, the battle was decided within the durable framework created by the losers.[3]

A third problem with the deterministic interpretation is that many vocal opponents of reform were strikingly similar to the proponents of change. They were middle- and upper-middle-class people who resembled their adversaries in occupation, age, education, social backgrounds, and group affiliation. This means that not all newspaper editors, professionals, or owners of large businesses condoned City Beautiful projects. Some belonged to the organizations that endorsed beautification programs in spite of their dissent. Endorsement of anything by a chamber of commerce meant endorsement by a majority of the group, however slender the majority. Usually a small committee of enthusiasts within the chamber carried on any campaigning or other activity resulting from the endorsement. It is possible though hardly demonstrable that those who secured group endorsements and group activism were a committed minority who swept along the indifferent majority in a burst of carefully orchestrated enthusiasm.[4]

A determinist might make two responses to this argument. The first is that differences between proreform and antireform groups are discernible if one probes effectively. Thus one finds "newcomers" and "old notables" clashing at times, or entrenched downtown property interests battling rising young businessmen. The problem with this response is that the situations may be true for selected issues in one city, but not for other cities or issues. Even if a firm interpretation may be drawn along the line of group disagreements within a single city, transferring the framework to larger, smaller, or different types of cities may produce negative results.[5]

The determinists' second reply might be that none of this makes much difference anyhow, because both the proponents and opponents of City Beautiful reforms really wanted the same things from the city. That is, both factions desired centralization, the dominance of expertise, and a powerful bureaucracy. No doubt this was true at some level of abstraction, but the City Beautiful battles were too earnest and intense for them to have been over minor or incidental matters. The struggles were between people who desired a rich, full life for the residents of a beautiful city and those who saw the city in strictly utilitarian terms, who desired economical government, and who wished to leave beauty or the acquisition of it to private quests.

What may be said with certainty is that the active leadership for and against urban beautification came from roughly the same group. Both sides had access to a citywide audience, both expressed citywide concerns, and both used the press, the courts, and other devices such as pamphlets and public meetings to express their views. The fact that City Beautiful proponents came from a certain social stratum is a generalization, nothing more. Nevertheless it will serve as a basis for examining the frankly class-and-culture-oriented concerns of the City Beautiful advocates.

City Beautiful Ideology

First, the City Beautiful solution to urban problems—transforming the city into a beautiful, rationalized entity—was to occur within the existing social, political, and economic arrangements. City Beautiful advocates were committed to a liberal-capitalist, commercial-industrial society and to the concept of private property. They recognized society's abuses, but they posited a smooth transition to a better urban world. City Beautiful proponents were, therefore, reformist and meliorative, not radical or revolutionary. They accepted the city optimistically, rejecting a return to a rural or arcadian past.[6]

The city was susceptible to reform because it was akin to a living organism. Thoughtful citizens could control and direct its growth somewhat as they could manipulate other organisms genetically and environmentally. McFarland wrote of an "endeavor to give us . . . in our urban habitations conditions . . . approximating those of the beautiful wild into which our forefathers came a few generations ago." Such a sweeping change could occur only if the city could be studied entire for the purpose of arranging its components in perfect symbiosis. The city had to be, as Liberty Hyde Bailey put it in 1903, "an organism." George A. Parker asserted that the city developed according to discoverable principles. "The starting point in the study of a city," he declared, "is to realize the fact that it is a living organism, whose life is not a series of accidents but conforms to the laws of growth, while undergoing constant modification in response to changing influences." If the city conformed "to biological laws," then its transformation could be understood and, possibly, directed. Guy Kirkham, a Springfield, Massachusetts, architect, suggested such a possibility when he added a Darwinian fillip. Solving architectural problems and creating a "safe" and "convenient" city would lead to a situation in which "finally the beautiful city will be evolved."[7]

The locale for all this evolutionary progress, it should be remembered, was the city. There was little interest among the devotees of the City Beautiful in the agricultural village, the Country Life movement, industrial utopias such as Pullman, Illinois, or the Garden City concepts of Ebenezer Howard. The beautification work of John H. Patterson of the National Cash Register Company and its transforming effect on Dayton, Ohio, was of vastly greater interest than any non-urban system or scheme. The city was the arena of the future, and there the City Beautiful enthusiasts focused their aspirations.[8]

Second, City Beautiful reformers recognized the aesthetic and functional shortcomings of cities. They sought beautiful buildings and scenes to help preserve what attractiveness remained in nineteenth-century urban settings. More, they wished to supplant the pervading ugly and unkempt atmosphere of the American city. McFarland called it "the crusade against ugliness" for good reason. Turn-of-the-century cities were ugly, and dirty too. Retail-commercial downtowns expressed their vitality by moving as they expanded, leaving behind aging buildings given over to secondhand shops, third-rate stores, light industry, or musty vacancy. Factories and business blocks vomited black, sooty smoke that lowered over Pittsburgh, Chicago, and St. Louis. The urban sections of rivers were treated as sewers, not waterscapes. Junk and rubbish littered their banks. Few cities could boast well-distributed or well-improved parks. In gross acreage or in the improvement of one or two large landscape parks, some older American cities could compare favorably with their English or German counterparts. More often parks were poorly located, undeveloped, or uncoordinated into park and boulevard systems. In 1890 Boston and Minneapolis could be proud of their parks, but Chicago displayed just over 2,000 acres of parkland and a pitiful 799 improved acres for its more than 1 million citizens. Rochester served 133,896 inhabitants with 76 improved park acres.[9]

Street paving of all types was often conspicuous by its absence. Boston boasted that 100 percent of its streets were paved, though 163 of its 408 street miles were only gravel covered. Boston was an exception, even for the eastern seaboard, and in cities farther west, paving conditions were much worse. In Kansas City 50 of its 267 street miles were surfaced; Dallas had paved only 5 percent of its streets. In 1903 a resident of Omaha bragged about his city's advances in street paving. Omaha, he said, embraced 350 miles of streets and alleys. Eighty-five miles were paved, and ten of those were "the remnants of what was once wooden block paving." The speaker, remember, was not criticizing. He was boasting of progress. Dirt streets—swirling dust in summer and gluey, sucking mud in spring, redolent with horse droppings—were the norm in many American cities.[10]

The beauty sought by City Beautiful advocates was scarcely ever specifically defined, except by such supplementary nouns as proportion, harmony, symmetry, and scale. Beauty was, however, often illustrated. Well-tended flower gardens, well-done landscape parks, street furniture of straightforward but gracious design, and single or grouped monumental public buildings, all in harmonious relationships, were the basis of civic beauty. City Beautiful leaders perforce did not usually go beyond a sort of generalized Ruskinism. They knew—by intelligence, breeding, and training—what was beautiful and what was not, be it natural or man-made. They wanted enough influence to exclude "costly blunders" and "amateurish experiment" from the urban landscape. The municipal art commissions established in many cities after 1900 gave them at least advisory powers over the design of public structures. While they thus asserted a cultural dominion over the city, they were hesitant to apply it without regard for neighborhood sensibilities, the existing urban environment, or the wishes of donors and experts. Embarrassing contretemps among arbiters of public beauty, such as the furor over the statue *Bacchante* in the courtyard of the Boston Public Library, occurred rarely.[11]

Third, those who endorsed the City Beautiful were environmentalists. When they trumpeted the meliorative power of beauty, they were stating their belief in its capacity to shape human thought and behavior. Some environmentalist statements, especially from the municipal improvement wing of the

City Beautiful, seemed to echo Olmsted. E. L. Shuey of the APOAA contended that "beauty and healthfulness" were as important as they were inseparable. McFarland declared that "beauty came even before food in Eden. And while we cannot restore man to the garden, we can . . . make the city garden-like." Civic design advocate Robinson urged preserving landscape parks, which "present the sharpest contrast to the artificiality of the city."[12]

City Beautiful environmentalism was not, however, a linear extension of Olmsted's. The impact of Darwinism[13] separated it from the analysis of Olmsted, a man whose fundamental ideas were formed in the first half of the nineteenth century. Endorsers of the City Beautiful were late-nineteenth- or twentieth-century people. They believed less in the Olmstedian view of beauty's restorative power and more in the shaping influence of beauty. Darwinism had compromised the old belief in man as a natural creature made in the image of God, who shared some of God's attributes and who required a beautified, naturalistic reprieve from his imprisonment in the artificial city. Man became remote from his Creator, more manipulable and malleable, a being conditioned by his environment. Therefore, the whole urban environment and the entire human experience within it were critical to the City Beautiful movement. City Beautiful advocates found secular salvation for humans in their belief in a flexible, organic city, in contrast to the intractable city of Olmsted's vision. The convictions about malleable humans and flexible cities underlay the City Beautiful insistence on a comprehensive plan, one that pervaded and unified the city and that addressed a significant number of its problems.

City Beautiful environmentalism involved social control, a subject over which a great deal of ink has been spilled. Two matters only need concern us about the City Beautiful style of social control. The first is, as Dominick Cavallo has written, that social control is an ahistorical concept. The forms and methods of social control are situational despite generalizations about their types. Considerations of social control must be specific to the intellectual and ecological setting. Paul Boyer's tour de force in urban and intellectual history (*Urban Masses and Moral Order in America, 1820–1920*) reveals how reformers focused on the problem of "moral control" of the masses from the Jacksonian era, when the city first emerged as a focus for reform effort. Boyer deftly illuminates the broad, general similarities in nonlegal, nonreligious social control, as well as some profound differences of strategy and goals.[14]

The danger of following Boyer's comparisons and contrasts to their conclusions is in losing sight of Cavallo's point. Both the City Beautiful's rhetorical flights and its varied attack on urban problems occurred within a particular context—namely, Darwinian views of humanity and the city. They developed amid the proliferation of large, rapidly growing cities and of rapid advances in the institutionalization and municipal socialization of such staple reform concerns as the juvenile problem, poverty, crime control, utilities, and housing regulation. Therefore, the connections among the Jacksonian reformers, Olmstedians, and City Beautiful advocates are limited and specific, not continuous.[15]

The second point about the City Beautiful's exercise in social control was that it was normative and behavioral. It was not coercive, the mechanism of the concentration camp, or utilitarian, the accommodation between the car corporation and the wage worker on the assembly line. The goal of the City Beautiful system was what Edward A. Ross, in *Social Control* (1901), termed the inculcation of "social religion," the idealized, transcendental bond among members of a community and among members of a nation or society. Ross claimed a deep emotional and instinctual basis for this civic religion, which was superior because it was an "*inward*," or internalized, control system. The problem with imputing overreaching or potentially fascistic sentiments to the City Beautiful reformers is that their system was severely self-limiting. Their rhetoric might soar, as McFarland's and Robinson's surely did, and they might occasionally overlook the individuals composing a community, but their claims for control rested upon the presumed effects of the urban environment. Effective socialization through the civic ideal was an unprovable proposition at best, tenuous or nebulous at worst. Environmental conditioning could be demonstrated in laboratory or quasi-laboratory conditions. The impact of the public environment upon such a complex organism as a human being—one subject to a succession of environments and playing a variety of social roles— was another matter entirely. The socialization of the urban dweller involved an elaborate network of circumstances and ideas, many of them beyond the reach of so exalted and transcendent a concept as the civic ideal. It would be fairer to the ideals of the City Beautiful advocates to say that they sought cultural hegemony by asserting control over the definition of beauty and the manipulation of civic symbols.[16]

There are other difficulties with setting too much store by the rhetoric of the City Beautiful. If its language was fervent, its actions often were prosaic: a cleanup campaign, a struggle for councilmanic hearts and minds concerning a local billboard ordinance, a suit over land condemnation for a park or civic center. Perhaps the City Beautiful's very fervor was its attempt to bridge the gap between desire and actuality. City Beautiful advocates dared not ignore or override individuals or categories of individual predispositions. Ross's doubts about the permanence of specific control systems extended to civic idealism: "Civic pride and public spirit are often hot-house plants." All this suggests how mistaken it would be to view social control as a sinister side of the City Beautiful: first, because social control was only one of several objectives; second, because it was normative only; and, third, because its rhetorical excesses, typical of the Progressive Era, were not translatable into a political program.[17]

The playground movement was more explicitly controlling and manipulative, for its goal was the socialization of youth. From early childhood to late adolescence, young people were to come under the sway of the organized playground and its director. The play movement was, like the City Beautiful, of middle-class origins, but it was focused on a particular reform, was more activist, and more militantly environmentalist. There were potential conflicts between the two movements. Park space designed for Olmsted's passive recreation and psychic restoration was, to some play enthusiasts, mere fallow ground waiting to be converted into playgrounds. Also, an active recreation movement would compete for public funds that could otherwise go to City Beautiful projects. The conflicts were muted during the earlier years, when the playground movement had developed an ideology but had not yet jelled organizationally. Active conflict would come in 1906 with the founding of the Playground Association of America.[18]

The playground movement was a feature of the child-saving impulse of the progressive years, but its thrust was universal. Playground advocates believed in reaching out to all children, irrespective of age and ethnic group. Team sports for the older children and adolescents taught them that what divided them was less important than what united them. Team play required the sacrifice or the tempering of individuality to a common goal. This training socialized the child, making the child receptive to the discipline of the work environment, to an efficiently organized polity, to national patriotism, and to civic idealism. A Darwinian ontogeny lay behind the inculcation of moral values, from the sandpile to team sports. Morality, in this view, was not independent and divine but environmentally conditioned. The playground movement saw itself as providing an alternative to the depraved, socially centrifugal city. The playground supplied the corrective for bad forms of recreation, including illicit drinking establishments, dance halls, and theaters of the vaudeville and burlesque types. The street gang's primitive civicism could be nurtured and its destructive appetites discouraged if only an innovative play director would inveigle it to the playground and seize its leadership.

Despite the conflicts between the City Beautiful and playground movements, what united them was more significant than their divisions. Their points of unity included social control, provided that concept is generalized to accommodate the differences, and agreement about the power of environmental influences on human nature, a nature less teleological than conditioned. Both subscribed to recreation and organized play. Urban beautifiers desired to reestablish community, a value that the playground movement sought to instill almost from the young citizen's cradle. Beautifiers and playgrounders believed in the expert and upheld efficiency. The City Beautiful advocated neighborhood playfields and was willing to concede a few acres of larger parks to playgrounds, provided the surrender did not involve the destruction of landscape values.[19]

Fourth, the City Beautiful leadership insisted upon synthesizing beauty and utility. Olmsted and other landscape architects had long argued for the role of beauty in creating a contented workforce, attracting a superior population, and raising property values. Burnham and others advanced the venerable argument partly for Olmsted's "pocketbook" reasons, for, whatever its intellectual permutations, American society remained materialistic. The champions of the City Beautiful realized that their vocal opponents, solid middle- and upper-middle-class citizens like themselves, were content with a smoky, noisy, unkempt city so long as it got the job done: distributed goods, provided housing, and brought together employer and employee. The trick, then, was to combine the beautiful, which was beyond value, with the functional, which paid off in discernible ways.[20]

But by the turn of the century the assertion that beauty and utility were inseparable meant something more palpable and design-related. No structure or scene could be truly beautiful without being functional as well. Jessie Good of the municipal improvement movement pinpointed the issue with an organic metaphor. "The old saying that beauty is only skin deep is deeply false," she wrote. "Beauty is as deep as the bones, the blood, the rosy flesh." The Harrisburg plan of 1901 united a report on parks and boulevards with two on mundane but essential street and sewer improvements. The city plans of Burnham and his associates concerned traffic circulation, railroad reorganization, cultural and civic centers, recreational improvements, and other functional matters. Arnold Brunner, a sensitive architect and planner in the classical mode, was so taken with the inextricable natures of beauty and utility that he coined the word "beautility" to express them. Fortunately, Brunner's neologism never gained much circulation, but it did epitomize City Beautiful functional and aesthetic aspirations.[21]

Beauty and utility were closely related to a fifth City Beautiful ideal, efficiency. Efficiency was a Progressive Era grail, talisman, and buzzword. The presumed efficiency of some private-enterprise factories and offices could be transferred to nonpecuniary concerns including the aesthetic. To McFarland, clouds of factory smoke and soot were not only ugly or distasteful. They were visible evidence of the "waste" of fuel, a waste compounded when fly ash "spread upon houses, clothes, goods and food." McFarland loved trees, but he believed that the proper tree was an "efficient" one. The idea of the civic center was promoted in part because clustered civic buildings would ensure the efficient, economical conduct of the city's business.[22]

Sixth, City Beautiful advocates sought expertise in the solution of urban problems. They responded to growing middle- and upper-class disgust with inept, piecemeal, patchwork efforts to stay abreast of urban needs. At the same time, experts in the youthful professional fields of architecture, landscape architecture, and engineering were available in sufficient numbers, training, experience, and eagerness to undertake municipal work.[23]

Several desirable aspects of planning clustered around the expert. From Olmsted's time, experts had predicted headlong urban expansion, called for the acquisition of public property before continuing urbanization drove up land prices, laid out functional designs of broad scope, subordinated and integrated details, and allowed for gradual improvement within the context of a grand scheme. Without a general plan, in the words of the 1893 plan for Kansas City, "the value of selections for public purposes, their most satisfactory distribution, and the dependence of one improvement upon another, cannot be appreciated." In 1901 the Harrisburg League for Municipal Improvements conceded that "the financial condition of the city will not at present permit the carrying out of Mr. Manning's system in all its details," but urged a "substantial beginning." Two years later the Local Improvement Committee of the APOAA listed "securing the services of an expert" as of first importance to a successful improvement campaign. An expert, the committee insisted, "must be employed if the community hopes to have a beautiful entity." In *Modern Civic Art*, Robinson called for a commission of experts to plan comprehensively and ensure that each year's construction fitted into the total plan. Burnham's aphorism "Make no little plans" distilled the experience of City Beautiful experts.[24]

Lay devotees of the City Beautiful upheld expertise for two other reasons. They were comfortable with the experts who matured before the second decade of the twentieth century, partly because they shared their solid middle- and upper-class backgrounds and achievements. Expert George Kessler could work intimately with layman August Meyer, expert Warren Manning with layman J. Horace McFarland, and expert Daniel H. Burnham with layman Charles D. Norton. This relationship was an important feature of the City Beautiful movement, but it faded as younger experts, more absorbed with professionalism, strove for some distance between themselves and the laity. Further, laymen liked an expert's cachet upon their plans for promotional reasons. City Beautiful bond issue campaigns stressed the practicality of expertly drawn plans. Expert certitude could deflect doubters and detractors. An expert who spoke well or who wrote in sprightly prose could provide an excellent prop for bond issue mass meetings and rallies.[25]

Seventh, City Beautiful ideologues were class conscious in a non-Marxian sense. They believed in individual mobility and in some class fluidity, but they accepted the reality of classes in urban America. For practical purposes they distinguished two classes split along functional lines. The upper group, composed of the owners and managers of substantial enterprises, would benefit from public improvements through a general increase in monetary values and ease of living. Through improvements the upper class would assume the obligations of class leadership. The lower group, composed of manual and nonmanual workers and their families, was oppressively citybound. Unlike the upper group, working-class people could not afford vacations, suburban residences, and surcease from the urban environment. These convictions reached back to Olmsted. New awareness of community needs, on the other hand, brought a rising emphasis on recreational facilities for the working class. These included playground parks and playgrounds within large landscape parks, public baths, baseball diamonds, picnic areas, tennis courts, and golf courses.[26]

In preparing these palliatives City Beautiful ideologues were not impelled by fears of working-class revolt. True, Robinson warned of "the city slum," where "smoulders the fire which breaks forth in revolution," but he was practically alone in raising the issue, nor did he pursue it beyond a sentence in *Modern Civic Art*. The ability of local, state, and federal governments to contain restiveness during the depression of the nineties, returning prosperity late in the decade, the relatively dispersed character of the country, the reformers' strong sense of community, all quieted fears of uprising. It does not follow, however, that the City Beautiful movement advanced without a sense of crisis. Environmentalism spurred the City Beautiful to forestall a demoralized and debased urban population.[27]

The movement's fervent optimism, its eighth ideological component, also blanketed the fears of class conflict. Its evangelical confidence bubbled up from a compound containing the convictions behind the social, cultural, and ethical outlook of the middle and upper classes. Other elements in the compound included the grand, if partial, beautification achievement of preexposition Chicago and a few other American cities, the adaptable grandeur of Paris ascribed to Napoleon III and Haussmann, and the importable architectonic triumphs of Venice and Rome. The urban transformation would depend upon the dynamics of charismatic leaders who were taming scandalous politicians, immigrants, and public service corporations. Robinson's rhapsodic opening of *Modern Civic Art* was more florid than most City Beautiful declarations but it captured the spirit of them all. "The darkness rolls away, and the buildings that had been in shadow stand forth distinctly," Robinson exulted. "The tall facades glow as the sun rises; their windows shine as topaz; . . . Whatever was dingy, coarse, and ugly, is either transformed or hidden in shadow. . . . There seems to be a new city for the work of a new day."[28]

Ninth, the City Beautiful shared in what has been called the American discovery of Europe. To thoughtful Americans of the late nineteenth century, Europe was more than a nicely arranged warehouse filled with classical models. European cities seemed to be as dynamic as any in America, yet they were, by American standards, clean, well-administered, attractive, even beautiful entities whose growth and development were well controlled. Political scientist Albert Shaw in 1895 praised the pre-Haussmannic and Haussmannic ruthless destruction of medieval Paris (there were plenty of medieval structures elsewhere in France, he wrote) but was less enthusiastic about Parisian administrative and sanitary arrangements. German cities, Shaw found, were masterpieces of administration. He praised the Viennese government for forging a beautiful and practical city. Chicago, he noted, muffed a vastly greater opportunity after the devastating 1871 fire. If the municipality had purchased the burned-out district and planned a civic area with public buildings, parks, and boulevards, it could have sold the leftover land for more than enough to pay for the improvements. Since the World's Columbian Exposition, "Chicago has had a clear comprehension of the magnificent effects that may be produced as the result of a large initial plan," but, alas, too late. As Shaw dourly concluded, "It is evident that Chicago would have been the gainer if it could have borrowed some of Vienna's genius for municipal administration."[29]

In the twilight years of the City Beautiful, Frederick C. Howe deplored the rampant individualism in American cities while he praised German municipal ownership, taxes on the unearned increment from urban land sales, and zoning. German cities' smooth, powerful administration, he explained, stemmed not from their great age as large cities, for they were in that respect younger than American and British metropolises. German success depended upon home rule and the psychology of responsibility that home rule engendered. Howe's paean to the German expert was an extreme example of American infatuation with European urbanism. Infatuations are impermanent. In 1913 McFarland revolted against an uncritical acceptance of all things German at the expense of a realistic awareness of heavy-handed Teutonic bureaucracy. Just as some municipal reformers stood in awe of European civic administration, so others imbibed European civic design. They were elements of the same awakening to those European advances adaptable to American conditions. The parallel is complete even to the later reaction against classicism.[30]

The tenth and culminating constituent of the City Beautiful ideology was its enthusiastic welcome of the city. The architects, landscape architects, and planners of the era worked in cities and often lived in them or their suburbs. Some rhetorical attacks on the unnatural city persisted, but they became rarer and more ritualistic as the twentieth century advanced. If cities could be made beautiful and functional, then they would no longer be running sores on the landscape. If the city became the locus of harmony, mutual responsibility, and interdependence between classes, mediated by experts, then it would be a peaceful, productive place, not a stark contrast to rural scenery. In its comprehensive view of the city and in its nonpartisan concern for improvement, the City Beautiful partook of a revived civic spirit.[31]

City Beautiful Aesthetics

City Beautiful aesthetics, considered separately from City Beautiful ideology, linked natural beauty, naturalistic constructivism, and classicism. Reverence for natural beauty and for naturalistic constructivism, its urban counterpart, stands first in the order of City Beautiful aesthetics. The priority may seem misplaced, given the traditional linking of the City Beautiful with neoclassical forms. When we examine what City Beautiful adherents really were thinking and doing, however, we find a reality richer than the neoclassic. It was no accident, as Henry Hope Reed, Jr., remarked, that the scenic preservation and urban beautification movements burst upon the country at the same time. There were precedents, including the rural cemetery movement, and Downing's call for ruralized homes. Olmsted personified the joining of rural preservation and managed conservation with the drive for urban beauty.[32]

As urbanization, mechanization, and commercialization roared into the twentieth century, their levy on beauty was too great to ignore. The preservation and accentuation of natural beauty were major motives for the Boston metropolitan park system, Robinson's plan for Raleigh, North Carolina, Kessler's for Dallas, and many others. City Beautiful crusader McFarland was a landscape zealot who fought to save Niagara Falls from continuing commercial threats, struggled unsuccessfully to preserve California's Hetch Hetchy Valley, campaigned for a National Park Service, and became one of the country's leading rosarians. The Olmsted brothers, Burnham, and McKim were among those architects and planners who traveled between intensely urban environments for living or work and suburban, exurban, or rural retreats. Sculptor Augustus Saint-Gaudens ultimately betook himself to New Hampshire. That appealing mixture of ebullience and exactitude Stanford White may once have paid a Long Island farmer fifty dollars per tree to leave standing a grove of potential firewood. Apocryphal or not, the story illustrates White's love of natural beauty. The landscape design and municipal improvement branches of the City Beautiful praised flowers, shrubs, and trees for their enhancing, softening qualities in city settings. Advocates from the landscape design–municipal improvement background espoused corporate beautification, too. They urged grass plots, ground covers, flowers, and plant groupings for the grounds of small railroad stations. They praised railroad executives and factory owners who adopted systematic beautification ideas for their properties. Such activities, they noted, often spread beyond the station or the factory gate to home improvement and heightened civic concerns.[33]

Civic designers embraced natural beauty and naturalistic constructivism in their urban improvement schemes. Burnham's plans suggested boulevards linking civic centers with waterscapes and park landscapes. They proposed new parks and parkways to unify and extend the existing landscape-recreational facilities. Robinson's plans for Denver (1906) and Honolulu (1906) offered similar recommendations; so did John Nolen's designs for San Diego (1909) and Reading, Pennsylvania (1910). City Beautiful planners typically treated naturalistic parks and parkways as precious assets, not as relics to be tolerated or disfigured by the imposition of their own designs. The charge that City Beautiful plans scorned or devalued natural beauty fits nicely with models of conflict or dichotomy in city planning, but the charge is simply untrue.[34]

Granting their interest in naturalistic themes, City Beautiful designers were drawn to neoclassic architecture. To them it represented the ultimate step in the late-nineteenth century search for an effective, expressive building style. As Carroll L. V. Meeks and others have written, nineteenth-century architects faced a new order of problems represented by the office building, the railroad station, and by the need to house expanding, differentiating governments. Architects increasingly concentrated on functional solutions at the expense of bizarre eclecticism. Gothic and gaudy Mediterranean styles gave way to a severe commercial vernacular and to the Romanesque. Over time, within the Romanesque, turrets softened and shortened, roofs pitched more gently, dormers retreated and lost some excrescences, and ornament flattened into walls. For all its vogue, however, the Romanesque suffered from fatal defects. It was ecclesiastical architecture originally, difficult to adapt to the public and semipublic buildings of a secular culture without severe modifications, for which there were no clear guides in proportion and arrangement. The genius of Richardson could impose discipline and order upon the Romanesque, as in the Allegheny County Courthouse and Jail. In weaker hands Romanesque buildings sometimes appeared ill-proportioned and fussily detailed. Their fenestration and the arrangement of horizontal and vertical elements were contradictory and confused. Even some great Romanesque buildings display features more compelling than their facades: the grace and massing of the rear of Trinity Church, the stylish severity of the Rookery's court, the powerful arch at the servant's entrance of the Glessner House, and the functional arrangement of the backs of Austin Hall and the old Kansas City Stock Exchange.[35]

Neoclassic architecture, in contrast, offered basic conceptions of proportion and arrangement. Because of its range in time and space from classic Greek to the Beaux-Arts, it was adaptable. "It was a flexible style," Christopher Tunnard wrote, "which could make a unity of a building by combining boldness of plan with refinement of detail. It made possible the handling of entirely new building types, frequently of great scale, that a growing democracy required. These were the new state capitols, the railroad stations, and the public libraries, which are part of America's contributions to world architecture." Neoclassic architecture enjoyed other virtues besides precedent and flexibility. It was ideally suited to any building requiring easy public access to a few floors, controlled vertical movement, and a high degree of functional utility. It was, in other words, a superb envelope for buildings low in proportion to their length and breadth, however much their monumental domes or interior spaces suggested height. Tunnard's list of candidates for classic treatment could be extended to include courthouses, city halls, museums, art galleries, theaters, banks, post offices, and newspaper offices. Gothic and Romanesque details became distended and trivial on their low, broad surfaces, but classic colonnades and arches throve.[36]

The neoclassical mode encouraged talented architects to pursue their experiments in arrangement and detail within the confines of a discipline. McKim, an architect whom the advocates of picturesque successionism dismiss as a talented copycat, did not "copy" or "derive" his buildings in any meaningful sense of those words. The Boston Public Library's multiple origins may be found in Henri Labrouste's Bibliothèque Sainte-Geneviève in Paris, Leon Alberti's San Francesco in Rimini, Richardson's Trinity Church and his Marshall Field wholesale store, and the Roman Coliseum. Charles B. Atwood, answering the charges of plagiarism leveled at his beautiful Art Building at the Chicago fair, snapped: "The difference between me and some other architects is that I know what to take and what to leave, and I know how to combine things that come from different sources, while they do not." The designs of these and other neoclassic buildings admittedly "come from different sources," but it is a legitimate question to ask how such selection should be distinguished from the obvious borrowings and adoptions among the members of the commercial Chicago and residential Prairie schools.[37]

The neoclassic approach encouraged skilled architects, but just as important, its discipline rescued a great many mediocre talents. So long as an architect followed precedent it was reasonably difficult for him to design a bad neoclassic building. Weak ones there were: those built without an adequate base above grade on city streets, or backed into hillsides, or covered with frivolous detail. Such errors are atypical. Devotees of the neoclassical realized that independent genius in facade design is a scarce commodity among architects. Any large city is infested with hideous buildings, failed efforts at originality, beside which a poised neoclassic structure is sweet respite for the eyes. Such contemporary failures do not settle the argument against modernism, but they do suggest that merely hurling words of dismissal such as "professional hocus-pocus" at neoclassical buildings does not end the "battle of styles."[38]

Lastly, neoclassic architecture evoked American history and spoke to the late-nineteenth-century urban elite. Classic construction evoked the American past because it was firmly in the architectural tradition from colonial times. It flowered through the late 1840s before giving way to eclecticism. Although the Greek orders were popular, Roman modes also found favor. The differences between the classicism of the early nineteenth century and the neoclassic buildings of the American Renaissance are differences of degree, not of kind. Classic architecture symbolized the historical heritage of the United States in a way that the Gothic, Romanesque, or commercial styles never could. As James Early, Neil Harris, and George Heard Hamilton have written, it expressed a romantic attachment to Greece and Rome and, by extension, to the Renaissance city-state. The attachment had less to do with governmental forms and more with assumed similarities of political thought and social achievement. At the dawn of the twentieth century it was still possible to believe the United States to be a republic governed in all important respects by European-descended, male-dominated elites. Despite growing suffragism women enjoyed relatively little political participation. Blacks were losing the right to significant involvement in Southern politics, and with some exceptions all racial minorities were confined to voting for whites. State houses of representatives as yet elected United States senators. State senators were chosen on a geographic, not a demographic, basis. By later standards, the federal government's role was circumscribed and remote from the citizen. It was reasonable to emphasize the greatness and the republican legacy of the United States by adapting the architecture of past republics.[39]

Several critics have treated neoclassic architecture and naturalistic constructivism as incongruities or curious appositions. Their explanation for the reality—that in many cities the naturalistic, and often approved, lamb lies down with the neoclassical, and frequently disapproved, lion—is twofold. First, neoclassicism characterized the City Beautiful, not naturalistic constructivism. The juxtaposition of classic and naturalistic represents a sequential development: all landscape work is of pre–City Beautiful origin or inspiration, while only neoclassical buildings are in the City Beautiful mode. Second, the origins of landscape design are definitely English, while those of the classic are distinctly French and Italian. Eclectic Americans mixed the two styles uncritically.[40]

These explanations have an appealing simplicity but they do not bear up under examination. Combining the classic and the naturalistic was not new to the City Beautiful but was a favorite device of the eighteenth and nineteenth centuries. European landscape gardening as imported to the United States was not merely Reptonian or simply picturesque but a complex heritage incorporating French and Italian survivals. Classic designs appeared in "romantic" landscapes and in "natural" English garden scenes. Olmsted, it will be recalled, learned from the English but also from Jean Alphand and Baron Haussmann. Charles Eliot and George Kessler absorbed important Continental influences. The Paris Universal Exposition of 1889 combined axiality, formality, and naturalistic constructivism, as did its American derivative, the World's Columbian Exposition. The inspired combination of neoclassic architecture and naturalistic constructivism disturbed few contemporaries. Nor did most of them object to the later civic blendings of the two styles. The romantic appeal of neoclassical architecture and the romantic yearnings expressed in naturalistic constructivism reconciled those modes of City Beautiful design.[41]

Indeed, the astonishment surrounding the Chicago fair's success focused as much on the celebratory aspect of the crowds in the Court of Honor as on anything else. Here was the Olmstedian ideal realized in a neoclassic setting, the friendly mingling of all classes and types of people. More than that, the crowd itself became an integral part of the spectacle, its spontaneous activity serving as counterpoint to the court's conscious artistry. The unprecedented success of the Court of Honor increased the reawakening interest in the square or city center as the focus of civic life. Urban celebrations such as New York's commemoration of Admiral Dewey fueled a taste for pageantry. Albert Kelsey's perceptive address to the Baltimore municipal art conference in 1899 related grouped public buildings to urban crowds. The buildings, he claimed, were "a perpetual exposition, drawing visitors to the city," while attracting "a desirable class of residents." The Pan-American Exposition, a financial failure remembered chiefly as the site of President McKinley's assassination, unified these conceptions of civic aspiration. The architecture of the Buffalo fair was a relatively restrained Spanish Renaissance, but the Court of Fountains was a carefully wrought, three-dimensional space of 1,400,000 square feet versus the Court of Honor's 563,000 square feet. Varied colors and colored-lighting effects heightened the sense of spectacle and pageantry, as did the careful design of the primary entrance at Buffalo. "The ensemble is full of suggestion of what may be done with open spaces in our cities," wrote Charles H. Caffin, "nor is any argument needed to prove how desirable it would be, if our great cities presented some such focal points of grandeur and human interest."[42]

Walter Hines Page saw in the Buffalo fair the latest indications of the "gradual evolution from the severely instructive type" of exposition to "play-places, places to which we go in a holiday mood, to see instructive things of course, but especially to see beautiful spectacles." The Buffalo fair was deliberately planned to include the crowd in the ensemble. People came "in family groups, . . . every type from all grades of life," Page wrote. He caught the interplay of individual and mass, of the fairgoer's simultaneously or successively assuming the role of participant and observer. "There was never such a sight under heaven as the people themselves. They gaze at the crowds. . . . And they are themselves the crowning glory of the spectacle." The same year Robinson, in his *Improvement of Towns and Cities*, urged the "grouping of public buildings," based on the discussions and plans in Cleveland preceding the 1903 civic center scheme by Burnham and his associates. The Senate Park Commission's stunning designs of 1901–2 gave visual expression to the yearnings for urban pageantry, community, and beautiful civic buildings.[43]

In the March 1902 issue of *Municipal Affairs* John DeWitt Warner drew together the historical and contemporary instances of "Civic Centers" to demonstrate how a traditional, useful, respectable idea was enjoying a renascence. Ostensibly, Warner's article was a criticism of the New York Fine Arts Federation. The federation had proposed to construct a single exhibition building to house its constituent organizations but had failed to plan a complete civic center for all the city's major public and semipublic buildings. But Warner's complaint was incidental to a historical review of the town center— the focus of civic life from the Acropolis and the Roman Forum, through modern European cities, to developments in Boston, Albany, and "current projects" in San Francisco, Chicago, and Cleveland. The Senate Park Commission plan for Washington came in for special attention. Through 1902, however, neither Warner nor anyone else had developed a theory of the civic center. Nothing existed beyond scattered mentions of European precedent, economy, civic efficiency, civic pride, and celebration. The concept of grouped public buildings was not yet fitted into the developing City Beautiful ideology.[44]

All that changed with five publications in 1903–4: Burnham, Carrère, and Brunner's study of the group plan of Cleveland; Robinson's *Modern Civic Art*;

Albert Kelsey's "The City Possible;" Charles Zueblin's "'The White City' and
After"; and the Municipal Art Society of Hartford's, *The Grouping of Public
Buildings*. These works, together with previous studies, brought the rationale
for the civic center to maturity.[45]

According to these publications, the civic center would supplement, not
supplant, the city's retail-commercial core. The center thereby deferred to the
existing social, political, and economic arrangements. The civic center would
respect the fact that most land near retail-commercial centers was too dear for
much of it to be given over to parks. In other words, there was no way to bring
the middle landscape to the urban core except in connection with public
buildings. An administrative and cultural center would focus citizen attention
and traffic near downtown, but major public buildings already were located
scattershot around most downtowns. The locational problem involved finding a site compatible with commerce, yet convenient for the public. Robinson
suggested a waterfront location but conceded the inconvenience in some cases
and, in others, the municipality's need to use "its waterfront space for other
purposes." His alternative location was on "an eminence." The elevation, if
not too steep, invited buildings. Robinson, however, did not consider the
convenience of collocating the civic center and the central business area. It
was up to George A. Parker, writing in *Grouping of Public Buildings*, to put
practicality over picturesqueness. The civic center, Parker declared, had to
leave main thoroughfares free and should not "intrude upon the business
center, but it should be in juxtaposition to it." The civic center, however
grand, "must not interfere with" but "be subordinate" to what "our modern
cities represent, commercialism and industrialism."[46]

The civic center was intended to be a beautiful ensemble, an architectonic
triumph far more breathtaking than a single building, no matter how comely,
could be. Grouping public buildings around a park, square, or intersection of
radial streets allowed the visual delights of perspectives, open spaces, and the
contrasts between the buildings and their umbrageous settings. Robinson
noted that public open space would push encroaching private structures farther away. Parker suggested that the influence of the civic center would spread
outward as the city developed. Burnham invoked the need for "uniformity of
style" and the "example of order, system and reserve" given to other building
operations in the city. Robinson wrote of the "stateliness," "dignity," and
"scale—the adoption of a certain module to which all the buildings must
strictly adhere, as they can do with no loss of individuality." Compatible
buildings could achieve "beauty and harmony of repose."[47]

Important as beauty was for itself, its role in environmental conditioning
was never far from the minds of civic center advocates. The civic center's
beauty would reflect in the souls of the city's inhabitants, inducing order,
calm, and propriety therein. Second, the citizen's presence in the center,
together with other citizens, would strengthen pride in the city and awaken a
sense of community with fellow urban dwellers. Burnham pleaded for "uni-

form architecture" to replace the "jumble" of buildings, which "sadly disturbs our peacefulness and destroys that repose within us which is the true basis of all contentment." Zueblin's retrospective on the relationship of world's fairs to city planning recalled the day when the "full majesty" of the Chicago fair's "Court of Honor and its greatest revelation to the makers of cities" arrived— the twenty-fifth anniversary of the Chicago fire. "Then the human mass" of fairgoers "gave life to the beautiful court with its background of majestic architecture, and man's latest civic triumph had been achieved." The mass participation and the interplay of people and buildings were the great accomplishments of the White City: "There was no loss of individuality, no place for individualism. The individual was great but the collectivity was greater." Similarly, the varied color and lighting effects of the Buffalo exposition "demonstrated that there need be no loss of individuality in collective activity."[48]

This collective activity needed some purpose beyond mere contentment. Robinson supplied the purpose—civic idealism and patriotism—wrapped in rhapsodic prose. Moving from the urban skyline, "a work of art which speaks not to the eye alone, nor to the head alone, nor to the heart alone; but unitedly, to senses, brain, and sentiment," he turned to the buildings of the civic center on their eminence. "There they would visibly dominate the town. To them the community would look up, seeing them lording over it at every turn, as, in fact, the government ought to do." Wherever located, however, a civic center would appear to be "a more majestic thing and one better worth the devotion and service of its citizens." J. G. Phelps Stokes was at least as hopeful of beauty's transforming, communal power when he wrote of the advantages of civic center groupings. "The wider the public enjoyment of the beautiful features of a city, and the larger the numbers of people who enjoy those beauties together, the wider the mutual thoughts and feelings and interests . . . and this tends to the development of a wider social morality. When we enjoy things together we for the time being feel and think together, and the more often we share the same thoughts and emotions the more unified in thought and feeling we become."[49]

Utility, efficiency, and expertise joined beauty in civic center theory. Stokes argued that "co-operation between the departments of a city is essential if the most efficient public service is to be had; and close co-operation is more easy . . . where distances are eliminated." The "ordinary citizen" benefited from the "concentration . . . for the same reason that the department store is of great convenience to the average purchaser. . . . It costs no more to group buildings," Stokes went on, "than to scatter them indiscriminately. Great economy is often involved in such grouping, particularly if all the land required for the proposed improvement can be purchased at once." Stokes's arguments echoed similar statements from Warner, Kelsey, and Robinson. Ford brought forth additional utilitarian reasons for a civic center. Proper spacing in a parklike setting would help to protect each building from fire, and their occupants from urban dust and noise. Their relatively close relationships would at the same time encourage the economy of a central heating plant. Only architects and designers could create such a complex urban artifact as a civic center. The manifold aesthetic and engineering details required it. The report on the Cleveland group plan by Burnham and his associates clinched the point in prose and graphics.[50]

The value of a civic center extended beyond its psychic and practical benefits. Burnham urged Cleveland's civic leaders to extend the "order, system and reserve" of the center outward to a uniform style for each type of public building, to the development of the city's parks and boulevard system, and to a new "really imposing" railroad station, "a beautiful vestibule to the town" to provide "the visitor" with a "favorable" "first impression" of Cleveland. While the city would emerge as the common artistic property of all citizens, the task of creating it fell on the cultural and political leadership, to whom Zueblin, Burnham, Robinson, and the others addressed their remarks.[51]

Finally, the civic center took its inspiration from Europe, ancient and modern. Warner's sweeping review of the history of the civic center was perhaps the most inclusive defense of precedent. Milo R. Maltbie argued that Berlin and Paris were beautiful principally because of the arrangement, location, and surroundings of their buildings. And it was their beauty, especially Parisian beauty, that drew so many Americans away from their own cities to spend "millions" in Europe. Burnham had similar entrepreneurial and aesthetic reasons for his forceful statement in favor of the neoclassic. He reminded Clevelanders of "the lesson taught by the Court of Honor of the World's Fair of 1893," that "the highest type of beauty can only be assured by the use of one sort of architecture." Burnham and his associates recommended "that the designs of all the buildings of this group plan should be derived from the historic motives of the classic architecture of Rome." They urged uniformity of materials, scale, mass, and cornice line.[52]

The neoclassical triumph should not be confused with the more fundamental reassertion of traditional Western aesthetics and cultural values. Robinson, in his earlier *Improvement of Towns and Cities*, had called for a public building to be "large, substantial, white, and pure . . . with detached columns and perhaps sculptured figures standing clear against the sky. So rose the Acropolis over Athens, and the opposing temples of Jupiter and Juno on the . . . Capitoline hill." By 1903 he was having second thoughts. In *Modern Civic Art* he labeled the classic "a *bourgeois* type" of architecture and wrote favorably of "the beautiful Gothic constructions of . . . Flanders." In any case, Robinson cautioned, "it would not be wise to limit the choice of architecture to a style that is alien in period and clime." Arthur A. Shurtleff's article on Harvard's college yard emphasized scale, mass, materials, and placement in relation to other buildings and to the sun's path, all part of a European tradition once acknowledged, then lost, in America. Irene Sargent's 1904 article in the *Craftsman* warned against adopting the externals of European municipal art. Sargent instead urged Americans to embrace its fundamentals: class harmony, patriotism, beauty, and civic-mindedness. Americans did not in fact confuse the externals and the fundamentals. City Beautiful aesthetics and sociology were, like the ideal civic building, a harmonious whole.[53]

CONCLUSION

By 1904 the advocates of the City Beautiful had forged an ideology that would serve them through the following decade. It blended earlier planning convictions, such as the psychic importance of natural beauty, with newer notions of evolution and environmentalism. It reinforced the experts' professional convictions and the leadership aspirations of the urban middle and upper-middle classes. Though incomplete and flawed, the City Beautiful ideology met one test of success. It effectively supported planning movements in cities across the United States.

II ◆

The Early City Beautiful

5 ◆ The Struggle for an Urban Park and Boulevard System in Kansas City

BACKGROUND

Officially organized in 1850, Kansas City lay at the great eastward bend of the Missouri River. Just to the west was the Kansas Territory and the confluence of the Missouri and Kansas (Kaw) rivers. The city was well positioned to become a trading and overland outfitting headquarters. What distinguished it from other prospering towns along the western Missouri was a determined, organized business community that pressed unremittingly for railroads. During the border troubles of the 1850s and the Civil War, the business leaders unified around the issues of law and order and economic growth. They did not permit the slavery question and sectionalism to disrupt the community. Their efforts met success in 1869, when the first railroad bridge across the Missouri opened at Kansas City.

Stockyards, packinghouses, grain handling, railroading, real estate, and banking were the obvious engines of the city's economic and population growth. From a population somewhere around 3,000 at the end of the Civil War, Kansas City claimed 32,628 in 1870, though the true figure was about 25,000. By 1880 the population had reached 55,000. In the succeeding decade the city spilled over its old limits, spurted past 100,000, and stood at 119,668 in 1890, larger than Denver, smaller than Omaha. The 1890s depression slowed growth, but the population reached 163,752 in 1900. By that year the city's pioneering park and boulevard system had begun to take shape.[1]

Kansas City's pre–City Beautiful park and boulevard campaign demonstrates how much the politics of the City Beautiful owed to the Olmstedian era. From the 1870s a significant number of the city's elite led a fight against people much like themselves to achieve a legal, political, and urban design framework for planning. Frustrated again and again, they at last succeeded in creating a powerful park board. Then they had to defend attacks on the board and its works along several legal-political fronts, a war they did not win until 1900, in the dawn of the City Beautiful movement. The board was fortunate to have George E. Kessler for its landscape architect. Young Kessler combined extraordinary talent with a thorough Continental education and Olmstedian sensibilities.

Kessler's park and boulevard proposal of 1893 was a forecast of future beautification and a culmination of educational, legal, and political campaigns for a park system. From 1872, when the first effort to secure a public park occured, the press detailed the rationale for parks and for a park and boulevard system. The relatively unrestrained writers of the era gushed forth descriptions of the lush rural atmosphere of parks, as well as references to their utility. Parks were a refuge for working people, whose contacts with nature made them more productive. Parkland should be purchased while open spaces were available and before urban expansion raised land prices. The interurban competition Olmsted invoked in his 1868 San Francisco report was an important "pocketbook" issue: Kansas City had to have parks and boulevards because other cities had them. No parks (other than the conversion of an old cemetery) or boulevards were secured during the 1870s, but the newspaper campaign demonstrated the diffusion of the Olmstedian rationale.[2]

WILLIAM ROCKHILL NELSON

The park movement gathered momentum through the 1880s and 1890s. One of its firmest supporters was a man with a dominating personality who did not come to Kansas City until he was middle-aged, who never held public office, and who shunned public appearances. He was William Rockhill Nelson, the owner and editor of the cheap and lively evening newspaper the *Star*. Nelson did not initiate the park and boulevard movement, but he made a significant contribution as a member of a powerful elite coalition. Born in Fort Wayne, Indiana, on 7 March 1841, Nelson grew up in comfortable circumstances. By age twenty he had overcome a boyhood reputation as a troublemaker and applied his quick, retentive mind to business. In the next two decades he made and lost modest fortunes while turning his hand to the law, real estate, farming, contracting, and, briefly, publishing. The last occupation appealed to him, but Fort Wayne's economic possibilities were limited. Nelson moved to Kansas City at the age of thirty-nine. He was starting over in a strange place, without friends or influence, with modest capital, in a profession about which he knew comparatively little. None of that bothered him, for he was a man of great energy and will and of unconquerable self-confidence.[3]

He was short and heavyset, but stood rigidly erect. His hair, already white, fell in long shocks over a massive head with a big mouth, bulbous nose, and heavy jowls and eyelids. His craggy face was smooth shaven and set on a bull neck, his shoulders sloped, and skinny legs supported his enormous body. Perhaps his most effective weapon was his voice. It was deep and booming, and when Nelson was excited he would thunder and roar "By God!" while he

William R. Nelson,
founder and editor of the
Kansas City Star,
campaigned for parks,
boulevards, a new union
station, and other
artifacts of the City
Beautiful. (Courtesy,
Missouri Valley
Collection, Kansas City
Public Library.)

pounded his desk with his pudgy fist. The performance produced the proper
degree of awe among his subordinates at the *Star*. Office histrionics probably
was a device to forestall familiarity, for Nelson's circle of close friends was
small. Yet he could captivate his employees with his loud and hearty laughter.
At home he was charming, a master of light conversation who could talk
engagingly on a wide range of topics. Nelson's admirers called him "Colonel,"
although he had never seen military service.

From its founding date, 18 September 1880, Nelson's *Star* steadily grew.
Nelson built the *Star* by a commitment to nonpartisanship and by well-written
local news prominently displayed on the front page. He insisted on a conservative appearance for his newspaper but had no objection to sensational
stories beneath the modest typographical dress.[4]

Nelson's systematic and resolute crusade for a park and boulevard system
and related improvements began in the mid-1880s. There were three reasons
for his crusade. The first was Nelson's love of beauty, expressed in his fondness
for art, natural scenes, and architecture. He created a rambling limestone
mansion, Oak Hall, in the southern part of Kansas City and later surrounded
it with an attractive residential development. His art collection became the

core of the holdings within the severe neoclassical gallery that now stands on the site of Oak Hall. Also, the park and boulevard movement dovetailed nicely with the "good roads" transportation campaign, the most venerable of all *Star* crusades. Lastly, Nelson wanted the rough-hewn Kansas City to match his vision of a progressive, stable community blessed with an active, corruption-free government.[5]

Nelson contributed to city planning achievements through the methods he used to lay well-worn arguments before his readers. The main tasks of writing and research he left to others, reserving to himself the decisions on the frequency and emphasis of stories. He directed staffers to compose "letters to the editor" commenting on park proposals and planted them in the *Star*'s columns to simulate a flurry of public interest. A long park story frequently was accompanied by a brief notice on the editorial page summarizing the longer piece and inviting the reader to peruse it. The *Star* employed humor effectively, too. In December 1890 it published a funny, fanciful narrative about a young Kansas Citian, "Jack Bestovit," who had lied to his prospective father-in-law, a New York resident, telling him false stories about Kansas City's beautiful parks, boulevards, and public buildings.[6]

The *Star*'s most effective technique combined repetition and adulation. The glories of other cities' parks and boulevards were illustrated in articles and elaborate line drawings. Interviews with out-of-town visitors and prominent local park advocates filled columns of the *Star* through the years. The *Star* devoted less attention to the achievements of European municipalities and concentrated instead on park and boulevard building in United States cities, which had more familiar tax structures and governments. New York's Central Park came in for favorable comment, as well as the city's smaller parks and playground squares near slum areas. There was publicity for the park systems of Minneapolis, Baltimore, Detroit, Milwaukee, Indianapolis, and many others. All aspects of those systems passed in review: legislation, financing, construction, beautification, and maintenance.[7]

No other city held the promise of Chicago. It had witnessed a stupendous growth, a devastating fire, and a breathtaking renewal. Its inhabitants lived with its dirt and stench while they threw boulevards across the prairie and fashioned parks from the marshes of Lake Michigan. This emergent Chicago was not the city of the World's Columbian Exposition. Eight years before the White City opened its gates, the *Star* examined the Chicago park and boulevard system in a cogent editorial that used Chicago and other cities as examples and set forth a succinct, Olmstedian rationale for a "park system." Kansas City, it said, was "destined to be a great metropolis," and parks were "an indispensable adjunct to a great city." The sooner parks were laid out, the more central, useful, and less expensive they would be. Their purchase and improvement should be financed by bonds, "assessing the current cost of maintenance upon the taxpayers." Finally, "experience in other cities has proved that the management of parks may be best entrusted to an independent

board or commission in order to separate it from the complications and con-
taminations of local politics."[8]

An 1886 page-one interview with "a gentleman from Chicago" told how
that city and its environs were divided into park districts assessed for improvements within their boundaries. Bond issues paid for the lands taken, and the
property that benefited from the improvements was taxed to pay the bonds as
they came due. The Cook County circuit judges appointed the park commissioners, freeing them from "the vicissitudes of city politics." In later years the
Star gave Chicago's parks and boulevards a large measure of credit for
Chicago's success in securing the world's fair. The city's "most effective weapon" in its struggle for the prize "was probably the vast and magnificent park and
boulevard system," the *Star* remarked. "Chicago projected and completed a
system of public pleasure grounds and driveways which eclipse in scope and
grandeur every other system in the country."[9]

The implication for Kansas City was clear: the city must follow Chicago's
lead and must beautify or fail in the race for civic amelioration. "The cities
which are seeking to rival Kansas City in population, progress and business
importance appreciate these auxiliaries of metropolitan life more fully than
they are appreciated here, and Minneapolis, St. Paul, Denver, Omaha . . .
are putting forth practical efforts to secure . . . parks and boulevards." Such
improvement would "render them the more attractive to people from the East
who are considering the choice of a Western city for future residence." Kansas
City offered excellent opportunities. Its rugged, well-drained hills lent themselves to beautification much more than Chicago's featureless marshes. Kansas City's superb climate amd its progress in industry and education would be
brilliantly offset by a park and boulevard system. Its citizens would benefit
from the increased property values that parks and boulevards would bring.
None of this was new, nor was it intended to be. Nelson's genius lay in
presenting acceptable arguments with system and variety. Often he did so to
buttress lengthy legal and political battles for beautification.[10]

EARLY LEGISLATION

Any public improvement beyond streets and basic utilities faced formidable
legal problems. The charter of 1875, an enabling act from the state legislature,
empowered the city to condemn lands for public use. The city applied this
provision to street openings, where relatively little land was taken, and owners of abutting property frequently donated the necessary rights of way. In such
cases the assessment against the owners of benefited property was relatively
low. If the land had to be purchased, the city was required to pay in full before
it could take possession. Condemning a score or more urban acres for a park
was difficult because of the higher cost to benefited property. The city could
not issue bonds for any improvement without permission from the legislature.[11]

The advocates of beautification had to develop legal formulas granting a park board the powers necessary to condemn and control the needed land; they had to create a board free from political interference, yet subject to checks, and they had to provide that board with an independent and adequate source of income. Next, they had to persuade the state legislature to grant the powers to the board, or they had to convince the people of Kansas City to incorporate them in a charter amendment. Then they had to wait until the state supreme court passed upon the constitutionality of their work.

Proponents of parks worked for both a charter amendment and state legislation. Success crowned their efforts in 1889, when voters approved a new charter creating a park board, but one powerless to issue bonds. Meanwhile, an attorney, John K. Cravens, was revising a previously drafted piece of park legislation. His draft allowed the mayor, city council, and county court roles in naming the park commissioners. The park board was empowered to create a park district within the county and to sell bonds up to one million dollars to pay for the purchase or condemnation of parkland, provided two-thirds of the district's voters approved. The board was granted control over the grades and improvement of boulevards. It could make rules for boulevards and parks and hire and manage its own staff. Each year the county court, on recommendation of the commissioners, was to tax the district real estate sufficiently to amortize the bonds.[12]

The Cravens law became effective November 1889, but neither the county court nor the city council took immediate action, because no funds would be available until July 1890. The city and county counselors further inhibited action with opinions against the constitutionality of the park law. Finally, the county court appointed two members; the mayor appointed two others, after the council could not agree within the time allowed by the law. The mayor himself served as the fifth member. The board did not have much to administer, for the only improved park belonging incontestably to the city was a five-and-one-half-acre tract perched on the north bluffs above the Missouri River. It had been improved by people in the neighborhood, not so much from a love of the beautiful as from fear that the city would use the site for a pest house. Boulevard building remained under the aegis of the Board of Public Works. Even this limited authority of the park board ceased in January 1891, when the state supreme court declared the law unconstitutional. The decision came in a friendly suit from the park board to compel the county to levy park taxes. The court struck down the law because of a defect in its title.[13]

The destruction of the legislatively sanctioned park board shifted attention to an alternative scheme, which was to organize a commission under the city charter. The new board was appointed in 1892, following a quick campaign by the newly formed Municipal Improvement Association to amend the park provisions of the charter of 1889. The amendments required the mayor to appoint a board and gave the board power to issue city bonds. August Robert Meyer, the president of the association, was also the president of the new board. Its other members were locally prominent. Simeon B. Armour headed the Kansas City branch of the Armour meat packing company. William C. Glass was a wealthy, retired wholesale liquor dealer and real estate operator. Louis Hammerslough, kindly and philanthropic, pursued mercantile and investment interests. Adriance Van Brunt was a successful architect.[14]

MEYER, KESSLER, AND THE PARK BOARD

The driving force of the board was its president, Meyer. A European-educated multimillionaire, he possessed a rich personality combining enthusiasm, gentility, and charm. A late portrait shows him with a high forehead, long sideburns on a thin face, intelligent eyes, a moustache, and a cleft chin. Like Nelson, he carefully surveyed Kansas City's prospects before relocating. Unlike Nelson, he was just into his thirties when he arrived in 1882, he had already laid the foundation of his fortune, and he delighted in the rough-and-tumble of public speaking. Meyer was born in St. Louis in 1851 to German immigrants who had lived in the United States for some time. His father was a woodenware manufacturer who sent his son, at age fourteen, to the polytechnic school in Zurich, later to the mining school at the University of Freiburg, and finally to the School of Mines at Berlin. Back in the United States, Meyer became a mining engineer in Colorado and he was for a time the government assayer there. He helped to found Leadville, Colorado, and is credited with naming it. While in Leadville he prospected, invested in real estate, and continued his studies.[15]

With some partners he took over a small smelting plant in Kansas a few miles from Kansas City and built it into the huge Kansas City Consolidated Smelting and Refining Company. His hand was everywhere. He bought real estate in Kansas City, and later built a mammoth brick house near Nelson's Oak Hall. He was active in the YMCA, the First Congregational Church, charity organizations, and the Commercial Club. At home Meyer was relaxed and genial, surrounded by his five young children. His desk was a clutter of mechanical contraptions and gadgets he bought from their inventors merely for the pleasure of toying with them. Meyer's horseback rides through the suburban hills filled him with a love for their beauty and an intense desire to preserve their natural state. Even before his appointment to the park board he was telling the Commercial Club that Kansas City needed beautification. He wrote to New York, Boston, and Buffalo for statistics on park development and traveled around the United States and to Europe. He looked, questioned, read reports, and gained new ideas for improving his adopted city. He recognized "that a good deal of our work will have to be educational"; therefore in the early days of the fight for parks he addressed civic groups, illustrated his talks with slides, and answered sharp-tongued questioners. At first Meyer was not adept at compromise but he learned quickly.[16]

By the end of 1894 the board had adjusted to a sharply curtailed, depres-

August R. Meyer, a
successful businessman
whose socially conscious
rhetoric adorned the first
Kansas City park board
report, and who
maneuvered the early
park ordinances through
passage. (Courtesy,
Missouri Valley
Collection, Kansas City
Public Library.)

sion-style budget. After a careful study of Kansas City's assessed real estate
valuation, topography, and population density, it divided the city into three
park assessment districts and persuaded the city council to establish them.
Later the council approved a one-mill tax on all property in each district, to be
used for park improvements in the respective districts. Next the Board of
Public Works gave the park board permission to beautify a small patch of
ground adjacent to the city hall, a gathering place for loafers and hucksters.
The park board also agreed to press for at least one scenic park as well as small
recreational tracts. The first significant piece of real estate it received was a
twenty-one-acre tract donated by a semiretired lawyer and politician. The
grounds lay east of the city and were little improved when Meyer's board
assumed control from the Board of Public Works. The greatest early achievement was the board's 1893 report, a product of the collaboration between
Meyer and Kessler.[17]

George Edward Kessler, whose work would reshape many cities, campuses,
and private lawns in the United States, was born in Frankenhausen, Germany, on 16 July 1862. Kessler's mother and father took him to America at

George E. Kessler, the landscape architect who designed the Kansas City park and boulevard system, as he appeared in later life, long after he had moved his practice to St. Louis. (Courtesy, Missouri Valley Collection, Kansas City Public Library.)

the close of the Civil War; they lived briefly in Missouri and Wisconsin before moving to Dallas, Texas. Kessler's father and an uncle invested in a nearby cotton farm. Shortly thereafter the father died, releasing him from the family pressures and the series of failed business ventures that had frustrated his artistic temperament. Her husband's unhappiness convinced Antoine Kessler that young George, who possessed strains of his father's character, should be educated to develop his creative powers, but with a practical element added. To introduce George to the ways of the world she got him a job as a bill collector, an adventuresome occupation for a teenager in a raw town. Meanwhile, after consultation with relatives, Antoine concluded that landscape architecture would combine the proper degree of creativity and practicality. Her son could cultivate his love of the beautiful through botany while the engineering curriculum disciplined his mind.[18] Antoine ended George's American schooling and his Dallas bill collecting and took him to the quieter precincts of the grand ducal gardens at Weimar, where he began private instruction in forestry, botany, and landscape design. Study at Potsdam and Charlottenburg followed, capped by a course in civil engineering at the University of Jena. Kessler spent his last year of Continental schooling on a study of civic design that took him to major cities from Paris to Moscow. No part of this education ever dominated the others. Though emotionally a naturalistic constructivist, Kessler could design plazas and axial boulevards or blend the curvilinear and the formal in the same parkway without breaking its continuity.

Back in the United States at the age of twenty, he worked briefly in New York's Central Park. Olmsted had left the city by then, but it is possible that the dean of landscape architecture met the neophyte and urged him to remain in New York. However, friends arranged for Kessler to become superintendent of parks for a little railroad in which they owned stock—the Kansas City, Fort Scott, and Gulf. Kessler got his first look at the craggy countryside around Merriam Park, in Kansas southwest of Kansas City, in 1882. Within four years he had developed it into a "beautiful pleasure ground" that included a small zoo. In addition, he had charge of the trees and shrubs around all of the railroad's stations; planted and supervised a 1,500–acre forest at Farlington, Kansas, which produced railroad ties and telegraph poles; and probably laid out and landscaped a residential development that the railroad opened near the park in 1886. In the meantime he established an office in Kansas City and searched for more work. His largest commission in the early years was landscaping a narrow, two-block-long hollow in Hyde Park, a new residential area about a mile north of Nelson's Oak Hall. To forestall the park's becoming a kind of collective backyard, he circled it with a road to encourage home builders to front their residences upon it. His plan worked. Land along Hyde Park sold well, and soon large houses presented gracious facades to the little park. After the first, short-lived park board organized, Kessler applied for the position of landscape architect. Meyer's board hired him, officially to be its "secretary," and as "Engineer to the Board to serve in said capacity without pay."[19]

REPORT OF OCTOBER 1893

The board's report of October 1893 was buttressed with visual material: a topographic map and several photographs as well as some finely done drawings. Its core was an extensive argument for improvements, contained in a careful, comprehensive examination of Kansas City's population density and growth; its industrial, commercial, and residential sections; and its prospects for future development. It included three sections: a letter of transmittal to the mayor, which served as an introduction to the second section; the report of the board, containing recommendations and supporting material; and the engineer's report, which discussed the recommendations in terms of topography, design, and construction. Meyer wrote the first two sections, and Kessler the third.[20]

Meyer's sections demonstrated his remarkable understanding of the park rationale. Discussing the "problem before us," he asserted that "we must deal with it in its application to the entire city." Piecemeal development, he wrote, "does not permit, on the part of the public, an intelligent judgment upon the value of such improvement. . . . The value of selections for public purposes, their most satisfactory distribution, and the dependence of one improvement upon another, cannot be appreciated without a general plan." He declared that "it is far better to plan comprehensively and broadly and proceed with actual construction leisurely, than to attempt economy in the original plans." Meyer developed four arguments for a park and boulevard system. His "pocketbook" argument—that parks advanced real estate values—showed how well he had absorbed the Olmsted and Vaux park reports of New York and Brooklyn. He dealt adroitly with the attraction and competition argument as well. Chicago, though topographically uninviting, had "created by purely artificial means, though with . . . the very highest skill, a beautiful and gigantic system of boulevards and parks" attracting "men and money." Beautiful surroundings were "a powerful attraction" to the "capitalist," whom Meyer defined as "a man, not only of money, but possessed at the same time of business experience, sagacity and knowledge." But "all classes" appreciated and were drawn toward attractive urban scenes.[21]

Meyer also demonstrated a sure grasp of social control issues. "We are but just beginning to realize that by beautifying our city, . . . we not only will do our duty to our citizens, but we shall create among our people warm attachments to the city, and promote civic pride, thereby supplementing and emphasizing our business advantages and increasing their power to draw business and population." He emphasized environmental shaping. "Life in cities is unnatural life," he declared. "It has a tendency to stunt physical and moral growth. The monotony of brick and stone, of dust and dirt, the absence of the colors with which nature paints, . . . write despair on many a face." "How," he asked, "is the poor man's boy to grow into a cheerful, industrious and contented man, unless he can play . . . on the green turf and under waving trees." Meyer insisted that a productive manhood required "the recollections of an innocent, joyous boyhood, instead of the impressions of dirty, white-faced and vicious gamins." The time had come for Kansas City to provide playgrounds for the young and larger parks for their elders.[22]

But not a "large scenic" park. Despite his high-flown rhetoric, Meyer was practical. Just as he did not hesitate to criticize land developers for "destroying much of the natural beauty of our city," he openly disagreed with Olmsted when the great landscape architect argued for a suburban landscape park. Olmsted paused in his World's Columbian Exposition and other work to come to Kansas City in March 1893. He drove around the city and inspected Kessler's plans, which were substantially complete by that time. Olmsted accepted the plans "in the main" but urged the park board to include a park such as Brooklyn's Prospect or Boston's Franklin. Meyer rejected the plea in favor of scenic preservation and recreation within the city. "While we are in the fullest sympathy with such wise and good friends of the people as Mr. F. L. Olmsted," Meyer wrote, "and willingly admit the great usefulness of large scenic parks in correcting and opposing the evil results of life in crowded cities, we . . . recognize that there exist within the boundaries of our city other special and urgent problems and peculiar conditions that . . . should engage our attention first."[23]

Instead of a huge landscape park the commissioners proposed what they believed would respond immediately to social problems and citizen desires. They suggested three parks, supplemented by boulevards, although they avoided a continuous boulevard loop through the parks apparently because of the expense involved in reaching the west bluff park west and south of the commercial district. The west bluffs were the target of long-standing beautification ideas and an example of the incorporation of old proposals into new plans. They were a notorious eyesore rising 200 feet above the Union Depot and rail yards, a blight of staggering billboards and weatherbeaten shanties. Yet the crest of the bluff commanded an impressive view of the Missouri as it turned east to sweep across the state to the Mississippi. An ornamented slope also would help impress travelers alighting at the Union Depot. All the city had done about the shanties was to place the area within the fire limits. The action stopped the shack construction, but the neighborhood remained run down and mostly a black housing district. Dr. Sam Scott, a successful black podiatrist and inventor of the herbal remedy "Scott's Blood Purifier," lived next door to the abode of "negro hellions and black loafers," an instance of the lack of class segregation in crowded black neighborhoods. Other parks were proposed for the north bluffs, which were steep cliffs cut by ravines high above the Missouri River on the city's northern rim, and for the broken, ugly Penn Street ravine in the southwestern part of the city. Three recreational grounds and a large "parade" for organized athletics and military drill supplemented the parks.[24]

Meyer revealed his keen understanding of the boulevard rationale. Establishing a boulevard system would end the "evils" he saw in Kansas City's residential-retail development. As soon as an attractive, if small, residence section was established, a flurry of neighborhood shops would arise, discouraging further residential construction of a high order. New residential establishments would be made elsewhere, followed by another new wave of shops, and so on, resulting in "a large sprawling combination of city and village" without focus or cohesion. A boulevard system would permit the "fixing and classification of residential sections" and help draw them together. "Such a system, . . . if it give due weight to existing conditions and adapt itself to the topography, avoiding as much as possible forced routes and forced construction, will give a permanent residence character to certain sections of the city." A "comprehensive, well-planned and thoroughly maintained" boulevard system would combine rural with urban advantages and "check the tendency to . . . build residences in the suburbs." Compact settlement would result in better sanitation, street maintenance, and streetcar service. Finally, the "best and most expensive residences will go up along boulevards," though Meyer expected a ripple effect spreading several blocks on either side of the boulevards, producing acres of pleasant housing. That done, "retail business that supplies the many and frequent wants of the family will find its legitimate foothold. . . . In the city the retail merchant will select, as the most advantageous location, the street that contains many establishments of the same character as his." Thus would housing and trade develop in an atmosphere of beauty and harmony.[25]

The proposed boulevards ran from the future North Terrace Park (now Kessler Park) overlooking the Missouri to the future Penn Valley Park in the southwestern section. The commission proposed a grand formal boulevard, the Paseo, in the central part of the city, including some ten narrow blocks between Grove and Flora avenues. The Paseo ended at the Parade, the proposed militia drill field. Suggestions for other recreation areas completed Meyer's statement. Kessler, though presumably writing an engineer's report, revealed his landscape training. A "great breadth of views" from a park was not always desirable, he explained, because the views "often include spots and objects not in harmony with park scenery." The solution was to arrange umbrageous screens "to cover undesirable objects" while opening vistas to "distant objects of interest," giving the impression that they were "portions of the park, although actually far beyond and out of control." Park buildings were essential for operations and public comfort but were "artificial and more or less out of keeping with natural scenery" and should not "be permitted to become conspicuous either in design or color."[26]

The immediate impact of the plan was an indication of its ultimate influence. Illustrated summaries and effusive editorials appeared in the daily press. The mayor told the park board to print the report and urged the city council to give its blessing to the plan. A favorable five-to-four vote in the lower house found James Pendergast, boss of the First Ward, for the report. No reformer, Pendergast consistently supported reform tangibles such as parks and boulevards. The Commercial Club called three meetings to discuss the plan. At the first session the city counselor and the park board attorney defended the board's legal structure and procedures before seventy-five querulous and somewhat dubious businessmen. Meyer fielded legal questions at the next meeting but saved his heavy ammunition for the third, semipublic gathering. At this assembly hundreds of people heard him tell how "the growth and improvement of a city must be symmetrical to be satisfactory" and thrilled as he flashed stereoptican slides showing the proposed plans. He talked for two hours. He stressed the relatively inexpensive cost of improvements compared with those in Paris, London, and other mature cities. He cited the rapid rise in land values on the perimeter of New York's Central Park. After the applause and cheers for Meyer's speech died away, the Commercial Club adopted a strong resolution calling for acquisition and construction "as speedily as practicable" for the sake of "all values in the city, promoting public health and comfort and emphasizing the culture and refinement of our people."[27]

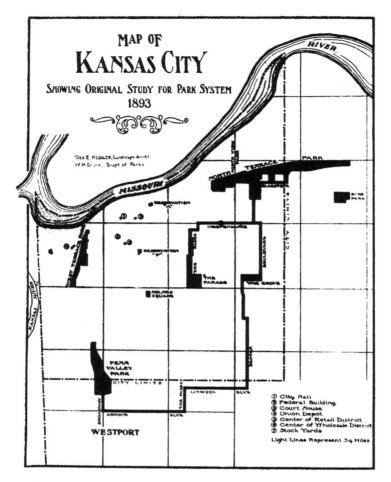

These three maps show the development of the Kansas City park and boulevard system from George E. Kessler's original design through the completion of the Union Station. (*Report of the Board of Park Commissioners of Kansas City, Missouri, 1914–1915.* Courtesy, Missouri Valley Collection, Kansas City Public Library.)

1895 Amendments to the City Charter

The next great victory for planning came in 1895 when voters approved an amendment to the city charter granting the park board its needed fiscal power. An understanding of the issues involved requires a look at the legal substructure so essential to the success of city planning and to the situation the park board faced after the charter amendment of 1892. That amendment continued and strengthened the park board but required the board to issue bonds for improvements, a device liable to the dual objection that it increased the city's bonded indebtedness and forced the assessed property holders to pay for land taken in a few quick and heavy installments. Kansas City in 1895 could

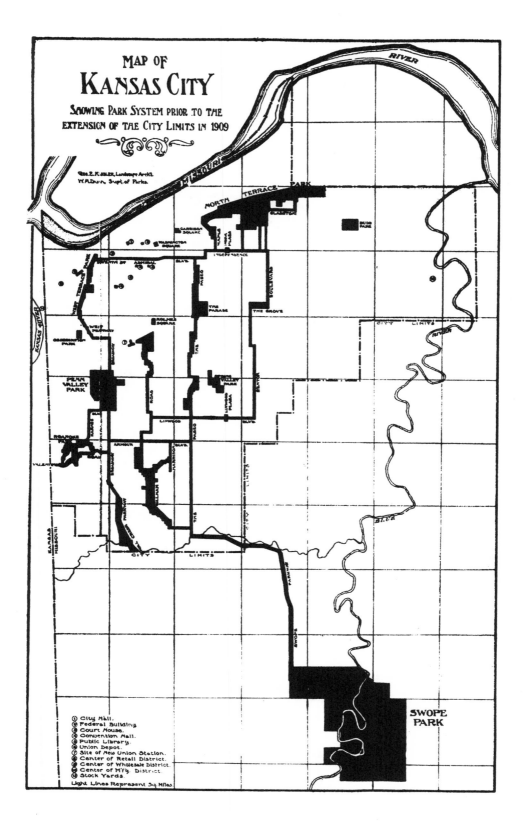

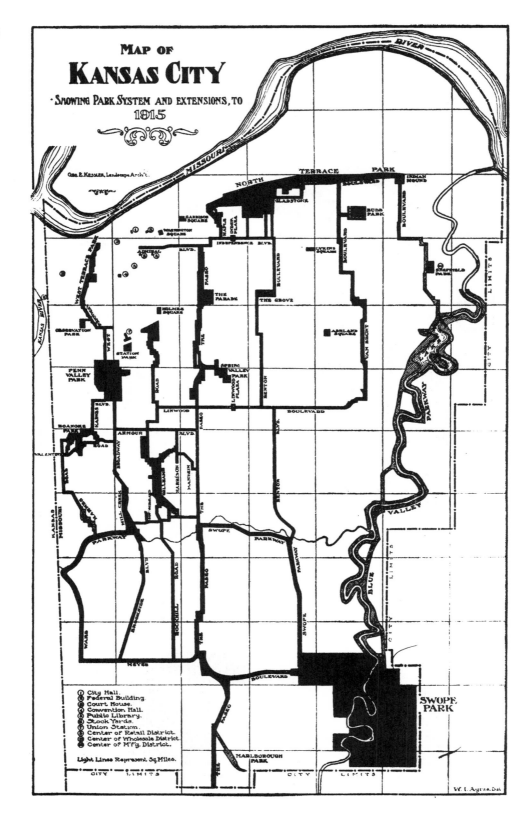

MAP OF
KANSAS CITY
· SHOWING PARK SYSTEM AND EXTENSIONS, TO
1915

Geo. E. Kessler, Landscape Arch't.

① City Hall.
② Federal Building.
③ Court House.
④ Convention Hall.
⑤ Public Library.
⑥ Stock Yards.
⑦ Union Station.
⑧ Center of Retail District.
⑨ Center of Wholesale District.
⑩ Center of M'f'g. District.

Light Lines Represent Sq. Miles.

W. L. Ayres, Del.

not afford park bonds. It could bond itself to but 5 percent of the assessed valuation of real and personal property. Though civic debt was moderate, the approval of pending waterworks bonds would push that debt to the limit. Finally, the board feared adverse public reaction to another "frequent and unpopular" special assessment of the type required for street paving and maintenance.[28]

The state law of 1893 circumvented these limitations by empowering the board to issue "certificates," really bonds on the land in the park districts rather than against the city's valuation. Other provisions of the act differed little from the future charter amendment. The Commercial Club was the principal supporter of the bill. Its quick passage was a comment on the club's enthusiasm and effectiveness and on the influence of Meyer in its councils. For the present, the important aspect of the legislation is its author, the young attorney Delbert James Haff. Before and during his tenure as general counsel to the park board, he forged the legal structure for the park system and the later City Beautiful. Like Nelson, Meyer, and Kessler, he was drawn to Kansas City in the 1880s, but unlike them he emerged from poverty.[29]

Haff was born in Oakland County, Michigan, on 19 February 1859. Left fatherless at six, he helped his mother scratch out a living from the family farm. He went to school and was qualified to teach at age fifteen. For six years he taught in a country school, farmed, and saved his money until he could enter the University of Michigan in 1880. After a year he went back to work, this time as a traveling salesman, returning to school in 1882. He made up the lost year by doubling up his courses and graduated Phi Beta Kappa with the class of 1884. The same year he graduated from the law department, passed the bar the next, and came to Kansas City in 1886. Haff cultivated moustaches, a Vandyke beard, a reputation as a skilled courtroom lawyer with a fine sense of the dramatic, and an interest in civic affairs. He helped to organize the Municipal Improvement Association and served as the chairman of its park and boulevard committee, probably because the first park board had retained him to fight its unavailing legal battle before the Missouri Supreme Court. He drafted the revised Article X of the 1892 city charter, which established the board presided over by Meyer. In 1893 he became general counsel to the board, drew up the law of 1893, and drafted the 1895 charter amendments. He became president of the park board in 1909.

In February 1895, however, his legislative masterpiece lay in ruins after a suit brought by property owners in the district surrounding the newly condemned North Terrace Park. The court struck down the 1893 law allowing the certificate issue because it was, in effect, an amendment to the city charter. The court reasoned that Section 18 of the act specifically altered the charter. Both the charter itself and the Constitution of Missouri declared that any change in the charter must be made by the people. The legislature could not; it was up to the people of Kansas City to act in the matter. Another charter amendment was not necessary to maintain the park board itself, but the board was, as Meyer phrased it, a "very useless ornament" without the finances to exercise its charter-given powers of 1892.[30]

The charter amendments of 1895 were the culmination of efforts to provide a board with administrative and fiscal autonomy, yet subject to some control. Under the 1892 charter amendment the Board of Public Works had to approve all of the park board's recommendations, a case of oversupervision. In the park board's eyes the Board of Public Works was a bottleneck through which its recommendations cleared but slowly. Haff's new charter amendments, in a brilliant stroke of omission, simply did not mention the Board of Public Works. The proposed amendments did provide for a condemnation jury to fix damages to owners of land taken for improvements and to distribute levies for payment of damages over the remaining land in the park district concerned, under the supervision of the state circuit court.[31]

The key to the document was the section granting the power to sell tax certificates—not to exceed the total assessment against private property for the improvement in question—to pay for the land taken. The certificates were actually a lien on the purchased land and bonds backed by the property values of the park district. Though the city treasurer was charged with keeping the assessment records and holding the tax payments, the certificates were not liabilities of the city. Thus the park board escaped the limitations imposed by the constitutional ceiling on civic debt and the voters' reluctance to tax themselves heavily for expensive improvements. Property owners could pay their assessments for certificate retirement in one lump sum, or, and this was important, they could spread them over a number of annual payments, as determined by the board. In practice this amounted to at least ten, and usually twenty, years. Investors had to purchase the certificates at par (some sold above par) and were granted a 7 percent annual interest rate. Because the park board received the face value of its certificates at once, it could make full payment to owners of condemned land and assume title without delay.

Sections of the amendments taken over with little or no change from previous acts and charters included those that set the board's membership at five, with no more than three from the same political party; provided for the board's control over parks and boulevards; continued the three districts; and required a minimum of one park in each district.

Supporters of the amendments left nothing to chance. On May 20, after the council had accepted the proposed amendments and set a special election for June 6, they announced a "citizen's association for the charter amendments" to develop propaganda and hold public information meetings. The chairman, Charles Campbell, was the wealthy president of a paint and glass company, while Robert Gillham, a feverishly active young engineer, served as secretary. Both would be named to the park board a month later. Other leading citizens, Meyer and Haff among them, composed the executive committee. The association shrewdly selected its spokesman for each ward. Big, friendly James Pendergast, boss of the First Ward, was a representative from his preserve. At the same time the association carefully included Joseph B. Shannon, leader of the opposition Democratic faction, as well as the venerable Republicans, James S. Cannon, an early advocate of a west bluff park, and R. H. Hunt. The necessary funds were to be solicited from businessmen.[32]

Quickly the citizen's association moved to stir up support for the charter amendments. Four days after its organization was made public, one of its committees appeared before the Industrial Council, the central labor organization, to plead the case for parks. The next evening the mass meetings and speeches began. Meyer spoke at a Tenth Ward gathering and addressed the Commercial Club on the following night. To ensure "the largest possible vote" Mayor Webster Davis declared a half-holiday for "all city offices and employees" and requested all employers to give their workers enough time off to vote. The next day he delivered an emotional, grandiloquent speech at the Stock Exchange Building, castigating wealthy property owners for their opposition to improvements.[33]

All this effort produced a thumping victory for the park amendments: 10,298 for, a mere 1,784 against. The amendments carried every precinct of every ward in their nearly six-to-one triumph. Such an overwhelming vote hardly begs for extended analysis. A few observations will, however, place the park and boulevard amendments in context. They were less popular than the other major issue, the waterworks buyout bonds, which posted only 482 negative votes, and slightly less well received than some proposed license changes, probably reflecting a view of parks and boulevards as superficial adornment.[34]

The results caution against a simple correlation between economic status and votes on improvement issues. Pendergast's First Ward, a potential beneficiary from a west bluff park, responded with 314 for, 58 against—almost the citywide ratio. The Second Ward—a river area of Pendergast influence and at the time the locale of downtown, saloons, gambling dens, and tenements—responded with a conclusive 242 yes to 27 no, or almost nine-to-one in favor. The Sixth Ward, a notoriously rambunctious district lying east of the Second, came through with a three-to-one vote, 579 to 199, below the citywide ratio but above the Fifth Ward's 533 to 263. The vote in the Fifth, site of the proposed Penn Valley Park, may have reflected modest property owners' fears of heavy assessments. On the other hand, the Seventh Ward, which encompassed river bottoms, fine homes, and most of the proposed North Terrace Park, gave its approval almost ten-to-one: 1,581 for, 161 against. The southeastern Tenth Ward, a developing, quality residential area, supported the bonds 1,309 to 158, above the citywide ratio but below the boisterous Second Ward's. Some of the ward-by-ward results read like an alliance between the city's least and most advantaged residents.[35]

The next step was a test of the new charter's constitutionality. The agent of the estate owning the block that later became Holmes Square playground appealed to the Missouri Supreme Court, singling out for heavy attack the concept of special benefit to property near an improvement. The suit was really a test of the methods of condemnation juries, which spread benefit assessments heavily on property nearby and more lightly on property farther away. In May 1896 the court upheld the idea of particular benefit to nearby realty and turned aside all other objections. Investors were assured that the park tax certificates were safe.[36]

SWOPE'S DONATION

The most spectacular change in planning fortunes came that June, when a rich recluse gave the city a vast park containing almost 1,334 acres—at the time, the second largest city park in the United States. Its donor was Thomas H. Swope, a shy, wispy bachelor who built a fortune on his shrewd real estate investments. His name would return to prominence thirteen years later, when a relative was tried for his murder but acquitted after a series of sensational trials and appeals. This shrewd, secretive man gave away more than two square miles of rolling, beautiful, wooded land, bisected by the charming Blue River, partly because he harbored tender feelings for the city that made him rich. He had dropped an earlier plan to donate a public building, perhaps because of premature publicity. When he heard of the park board's interest in a large suburban park to supplement its projected interior parks, he went to the mayor's office and, after a two-hour conference, offered the property. Another, less altruistic motive may have impelled Swope's donation. He probably foresaw that improvements meant heavier taxes on his real estate holdings and hoped to forestall comprehensive development by the dramatic donation of a mammoth park. His later leadership in the antipark movement suggests that crass and charitable motives mingled in his decision to deliver the land to the city.[37]

The new parkland, roughly a rectangle with a westerly extension at its northwest corner, lay southeast of the city, four miles from the nearest city limit and seven from the center of the business section. There were no improvements save a country road, a railroad track, and a scattering of indifferent buildings. No trolley line ran that far out. Anyone equipped with "a young active horse" might make the trip in an hour. None of this dimmed the enthusiastic reception of the gift. After all, Swope's conditions were light. The deed required that the land be used as a park forever, that it be called Swope Park, that the city present a plan of improvements by 1 January 1898, and that, beginning the same date, it spend for improvements $5,000 a year above expenses, a stipulation Swope later waived. The council suspended its rules and passed an ordinance accepting the park with a rush. The most enthusiasm went into a plan, first developed in the *Star*, for a grand holiday and pilgrimage to the park. The city council declared a holiday and the Clearing House Association resolved to close the banks on the day of celebration.[38]

The celebration began with a parade at ten the morning of 25 June. Then came the exodus to the park. On anything that would roll—excursion trains, buggies, carts—on horses, burros, and on foot, people jammed the rail line and roads leading to Swope Park. A flag-raising ceremony preceded an afternoon of speeches. The crowd was huge, estimated at 18,000, so two men spoke simultaneously from separate platforms to different sections of the audience. Almost everyone of community importance made a speech. Nelson Crews, the popular black politician, quipped, "I am here to add a little color to the proceedings." He kept the delighted audience in the palm of his hand, paid a moving tribute to Swope, and then led his hearers in singing "America." The speeches lasted two hours. After the last of them, the crowd filled the roads leading back to Kansas City, their progress marked by the dust raised by thousands of wheels. Through it all, Thomas H. Swope lingered on the fringes of the crowd. He had been too shy to ride with the mayor at the head of the parade, and he was too reserved to mount a speaker's platform to receive acknowledgments from the throng gathered in his honor. A reporter approached him and asked him for a comment. He shook his head but scribbled a statement: "I have often heard it said that gratitude is a scarce article in this world, but from this time on I shall reject & ignore that pessimistic sentiment."[39]

The jubilee was a great day. A few thousand more people would have gone to the park had there been trains enough to carry them. Beyond maintaining interest in the park movement, however, the new gift had little value. The lessee refused further public entry, and even had he not, the park was too remote. Its real importance was for the future.

The rise of neighborhood improvement associations was a local manifestation of the municipal improvement movement. One group petitioned the county court to build a boulevard to Swope Park. Another asked the city to convert to parkland the unused portion of the reservoir overlooking the Kansas River south of the west bluffs. A third wanted part of the workhouse grounds improved with flowers, walkways, a fountain, and seats. A fourth concentrated upon securing the Penn Valley Park condemnation ordinances through the council. An association delegation followed the ordinance through both houses of the city council. Then it marched triumphantly into the mayor's office, where the document was signed. The delegates cheered, whereupon the mayor treated them to cigars and an impromptu speech. The improvement club was so proud of its role that it hired a hall and held a celebration.[40]

Boulevard building continued in the midst of the excitement. Unfortunately almost all of it was concentrated along the north bluffs, where a view required a long walk for most citizens. The few acres of accessible donated parkland and the handful of boulevard miles built could not compete with the streetcar parks and their plays, Hawaiian bands, and performing elephants. That was so much the worse for the friends of planning, who were about to plunge into a long, bitter struggle for their ideas and hopes. In the afterglow of the Swope Park jubilee, the antipark men quietly gathered strength for their big battle against the plan.[41]

OPPOSITION TO THE PARK MOVEMENT

The opponents of planning fought with tenacity and skill, giving the friends of parks lessons in how to exploit the mechanisms of democracy. Ultimately they lost, but not before they delayed plans, drove wedges in their adversary's ranks, and even caused one notable defection. At the outset the antagonists were closely balanced. The propark people had a plan, a charter amendment, a remote park, and a record of surviving the legal challenges that mattered. It was difficult to organize a sustained opposition to what they had so far accomplished. On the other hand, the first evidence of park and boulevard planning was a benefit assessment in a park district, a weakness that the enemies of improvements turned to their advantage. If they could delay construction, citizens would note only one tangible, the deflation of their pocketbooks, in return for which the propark people could offer only future benefits.

For almost four years, from the autumn of 1896 to the summer of 1900, the opponents of parks organized a series of petitions, public meetings, delegations to the council and the park board, court fights, substitutes for Kessler's plan, and an attempt to remove Meyer from the park board. The antipark faction was not composed of vicious or mean men intent on destroying a beautiful plan. They did care for money. They were vitally concerned about the expense involved in creating a park system, which they honestly believed was superfluous to the city as an economic organism. Not all of them were well-to-do. The *Star* staff's 1915 biography of Nelson, which is inclined to view the editor's enemies as evil or stupid, admits that the antipark leadership "enlisted many home-owners who really believed that the building of these improvements would entail an expense that would sweep away their homes and ruin them." The leadership was, however, remarkably similar in occupation and community position to the propark group. The president of the Taxpayer's League, the principal antipark organization, was also president of the National Bank of Commerce. Of the remaining sixteen leaders of the organization, six were attorneys, four were real estate men, one was an insurance agent, and another operated a drugstore. Others included the president of a medical school and the treasurer of a large hardware company. Bernard Corrigan, listed as a contractor, later headed the Metropolitan Street Railway Company and built a stunning poured-concrete house in a fashionable district, activities scarcely qualifying him for membership in the faceless masses. One man identified with the Taxpayer's League leadership called himself a carpenter, which may or may not have been a Franklinesque listing.[42]

The struggle over the parks foreshadowed many later battles for the City Beautiful. It was a complex, five-cornered contest involving the park board (which was willing to compromise its original land takings but not to surrender Kessler's plan), uncompromising friends of parks such as Nelson's *Star* and some affected property holders, a city council committed to park development, the Taxpayer's League and other park opponents, and the Missouri Supreme Court. The opposition's first call to battle against a specific project came on 13 August 1896, when the North Terrace Park condemnation jury awarded damages of $603.113.04. This meant that residents of the North Park District would be taxed that amount for 200 acres, much of it steep, wild bluffs. Less than two months after, the verdict for West Terrace Park came in, $866,237.32. Even before the second award, the already-organized Taxpayer's League was circulating petitions asking the city council to "proceed slowly" with park improvements. Immediately after the West Terrace Park condemnation, the league prepared petitions against both bluff parks. Among those reported "busily canvassing for signatures" was Thomas H. Swope. Propark leaders assembled counterpetitions. The park board late in 1896 received the petitions, and the council's upper house heard arguments for and against the parks.[43]

On 24 March 1897, the *Star*, already referring to the park opposition as "mossbacks," let fly with two humorous sallies against the league and Swope. The attack on Swope stemmed from his opposition to planned improvements and from his ownership of an unimproved corner across the street from the *Star*. Two rows of garish billboards formed a right angle at the corner, concealing a muddy hollow behind. The property was the antithesis of Nelson's ideals of civic beauty and personal responsibility and an affront to his ambitions for Kansas City. Readers of the *Star* on that March day saw a drawing of a bald man standing on a raft in the middle of a stagnant pond. His back was to them. He was addressing an audience of elfin creatures perched high above him on a row of billboards. Retail stores occupying other corners opposite Swope's property were visible above the billboards. The accompanying story was a fanciful account of "Colonel Stope's" speech. (Swope, like Nelson, enjoyed the complimentary but unearned title of "colonel.") "Stope" addressed his "fellow taxpayers and downtrodden millionaires," who cheered his claim that "we have many times opposed propositions of a public nature which did not cost a cent." The speaker denigrated Kessler's plan with "What use have I for parks? I have [no] carriages and horses to display on the boulevards and never will because carriages must be bought."[44]

The companion story attacked the Taxpayer's League. The humorous, largely fictional account of one of its meetings appeared under a drawing of a character similar to those in "Stope's" audience. This bearded creature, attired in a top hat and a coat reaching to the knees of his pipestem legs, gripped a padlocked pocketbook in his left hand and brandished a hammer in his right. His exposed right arm was heavily muscled in contrast to the rest of his shriveled body. He was the "President of the Hammer and Padlock Club." The *Star* explained that the locked pocketbook was a safeguard against taxes and the hammer was used to "knock" improvements and progress. The imaginative text told how one member of the club called for "a law that only property owners may vote on questions of taxation and let the rabble vote for mayors and the like and thereby have fun with themselves." The *Star* later adopted a mock heraldic device of crossed sledgehammer and padlock on a field of repeated "No!" It printed this "coat of arms" in an insert beside accounts of Taxpayer's League activities.[45]

The propark campaign also gathered momentum. On 28 March, the Industrial Council, the central labor organization, declared that the "establishment of such parks and improvements will tend to relieve the congestion of the labor market" and protested "most solemnly against the repeal of the ordinance establishing parks." Two days later the Commercial Club reaffirmed its support when it passed a resolution expressing confidence in the park board and remonstrating against repeal. School principals, in a separate meeting the same evening, resolved their opposition to repeal of the park ordinances. On the last day of March a group with a direct interest in the plan met and endorsed the park commissioners' proposals. Architects, builders, and materials men composed that group. Resolutions and further meetings meant little, however, until the third condemnation jury reported on Penn Valley Park.[46]

On the morning of April 24 the jury gave over a fat file of Penn Valley Park documents to the circuit court. The verdict was staggering: $870,759.60, the highest figure yet declared for Kansas City parkland. Clearly the friends of parks were in a bad situation. Both West Terrace and Penn Valley parks were in the West Park District, a relatively small area of roughly three square miles. Though it contained sizable wholesale and retail sections and had an assessed valuation of $10,847,000, the district was asked to bear an enormous tax load of well over $1,700,000 for the two parks. Important interests were affected. The Union Depot Company was assessed almost $15,000 for Penn Valley Park alone, while the New York Life Insurance Company was charged more than $7,000 on its graceful office building.[47]

Meyer decided upon compromise. He threw his energies into reducing the size of the parks, a decision that cost him the unconditional support of the *Star*. Editor Nelson could not compromise or tolerate compromise. Meanwhile, the "knockers" attempted to defeat the North Terrace Park with an alternative proposal. Under the terms of this offering, the city would lease a large street railway park outside the northeastern city limits for five years, while it sought a constitutional increase in its bonding power enabling it to purchase the tract at the end of that time. The "knockers'" most audacious move, however, was their attempt to remove Meyer from the park board. The Taxpayer's League based its case on the undeniable fact that Meyer maintained a large estate a block from Nelson's Oak Hall in what was then the town of Westport. According to the petition filed in circuit court on 2 July, Meyer's legal residence was in Westport and not in Kansas City, as required by the city charter. The mayor answered that Meyer voted, paid taxes, and maintained a residence at a fashionable club in the city. Both Taxpayer's League campaigns failed.[48]

Simultaneous action went forward on the city council and the park board. At one point, Meyer threatened to resign, but he wisely reconsidered. However, in September 1898, Charles Campbell, the paint and glass merchant who had served the park board for almost four years, resigned. Campbell resigned because of the failure, at the time, to reduce the West Park District assessments. The upshot was that the council approved the original North Terrace and Penn Valley condemnations. The latter decision was at least partly the result of intensive lobbying from residents in and around the Penn Street ravine. In April 1899 it reduced the area of West Terrace Park, dropping the assessment against the West Park District from about 17 to 11.5 percent of assessed valuation.[49]

Court decisions made up the legal backdrop of the local struggle. The Taxpayer's League and its allies fought with ingenuity on the legal front, but they lost every battle. In 1898 the state supreme court upheld the city's right of eminent domain in a case involving boulevard extension. The court upheld the 1895 charter, as it would do time and again. "A constitutional provision authorizing a city . . . to form its own charter," it declared on this occasion, "implies the power to adopt a complete and harmonious system of local government," including the power to condemn. In June 1899 the court issued a decision in the North Terrace Park case. To a general challenge of the city charter it replied that the document's constitutionality was firmly settled, and it once more upheld the idea of the benefit district against the allegation that it operated unfairly in practice. In March 1900 came a triumph in federal court. This decision affecting the North Terrace Park resulted from a federal suit by Frederick G. Bonfils, the eccentric co-owner of the *Denver Post* and one of Nelson's bitterest enemies. Bonfils bought property in the North Park District apparently for the purpose of contesting his old enemy's pet projects, a situation that did not help his case in court. The state supreme court decision that virtually doomed the antipark forces came in June. Appellant briefs once more challenged the condemnation and benefit process, but the court rejected their arguments. Three years later the court ruled in the city's favor in a West Terrace Park case. A 1908 decision upheld the park and boulevard maintenance tax.[50]

TRIUMPH OF THE KESSLER PLAN

Effective opposition to the park and boulevard plan was over by 1900. The assault failed not because the attackers lacked determination and resourcefulness, but partly because they were fighting opponents with more experience than they in the techniques of mass persuasion, in the council chambers, and in the courts. Essentially their program was a negative one, and it proposed little to replace the plan. Its allegations of oppressive taxation were spurious,

Top, looking northeast across the sunken garden in the Paseo, an elaborate dual boulevard and a showpiece of Kessler's original design, about 1900. *Bottom*, looking south along the sunken garden in the Paseo from the Terrace, a structure including stairs, an outlook, and a retaining wall designed to compensate for a change in grade, about 1900. (Courtesy, Missouri Valley Collection, Kansas City Public Library.)

although there may have been isolated, individual examples of financial distress. A final reason for the failure of the antipark movement was the growing visual impact of the Kessler plan.

The Paseo was the jewel of the developing system. As originally constructed, the Paseo ran north to south, dropping down a generally easy grade from Ninth to Eighteenth Street in the north-central section. The intersecting streets formed rectangles, each one of which Kessler fashioned into a distinctive park. At Ninth Street a small stone fountain bubbled; the Pergola, a double colonnade with a trellis roof, stood between Tenth and Eleventh; at Twelfth Kessler designed a high stone terrace to ornament and compensate for a steep grade; across Twelfth, a Spanish cannon captured during the Spanish-American War overlooked a formal sunken garden; at Fifteenth stood the wonder of the Paseo, an enormous stone fountain that Kessler designed after a fountain at Versailles. A small fountain at Eighteenth completed the original Paseo. Though each park was individual, all were harmonious and subordinated to the whole. In a day of slow travel, the Paseo presented a delightful pattern of colorful, shifting scenes to the pedestrian or carriage passenger.[51]

The planning story through 1900 was not all progress. Kansas City's chronic financial problems hampered the park board. Vandalism was a continuing problem. On 10 May 1897 Kessler asked for police protection of the parks, pointing to damage done in areas of North Terrace Park not yet city-owned. "At Holmes square we have the same experience," he complained, "shrubbery is being actually carried away." The popular band concerts along the Paseo had to be discontinued because there were not enough police to control the rowdies, who capped one evening of unrestrained fun by throwing a hapless girl into the big fountain at Fifteenth Street.[52]

Despite these problems, the park and boulevard system had moved from rhetoric to reality. The struggles of the eighties, the legal reversal of 1895, the charter triumph of the same year, the battle against the "mossbacks," all were past. A loosely organized and sometimes warring elite group had overcome their legal and political obstacles and laid the foundation of the City Beautiful movement. About the time the phrase *City Beautiful* came into common use, these friends of urban planning could boast of a park and boulevard system whose slowly ripening beauty foretold the mellow symmetry of the twentieth century.

6 ◆ An Elite Campaign for Beauty and Utility in Harrisburg

BACKGROUND

Harrisburg is an old city by American standards, with white occupation dating back to the 1720s. It is located at a bend of the Susquehanna River, some 100 miles west of Philadelphia. Thousands of westward emigrants knew the site as Harris' Ferry. A town laid out in 1785 was incorporated in 1791, and Harrisburg became Pennsylvania's capital twenty-one years after. Late in the 1820s its career as a transportation center began with the opening of a segment of the Pennsylvania Canal.[1]

Population grew slowly at first, from 1,472 in 1800 to only 7,834 fifty years later. In the 1850s Harrisburg experienced a population takeoff of sorts, and its count reached 13,405 in 1860. By 1890 its population was almost 40,000. When the City Beautiful campaign began in 1900, the population had reached 50,167, making it the seventy-seventh largest city in the country. The inhabitants increased to 64,186 in 1910 and to 75,917 in 1920, after which rapid growth ceased.[2]

The older section of the city lay some five miles north to south, between the Susquehanna's eastern shore and the western bank of Paxton Creek, a flood-prone tributary. A gentle westward river bend defined the city's distinctive stretched-ovoid shape. Although it was the state capital, much of Harrisburg wore the look of a railroad town or an industrial village. Many streets were poorly paved or unpaved, even at intersections. The riverfront, saved from railroad tracks by its abrupt banks, was defiled instead by sewage spewing at its base and by trash dumps cascading down its bluffs. The bluffs forced the Pennsylvania Canal, the Pennsylvania and the Reading tracks and yards, and industry into the Paxton Creek basin, where the threat of flooding menaced them. Sewage from the eastern slope of the older oval area and from the western slope of a newer, eastward residential section poured into the Pennsylvania Canal and Paxton Creek. The city pumped its unfiltered and untreated water from a Susquehanna laden with sewage from upstream cities and

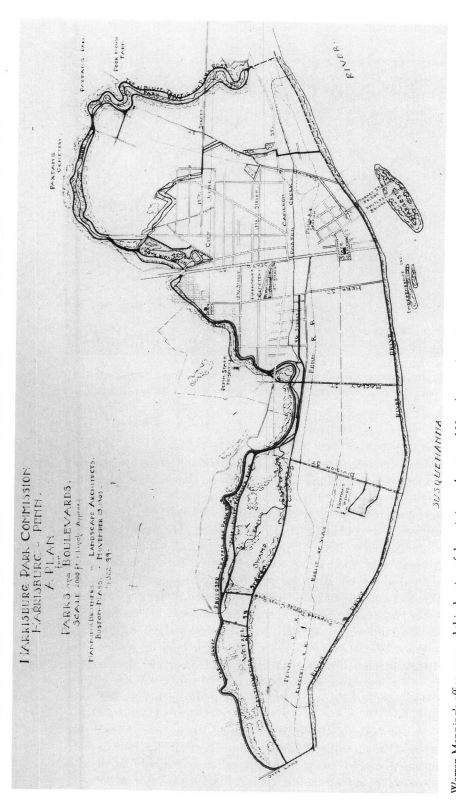

Warren Manning's office prepared this drawing of the existing and projected Harrisburg park and boulevard system in 1903. It is similar to one displayed during the bond improvements campaign of 1901–2. The long axis of the map runs north to south, with east at the top of the map and west at the bottom. Manning planned a practically circumferential boulevard. His "River Drive" along the Susquehanna's eastern shore became the Front Street improvement. Much of the eastern boulevard was constructed but it has since fallen into disrepair and virtual abandonment. Prominent among the major parks is the future Island Park, here labeled "Hargest's Is" in the Susquehanna River. Capitol Park is east and north of the island, while Reservoir Park is due east of Capitol Park. The Twelfth Street Playground is north of State Street about midway between Capitol Park and Reservoir Park. Paxtang Park is in the southeast corner, along the eastern boulevard. Wildwood Park, later a sizable landscape park with a large lake, is shown as "Wetzel Swamp," in the northeastern sector of the map. Noisome Paxton Creek flows southward through Wetzel's Swamp and Harrisburg's industrial valley to the Susquehanna. (Courtesy, Warren H. Manning Collection, Department of Landscape Architecture, College of Design, Iowa State University, Ames, Iowa.)

Harrisburg's Paxtang Park at the turn of the twentieth century, a busy clutter of buildings clashing with the landscape idealism of Frederick Law Olmsted and the City Beautiful. (*Harrisburg, Pa.* Courtesy, Dauphin County Historical Society, Harrisburg.)

towns and with culm washed down from anthracite mines. Low water in the river brought murky, foul-smelling liquid to spigots in Harrisburg's homes and businesses.[3]

There were some unexploited scenic advantages. The few patches of parkland on the river bluffs could be extended and unified. The newer, eastward business and residential section, Allison's Hill, was the site of the only well-developed recreation ground, twenty-six acre Reservoir Park. The park could be expanded and improved, but it lay well beyond the 2,000-foot swath of canal, tracks, and creek separating the more crowded, older city from Allison's Hill. Four-acre Capitol Park was crowded with picnickers and strollers on warm weekend afternoons. Citizens with the time and means to escape chose picturesque Wetzel's Swamp just north of the built-up section, the hamlet of Rockville and its environs farther north, or some other place outside the city. Harrisburg's greatest advantage was its relatively small size, for projects of modest scope could raise its level of sanitation, aesthetics, and commercial utility.

The improvement campaign in Harrisburg began late in 1900 and probably was the first to use the inspiring, vivifying phrase *City Beautiful.* It was a more unified campaign than Kansas City's, even though the Harrisburg elite had no more ultimate success in maintaining cohesion and enthusiasm. It was also more ambitious, bringing utilitarian projects such as a huge intercepting sewer under the wing of the City Beautiful.

The Harrisburg struggle illuminates once more the central role of politics. City Beautiful advocates could publicize and educate concerning urban environmental change, but the implementation of reform once again depended upon a group of related successes in administration and popular legislation. Had the City Beautiful movement not been political, there would have been little environmental reform in Harrisburg. Women's role was especially important. A woman began the public movement, and women helped to sustain it in significant individual and organizational ways. The battle catapulted J. Horace McFarland into nationwide prominence. He became the leading lay spokesman for the City Beautiful, publicizing the Harrisburg experience at about the same time that the famous Washington plan came into public prominence.

Mira Lloyd Dock and the Beginning of the City Beautiful Campaign

The improvement campaign opened with an informed, insightful speech from a woman as remarkable as the plan she later espoused. Mira Lloyd Dock was born in 1853 into an old, financially comfortable Pennsylvania family. She epitomized the energetic "new woman," who was abandoning parlor studies for practical civics. A heavy-featured, stocky spinster, she compensated for her lack of physical beauty by an abundance of wit and charm. She became involved in a wide range of activities from feminism to photography and related almost all of them to her chief concern, botany. Hers was no armchair interest. A bluestocking, she studied at the University of Michigan, wrote, and lectured, developing a large acquaintance among landscape architects, foresters, and conservationists. Her concern for conservation did not stop at the city limits. In common with other forest conservationists, Dock believed in saving rural environments and in introducing them, properly tended and idealized, into the urban milieu.[4]

Dock believed that Harrisburg should enjoy the rural delights of parks, landscaped views, and pure water. With verve and skill she exploited the two means of gaining a beautiful city that were available to the leisured, middle-class women of her day, organization and publicity. Teas, polite conversation, and literary exegesis were not, for her, the proper ends of a women's club. By 1896 she was seeking advice on how to found a civic organization that could do something about cleaning up Harrisburg's dirty streets. Two years later she became one of the founders of the Civic Club of Harrisburg, serving as chairperson of its Department of Forestry and Town Improvement. Soon she was importuning councilmen and other public-spirited males to rid Pennsylvania's capital city of its village atmosphere.[5]

Dock's opportunity for publicity came when a correspondent, Miss F. R.

Wilkinson, the landscape gardener of the London Public Gardens Association, invited her to attend the horticultural section of the International Congress of Women at London in June 1899. Then the Federation of Pennsylvania Women and the Parks Association of Philadelphia named her to be their representative to the congress. Later the Pennsylvania Department of Agriculture agreed to expand her visit into a study of forestry and urban arboriculture in England and the Continent. The results of her travel and investigation appeared in 1900 in her *A Summer's Work Abroad*, Bulletin no. 62 of the state Department of Agriculture.[6]

European travel broadened Dock's knowledge of forestry and heightened her concern for civic beautification. A first-rate amateur photographer, she returned with dozens of negative plates of urban parks, squares, and riverine improvements. Even before completing her booklet, she had been discussing the possibility of major improvements in Harrisburg with two friends. One was McFarland, the aggressive businessman, preservationist, and fellow Harrisburger. The other was Warren H. Manning, a Boston landscape architect and Olmsted trainee. After writing *A Summer's Work Abroad* Dock prepared a lantern-slide talk, comparing the manicured parks and riverbanks of European cities and the natural beauties of the Harrisburg area with Harrisburg's trash-strewn bluffs, foul sewers, and generally unkempt appearance. Slides of improvements in other American cities heaped more humiliation on the smug little city alongside the Susquehanna.[7]

By December 1900, Dock was ready for a major appearance. On the twentieth of that month she spoke on "The City Beautiful" to a "large audience" composed of members of the city's elite Board of Trade and their guests. Her graphic descriptions, her more than one hundred striking slides, and her "graces that give so much charm to the successful public speaker" compelled her audience's attention. The talk, stripped of her vibrant animation, consisted of well-worn, but well-presented, arguments for the City Beautiful. Harrisburg, Dock averred, was blessed with a beautiful setting but it had abused some of its natural beauty spots and had failed to preserve others. Some cities with fewer natural advantages had achieved more beauty. Her "vivid description of the roughness, slime and filth we create for ourselves, caused applause and then the hush of full comprehension."[8]

She appealed to civic pride and to interurban competitive spirit but also played on the theme of organic social unity. She reminded her audience that classes were interdependent and that working-class people and their children needed beauty spots and recreation areas as much or more than anyone else. The city should build playgrounds, parks, and public baths (swimming pools with tubs, showers, soap, and towels available in the dressing rooms) for those citizens who lacked the means to provide for themselves. Dock insisted that parks, recreation, clean streets, and clean inhabitants were compatible with a city's business success, denouncing the idea that such improvements had "no place in a busy manufacturing town." She made deft comparisons between

Sewer outfalls along the Susquehanna and unsupervised swimming in the polluted river threatened the health and safety of these young swimmers in 1900. (Dock Family Papers, Manuscript Group 43, Pennsylvania State Archives. Courtesy, Pennsylvania Historical and Museum Commission, Harrisburg.)

local "hideous conditions" and attractive scenes in Milwaukee, Boston, Hartford, Dayton, and European cities. Through her slides of progressive communities "the cash value of cleanliness and beauty in busy places was strongly shown." She praised voluntary ameliorative work but urged more citizens to take an interest in Harrisburg's development.[9]

The success of Dock's address suggested that some members of the elite had already begun to worry about the city's situation and prospects. She could not have delivered her lecture at the Board of Trade and received a resolution of "heartily tendered" thanks without some budding sense of inadequacy already present in the minds of her audience. After Dock's galvanic speech, the Board of Trade, other groups, and individuals proposed a variety of improvement projects. It was not until late April 1901 that the *Harrisburg Telegraph* announced the possibility of a comprehensive attack on the city's problems. The text of the *Telegraph*'s front-page article, together with subsequent activities, indicated that the sponsors of the *Telegraph* idea had already decided upon the elements of a city plan and a scheme for their implementation. The *Telegraph* article reinforced Dock's themes of beautification, recreation, and citizen activism. It asked for parks, pure water, paved streets, a city hall, and increased taxes to pay for them. It called for combining beauty and utility in a covered interceptor sewer along the river, to carry sewage away from banks converted to parkland. The essentials of the *Telegraph* suggestion, and more, were in place fifteen years later. An analysis of this success requires answers to three questions: Who sponsored the plan? Why did they identify the problems that they did? How did they maneuver the passage of the necessary bond issue?[10]

HARRISBURG'S CITY PLAN

The sponsors were members of the city's business elite. Twenty-one people were actively involved in the bond issue campaign or served on the first citizen boards established to spend and oversee the bond funds. Of the seventeen whose occupations could be identified, ten were industrialists, two were attorneys, two were bankers, one was a publisher (of the *Telegraph*), one was a writer-lecturer (Dock), and one was a businessman-inventor. All but Dock were male. Of fourteen whose lineage could be traced, the paternal families of eight had been in the United States two generations or more prior to their birth; of four, two generations; and of two, one generation. It is almost certain that none was an immigrant and that they represented no racial or ethnic groups besides Anglo-German. Among the thirteen sponsors who recorded their highest educational level, two attended common schools, one attended college, five graduated from a college or university, and five received a secondary or advanced specialized education. This was an extraordinary group record for mature persons in 1901, a year when only 6.3 percent of seventeen-year-olds graduated from high school. Of eleven sponsors, eight were Republicans and three were Democrats. Religious affiliations among eleven leaders were predominantly middle or upper class: there were five Presbyterians, one Episcopalian, three Methodists, one Roman Catholic, and one Lutheran. The ages of twelve of the leaders as of 1 January 1901 are known and have a mean of 41.8 years and a median of 39.5 years.[11]

The elite organized a City Beautiful campaign because of Harrisburg's palpable defects. Poor paving and planning impeded journeys to work, hindered communications, slowed the growth of newer areas, and fragmented the city into self-concerned neighborhoods. The successful bond issue campaign and the election of the young, wealthy, reforming industrialist Vance C. McCormick to the mayor's office were more than coincidental. McCormick promised and delivered an effective, efficient, honest city administration and oversight of public improvements, the necessary framework for the social, economic, and physical rationalization of the city. The elite were determined to accomplish through public authority and funds what they could not achieve by private means. In a smaller city the transformation appeared to be, briefly, within their grasp. The elite's self-interest was not, however, either narrow or negative. There was concern for the quality of urban life and for the uplift of the citizen in the demands for pure water, parks, and improved streets. However, their dependence on popular support, not to mention the limited means deployed in the battle for environmental ends, frustrated their social goals.[12]

The answer to the question, who were the City Beautiful advocates? largely determined what sort of improvements they would sponsor. Harrisburg's leaders firmly believed in the rights of private property. They were unlikely to approve any plan involving its taking or limiting except as needed for the improvements themselves. McFarland, despite his relatively advanced social impulses, pressed the hoariest of defenses for municipal improvements—the rise in surrounding property values. The elite's sense of civic responsibility and grasp of political realities prevented it from advocating any development that benefited only one group, class, or area of the city. Extensive street paving, a park and boulevard system, and a safe water supply were tested means of downing any charges of urban sectionalism or class favoritism.[13]

The City Beautiful leaders' carefully planned, thoroughly controlled campaign was of a piece with their backgrounds and attitudes. Possibly because of Harrisburg's smaller size and increased sophistication of technique, the campaign appeared less spontaneous than Kansas City's. The 27 April 1901 *Telegraph* article came first. On 3 May John V. W. Reynders, the superintendent of the Pennsylvania Steel Company, published a letter in the *Telegraph* recommending that a private fund be established to retain "specialists" who would study Harrisburg's municipal needs and make a report. Reynders made suggestions for the selection of experts and the topics to be studied and offered $100 to begin the fund. McFarland's letter of support and offer of $50 appeared the next day in the *Telegraph*, followed by a drumfire of *Telegraph* articles and editorials and the pledging of $5,000 within ten days. McFarland described how the leadership dealt with recalcitrants among the elite. "The money came 'voluntarily,'" he wrote, "but I never did notice the voluntary part of it, because Mr. Reynders and several other men with nothing to do but run big industries simply came into your office and looked pleasant until you cashed up, or signed up!"[14]

Having raised the private fund, the elite were determined to control its disbursement. It carefully arranged, however, for the appearance of increased citizen involvement. On 17 May the fund contributors established a permanent organization and appointed a seven-man committee to choose the experts, a committee including the future mayor McCormick, Reynders, and McFarland. An overture to the city government that the mayor, the city engineer, and representatives of each house of the council join the committee was accepted. The arrangement identified important city officials with planning but without compromising elite control. The committee chose James H. Fuertes, a consulting engineer from New York City, to study water supply, sewage, and drainage problems; and M. R. Sherred of Newark, New Jersey, to report on paving. Manning was selected to recommend park and boulevard treatments. Manning wanted the job and acknowledged efforts of his friends McFarland and Dock to land it for him.[15]

By late November the reports were complete. Fuertes urged a low dam in the nonnavigable Susquehanna to raise the river above the sewer outfalls and to provide a wide expanse of water by the city for swimming and boating. He called for a water filtration plant with a capacity of ten million gallons per day and a new reservoir to solve the health problems posed by the culm, clay, and sewage in the Susquehanna. He proposed a flood control system for Paxton Creek and an intercepting sewer to divert wastes from the creek. The creek, Fuertes found, carried five to twenty times the sewage it could safely accept. Manning recommended a parked river front, expansion of Reservoir Park, the creation of a large landscape park in Wetzel's Swamp north of the city, playgrounds, and a ring boulevard connecting the large parks. Sherred presented a paving plan giving careful attention to the proper surfaces for all conditions of traffic and grade.[16]

PASSAGE OF THE BOND ISSUE

After receiving the reports, the contributors further broadened their base of support. They secured the councils' approval for a $1,090,000 bond issue vote to be held concurrently with the municipal election in February 1902. They created the Harrisburg League for Municipal Improvements (HLMI), which opened downtown offices in January, to promote the bond issue. Anyone could join the HLMI for $1.00. An executive committee and other committees organized and conducted the HLMI campaign. Finally, the HLMI in January began a second $5,000 fund drive to raise money for publicity expenses. Large contributions formed the backbone of the second fund but the HLMI also solicited and received small amounts.[17]

The elite systematically propagandized the improvements and promoted them in one City Beautiful package. Sympathetic newspapers used the HLMI releases while they followed the organization's carefully orchestrated neighborhood meetings and mass rallies. Movement luminaries as well as public officials spoke on those occasions. They answered audience questions, not all of them friendly. From Dock's December 1900 speech onward, the *Telegraph* and Harrisburg's two other dailies played on fears that comparable Pennsylvania cities would outstrip Harrisburg in wealth and population; printed statements and letters about the importance of the improvements from prominent local people; ran articles on beautification and improvement projects undertaken elsewhere; and attacked urban sectionalism and its cry that the park projects were merely a "Front Street scheme" to benefit the fine residential area along a section of the riverfront. They countered threats of higher taxes and rent with assurances that rents were rising because of a housing shortage; insisted that the improvements' impact on local taxes would be modest; and used the experts' reports to counter attacks on the parks, proposed water filtration methods, and the low dam on the Susquehanna.[18]

HLMI members investigated how drinking water from the sewage-laden Susquehanna was affecting the incidence of typhoid and were dismayed to learn of no dramatic increase in the disease. They did discover lax reporting among local physicians. The doctors were encouraged to bring their reports up to date in January. The result was a manufactured typhoid "epidemic" of thirty cases in one month, double the number of the previous quarter. After the successful bond issue campaign in February, the reported cases dropped to nine, and in March they fell to four.[19]

The HLMI's downtown office displayed and dispensed material. The league published and sent summaries of the experts' reports to "each house." From early January to the election, it hired high school boys to distribute additional propaganda to every home. It isolated the ineffectual opposition to the improvements, stigmatizing the opponents as "clams," tightfisted landlords who refused to consider reasonable increases in their property taxes. It persuaded the councils to create a Board of Public Works in advance of the vote. After the councils appointed three elite businessmen to the board, the league claimed that the bonds should be approved because the board's portion of the funds would be in competent hands.[20]

Women aided the league. Dock was as active during the improvements fight as she had been in starting it, though her role and the role of the Civic Club were different from those of the men's organizations. The distinction can be laid in part to late Victorian ideas about the separate spheres of women and men, for participation in formal decision-making and leadership in major public meetings were closed to females. Dock contributed to the experts' fund but neither she nor any other woman served on the selection committee. Nor did women address the capstone rally at the courthouse. Although they were not allowed key roles, the women were welcomed by the male civic leaders, who depended upon their experience and expertise and expected them to carry a significant part of the propaganda fight. The Civic Club, composed of middle- and upper-class women, already had contributed to local beauty and cleanliness by setting up trash receptacles and by hiring a man to keep a city block clean after the manner of New York's "white wings." The action prompted the city to improve its street cleaning. During the bond issue campaign the club and the Board of Trade sponsored a stereoptican lecture by Manning in October 1901.[21]

Later, during the final, intensive propaganda phase of the campaign, the Civic Club pressed the councils to inaugurate a municipal garbage collection service and passed a resolution calling "the attention of Councils to the unsightly and unsanitary condition of the river bank, caused by the violation of the ordinance against dumping." Meanwhile its members were collecting a $175 donation to finance the publicity campaign. Dock lectured on the improvements at the club's annual meeting. On 20 January 1902 she spoke at a neighborhood meeting in the Bethany Presbyterian Church. On the last night of the month she braved bitter cold to deliver a "rather sparsely attended" stereoptican lecture at the high school. Early in February, when overnight temperatures were falling below ten degrees, she spoke again at the All Saints'

Mission. Her message emphasized both the potential beauty of Harrisburg and the functional relationship of beauty to cleanliness, health, and civic prosperity. In content, her speeches were similar to those of the male orators, but she emphasized beauty and the interdependence of beauty and utility more than most of them did.[22]

Men praised the work of the women campaigners both before and after the bond issue vote. "The Civic Club of this city has demonstrated the power of organization among the good women of any community," the Telegraph editorialized in January 1902. "I don't know whether any of us could have accomplished anything had not the Civic Club paved the way," McFarland wrote to Dock in late February. "Back of the Civic Club is your own effort and enthusiasm, and I think, when this thing is hunted down to sources, you and [a male organizer] will have to stand as the sponsors of the whole movement." Although his remarks were tinged with an unconscious condescension, another of Dock's admirers introduced one of her talks by saying that the Civic Club had done "more almost than the men" to launch the movement for a beautiful Harrisburg.[23]

Proponents of the improvements capitalized on other circumstances. In 1901 the Pennsylvania Canal company abandoned the last section of the "main line." Odors from the sewage-clogged segment near Paxton Creek underscored the need for a collector sewer. A determined but unsuccessful effort to move the capital to Philadelphia pointed up the desirability of an attractive capital city with contemporary amenities. Two brief floods in Paxton Creek during December 1901 and January 1902 demonstrated the worth of the flood control proposals.[24]

On 18 February the voters went to the polls. They voted for the bonds by almost a two-to-one majority: 7,319 to 3,729. The bonds carried all but six of thirty-six precincts and each of the ten wards but the Tenth, a sparsely settled ward undivided into precincts, where the measure failed by four votes. In table 1 the mean house values and the number of high-value houses by ward—a rough index of the economic status of ward residents—are compared with the vote in each ward. The table refutes the easy assumption that high economic status and a favorable vote (or low economic status and a less favorable vote) were closely related. True, the voters of the First Ward, with the lowest mean house value, rejected the bond issue in one of three precincts and voted favorably by less than 54 percent. The Fourth Ward, where mean house value and the percentage of high-value houses were the highest, voted over 82 percent favorably. Two wards returned votes below the citywide favorable majority of 66.2 percent, as their position below the citywide mean house value of $1,827.64 might suggest. However, five wards of the nine in which house values could be determined do not follow that pattern. The Second, Eighth, and Ninth wards were below the mean house value, yet they returned favorable majorities of 76.9, 83.4, and 78.8 percent. The Fifth Ward, with a house value above the mean, delivered a favorable vote lower than the

TABLE 1. Comparison of Economic Status of Ward Residents and Their Vote on Improvements

Ward	Number of Houses	% of Vote	Mean House Value ($)	High-Value Houses (Valuation $5000+)		Vote		Favorable Vote (%)
				Number	% of Citywide Total	For	Against	
1	747	7.8	930.50	5	1.0	615	527	53.9
2	845	8.8	1,754.36	28	5.7	714	214	76.9
3	—	—	—	—	—	513	92	84.8
4	858	8.9	3,722.74	186	37.8	761	161	82.5
5	959	10.0	2,240.56	78	15.9	571	338	62.8
6	2,570	26.7	1,653.20	74	15.0	1,102	1,094	50.2
7	1,327	13.8	1,339.43	16	3.3	721	624	53.6
8	846	8.8	1,363.16	8	1.6	940	187	83.4
9	1,165	12.1	1,717.82	42	8.5	1,196	321	78.8
10	294	3.1	3,270.51	55	11.2	216	220	49.5

Sources: Table 1 is constructed partly from the 1900 Dauphin County Triennial Assessment, the last complete assessment before the improvements, or their anticipation, might have affected property values. Vote totals by ward are the sums of the precinct vote as recorded in the Harrisburg *Telegraph,* 21 Feb. 1902. The precinct ward totals add to 35 more "for" votes and to 50 more "against" votes than the totals recorded in the *Telegraph.* The official tallies are no longer available.

Note: Number of houses = 9,611; Harrisburg mean house value = $1,827.64; high-value houses = 492; total "for" vote by precinct = 7,319, total "against" vote by precinct = 3,729; citywide percentage favorable vote = 66.2. Mean house values could not be determined for the Third Ward because it was the principal retail-commercial ward and the assessor usually did not distinguish between houses and businesses. The few surviving houses approximate those in the Fourth Ward, as the vote suggests that most Third Ward houses did in 1902. Mean house values tend to obscure the enormous range of values within each ward, as reflected in large standard deviations. For example, the standard deviation for the First Ward is 1,040.

The Early City Beautiful

TABLE 2. Bond Results Compared with Electoral Partisanship

	Vote for Mayor, Treasurer, Comptroller[a]		Greater Percentage Vote, Common Council[b]		Total		Mean Vote	
Ward	Repub.	Demo.	Repub.	Demo.	Repub.	Demo.	Above	Below
1	3	6	2	0	5	6		X
2	5	4	1	1	6	5	X	
3	5	4	2	0	7	4	X	
4	6	3	1	1	7	4	X	
5	4	5	0	2	4	7		X
6	3	6	1	1	4	7		X
7	0	9	1	1	1	10		X
8	6	3	1	1	7	4	X	
9	6	3	2	0	8	3	X	
10	5	4	0	2	5	6		X

Note: The mayor, treasurer, and comptroller were the leading officers of administration and oversight. They were elected concurrently every three years. Representatives to the common council were chosen each year, with half the wards selecting two councilmen every year. Thus each ward chose its common councilmen every other year. The two parties typically placed two names in nomination in each ward. The greater percentage of the vote for the pairs of nominees is listed under Democratic or Republican, irrespective of the party affiliation of the individual winners.

[a] 1899, 1902, 1905.
[b] 1900, 1901, 1903, 1904.

citywide percentage. The sparsely populated Tenth Ward, with only 3.1 percent of the houses but containing 11.2 percent of the high-value residences, defeated the bonds.[25]

The bond issue vote paralleled partisanship to a remarkable degree. In table 2 the bond results are compared with the election of certain Republican and Democratic candidates and with the percentage of votes by party for the common council during the three years preceding and following the bond election. The wards ranking above the citywide mean shared a partisan characteristic. All of them gave the majority of their votes to Republicans, when the votes for the candidates for mayor, treasurer, comptroller, and common council are taken together. Extreme partisanship was not typical of any ward except the Seventh, which was heavily Democratic. Wards preponderantly Republican, for instance, gave comfortable majorities to some Democratic candidates. The generally mild partisanship of the Harrisburg electorate precludes absolute statements about the relationship between Republicanism and a strongly favorable vote on the bond issue. Possibly there is an ethnocultural or historical connection. Perhaps the vote reflects some partisanship. The campaign leadership, predominantly Republican, may not have been entirely successful in giving the bond issue a nonpartisan cast. Perhaps the voters who favored the bond issue for its progressivism also imagined Republicans to be more aggressive, enlightened public servants than their Democratic opponents.[26]

Additional reasons might be adduced to explain the vote, such as the presence of Paxton Creek in the Eighth and Ninth wards or the large lots artificially inflating house values in the Tenth Ward. The facts remain that there was no consistent relationship between economic status and the vote, that the total vote was decisive, and that the measure carried every ward but one. Dock, McFarland, McCormick, and their cohorts argued for improvements to the community's public health, transportation, recreation, and aesthetics. Individual benefits would accrue, they insisted, without respect to economic status. Almost two of every three voters believed them.

IMPLEMENTATION OF THE IMPROVEMENTS

During the next decade and a half the bond funds brought extensive improvements to Harrisburg. Park acreage grew from 46 in 1902 to 958 in 1915. A 140-acre lake in Wildwood Park, the old Wetzel's Swamp, served recreational needs while it impounded floodwaters above the urbanized banks of Paxton Creek. Concrete steps topped by a broad walkway defined the base of River Front Park for almost three miles along the Susquehanna. They provided a seating and strolling area while protecting the bank from the river's fluctuations. Despite a rise in the city's population from about 51,000 to about 73,000, park area had grown from one acre for every 1,260 people to one for every 76. A Capitol Park expansion program under state auspices, in which McFarland was unofficially but deeply involved, promised to increase the city's scenic area. Recreational opportunities had developed from band concerts and children's play equipment in Reservoir Park to eleven public playgrounds, including one large playground park. Island Park in the midst of the Susquehanna boasted swimming facilities, athletic fields, and a grandstand. Athletic fields were included in other play areas, while a nine-hole golf course was developed on the eastward extension of Reservoir Park. Park visits rose to an estimated 1,599,000 in 1912. Landscape architect Manning consulted with the park commission during the implementation of his 1901 plan.[27]

Nor had the utilitarian side of the City Beautiful been neglected. Four and one-half miles of streets were paved in 1902, and more than seventy-four miles by 1915. Filtered water, intercepting sewers, and flood control had raised municipal sanitation to levels merely imagined in 1902. The citizen water, park, and public works boards had overseen all construction, cooperating when necessary. McFarland insisted that "the national importance of this lies in the completeness and co-ordination of the effort." Other cities had made significant improvements, but "no other city in all this broad land has done all these things concurrently, harmoniously, and entirely upon the plans of ex-

Top, Front Street and its narrow parking aside, the Susquehanna river bluff at Harrisburg presented a ragged, unkempt appearance in 1900. It drew visitors despite its shortcomings. (Dock Family Papers, Manuscript Group 43, Pennsylvania State Archives. Courtesy, Pennsylvania Historical and Museum Commission, Harrisburg.) *Bottom*, Front Street after the bluffs beautification project was completed, about 1913. (*Art Work of Harrisburg Pennsylvania: Published in Nine Parts* [Harrisburg: Gravure Illustration Co., 1914]. Courtesy, Dauphin County Historical Society, Harrisburg.)

A 1928 perspective of Harrisburg's projected Capitol Park reveals how the park tied into such city improvements as the Memorial Bridge across the Paxton Creek valley, State Street and its obelisk, the Front Street and bluffs development, and the widened and stabilized Susquehanna River. Unfortunately, the demands of the private automobile required the sacrifice of the projected grand staircase, balustrade, and plaza at the rear of the capitol to an unlovely asphalt parking lot. (Records of the Department of Property and Supplies, Record Group 20, Pennsylvania State Archives. Courtesy, Pennsylvania Historical and Museum Commission, Harrisburg.)

perts so that a baker's dozen of years shows a made-over town with a degree of efficiency . . . much more characteristic of the average German city."[28]

The Maturing City Beautiful Movement

From 1906 through 1914 Harrisburg's citizens approved three additional bond issues for projects totaling $1,341,000. Most of the projects of the last bond issue were related to the first City Beautiful construction. McFarland credited the bond issue successes to the good record of the citizen boards, which generally remained in the hands of the elite. Despite the elite's continuing involvement, its members soon became immersed in routine. Their unity and City Beautiful fervor faded rapidly, although McFarland retained his first enthusiasm for the City Beautiful. His hyperactivity helped to realize Har-

A monument in Reservoir Park, Harrisburg, in the early twentieth century. (*Art Work of Harrisburg Pennsylvania*. Courtesy, Dauphin County Historical Society, Harrisburg.)

risburg's beautification, but it brought him into conflict with others, including his former allies in civic improvement.[29]

McFarland was not named to the first park commission of 1902, but he was appointed to fill a vacancy in 1905. He remained on the park commission until Harrisburg's mayor-council government and boards were superseded by the commission form in 1913. Soon after his first appointment he was actively involved in every phase of the park commission's work. McFarland credited his interventionism partly to the ignorance of some fellow commission members, who did not "know a pine from a pumpkin." "These people," he wrote to Dock, "give me almost a free hand, and the way in which I am meddling . . . would make your hair stand on end if it was as short as mine!" Much of McFarland's "meddling" was constructive. He urged landholders along the proposed circumferential parkway to donate right-of-way to the city and probably tried to wheedle land for Wildwood Park as well. He lobbied with councilmen for a park extension. On at least one occasion, in 1905, he delivered an illustrated address on municipal improvement and argued the necessity for continued citizen involvement. In 1906 and 1907 he labored to put through a bill providing for the municipal control of shade trees on the streets of every first-class city accepting the responsibility. The governor approved the bill in May of 1907. When, in 1912, sewer-laying crews began cutting down trees

The utilitarian side of the City Beautiful was well expressed in Harrisburg's water filtration plant. Plantings, tidy lawns, and trim sidewalks surround the structure. By the late 1970s the plant was abandoned and became the victim of vandalism and overgrowth. (*Art Work of Harrisburg Pennsylvania.* Courtesy, Dauphin County Historical Society, Harrisburg.)

along the riverfront, McFarland rushed to the rescue of the remaining timber.[30]

He inveighed against billboards and signs. Political signs adorning telegraph poles, he told the mayor, were "very much against the idea of the city beautiful." "I have personally torn down a great many posters," he proudly informed a friend. By 1910 he and others had persuaded the Harrisburg councils to pass a billboard ordinance restricting the size of the boards and requiring adequate bracing and inspection. He continued to serve as secretary of the renamed Harrisburg Municipal League, helping to mobilize it in favor of subsequent improvement bond issues. In 1908, a typical year, he or his company donated prizes for the park commission's water carnival on the Susquehanna, contributed to the Reservoir Park concert fund, and loaned a slide projector, screen, and some of the slides shown during concert intermissions. One of his great delights was showing visitors over the expanding park and

Top, prone to flooding, choked with sewage, and lined with rubbish, Paxton Creek made its noisome way through a Harrisburg industrial district, about 1900. *Bottom*, by about 1910 Paxton Creek was tamed into a concrete bed. Sewer lines formerly ending at the creek were diverted to outfalls in the Susquehanna below Harrisburg. Such dramatic environmental improvements demonstrate how far the City Beautiful movement went beyond merely decorative effects. (Dock Family Papers, Manuscript Group 43, Pennsylvania State Archives. Courtesy, Pennsylvania Historical and Museum Commission, Harrisburg.)

boulevard system and receiving their favorable comments.[31]

McFarland's pride in the new Harrisburg was tempered by failures and disappointments. His "meddling" was not always viewed as joyously as he pursued it. It hurt him when other park commissioners did not wish to proceed as rapidly as he in land acquisition. He suffered when other members of the elite subordinated his love for urban beauty to their self-interest. When the president of the park commission, a prosperous shoe manufacturer, allowed billboards on some property he owned, McFarland offered to buy the advertising rights at the rental paid by the billboard company. McFarland would have placed no signs on the property. When he discovered that the park board president had renewed the lease at a higher price without first informing him, he was furious. Recalling that the offending manufacturer had promised not to renew the lease, McFarland wrote: "It is, however, just a little anomalous for you as President of the Park Commission, supposedly interested in making the city more beautiful, to be taking a comparatively small sum for making it more ugly." At about the same time McFarland "upset a scheme . . . to girdle Front Street by a trolley line and practically destroy our city entrance." Then he learned that the "scheme" was a project of a fellow member of the elite, who "himself gave me the most unpleasant, personal lambasting of the tongue I ever received."[32]

By 1910 McFarland was tired of his park work, but he stayed on until the commission-type council took office late in 1913. The commissioner for parks, M. Harvey Taylor, was an effective politician who persuaded the old park commission to remain in an advisory capacity. McFarland regarded Taylor as a well-meaning incompetent at best. When a disagreement led to the advisory commission's resignation, McFarland privately denounced Taylor, "exceedingly shallow, vacillating and uncertain," whose chief accomplishment was "to arise to the dignity of running a cigar store." McFarland was also distressed over Taylor's refusal to implement his pet project, the Pennsylvania shade tree law.[33]

The council delivered another blow to McFarland when it failed to name him to a city planning commission appointed in April 1914. By then he had been president of the American Civic Association for a decade, widely publicized the Harrisburg achievement, and enjoyed a national reputation in city planning circles. He could not resist "educating the amiable gentlemen" who composed the commission "as to what city planning really is." His efforts did not lead to an appointment, but he could not be ignored when, in 1915, the city celebrated its progress under the plan. The man who had contributed so much to the plan's success admitted that he was "between two fires." He was proud to be a center of attention, but his beforehand description of the affair revealed a weariness characteristic of his later discussions of Harrisburg events. "The whole celebration is based on a vaudeville idea," he wrote, "and I am tired of it in advance." McFarland's bustling activity, his desire to dominate, and his sometimes scornful approach to those he considered his inferiors partly explain his loss of popularity and place. His continuing commitment to urban beautification was also responsible, for it was not shared by most others in Harrisburg's elite.[34]

Dock's activities rapidly moved away from the urban aspects of the struggle for planning, preservation, and beautification. She was appointed a member of Pennsylvania's Forestry Reservation Commission and served in other organizations. She maintained a large and active correspondence with a remarkable range of people, including Gifford Pinchot and her "Dear Cousin," William Dean Howells. Meanwhile she began spending more time in the South Mountain region a few miles north of the Maryland line. In 1903 she left her family's spacious, late Victorian frame house, with its beautiful view of the Susquehanna and Blue Mountains beyond, and moved to an obscure hamlet.

For Manning, the landscape architect, his planning and consulting work developed "in ways and with results that make this project one [of] the most important in my career." Harrisburg was the first large independent project in a varied professional life that included several schemes for Billerica, Massachusetts, and the organization of "Community Days." The object of the Community Day, Manning explained, was to "bring people together for a specific undertaking that will . . . stimulate mutual helpfulness and good fellowship." The resulting "spirit" would be "of far greater benefit than the actual work accomplished." After conducting Community Days elsewhere, Manning returned in 1926 to supervise the improvement of a Harrisburg hospital grounds. In addition he ventured into publishing and the preparation of a national plan that included what, to him, was the rational redrafting of state boundaries.[35]

McFarland's isolation, Dock's move out of Harrisburg, and Manning's shift to suburban, piecemeal urban, and national planning typified the fragmentation of the City Beautiful movement. Harrisburg's civic spirit did not languish, however. The Park Department developed an elaborate recreational program capped by a "Romper Day" at Reservoir Park at the close of the summer season. Beginning in 1916 the "Kipona," a combination of daytime water sports and a nighttime boat parade, graced the broad river while viewers watched from the steps and esplanade. In 1919 the modern Penn-Harris Hotel opened, financed after an intensive chamber of commerce fund-raising campaign. The civic spirit lived, but it was no longer guided and informed by the unified, comprehensive vision of the City Beautiful.[36]

7 ◆ John C. Olmsted's Plan for Seattle

Origins

Seattle is one of the most scenic cities in the country. Founded in 1852 in the shelter of Elliott Bay, an indentation of Puget Sound, this unkempt town amid almost incredible beauty grew slowly at first.[1] The little city's active inhabitants built up lumbering, sawmilling, and shipping industries and secured the territorial university. Salmon canning, railroad promotion, and a brisk coal trade followed. The city had to wait until 1891 for transcontinental railroad service, but other railroads, notably the Great Northern, followed soon after. The withering depression of the nineties lifted dramatically in 1897 when the steamer *Portland* docked with $800,000 in gold from Canada's Yukon Territory and stories of the amazing wealth there, obtainable at the flip of a gold pan. Almost overnight Seattle became the premier outfitting and shipping point for Alaska and the Yukon, a position it never relinquished.

Population figures reflected these economic developments. In 1880, after almost thirty years of existence, the city held fewer than 4,000 people. In the next decade it grew to 42,837, an astonishing 1,112.5 percent increase. The years to 1900 saw an absolute population gain almost as impressive, which lifted the total to 80,671. The real boom, however, occurred in the first ten years of the twentieth century. In that delirious decade, Seattle's net growth was 156,523, boosting its population to 237,194, an increase of 194 percent. In those ten years the city annexed large areas, spilled over hills and into valleys, and flung out suburban extensions north and south and around the margins of Lake Washington. The process of neighborhood differentiation and segregation by occupation or income accelerated.[2]

The stunning natural environment might best be recaptured as it was in 1903. That was the year John Charles Olmsted first saw it, when he arrived to design the park and boulevard system. Seattle's site resembled a giant hourglass, pinched at its waist by intrusions from saltwater Puget Sound on the west and freshwater Lake Washington on the east. A series of bays and inlets,

147

plus Lake Union just north of the city's waist, created a richly varied pattern of
land and water. Steep hills, plateaus, and ridges offered spectacular views of
deep ravines, lakes and sound, the Olympic Mountains on the west, and the
Cascade range to the east. Mount Rainier's near-perfect cone, visible to the
southeast on a clear day, was the centerpiece of this visual delight. Puget
Sound and the nearby Pacific moderated the temperature. A well-distributed
rainfall supported luxurious coniferous and deciduous vegetation. Cloudy and
cool days and mottled days varying from light rain and clouds to mostly clear
conditions occurred along with more typically midcontinental days of sun or
rain. This meteorological mixture varied still more the optical experience of
water and land. The weather, Olmsted wrote, "was like England or Ireland."[3]

In some respects Olmsted's impact on Seattle was less than could have been
expected from so prestigious a landscape architect. The first explanation is
one often overlooked. An indigenous park, boulevard, and beautification
movement already existed in Seattle. It had developed expectations about the
improvements to be included in any comprehensive scheme, and these expectations limited Olmsted's initiative. Another difficulty lay in society's rapid
abandonment of Olmstedian limits, particularly those on active recreation in
parks. Neighborhood demands for a district playground pressured the park
board and created tension between that body and Olmsted.

EUGENE O. SCHWAGERL AND EARLY PLANS
FOR CIVIC IMPROVEMENT

Many years of beautification agitation preceded Olmsted's visit. Much of it
revolved about the plan or plans of a landscape architect and early superintendent of parks, Eugene O. Schwagerl. Schwagerl, born in Bavaria and educated
mostly in France, was credited with work at the Centennial Exposition of
1876. Designs in Cleveland and St. Louis followed. By 1892 he had completed
a draft plan for a Seattle park system, which he unveiled before a "meeting of
business men" called "to perfect a general comprehensive plan for the securing
of public parks for the city." Schwagerl proposed four anchor parks that later
became public reservations, though not necessarily with the boundaries he
envisioned. Beginning at the northeastern corner, he proposed enclosing the
peninsula jutting into Lake Washington across from Kirkland (now Warren
G. Magnuson [Sand Point] Park). On the southeast he recommended taking
the Bailey Peninsula (now Seward Park), and on the northwest what was then
known as West or Lighthouse point (now Discovery Park). For the southwestern anchor he selected the Alki Point area of West Seattle, now largely in
private development, but with Alki Beach, Schmitz Park, and a playground
nearby.[4]

Schwagerl also presented an elaborate boulevard plan. In this scheme a
boulevard left Lake Washington, running northwest to Green Lake and the
then private Woodland Park. Then it dipped southwest to Salmon Bay and

Queen Anne Hill, continuing south and west to Alki Point in West Seattle. He proposed another boulevard along Lake Washington from the Bailey Peninsula northward to the site of the park across from Kirkland. The plans, endorsed by the park commission, the mayor, and "in a general way" by the meeting, inspired an effort to secure a boulevard around Lake Washington. In their annual report of 1892 the park commissioners proposed a parkway from the then private Madison Park south of Lake Washington's Union Bay, looping around the southern end of the lake, and running up the eastern shore to Evergreen Point. In July 1893 two meetings of the park board, landowners, and other interested citizens produced a letter to the city council, urging the replatting, acceptance of land gifts, and condemnation of a portion of the necessary boulevard right of way. The council took no action.[5]

Schwagerl's plans and related activities raised public expectations of an eventual boulevard along Lake Washington and a link with Green Lake and Woodland Park. George F. Cotterill, an assistant city engineer and, in later life, a reform politician, heightened anticipation by constructing a series of bicycle paths during the later 1890s. In 1900 the council discussed buying the property along the Lake Washington bicycle path and building a boulevard.[6]

Meanwhile the city's parks grew by gift and purchase. By 1902 they amounted to almost 500 acres scattered around the city. The largest, Woodland, comprised almost 200 acres adjoining Green Lake in the far north central section. Its purchase in 1900 stirred controversy because of its cost and remoteness but it soon proved to be a popular resort. Washington Park south of Lake Washington's Union Bay, Volunteer Park with magnificent views of Lake Union and the retail-commercial district, Denny Park just north of downtown, and Kinnear Park on the southwest slope of Queen Anne Hill, all were distinct in function and size. Olmsted blamed Schwagerl's trite and undifferentiated landscaping for masking their individuality. Denny and Kinnear parks, he wrote his wife, "have been laid out and planted by a local landscape gardener, . . . but his walks are very crooked often & his banks steep & high and his planting very mixed but pretty much the same selection for every place."[7]

Neither Schwagerl's unrealized plans, nor his executed work, nor the bicycle paths, nor the erratic and disconnected park growth provided the immediate impetus to systematic urban beautification. The drive for comprehensive planning resulted from the convergence of four circumstances in 1902. The University of Washington was negotiating for a plan of its new campus with the Olmsted Brothers landscape architects. Their exchanges, if successfully concluded, would bring a representative of the prestigious firm to the city. About the same time the park commissioners became aware that their rival, Portland, Oregon, had approached the Olmsteds for a park and boulevard system plan. The third and fourth circumstances were entirely local. Elbert F. Blaine, a dynamic real estate man, joined the board in 1902 and became president in July. Blaine, whom Olmsted would term "the broadest man of the lot," wanted park and boulevard system plans and a stronger legal authority so the board could effectively plan and build.[8]

Lastly, by 1902 Seattle's neighborhood improvement clubs numbered about ten. The clubs may have been especially active in Seattle because of the way the topography divided the city into distinct areas. The peculiarity of one's own hilltop, ridge, lakeshore, or vale may have heightened the sort of neighborhood consciousness that makes for a keen awareness of utilities extension and improvements, tax and assessment policies, and the like. In any case these prototypical examples of the municipal improvement urge had united in a "conference committee." Its chairman, Joseph Shippen, arranged a February 1902 meeting at which Schwagerl, then in private practice, explained his plan of a decade before. Frank N. Little, the current superintendent of sewers, streets, and parks, and others also spoke. A letter was read from the Reverend Thomas L. Eliot, head of Portland's park commission, explaining beautification development there. The consensus of the meeting was that Seattle should begin a park and boulevard system while land costs were relatively low and that the park commission should have "full authority" to carry on the work. Little continued a close association with the improvement clubs. Discussions of a park and boulevard project and of the proper organization of the park board appeared in the press.[9]

The initiative to Olmsted Brothers came neither from an improvement club nor from a public official but from J. D. Blackwell, the superintendent of the Seattle Electric Company. The company owned a trolley line and some acreage around Green Lake that it and the city hoped to develop jointly with Woodland Park. In March 1902 Blackwell wrote to Percy R. Jones, an Olmsted employee, for himself and "on behalf of the Superintendent of Parks of Seattle" to discover "under what conditions we could get Mr. Olmstedd [sic] or some good landscape architect, to design a scheme of general improvement for the parks here." Soon the city assumed both the design project and the negotiations with the Olmsted firm. The Olmsted organization proposed a preliminary plan for Woodland Park based on maps supplied by the park commission, a service that further strengthened its hand.[10]

By January 1903 the commissioners had survey parties in the field to prepare the way for a park system study. They had sent information on the city to Frederick Law Olmsted, Jr., but teaching duties at Harvard University restricted the junior Olmsted's movements. Olmsted Brothers pressed the commissioners to accept John Charles, the senior partner. In late December Olmsted Brothers made a formal proposal "for a preliminary visit and report" involving a lengthy stay by "Mr. Olmsted" (either Mr. Olmsted would do, the commissioners had said), and an assistant, study of the problem, and preparation of a narrative report and accompanying map; followup consulting visits might also be necessary. By mid-January 1903 the commissioners and the city council had all but formally agreed to a contract. In April John Olmsted began the first of many visits to Seattle.[11]

John C. Olmsted and His Park
and Boulevard System

The man who came to the Pacific Northwest city carried both the banner
and the burden of the premier landscape architecture practice in the United
States. Olmsted suffered the fate of developing in the shadow, first, of his
pioneering stepfather, Frederick Law, and then of his younger half-brother,
the hyperactive Frederick, Jr. He was born in Geneva, Switzerland, in 1852,
during his father's futile odyssey in search of health. After the death of his
father, John Hull Olmsted, his mother married his uncle, Frederick. John was
raised practically as Frederick's son and entered the older man's practice upon
his graduation from Yale's Sheffield Scientific School in 1875. Three years
later his stepfather granted him a share of the business, and a partnership in
1884. The younger Olmsted was deeply involved in planning the Boston
parks, including Franklin, the Arnold Arboretum, and the Riverway. After
his stepfather withdrew from active practice, John took "the lead" in planning
and developing the Essex County, New Jersey, park system. By 1899, the year
of the founding of the American Society of Landscape Architects, "he was
unquestionably the most widely experienced in the group and probably the
ablest." Unfortunately for John's contemporary reputation, his half-brother
was chosen to prepare and head Harvard's new curriculum in landscape architecture, the country's first university training in the discipline. The next year
Frederick, Jr., joined Burnham and McKim on the soon-to-be-famous
McMillan Commission. He, not John, possessed all of the illustrious name.[12]

John Olmsted was cool and aloof, with a shyness that sometimes toppled
into snobbishness. Although capable of normal business relationships, effective public speaking, and even a few friendships among the outlanders with
whom he dealt, he was basically an inner-dwelling and inward-looking man.
"I am not very shy in business but the effect is ingrained & I rarely can be at
ease in company," he wrote his wife after his first visit to Seattle. "I tend
always to keep by myself and make no friends." On another visit he described a
barely tolerable dinner preceded by "considerable standing around in entirely
unheated rooms with the doors mostly open & being introduced to various
men whose names I either did not hear or promptly forgot" and followed by
introductions "to many more people to whom I had little to say." Olmsted,
introverted, fastidiously dressed, with a neatly trimmed beard, appeared to be
an aesthete, but the appearance was deceiving. Harnessed to a far-flung clientele and months of travel to feed the Olmsted domestic fires, he well understood the value of money and of a financial windfall. In 1906 he learned of the
1903 purchase, for $35,000, of a Seattle lot worth $125,000 three years later.
"There is a rise for you," he exclaimed. Clearly he had no objection to
unearned increment so long as avaricious manipulation or deceit played no
role.[13]

Olmsted and his assistant Percy R. Jones spent two months in Seattle and

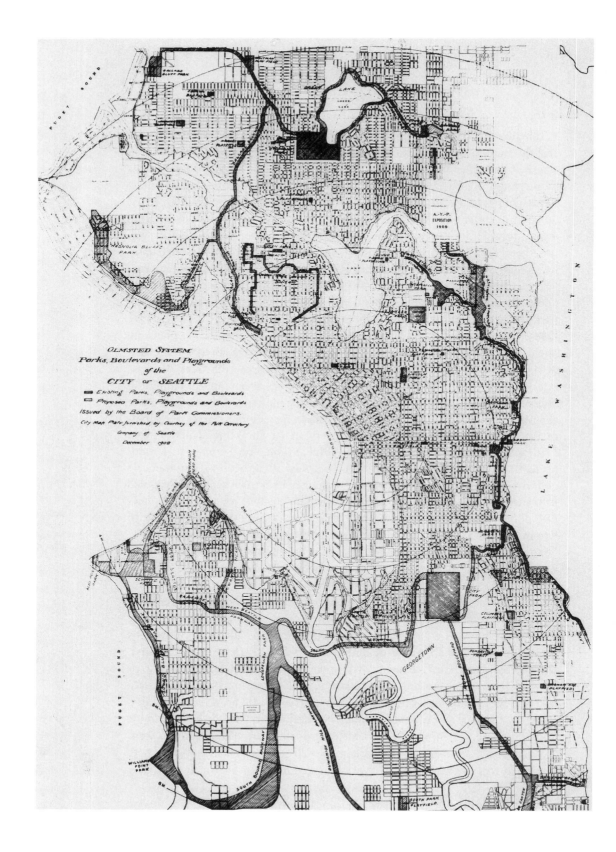

OLMSTED SYSTEM
Parks, Boulevards and Playgrounds
of the
CITY OF SEATTLE

Existing Parks, Playgrounds and Boulevards
Proposed Parks, Playgrounds and Boulevards

Issued by the Board of Park Commissioners.

City Map Plate furnished by Courtesy of the Polk Directory
Company of Seattle
December 1908

Portland. In the course of discussions with various Seattle officials and land-owners, Olmsted pointed out that Seattle's spectacularly scenic landscape would exact penalties. The abrupt hills and steep slopes would involve heavy construction work. The expense of bridging waterways virtually ensured that boulevard traffic would enter major commercial streets amd mingle with commercial traffic before returning to a boulevard route. Olmsted was also constrained by public expectations of particular improvements, such as the boulevard running south from Union Bay on Lake Washington, and by the rapidly growing demand for active recreation within the traditional park and boulevard system. Finally, he had to bring the existing public parks into the system, and he had to arrange for the eventual absorption of most of the private amusement parks. He completed his report in June, and the city council accepted it in October.[14]

Olmsted proposed, as an ultimate goal, an ambitiously conceived "comprehensive and satisfactory system of parks and parkways," with supplemental drives and playgrounds. He began at the undeveloped Bailey Peninsula, almost 200 acres jutting like a cocked thumb into southern Lake Washington. He proposed taking and preserving the peninsula and then laying out a parkway that, for the most part, hugged the lake's western shore until it reached Washington Park across Union Bay and southeast from the new University of Washington grounds. Olmsted drew a proposed boulevard from a suggested expansion of Washington Park, west to a crossing of the future canal between Lakes Union and Washington, then north through the university grounds along the bluff overlooking Union Bay. The boulevard continued to the east end of the privately owned Ravenna Park, a park he advocated bringing into the system.[15]

Opposite, this Board of Park Commissioners map of 1908 shows Seattle's prominent features. The northernmost lake is Green Lake, while the lake directly south of it is Lake Union. Lake Washington's Union Bay lies east of Lake Union, with Lake Washington proper beyond. Queen Anne Hill, a boulevard loop on its west, north, and east summits, is immediately west of Lake Union. Magnolia Hill, with Fort Lawton at its northwest corner, is west of Queen Anne Hill. Salmon Bay of Puget Sound is north of Magnolia Hill, while Elliott Bay is south and east. West Seattle is south across the mouth of Elliott Bay from Magnolia Hill. Woodland Park is at the southwestern corner of Green Lake. Ravenna Park is east of the lake at the end of the boulevard running eastward from the lake. The university grounds are south of Ravenna Park and are marked "A.-Y.-P. Exposition 1909." Washington Park is directly south of Union Bay. Volunteer Park is the darkened square between Washington Park and Lake Union. City, or Beacon Hill (now Jefferson), Park is the large oblong a few miles south of Volunteer Park. Except for the boulevards west of Woodland Park and most of the complex west and south of City Park, the system was eventually built. Seward Park, occupying Bailey Peninsula farther south along the shore of Lake Washington than the map extends, was one of the significant later additions not shown. (Courtesy, Special Collections Division, University of Washington Libraries.)

At Ravenna Park the proposed boulevard swung northwest along the edge of the ravine and, continuing in the same direction, followed the creek then running between Green Lake and Ravenna Park. At Green Lake Olmsted suggested an extension around the western shore of the lake, to Woodland Park. From there it would continue in a generally southwesterly direction to near the head of Salmon Bay, where a bridge would carry it to the northwestern flank of majestic Queen Anne Hill. From Queen Anne Olmsted would have had a boulevard run southerly to a cove between Queen Anne and Magnolia hills, thence west and north along the upper shore of Elliott Bay and the rim of Magnolia Bluff to the Fort Lawton military reservation (now Discovery Park). A branch of this boulevard would run south and east along the base of Queen Anne Hill to Kinnear Park. Olmsted planned a boulevard loop around the summit of Queen Anne, except on the south summit, where pleasure drives would follow existing streets. Branch parkways from Washington Park to Volunteer Park and from a point on the boulevard along Lake Washington to City Park or Beacon Hill Park (now Jefferson Park) and a speedway for equestrians south of City Park rounded out the proposed driveways. He suggested several smaller takings, among them the site of the present Gas Works Park at the junction of the arms of Lake Union and six playgrounds mostly in the east central or southern part of the city. The main parkway system, including its major intrapark drives, would have reached almost twenty-four miles. Unfortunately it could not be made continuous, to prevent doubling back over the parkway routes. Olmsted, to achieve a true loop, would have had to draw a boulevard through expensive property at the city's waist, north of the commercial-retail core and south of Lake Union, to say nothing of additional miles to the east and south.[16]

Olmsted laced his report with sound advice based on the prevailing concern about land values. Writing of the boulevard along Lake Washington, he warned that there was "a strong probability of many conflicts of opinion with the land owners." Unless the park commission were firm, "each land owner, for the purpose of keeping as much of his land as possible, will agree to nothing more than a broad street." Landowners with limited experience should "study the effect of long, wide and handsome parkways on the value of adjoining land"; then they might realize "that rather than lose such a chance for profit entirely it will pay to agree to the city's terms." He urged the city to buy all of the "Rainier Heights Landslide Section," an area along Lake Washington extending roughly from the middle of the present Colman Park to the north boundary of the present Leschi Park, and irregularly westward of the lake. Part of his concern was simply utilitarian. The instability of the soil would cause sagging streets, broken utility lines, and displaced houses. If the land were not converted to a park, probably it would be "occupied by cheap houses, the existence of which in the immediate proximity to one of the best residential districts of the city, would tend to retard the rise in value of that district, which its natural advantages should otherwise ensure."[17]

Olmsted has been criticized for upholding income-segregated housing and for making a blatant class appeal. The criticism is true to a degree, but it misses larger points. Olmsted and others of his generation had seen too many prime residential areas inundated by commerce, conversions to rooming houses, or cheap fill-in houses to be very romantic about mixed-income neighborhoods. Olmsted did have a class bias and he did wish to create a pleasant urban environment for the well-to-do, but his proposed takings, including playgrounds, were by no means sited to appeal only to one economic group. Finally, Olmsted argued for variety in both parkways and parks. Depending on the location, he advocated parkways combining driveways, footpaths, bridle paths, and bicycle paths; those combining bicycle and bridle paths and driveways; or a boulevard with one roadway reserved for "pleasure driving solely" amd the other for "ordinary traffic." He urged a break with the prevailing similarity of improved park landscapes. Concerning Volunteer Park, he noted the lack of "rugged topography" in its ridgetop location and predicted that it would "be surrounded by a highly finished style of city development"; therefore, "it will be best to adopt a neat and smooth style of landscape gardening throughout, thus harmonizing the park with its surroundings and making it contrast with the outlying parks, and those having rugged topography, in which a wild style and greater respect for the preservation of the natural forest undergrowth would be appropriate."[18]

The costs of the system—$1,198,000 was estimated for the major parkways and park acquisitions—were too high for an immediate, broad-scale undertaking. Only about $280,000 was available for purchases. Under the press of these circumstances Olmsted and Jones met with some park commissioners and interested landowners at the end of May, before Olmsted completed his report. It was a private meeting at the home of Blaine, the park commission chairman, called to discuss what the report would characterize as a "reduced system for the near future." Gradually the others drifted away, and for perhaps an hour only Blaine and Olmsted conferred. Olmsted's terse notes and his report revealed how seriously his comprehensive system was compromised. The truncated plan dropped the Bailey Peninsula and the southern portion of the Lake Washington Boulevard (both outside the city at the time), an expansion of Washington Park, and the boulevard through the university grounds from the university to Ravenna Park, to and around Green Lake. It excised Ravenna Park. Olmsted dropped the boulevard from Woodland Park to Queen Anne Hill, modified the Queen Anne boulevard, and eliminated the drives through Fort Lawton. The recommended playgrounds he reduced to three. He retained a few spur or substitute boulevards of no great consequence.[19]

The reduced system symbolized the juncture of the Olmstedian and the City Beautiful approaches to the problems of city planning. Neither John Olmsted nor the park commissioners ever abandoned the Olmstedian vision. The comprehensive system remained the ultimate goal. The reduced system

represented an empirical solution, a tough-minded application of the Olmstedian injunction to make a beginning on an elaborate plan. This time there
would be no dazzling vision of a resplendent parkway such as the senior
Olmsted and Calvert Vaux offered the Prospect Park commissioners in 1868,
but without any concrete suggestions for its realization. Instead, the younger
Olmsted explicitly pointed to ways of making beginnings. The influence of the
playground movement showed in the reduction but not the elimination of the
playgrounds.

The Park Board's Struggle for Power

With Olmsted's report in hand, the commissioners plunged into a battle to
strengthen their board's finances and independence. Their problem was similar to the one that the Kansas City park board confronted a decade before. The
Seattle city charter severely limited the powers of the park board, providing
only that the mayor would appoint a "park committee" of five, with the advice
and consent of the council. The "committee" was to play a strictly advisory
role. It was to "exercise inspection over" and once each year report to and
advise the council on the "maintenance, extension, ornamentation and improvement of the city parks, drives, boulevards, and public places." The
council held the real power, having the "management and control" of all park
and boulevard properties. It was authorized to accept gifts of park property. It
could spend the park funds, that is, money generated by a property tax levy of
up to one mill on a dollar's valuation, ten percent of "gross receipts from all
fines, penalties, and licenses," and any other sources. The Board of Public
Works, not the park board, was charged with improving park properties once
they became the "unencumbered property of the city." The city could condemn property for park purposes, and the council make contracts for purchasing park lands, but any mortgage payment was limited by the available park
funds and the mortgagee's legal remedy was "confined to the property mort-
gaged." Olmsted's report was an almost useless document in the hands of such
a powerless board.[20]

The board opened discussions with the council about a charter amendment
increasing the board's executive authority. It soon developed that power to
the board meant a corresponding reduction in the powers of the council and
the Board of Public Works. The council's reworking of the board's draft
amendment rendered it "practically valueless" in the board's opinion. The
park commissioners then decided to use the recent initiative legislation allowing a charter amendment on a ballot, provided it was supported by a petition
with signatures equal to 15 percent of the qualified voters in the previous
municipal election. The commissioners needed some two thousand signatures. They distributed petitions among the improvement clubs, by then
twenty-two strong, and began collecting signatures. With the support of the
daily press, this active merging of the landscape beautification impulse, the

play movement, and municipal improvement produced more than three thousand signatures. The amendment, "stronger and more sweeping" than the one first proposed to the council, was scheduled for the 8 March 1904 ballot. The first sections continued, clarified, and strengthened the previous charter language providing for a park fund and provided for a "board of park commissioners" of five appointed for terms of five years. The heart of the proposed amendment transferred control of park properties and funds from the council and Board of Public Works to the park commissioners. It made mandatory an appropriation of at least three-fourths to not more than one mill annually for park programs. The board continued to be subject to the current and anticipated money in the park fund. The council retained its power to advise and consent to mayoral appointments and to approve the purchase of park property selected by the board, a significant control. Unlike the Kansas City board, the Seattle board would enjoy no independent power of park selection.[21]

The park commissioner's proposed authority engendered substantial opposition. Some council members and well-meaning citizens fought it. Concerted opposition came from the Board of Public Works, whose powerful chairman, City Engineer Reginald H. Thomson, had been continuously in office for more than a decade. Except for a brief period in the 1890s, the parks were practically the fiefdom of the Board of Public Works, and Thomson intended to keep it that way. The superintendent of sewers, streets, and parks, whose office would lose jurisdiction of parks and boulevards under the proposed amendment, and who was also a member of the Board of Public Works, joined the city engineer. Thomson's antiamendment letter published in the *Seattle Post-Intelligencer* denounced the lack of an external control over the park board's expenditures, although Thomson did not object to similar freedom for his own board. He disagreed with large grants of power and fiscal autonomy to unpaid and appointed officials despite the fact that he, a paid official, wielded almost absolute power over street and utilities development and extensions. He objected to the "compulsory" minimum levy of three-fourths of a mill. The council's control of park board appointments and land purchases notwithstanding, Thomson found the amendment "repugnant to good morals" and "repugnant to a democratic form of government." As Charles W. Saunders, the secretary of the board, wrote to Olmsted, the "election is very much in doubt. We are hoping our friends will be stronger than the politicians."[22]

They were stronger, but barely: 3,825 to 3,732. While capsule characterizations of neighborhoods are imprecise, the ward-by-ward vote supports a conclusion that workingmen and their families were skeptical of transferring power to an assertive elite determined to spend a lot of public money, even if cumulatively, and even if, as the board members asserted, on "the gardens of the people." The measure passed in the low-income First Ward, perhaps because it was perceived as a jobs-producing public works initiative. It also carried the economically mixed Third, Fourth, and Fifth wards, areas includ-

Above and right, these scenes of Volunteer Park by the premier Northwest photographer Asahel Curtis show examples of the frequent juxtaposition of formal and naturalistic elements in parks. Volunteer Park overlooks downtown Seattle and Puget Sound. (Special Collections Division, University of Washington Libraries, negatives 58302 and 27201. Negative 58302 is copied from the Governmental Research Assistance Library, Seattle Public Library. Negative 27201 is reproduced by permission.)

ing downtown and settlements to the east and northeast. The Seventh Ward, bounded by downtown, Madison Street, and Lakes Union and Washington, was home to some workingmen but was one of the better residential wards. It approved the amendment, as did the Eighth, another good residential ward that included Queen Anne Hill. The amendment failed in the Second Ward—the locale of unskilled and semiskilled labor and a few middle- and upper-middle-class homes—by 200 of the 706 votes cast. The vote was close but against the proposition in the Sixth Ward, an industrial and blue-collar area. The sprawling but largely upper-blue-collar Ninth Ward overturned the amendment by almost two to one. In sum, wards dominated by regularly employed workingmen defeated the amendment, while those wards with a substantial mix of casual laborers and white-collar types approved it.[23]

This blue-collar bias against parks and boulevards diminished later in the decade. One reason it did, as Mansell Blackford has observed, was that the park board approved neighborhood demands for playfields in parks and adjacent to schools. Another reason was the growing accessibility, through improved streetcar service, of such parks as Woodland—Green Lake, Volunteer, and Washington. In a special vote during the holiday season of 1905, a $500,000 property acquisition bond issue secured a majority in a light turnout—1,348 for, 1,275 against—but not the required three-fifths. The proposition was narrowly defeated in the First Ward and lost decisively in the Second and Sixth. The Ninth defeated the amendment, as it had the park board reorganization, by almost two to one. Of two newly added middle-class

wards, one barely passed the amendment and the other defeated it. Asserting
that the showing did not reflect the popular will, the park board asked the
council for another vote. The council assented. Among the organizations
endorsing the $500,000 proposition were twenty improvement clubs, the
conference committee of the improvement clubs, the chamber of commerce,
the Seattle Real Estate Association, the local chapter of the American Institute of Architects, and the Central Labor Council. In March 1906 the bond
issue carried every ward but the recalcitrant Ninth, failing there by only 69
votes of 995 cast. The totals—7,501 for, 4,188 against—easily topped the
required three-fifths.[24]

In a December 1908 special election, a $1 million bond issue swept all the
wards, which annexations had increased to fourteen, a victory including the
no-longer-incorrigible Ninth. In the absence of a precinct-by-precinct comparison correlated with occupation and assessed valuations, generalizations
must be limited, but the Ninth's 552-to-299 approval compares favorably with
that of two middle-class wards: the Tenth, 318 to 120; and the Eleventh, 386
to 169. Wards similar to the Ninth—the Thirteenth and the Fourteenth—
passed the bond issue 372 to 203 and 333 to 50, respectively. By comparison
the mixed but declining Fourth Ward registered an overwhelming 315 to 48 in
favor. The totals once more readily cleared the three-fifths barrier, 6,688 to
2,359. In 1910 the emboldened board asked for a $2 million bond issue, a
considerable sum at the time and more than the total expenditures on parks,
playgrounds, and boulevards during the previous decade. Again the issue
carried all wards, although the total vote, 13,311 to 7,549, probably reflected
tempered enthusiasm for the large amount involved. What may be asserted
from this record is that parks, boulevards, and playgrounds were democrat-
ically and repeatedly approved in Seattle by people of all income and occupational levels.[25]

THE PLAYGROUND MOVEMENT

Whatever their Olmstedian predilections, the park commissioners could
not ignore the pressure for expanded playground facilities. The improvement
clubs, the press, and the active Seattle Playgrounds Association all worked for
the change. The earnest reformer Austin E. Griffiths supplied the leadership
as president of the playgrounds association. The commissioners plunged into
construction and kept Olmsted busy responding to requests for designs and for
advice. They benefited from Olmsted's counsel to a degree unusual for a
commission so remote from Brookline. But because Olmsted had been chosen
to design the University of Washington grounds and, later, the plan for the
Alaska-Yukon-Pacific Exposition of 1909, he was in the city fairly frequently
and kept up to date by correspondence when away.[26]

In 1906, 1908, and 1910, Olmsted wrote supplementary reports on parks,
parkways, and playgrounds. The reports revealed a distinct difference be-

tween the commissioners and their adviser. Contrary to the park board's wishes, Olmsted pressed to resolve any conflict between traditional parks and playgrounds in favor of perpetuating the Olmstedian ideal. In his 1906 park and playground report he conceded that "the time is now near when some of the expenditure for improvements can advisedly be made in the play grounds" but cautioned against capitulation to the popular desire for small parks and playgrounds in each neighborhood. Delays in providing larger, close-in land-scape parks and parkways would deprive the masses of their benefits and would hold the commission hostage to the demands of urban sectionalism. Besides, he wrote, "I do not think the city is yet so large and the working population so crowded as to make it so vitally essential to provide play grounds in the midst of the dense population as it is in cities of two or three times the population of Seattle." Therefore, "I do not believe that even such play grounds as have already been acquired, or will be secured in the immediate future, should be improved in any comprehensive or expensive manner." He discussed the improvement of only two playgrounds already in the board's possession. Not surprisingly, the bulk of his report concerned park and parkway improve-ments. Olmsted urged an addition to Washington Park and acquisition of a park in the Mount Baker area along Lake Washington, of Bailey Peninsula, and of the parkway between Green Lake and Cowen Park adjoining the west edge of Ravenna Park. He made extensive recommendations for the improve-ment of Frink, Cowen, and Washington parks.[27]

Olmsted's 1908 report followed an active annexation program incorporat-ing large suburban areas, including Ballard to the northwest, Ravenna to the northeast, West Seattle, and districts to the south. Accepting the board's charge to examine these areas, plus Magnolia Hill, Olmsted devised a park-area formula for each, based on the percentage of preannexation-Seattle's total area in parks, playgrounds larger than an acre, and parkways. Then he suggested smaller parks, parkways, and playfields for every district, their acreage of improvements following the formula in each case. For instance, the proposed area of parks and related improvements in Ballard was 3.1 percent of the area of Ballard, which compared with 3.25 percent for the whole of preannexation Seattle.[28]

Olmsted recommended thirteen play spaces, but his commitment to land-scapes and to City Beautiful practicality dominated the report, although the board generally failed to follow these more elaborate recommendations. Olmsted's parkways around and through the southern portion of the city, winding west to West Seattle and looping around the peninsula, remained unbuilt except for some West Seattle segments. A "Ballard Bluff Park"—forty-five acres on Puget Sound south of Golden Gardens (the present Golden Gardens Park)—and a parkway connecting to Woodland Park were never constructed. The board never adopted his suggestion for funding most of the parks and playgrounds from special assessments on the newly annexed areas. The special assessments were fiscally fair, particularly because Olmsted's recommendations involved mostly smaller parks or play areas located near their potential users. From another perspective, however, they were inequitable, because the concept of benefits and assessments had not been employed in preannexation Seattle. Instead, park fund monies or bond revenues paid for land improvements. One system for the pre-1907 city and another for the areas recently annexed smacked of favoritism.[29]

Ultimately the commissioners purchased land at or near eighteen of the twenty-five locations designated as play areas or smaller combination park and recreation grounds. With the exception of the present Lincoln Park in West Seattle and of some earlier Olmsted suggestions, the commission did not buy any new large scenic and recreation grounds. The principal lesson from the 1908 report and the board's response is the divergence between Olmsted's continuing emphasis on naturalistic constructivism and the commissioners' concern with meeting the popular demand for active recreation.

The contrast was more pronounced in 1910, when Olmsted presented the last of his formal reports. With unconscious irony the commissioners had instructed their advisory landscape architect to prepare recommendations on playground sites throughout the city. Olmsted chided them for "yielding to public pressure" by maintaining playgrounds in school yards. "The primary duty of the Park Board is to provide parks—not school playgrounds," Olmsted reminded his readers. Then he coupled a concession to play ideology with a call for administrative and functional clarity. He agreed that "the City needs and must have playgrounds," because "they surely are necessary as a matter of public health and good morals. But . . . most of them ought to be provided and all of them should be managed . . . by the School Board as a matter of right education of the physical, mental and moral natures of children. . . . If the Park Board diverts its income from park work to teaching children in playgrounds, it is not accomplishing what it should in its proper line and is doing . . . what could probably be better done by the School Board."[30]

Olmsted advised the board "to go on providing playgrounds" but "only incidentally and subordinately to parks." He urged the park commission to surrender its small playgrounds "bodily to the School Board whenever that Board is prepared to take them." And he recommended combined landscape treatment and play space development for each subsequent acquisition. He insisted "that the local parks should be larger and more park-like than several which have been acquired and improved by your Board under the name of playgrounds." He advised the board, where possible, to locate the parks "on steep hillsides or on the shores of lake, harbor, or river where they will afford the pleasure and refreshment due to their command of views, even at some sacrifice of advantage of shortest distance from the greatest number of homes or of uniformity of distribution." Olmsted made fifteen recommendations for playgrounds or other active recreational spaces, including his call for a waterfront park repeated from the 1903 report. Of these, the city eventually provided eleven, counting partial and nearby purchases and provisions for recrea-

tion within the same general area. A few, such as the Hiawatha Playfield in
West Seattle, were elaborately landscaped, fulfilling Olmsted's vision. Walks,
shelter houses, field houses, and toilet houses, surviving trees, planted shrubs,
and grass relieved the stark outlines of a few others, but most were play areas,
not small neighborhood parks with play apparatus integrated into landscape
design.[31]

IMPROVEMENT DEVELOPMENTS AND PROBLEMS

Seattle's park, boulevard, and playground system did not develop in a
vacuum but in tandem with other beautification efforts. There was some
interest in the convenient location and effective design of public buildings.
The conference committee of the improvement clubs resolved in favor of
"play-grounds in various parts of the city" and actively favored street trees and
opposed industrial smoke. The Washington State Chapter of the American
Institute of Architects promoted civic art and city planning. During the spring
of 1904 the *Post-Intelligencer* conducted a cleanup and beautification drive.
The next year it sponsored a more elaborate, pictorial "Cleaner Seattle"
campaign. The most vigorous of all the beautification fights was waged against
the billboard, although without many conclusive results by the end of the
twentieth century's first decade. Thomson and the Board of Public Works
were busy in 1904 with taking down illegal signs, but these were a small
percentage of the total. The Commercial Club, the Association of Collegiate
Alumnae, and the improvement clubs came out against the practically unrestrained proliferation of signs. No group was more indignant than the faculty
and students of the Franklin High School, who protested the erection of
boards facing the school grounds. The boards, they told the council's fire and
water committee, attracted "rubbish" and, worse, "hoodlums, who insult the
girls."[32]

As beautification and its struggles continued, the park, boulevard, and
playground system brought satisfaction to its principal designer. In January
1909 Olmsted sent home some newspaper clippings, one of which, he wrote
his wife, "is an example of what a lot of free advertising I get here because
people fall into the way of referring to the whole park system as the 'Olmsted
System.'" He supported the park commissioners' 1904 initiative for greater
autonomy and had the satisfaction of learning of its success. In 1904, too, the
park board hired the Olmsted firm's second choice for park superintendent,
John W. Thompson, who was a driving man and willing to accept a lower
salary than a distinguished rival, George A. Parker. Thompson was once
described as "a rough abrupt individual, and not as literate as he might be," but
who was an economical, capable administrator with an "unusual ability to
handle men." Thompson served the commission for almost a generation. A
number of private landscaping commissions came Olmsted's way because of
his public work. His greatest "moral" victory came in 1910, when the park

Colman Park, Seattle, along Lake Washington Boulevard, about 1910. John C. Olmsted created the Seattle park and boulevard system but could not control the details of design and construction. He ridiculed such a horseshoe curve as more suited to a railroad than a park drive. (Special Collections Division, University of Washington Libraries, negative UW 876. Reproduced by permission.)

board accepted his advice to deny space in Volunteer Park to an art museum. It was a triumph for the idea of the inviolate landscape park.[33]

Otherwise, Olmsted suffered the frustrations of a consultant working in a remote city with an alien climate and boomtown culture. Seattle was simply too far away. "I wish I could get going with good business at St. Louis and Kansas City and Omaha and Indianapolis so I could refuse work out here," he wrote. Although he admired the spectacular views of Puget Sound and Mount Rainier, he disliked the too-frequent overcasts obscuring distant scenery and the damp, chilly weather. "The total rainfall at Seattle is not heavy but it keeps everlastingly at it," he complained.[34]

Seattle's rapid growth produced rising real estate values but it also encouraged speculative greed, and expenditures on essential utilities combined with parsimony toward the park system. The board's resulting stingy habits bothered Olmsted. He balked at planning small sections of Woodland and Washington parks, when the whole had to be considered in order properly to design the small portions. It was no more correct to ask him to design small sections of parks, he wrote, than to request an architect to draw plans for thirty or forty percent of a building. Economy-minded compositions upset him especially.

Seattle's Frink Park, about 1910. Straight cement stairs of the type to the left and to the right forward of the automobile came in for criticism from Olmsted, who believed them to be out of place in a park landscape. (Special Collections Division, University of Washington Libraries, negative UW 877. Reproduced by permission.)

He was critical of the cheap construction on Interlaken Boulevard, which had in addition ruined much of the natural scenery in the ravine. Of Washington Park Boulevard he wrote, "What between economy of land and construction, and trying to suit the ideas of individuals, the boulevards are narrow, crooked and with unscientific boundaries." Poor design occurred even when conditions did not impose it. After a 1909 visit he wrote the president of the park board about the regularity and uniformity of tree plantings and steps of "a stiff and formal appearance." Similarly, "the lines of the drives were in many cases conspicuously stiff and formal, consisting of a succession of simple radial curves and straight lines, as is customary in railroads, instead of gracefully varying curves as is customary in the best parks."[35]

Design procedures affronted more than the artist in Olmsted. He knew that boomtown avarice could influence design as much as the shortage of public funds or the ineptitude of local draftsmen. In May 1907 he anticipated, with considerable distaste, helping to lay out a boulevard. "The landowners, as usual want to squeeze the parkway down to a mere avenue in width so as to retain more of their own land to sell when the expected rise in value resulting from laying out the parkway occurs. It is all very sordid and lacking in any aspect of patriotism on the part of the landowners. It is a disagreeable task for me to try to persuade Councilmen to approve the acts of the Park Commission when I feel that the Councilmen regard it as for their interest to assist their constituents in plundering the park funds." Olmsted's outburst was not fair to all landowners or councilmen, but his exasperation was legitimate.[36]

Nor were park commissioners exempt from criticism. Later the same year Olmsted noted in his conference log that one commissioner "did not ask me what I thought on any subject, but told me a multitude of things he thought." The landscape architect also suffered the indignity of having his advice ignored, as in the case of the assessment districts in the newly annexed areas. Some of his private work went well but some did not. "Lots of people," he complained, "employ me out here just from curiosity to hear what I will say (as they might employ a fortune teller) and do little or nothing that I advise."[37]

There were other problems not necessarily involving Olmsted. The weekly *Argus* never accepted the Olmstedian–City Beautiful argument that parkland should be purchased as soon as possible to forestall a rapid rise in land values. Olmsted's May 1903 plea to the council to provide parkland brought the response from the *Argus* that "there are some things that posterity should do for itself. When Seattle has a million inhabitants it can better afford to pay millions of dollars for parks than it can afford today to pay a hundred thousand dollars in bonds." For Seattle to begin "the purchase of park lands on a wholesale scale would be the height of folly."[38]

Four years later the *Argus* insisted that the city needed more paved streets, "sewers, water mains, sidewalks, a city hall, more school buildings," and other utilitarian improvements. Land taken for parks ceased producing tax revenue and began consuming money and interest payments. On the other hand, land values rose generally no more rapidly than a city's taxable wealth, so land purchases could be postponed without harm. The *Argus* argument suggested that the beautification ideology did not hold sway universally. So did the defeat, at the 1910 election, of a bond issue for a "Central Park" on "Courthouse Hill" southeast of downtown. The park board's position was neutral, but a citizen group generated publicity and petitions for the purchase. It failed (9,060 for, 9,793 against) in the same election that carried the park board's $2,000,000 bond issue. The park board's jurisdictional disputes with the Board of Public Works and its struggles with the city council were further indications that others doubted beautification or did not regard the park board as its institutional embodiment.[39]

The most difficult struggle with the council came over acquiring Ravenna Park. This private recreation ground, north of the state university campus, was a steep ravine containing a stream and dappled pools beneath towering evergreens. Its owner had generated much enthusiasm for its preservation and purchase among individuals and groups, including the Seattle Federation of Women's Clubs and the Ravenna Improvement Club. The proposal, however, invoked a bitter display of the urban sectionalism that the advocates of beautification deplored.[40]

Councilman Eugene Way of the Second Ward in southeastern Seattle insisted on the purchase of Bailey Peninsula for his section of the city before any more purchases were made in northern districts. Way could "enforce his blockade" as chairman of the council's parks and boulevards committee, which recommended approval or disapproval of sites selected by the park board. When the board held a late September 1908 meeting to discuss buying Ravenna Park, Way led a phalanx of southsiders against the purchase. "You buy Woodland park for the north and you give us a new pesthouse," Way cried. "You put the exposition in the north end," he continued, referring to the Alaska-Yukon-Pacific Exposition then in progress, "and you build a rat incinerator in the south end. Now you want to buy Ravenna for the north end and for the south end you promise a new restricted district." Way was nothing if not honest. He promised to support Ravenna if the park board would also propose to purchase the Bailey Peninsula, but otherwise he would "exert every effort" to defeat the Ravenna sale. Way soon extended his embargo to include all park purchases anywhere, until Bailey Peninsula was brought into the system. The park commissioners were furious but they were powerless to lift Way's blockade. By April 1909 they had arranged with the obdurate council-man for the condemnation of Ravenna, the Alki Point bathing beach in West Seattle, and Bailey Peninsula.[41]

Meanwhile the park system grew. By the end of 1909 it comprised nineteen parks of significant size; the largest, Woodland Park, was 179 acres. The total park acreage was almost 684, but about 170 acres were unimproved, mostly in small tracts. Even Olmsted argued that Seattle's exceptionally scenic setting negated the need for a large landscape park. The park commission had worked hard to develop the boulevards for visitors to the Alaska-Yukon-Pacific Ex-position and had succeeded in completing more than twelve miles. A contin-uous boulevard along most of Lake Washington ran from about a mile north of the Bailey Peninsula to the exposition in the southern part of the state univer-sity grounds. From the north edge of the university grounds a landscaped street ran to a point near Cowen and Ravenna parks. A short boulevard had been built in West Seattle, and many others were being planned. Ten playgrounds existed outside play areas in the larger parks, and others were in various planning stages. It was a remarkable record considering the compression of many improvements into the preceding three years.[42]

There were other signs of concern for civic improvement, including a movement to preserve the grounds of the Alaska-Yukon-Pacific Exposition as a park. An active drive among architects, other professionals, and business-men for a mandated comprehensive plan was auspiciously launched. Mean-while, Seattle enjoyed a planned beautification and recreation system that combined traditional design, playgrounds, and the preservation and enhance-ment of the Pacific Northwest's scenic wonders.[43]

8 ◆ Bossism as Civic Idealism, Planning, and Reform in Denver

BACKGROUND

Denver shares some of Seattle's qualities. The Colorado city rests on the verge of the eastern foothills of the Rocky Mountains, which dominate the western horizon. The Rockies' sublimity may be seen from many elevations in the city, including several parks improved or purchased during the City Beautiful era. Denver's site, a high tableland, is pleasant rather than scenic, but much of it is topographically varied and umbrageous enough to frame distant views. Like Seattle, Denver depended on regional industrial developments. It was founded in 1858 on the strength of a nearby gold rush, and despite three smelters and miscellaneous manufacturing in town, its growth resulted from the development of trade, transportation, and financial services to the region. Energetic boosters promoted Denver as a health resort and, by the twentieth century, were encouraging tourism.[1]

Denver's population pattern was similar to Seattle's, slow growth at first, followed by decades of boom. In 1870 the population was 4,759, scarcely more than what it had been ten years before. The decade of the seventies brought that Western urban phenomenon, the huge percentage increase, 648.7, and a rise to 35,629. Before 1890 the population crossed the 100,000 mark, rose to 133,859 during the depressed nineties, and soared to 213,381 by 1910. In 1920 it reached 256,491. A major expansion in 1902 brought the city to some 60 square miles, most of it in a roughly rectangular area of 5 by $7\frac{1}{2}$ miles, with a nearly square extension about $2\frac{1}{2}$ by $2\frac{3}{4}$ miles on the south.[2]

Though Denver resembled Seattle in its scenic attractions (except for its site) its economic organization, and its population growth, there were important differences. Denver's climate was semiarid, a condition conducive to drawing settlers suffering from tuberculosis, bronchitis, and asthma, but antithetical to beautification. Stream bottoms sprouted cottonwoods and wild fruit trees, but only sparse scrub grew on the dusty, barren tablelands. This circumstance made the quest for urban beauty, with its emphasis on planting, all the more poignant. In 1865 a City Ditch with branches to different parts of town was dug from the South Platte River, opening Denver to irrigation. Within two years, young trees were numerous enough for a French visitor to remark on them. The City Ditch was improved and covered, and eventually its function was largely assumed by other systems. Irrigation remained essential. The bill for watering the two blocks of the Colorado State capitol grounds was seven thousand dollars annually at the price levels of 1908.[3]

Denver's shortage of readily available natural water supplies also distinguished it from Seattle. The only river in Denver, the South Platte, was an unremarkable stream usually 100 to 150 yards wide along its traverse through town. Industry soon claimed most of its banks and bottoms. The South Platte flowed northerly until, a few blocks west of the commercial-retail district, it swung northeasterly. Just downstream from the northeastern bend was the confluence with Cherry Creek, where the creek ended its northwesterly ramble through the city. Save for its infrequent, devastating floods, Cherry Creek was as insignificant as the South Platte was unremarkable. Small natural lakes provided the still water. Less than fifty acres, most were located in an arc southwest to northeast of the confluence of the South Platte and Cherry Creek. They represented the only opportunity to combine water and mountain views, but unlike Seattle's vastly larger bodies of water, they could not be left to private shoreline development and yet be incorporated into stunning vistas.[4]

Robert W. Speer

The third difference from Seattle was personal and human—the catalytic mayor, Robert W. Speer. Speer oversaw or encouraged almost every City Beautiful improvement from before his election as mayor in 1904 to his death in 1918. Speer was a boss; "I am a boss, and I want to be a good one," he was quoted as saying. He looked the part. Heavyset, balding, jowly, and steely-eyed, with a commanding voice, Speer lacked only ever-present cigars and checked suits to complete the stereotypical boss image. His biographers and other commentators have variously analyzed him, but most agree that he was a broker who unified Denver's disparate elements into an effective polity. Stated or implied in the boss-broker image is the concept of Speer the centralist who gathered the power of city government into his hands, through formal or informal means of control. Speer's genius forged an unlikely coalition of gamblers, saloon keepers, notorious madams, bankers, utilities executives, other businessmen, blacks, immigrants, and urban beautifiers. This is not to say that everyone in each category was in Speer's camp, but many were, and almost all the gamblers, saloon keepers, and notorious madams were. Speer's open alliance with vice activities has kept him from the pantheon of Progressive Era boss-style mayors—Samuel M. "Golden Rule" Jones of Toledo, Thomas L. Johnson of Cleveland, and Hazen S. Pingree of Detroit.[5]

Speer was a realist who took humanity as he found it, while hoping for its

Mayor Robert Speer labored long and successfully for a beautiful Denver. (Photograph by DeLux Studio. Courtesy, Colorado Historical Society.)

gradual elevation. He was also a civic idealist who argued that one way to improve humanity was to offer it an uplifting urban environment. His apparent moral dichotomy may suggest a cynical policy of using "the beautification of 'Speer the Builder'" to mollify "the garden-club crowd and other civic ostriches who saw only the lovely new parks and public works." That judgment may be faulted on two counts. First, almost everyone who knew Speer and who recorded a view of the man, and almost every Speer scholar, has testified to what J. Paul Mitchell termed Speer's "deep sense of civic patriotism." Second, the criticism begs the question of why the "garden-club crowd" had to be included in Speer's coalition. The answer is twofold. Speer accepted City Beautiful idealism and yearned to reshape Denver into a personal monument. Further, the garden-club crowd was too large, well-organized, and powerful to ignore. Speer included it for the same reason that he did not wish to ignore the influence, votes, or money of the public utilities executives, blacks, or notorious madams. Also, the garden-club crowd had already shaped the possibilities and perceptions of the future of Denver by the time Speer took office.[6]

The city had acquired twelve parks by 1903, though not a park system. The three largest were east and south of the original settlement. They were Congress Park, purchased from the federal government in 1873 and originally a burial ground; City Park, the largest at 320 acres, purchased from the state in

1880; and Washington Park, bought from a series of private owners beginning in 1889. All were in what was rapidly becoming the fashionable residence section of Denver. This circumstance was not the result of a deep-laid plot but rather because the lands were high, remote at the time of purchase, and, in the case of Congress and City parks, cheap. From 1887 the parks received the benefits of a mandatory park fund, the levy for which gradually increased over the years. In 1893 the state legislature created a park commission, although the legislatively created Board of Public Works continued to have charge of such boulevards as existed and of most of the construction of public improvements in the parks and elsewhere.[7]

The garden-club crowd had made significant progress before Speer became mayor. And, as in Harrisburg, women were active in beautification and its politics. Speer built on their work but made critical personal contributions. He demonstrated, better than any citizen activist or planner, the critical importance of administrative and electoral politics to City Beautiful success. He was able at times to combine City Beautiful goals with others, however distantly related. He articulated the goals of the City Beautiful and made many bold moves on their behalf.

EARLY BEAUTIFICATION EFFORTS

While Speer was winning his political spurs, some Denver citizens made several efforts to expand and develop the park system and to pursue other goals related to the City Beautiful. John Evans, a former territorial governor and founder of Denver's street railway, the Denver Tramway, in 1894 proposed land purchases for a "comprehensive" system of parks and boulevards. His son, William Gray Evans, a rising member of the Denver business elite, went to the city council with his father's plans and secured approval of the idea. The council's action precipitated newspaper opposition and a protest meeting. Opponents criticized the costs of acquisition and irrigation and the benefits to the Tramway company from hauling passengers to the parks. Father and son attended the protest meeting, where the elder Evans asked to present his arguments and answer his critics. The chairman of the meeting denied Evans's request because, he said, the influential politician and businessman would dominate the proceedings.[8]

Although Evans's effort failed, other men and women carried on the fight under the rubrics of municipal improvement and civic design. Women were especially active, encouraged by general social trends but also, probably, by gaining the vote in Colorado in 1893. The Civic Federation of Denver, a women's club with no relationship to the National Civic Federation, flourished in the 1890s. The Civic Federation espoused good government, high public morals, and municipal nonpartisanship, but it also allied itself with the "village improvement" work of the Woman's Club of Denver. In 1900 it asked the park board to improve the entrance to City Park and received a commissioner's reply "that the land immediately adjoining the Park belonged to a private party, so the Commissioners had no jurisdiction over it and would be obliged to endure the annoyances until they could purchase the property." Early in 1901 a member spoke to a general federation meeting on "Municipal Art."[9]

The Woman's Club of Denver (organized 1894) carried on cleanup campaigns, agitated for a park "in the heart of the city," encouraged vacant lot gardening, redecorated school rooms to impart "dignified beauty" to them, and worked generally "for a more beautiful and wholesome city." Dr. Mary E. Bates, "for years an enthusiast on the subject of clean streets," organized the Clean City Club among west Denver schoolchildren. By February 1903 the club had more than one thousand members. No improvement group was more dynamic than the Civic Improvement Society (CIS). The CIS grew out of the reform department of the Woman's Club and held its first meeting in April 1896. Membership was open to men, but women led the organization "to create public opinion against existing evils, to awaken a civic ambition for [a] cleaner, healthier, and more beautiful environment," and to serve as ombudsmen for citizens with complaints. The CIS first concentrated on street cleaning, securing pledges from merchants on one downtown block to hire a private street cleaner for a month. The improvement induced the city to increase its own street-cleaning force. Next the CIS successfully agitated for trash cans at street corners, seats on the courthouse lawn, weed trimming, tree watering, antispitting notices in public places, and other public improvements combining practicality and uplift.[10]

The CIS soon moved on to more general beautification concerns such as uniform street tree planting and the billboard problem, in answer to which it helped secure an early, if ineffectual, regulatory ordinance. It cooperated in various projects, such as a proposed commemorative fountain, with the Artist's Club, the chamber of commerce, and neighborhood improvement societies. It corresponded with similar organizations in other cities. Attendance at special meetings sometimes included city officials. The women and men of the CIS unabashedly sought a modest social control through some of their reforms. They attacked "the small store in the vicinity of schools, and its sale of cigarettes and frivolous literature." In 1899 the secretary of the CIS noted with satisfaction how "one of our most recent efforts" resulted in an iron fence around the post office. "It is scarcely necessary," she asserted, "to call attention to the beauty of the fence in contrast to the row of men who daily sat on the coping and who incessantly smoked, chewed, and spit [sic] to the disgust of every right minded passer by."[11]

While it pursued these municipal improvement objectives, the CIS was preparing to embrace civic design matters through the creation of an umbrella organization, the Municipal Art League, "to secure united action in the promotion, erection and protection of public works of art and of artistic municipal improvements." The constitution the CIS drew up shrewdly included the mayor and representatives of the park commission and Board of Public Works ex officio and a member of the state capitol commission. Having taken the government partway into camp, the CIS was careful not to load the league with more representatives from its own organization than from others equally interested. The constitution provided for three representatives each from the CIS, the Woman's Club, the Colorado State Chapter of the American Institute of Architects, and the Artist's Club. Nine groups were allowed one member each, including the chamber of commerce and the influential Real Estate Exchange. Five members were selected at large. By April 1900 the league was established. Soon it was concerned about the lack of a city seal and with urban beautification generally. In May 1902 the league was discussing, among other issues, building height limitations. Its concern inspired the comment that it was "positively suicidal for the intelligence of the community to remain silent while the city develops at hap-hazard."[12]

All this activity indicates a high level of awareness about Denver's aesthetic problems and potential by 1903. Nor were the efforts of the "garden-club crowd" naive or unrelated to economic realities. In March 1903 the Real Estate Exchange, the CIS, and "other organizations of Denver" urged the city administration to begin using at once an enlarged appropriation for street cleaning. They made their demand partly because the coming influx of tourists and visitors would be repelled by dust and dirt, but also because the transients would bear tales of repulsive, filthy Denver to all corners of the country. While the state of Denver's parks and boulevards was primitive by later standards, they were being improved in the midst of repeated calls for their extension and betterment. The improvement effort was intellectual as well as organizational. In 1901 Jerome C. Smiley edited a *History of Denver*, in which he reviewed previous beautification efforts and suggested some present needs, including the Cherry Creek improvement and the parking of nearby lakes. The urban beautification movement, in sum, was well formed when Speer became prominent in Denver's partisan politics.[13]

SPEER'S RISE TO POWER

Speer's prominence antedated the struggle over the 1903 home rule charter, but after the charter lay in defeat, there could be no doubt of Speer's power, his partisan sympathies, and his bipartisan alignment with the banking and utilities interests of Denver. The defeated charter developed from a 1902 law and state constitutional amendment allowing home rule for Denver and the consolidation of a city and county of Denver, although true consolidation was not achieved until 1911. Denver's citizens selected a slate of reformers to write the new charter. The reformers included provisions that were an anathema to the traditional economic and political interests. They included provisions for an easy municipal takeover of the public service corporations, civil service, recall, and a short ballot. Speer worked with the heads of large corporations, prominent attorneys, and others, whether Democrats or Republicans, to defeat this threat to their mutual interests. The corporate chieftains provided cash and influence while Speer marshaled the voters, including those quick, dead, and nonexistent. The outright illegalities probably were unnecessary, but Speer and his allies were taking no chances. Another charter, drawn by a new, more traditional slate of electors and containing much more traditional provisions, was approved in March 1904, comfortably and without fraud.[14]

Two provisions from the defeated charter were included in the 1904 charter, though their survival would have been doubtful had Speer opposed them. The park commission article, carried over with some changes from the reform charter, divided Denver into four park districts and increased the park board from three to five members, one from each district plus a president chosen at large. All were mayoral appointees. The second provision, the result of successful pressure from the Municipal Art League, created an official Art Commission. The membership of seven was split among professionals and nonprofessionals. Two artists, "one of whom shall be a sculptor," were to be chosen from lists presented by the league or by the Artist's Club. The third member was to be a professional architect, while three others "shall not be persons pursuing the profession of art or architecture." The same shrewd co-option of government seen in the creation of the art league prevailed with the Art Commission: the mayor was made a member ex officio. He also appointed the other members. The commission was to "have control of all matters of art" in Denver, including the acceptance, location, relocation, or removal of all public works of art. A work of art by charter definition included paintings, stained glass, murals, statues, fountains, arches, gateways, and the like but did not include buildings.[15]

A month after the 1904 charter was approved, Speer ran as the Democratic candidate for mayor. He won, assisted by a padded and selectively purged electorate. Whether or not such chicanery was necessary, Speer believed that it was. One report has it that Speer's Republican opponent of 1904 visited him years later, when the stricken mayor lay on his deathbed. Speer confessed to his old adversary that he had been the "acting mayor," meaning that he had won through fraud. Speer's path to that election was a long, carefully taken journey in public and private realms.[16]

Speer was born in Mount Union, Pennsylvania, in 1855. He attended Dickinson Academy in Williamsport, an unusually advanced education for the day. In 1878 tuberculosis brought him to the uplands near Denver, where the air and exercise worked their advertised cure. Thereafter Speer went to Denver and soon was in the real estate business. Aggressive, ambitious, intelligent, hardworking, and genuinely friendly, Speer rapidly expanded his circle of business and political acquaintances. His formal political career began in 1884, when he won the city clerkship. Two years later Grover Cleveland appointed him postmaster, a strategic position. When, in 1889, the Harrison administration came in, Speer went out, but to the sounds of praise for his efficient, improved service. Two years later the governor appointed him to the fire and police board, a unit of city government but one controlled by the governor in the days before home rule. Speer served two years, then returned in 1897 for a four-year stay. He came to wield enormous influence on the three-man board, if not to dominate it, while maintaining a policy of protected gambling and prostitution and judiciously lax enforcement of municipal codes, if the case involved a prominent businessman or a genuine hard luck situation.

In 1901 the governor appointed Speer to head the Board of Public Works, another state-controlled city agency. Here Speer, working with about half the Denver budget, continued his policies of effective administration, partisan appointment, and the cultivation of friendship. By 1904 he enjoyed widespread support among the city's blacks, ethnic groups, middle class, and powerful financial interests, even though some people in each category might prefer the Republican candidate or criticize Speer's compromises with stern public morality. Money to fuel the Democratic machine's operations and elections came from those who benefited from Speer's policy of partisan appointments and vice protection. Through the years Speer maintained his party activity whether in or out of office and continued his real estate business. His machine was corrupt, but Speer apparently made enough from his official positions and his real estate business to live in a fashionable residence district without the benefit of personal graft. In 1904 he was ready to use the considerable power of the newly strengthened, home rule mayorship.

Speer and the Beautification of Denver

Speer placed his varied talents at the service of the City Beautiful movement. He deftly applied his previous experience to the problem of public improvements. His difficulties with real estate investments in the Arlington Park area included the untamed Cherry Creek, for his property straddled the creek in an area roughly equidistant from Washington and Congress parks. Early on he recognized the advantages to abutting property and, indeed, to the entire city to be gained in beautification and flood control from boulevarding and walling the stream.[17]

Speer well understood the relationship between improvements, land values, and boosterism. While president of the Board of Public Works Speer apparently practiced "honest graft" on one occasion, when he sold land owned by himself and his associates to the city for public as well as private benefit. He profited little or not at all from such transactions while mayor, preferring to use land purchases to reward political allies when there was also some benefit to the city. That he helped them substantially is doubtful, for the beneficiaries of his widely known improvements would hardly have required inside information to buy land at strategic places. As early as 1895 Speer was drawn into the "booster" activities existing in symbiosis with public improvements when he was chosen to be chairman of an Autumn Festival designed to commemorate the city and its development and, probably, to lift spirits sagging under the weight of the 1890s depression.[18]

While a member of the works board he had to deal with the urban sectionalism so antithetical to the City Beautiful, when a group of north Denver residents complained of overvalued property relative to commercial and elite residential sections. Finally, Speer learned of the interest some citizens had in boulevards, because the board in those days established boulevards at the request of abutting property owners.[19]

Speer's past experiences would have meant little without his organizational and executive ability. The park board is a case in point. The president of the park commissioners, Jacob Fillius, was a long-time political associate whom Speer could trust. Saco Rienk DeBoer, the Dutch immigrant who became the board's landscape architect, remembered that Speer and Fillius were "close" and that Speer told Fillius what to do. He also told DeBoer what to do. The Dutch landscaper recalled one such incident, involving DeBoer's orders to one man with a team to level a portion of the new Cherry Creek improvement, a slow job. The activity caught Speer's attention because the mayor walked by the job site each morning on his way to work. One of those mornings DeBoer received a summons to Speer's office, where he arrived "trembling." Speer told him, "You have one team working there, going around in circles. It'll take him a hundred years to level off that boulevard." Characteristically, Speer listened to his subordinate's defense of the situation. "Mayor, we don't have much money," DeBoer replied. Speer resolved that dilemma in a trice. "Who told you to worry about money? I do that. Now get out of here and get that thing done." DeBoer reported the incident to his supervisor and the "next day we had more teams there than we had room for."[20]

Speer's executive style had its weakness, for it encouraged all sorts of official interference in the activities of the professional staff. Frederick Law Olmsted, Jr., deplored this habit in a 1913 advisory letter. Among other administrative defects he found no clear lines of responsibility and authority, with the department's work "directed far too impulsively for the best efficiency in the long run." The board should leave methods to the superintendent while judging their efficiency. "But keeping in close touch with the methods of an employee is one thing, and doing his work for him or tying his hands by detailed orders is another." Olmsted's reasoning would not have impressed Speer. To the paunchy, hard-eyed boss, the important thing was to "get it done." In a speech delivered a year before his death, Speer confessed that "I am weak on theories. The practical side of an administration appeals to me. Results count for more than the conveyance in which they are delivered."[21]

Another instance of Speer's executive ability concerned the Art Commission. Here the case was somewhat different from the park board. The Art

Commission was not a policy-making board but was reactive, approving or denying the initiatives of others. Yet it could exert considerable influence when passing upon artworks, offering advice, or urging action on other public or private groups. The path from an Art Commission decision to its implementation, however, was relatively swift and simple and did not invite Speer's active intervention. He no doubt made his views known in his ex officio role, but he appears to have acquiesced in decisions. He used his executive talents in other ways. He made excellent appointments to the commission from among the city's cultural elite, including Anne Evans, the sister of Speer's friend, the business tycoon William G. Evans. The commission chairman, Henry Read, was an artist but was better known as an art entrepreneur. Read seized the opportunity to plunge the Art Commission into the swirl of civic life. Speer supported the commission's decisions to request a city seal, urge the development of a civic center, and bring the celebrated planner Charles Mulford Robinson to Denver. He supported the commission when it "strenuously opposed" the plans of the Denver Gas and Electric Company to light downtown's Sixteenth Street with a series of illuminated arches. The idea failed, and Read worked out a better system. Speer remained politically close to the utilities, but in matters of municipal art the Denver Gas and Electric Company's bright ideas would have to stand the scrutiny of the experts.[22]

The experts, in their turn, understood and appreciated Speer's risks on their behalf. "We have turned down so many things," Anne Evans told the First National Conference of Art Commissions in 1913. "It may get us into trouble." During Speer's first two terms Chairman Read "familiarized himself with several industries" and "made it a point to stay in close touch with the City Hall. Further, we found that we were very effective when we could work in close connection with the City administration and we were very fortunate to have a Mayor who referred things a great deal to the Art Commission." In backing his Art Commission, Speer revealed an understanding of his own deficiencies in the realm of art appreciation and a willingness to follow, most of the time, the advice of appointees whose expertise he trusted. Speer's taste in municipal art ran to ostentatious park gates, sentimental statuary, and other reminders of what Robinson called "the period of iron stags on lawns, and patent rockers and plush albums."[23]

For all their freedom and initiative, however, the art commissioners recognized a reciprocal obligation. They approved, for example, the erection of the Welcome Arch, an illuminated iron and bronze monster facing the Union Station at Seventeenth Street, sixty-five feet high and eighty-six feet wide. It allowed two traffic lanes through the blocky central portion and pedestrian passage through each of two lighter, lower wings. The arch looked roughly like a suspension bridge tower with a huge filigreed clock on the crossbar above the words *Welcome* on the station side, *Mizpah* on the other. The structure was not ugly, exactly, but as a piece of municipal art it was redolent of the iron stag. It was funded by local subscription, designed by a Denver artist, and

Formal gardens in Denver's City Park, a mode of decoration favored by Mayor Speer. (Western History Department, Denver Public Library. Reproduced by permission.)

enthusiastically received by the mayor, so the commission accepted it. At its dedication in 1906 Speer announced that the arch would "stand here for ages," but by 1931 it was in bad repair, battered by vehicle collisions, and burning nine thousand dollars' worth of electricity per year. The city tried to give it away but nobody wanted it. It was demolished. Despite the fate of the Welcome Arch, Speer usually struck the right balance between intervention and restraint.[24]

Speer also read, understood, and repeated the public rhetoric of the day but with a measure of realism often lacking in the platitudinous expression of the civic ideal. Although Speer is thought to have first articulated his plans in a 1907 speech, he packaged much of his subsequent civic improvement program into a speech given in November 1904, about half a year after he took office. The occasion was a conference held under the auspices of the Artist's Club, and it was important to Speer. He gave few formal speeches, lavishing care on each one, reworking and revising until his earnest prose conveyed his intentions and meaning precisely. By accident or design his remarks dovetailed with a speech from John Parsons, the president of the Municipal Art League. Speer surely listened with approval while Parsons delivered a stereotypical

City Beautiful address, applying its ideology to specific beautification projects such as street tree planting, park improvement, and new, grouped public buildings. Parsons sat down to an ovation, and then Speer heard himself introduced as the former president of the Board of Public Works, who had done so much "good work" for streets and parks.[25]

"Nature has done her part for Denver," Speer declared. "She has given us as pure air, as bright a sunshine and as blue a sky as can be found anywhere. The two-hundred-mile view of the Rockies . . . is truly grand. We do not half appreciate these gifts; in fact, we seldom think of them." Referring to the work of humans, Speer also found it good, considering Denver's comparative youth. "In all new cities necessities must come first," he said, but added that in a contemporary new city "we would all try to see that the necessities were made a little more ornamental." Turning to Cherry Creek, Speer likened it to "an abandoned stream in the wilds of Arizona." Walling the creek was a "necessity," but "a shady driveway along its banks" was required "to improve values of surrounding property, and make ornamental what is now the perverse [sic]." Then he spoke of the need for street improvements, the control of weeds in vacant lots, the problem of dusty streets, and the need for ornamental street lighting, about which "the city administration would be very glad to have suggestions . . . from the Municipal Art League and others." Next he mentioned placing the electrical wires in the business district underground and then turned to the problem of signs, calling business signs over the sidewalk "a nuisance, and in many places, dangerous." Speer knew his municipal improvement literature and its principle of the control rather than the eradication of a device businessmen considered essential. "We are going to ask the business men to join with us in having all [signs] extending over a certain distance removed. Ugliness is not necessary to business."[26]

After outlining acceptable sign designs, he mentioned the need for ornamental drinking fountains and called for what became a focus in his successful drive for municipal art, "a statue to the pioneers of the state." Forecasting by many years his 1916 "Give While You Live" speech, he called on "public spirited citizens to pay for" the erection of municipal monuments. "How many men of wealth residing here could build one or all without feeling the cost! Let us keep up the agitation that they may not neglect the opportunity of helping to beautify their city, while they are yet alive to enjoy it. A man deserves more credit for erecting fountains and statues while he lives and can enjoy his money than providing for them after he is dead and cannot use it."[27]

Speer next enumerated the "total of little things which makes or mars the beauty of a city," such as clean streets, trimmed trees, neat fences and business buildings, painted wagons, and regulated billboards. Then he made a mild reference to attacks on his policies of protecting gambling and prostitution. "No city administration can meet the views of all classes or satisfy all interests, but if an administration amounts to anything it must have the courage of its convictions." He concluded with a rhetorical bow to his hosts: "The Artist's

Club can do much by arousing public interest, stimulating local pride, encouraging the desire and determination to make Denver more beautiful."[28]

Speer did not confine himself to socioenvironmentalism or to practical civic idealism. He took bold action on behalf of the City Beautiful when he approved the Art Commission's decision to invite Robinson to Denver. As Robinson himself wrote, "I was not brought here to praise." Robinson's major recommendation, a civic center, will be considered in chapter 11. His January 1906 report urged a boulevard linking Cherry Creek (now Speer) Boulevard with boulevards connecting, in their turn, City, Congress, and Washington parks. He suggested a connection of Cherry Creek Boulevard northwest to Boulevard F (now Federal Boulevard), thence north to Rocky Mountain Lake, and the development of "Mountainview" (Montview) Boulevard east of City Park. All of Robinson's boulevard recommendations were in place several years later. Beyond his major concerns, he made many typically Robinsonian City Beautiful suggestions, including improvements in City Park, expanded playgrounds, a city forester, billboard and sign control, and smoke limitation. It was a thoughtful, sensible report, if, because of its expensive civic center proposal, not a popular one.[29]

Meanwhile Speer was planning another bold move, offering to convert a park into a monument to a wealthy citizen in return for a substantial donation to the park's improvement. The mayor remained dissatisfied with Denver's public development despite park and boulevard expansion, a new library, civic auditorium, and museum of natural history, gains in ornamental street lighting, and the approval of designs for a pioneer monument. His January 1907 address to the combined commercial bodies of Denver went beyond these disparate projects to call for "a complete system of boulevards," view preservation, purchasing what later became Inspiration Point, and an "Appian Way from Denver into the Rockies." Turning to his theme of the wealthy donor, Speer enumerated several possible objects of benefaction, including an "observation pavilion in Congress Park, with verandas north, west, and south, from which the 200-miles view of the mountain range cannot be equaled—inspiring men and women to greater and nobler deeds in life." After enumerating other possible donations, Speer returned to Congress Park. "On account of its magnificent location," he said, "Congress Park could be made the Inspiration Park of the West. An opportunity is presented for someone to furnish the money to beautify and adorn it. The name of the park should be changed," Speer added, almost as an afterthought, "and no name could be more fitting than that of the person endowing it."[30]

Speer's earnest, enthusiastic speech struck a responsive chord in the cumbrous breast of Walter S. Cheesman, a real estate and railroad investor, banker, and major stockholder in the Denver Union Water Company. The rotund magnate had no opportunity to act on Speer's suggestion, for he soon fell ill and died in May. His widow and daughter took up Speer's invitation, offering $100,000, a large sum in those days, for an outlook pavilion. The city council compliantly changed the name of Congress Park to Cheesman Park in June. The council moved despite a blast from Thomas M. Patterson, a political foe of Speer's, publisher of the *Rocky Mountain News*, and one of the rich personalities enlivening Denver's past. Patterson likened Speer's action to "putting the second most beautiful park of Denver up at auction" to wealthy men or their heirs. Individual monuments appropriately memorialized individuals, Patterson noted, but in this case heirs were donating a $100,000 monument and having a park worth $1,000,000 renamed. They were getting a park at cut rates. If the heirs wanted a Cheesman Park, they should buy a park and donate it to the city. "I don't in any manner criticize the widow and daughter of Mr. Cheesman," Patterson continued. "They heard of the foolish and unwarranted speech made by Mr. Speer at the business men's banquet, and they have not stopped to think of the imposition such an arrangement would be on the people of Denver." Patterson had a point, but Speer had the audacity to propose the change, and he had the votes in the council. In time, the people of Denver acquired a graceful "Renaissance parthenon" with a magnificent view of the Rockies across a broad lawn.[31]

Speer next secured the services of George E. Kessler to plan the "complete system of boulevards" he envisioned in his January speech. Kessler's reputation as a planner was by then equal to Robinson's. Robinson was the abler publicist but Kessler was a skilled landscape architect who could call on the support of an expert office staff. The German-born planner first arrived in Denver in the spring of 1907 and worked with the mayor, the architects of the Cheesman Memorial pavilion, and the Cheesman estate at least through 1908. Kessler prepared plans for Berkeley and Rocky Mountain lakes, a connecting boulevard to the future Inspiration Point, boulevards including Monaco and Cherry Creek, the City Park Esplanade, and the Isle of Safety at Broadway and Sixteenth Street near the capitol grounds. Close collaboration with Speer restricted the scope of Kessler's originality, for Kessler was "of course to take up with him in detail" the plans and drawings. On the other hand Kessler was able to head off a major change for the Cheesman Memorial that would have shorn it of its wing pavilions and disrupted the design purpose of its elaborate base and proposed plantings.[32]

Speer best epitomized his civic-minded valor when he secured Inspiration Point, a promontory just beyond the northwestern city limits in adjacent Jefferson County. It enjoyed a breathtaking view of the Rockies, their foothills, and the Clear Creek valley below. As Edgar C. MacMechen, Speer's most sympathetic biographer, described it, Speer early in 1910 asked the city attorney for an opinion on whether the city could buy property outside its boundaries. The counselor ruled against such purchases, but Speer, who had desired the land for at least three years, was not so easily thwarted. He turned to John McDonough, a park commissioner and real estate man. Speer gave McDonough the money to pay the taxes on the land, which were seven or eight years in arrears. After McDonough had redeemed the land for about

Top, the graceful Cheesman Memorial pavilion in Cheesman Park. In 1907 Mayor Speer offered to change the name of Congress Park to that of the donor of a suitable memorial. The heirs of Walter S. Cheesman, a utilities magnate, accepted Speer's offer. (Courtesy, Colorado Historical Society.) *Bottom*, looking through the Cheesman Memorial toward the Rocky Mountains. A high-rise building later thrust into this scene resulted in a view preservation ordinance. (Western History Department, Denver Public Library. Reproduced by permission.)

eight thousand dollars, the mayor again addressed the city. "I now have title to Inspiration Point," he wrote. "If the city desires to acquire and improve this point for park purposes I will give it a deed at the cost of acquisition; if not I will keep the land myself." Speer was more determined than his language suggested. DeBoer remembered him as saying, "I'd be willing to go to jail for it as long as the people of Denver got the use of it." Despite the legal doubts Speer's park board accepted his offer of the twenty-one-acre tract. Before the year was out, workers walled the promontory and built an auto road from nearby Berkeley Park.[33]

Speer's bold promotion of civic values extended beyond park issues. In 1909 he founded *Denver Municipal Facts*, a 9- by 12-inch newspaper, lavishly illustrated, detailing the city government's work as well as private civic endeavors, and sent free to every taxpayer. *Municipal Facts* attentively followed Speer's mayoral activities, but it also reprinted beautification scenes and improvement articles from other publications and kept local residents informed on improvement projects, pending and progressing, in Denver. An annual municipal parade showed off workers and equipment in each city department.[34]

The most striking of Speer's lesser beautification activities reflected his love of trees. He laid the groundwork for urban arboriculture carefully if indirectly when in 1906 he advocated voter approval of new utility franchises. The franchises included clauses requiring the Tramway to pay $60,000 annually and the Gas and Electric Company $50,000, for park and boulevard maintenance. The voters approved. Speer then used about $5,000 annually from the Tramway's donation to buy trees to be given away to the public. Each recipient received planting instructions and a suggestion to place the trees in a street parking, but in fact there were no restrictions on planting. Any citizen of Denver who came to a distribution station and presented a card signed by his alderman or by Speer was entitled to three trees: one elm and two maples or one maple and two elms. From 1906 through 1912 the city gave away about 100,000 saplings. Some 75,000 reached maturity.[35]

On occasion Speer's defense of trees was more spontaneous and spirited, if not entirely rational. DeBoer recalled an incident in 1914 when he was planting the Third Avenue parkway in the fashionable southeast section. He placed lofty English elms on the south side of the street, to frame a "beautiful view" of the Rockies. But when he attempted to take out a line of "poor soft maples" on the south side and replant with English elms, Speer and his neighbors, who lived nearby, appeared in protest. "We have shotguns," Speer announced. DeBoer retreated before the formidable politician. He need not have done so, for Speer in 1914 was out of office, but the mild-mannered little Dutchman revered his former chief. "We surrendered and left the maples in," he recalled. During Speer's third term the city forester wanted to cut down the poplars lining Speer Boulevard along Cherry Creek. The very idea angered Speer but he listened to the reason, which was to remove temporary trees and give the elms room to grow. Then he made his decision, no poplars would be cut, not even for elms. "And that ends it, plunk!" he bellowed. Speer's fanatical concern for trees reflected a heightened regard for them in arid Denver. When DeBoer revised the meretricious design of City Park, with its looping walks and drives, heavy stands of trees, and lack of lawns, he ordered the trees cleared during snowstorms so few would observe. Despite his precautions he "sure caught hell when we cut down those trees."[36]

In 1911 Speer went to Europe as a member of a group sponsored by the Boston Chamber of Commerce. It was a tour done up in the grand manner of Edwardian Europe, with banquets and sightseeing. Speer, with his geniality and quick mind, became a favorite of the group and was named head of the committee on "How Foreign Cities Are Governed." Through England, France, Germany, Austria-Hungary, and Switzerland, Speer looked, questioned, considered, and collected photographs of European cities' grand public improvements. A politician who sought power, Speer was most impressed with the regulating and entrepreneurial powers of German cities, which could enter virtually any business, including real estate. He learned much, to the delight of Lincoln Steffens, the cynical yet hopeful muckraking journalist. With Frederick C. Howe, another writer on urban reform, Speer and Steffens formed a trio that sometimes skipped banquets to ferret out city officials and ask probing questions about methods and techniques of government.[37]

So far as beautification was concerned, "Mayor Bob," as Steffens called him, confirmed and strengthened notions long held. What appeared to be the German city's benevolent dominion over the individual citizen and every business in the city intrigued him for the way such power could realize the City Beautiful. "If Denver were a German city," Speer told a banquet in his honor after his return, it would have a new or remodeled Union Station "without delay." The city would acquire "a large mountain park, and a ribbon strip would be annexed to Denver, connecting the city with the park, upon which a shaded drive and electric road would be constructed." The "Platte River would be walled and a drive built along each bank," and so on. Beyond these matters, the trip may have made Speer more aggressive in seeking out, or more receptive to a suggestion to retain, Frederick Law Olmsted, Jr. Olmsted advised on the planning of city parks, developed a mountain parks plan, and planned a civic center.[38]

The Denver mountain parks that Olmsted surveyed were, and are, a series of landscape, landscape preservation, view, and recreation areas southwest of the city, in the foothills of the Rockies. As originally conceived the parks embraced a roughly rectangular area of about forty-five square miles, bounded by Lookout Mountain on the northeast, the Bergen Park community on the northwest, an area south of Evergreen on the southwest, and the town of Morrison on the southeast. The original final proposal called for a series of "five natural parks of about 1,200 acres each," an "elegant fifty-five mile circle drive on easy grades" to and from Denver, and "forests, hills and valleys in natural state." In time the mountain parks and their connecting roads expanded far beyond the initial conception. The system was unique. No other city save Denver so boldly exploited a nearby scenic resource. The mountain parks movement borrowed heavily from the City Beautiful ideology, especially its emphasis on tourism, boosterism, and urban competition, its concerns for landscape and scenic values, and for the passive recreation involved in their appreciation. The men who orchestrated the movement came from Denver's commercial elite. Their 1912 campaign for the necessary city charter changes was similar to those of past City Beautiful drives, and it succeeded. Construction began in 1913.[39]

The junior Olmsted reported on the mountain parks in 1912 and in 1914, but he had a much greater influence on Denver's growing urban park and boulevard system. His 1912 preliminary recommendations were general with, sometimes, a specific application suggested. The "tendency to monotony of effect" in the boulevards could be varied by "a different treatment, even if it is no better in itself" or by "interrupting the continuity of the design at certain critical points." For height and use restrictions along parkways, a topic he expanded in a later report, he urged the commission to consider "each locality, often a very small locality, . . . on its own merits" and to adapt restrictions "in detail to the local conditions." He suggested planting more trees in City Park around the museum and shrubs around the base of the Cheesman Memorial, but in the case of Inspiration Point he called for keeping most of it "in its natural condition as a typical dry Colorado hillside." He argued for a locally naturalistic landscape treatment, writing "that it ought to be possible in Colorado and in the dry Southwest to develop certain types of landscape treatment . . . that would be more nearly indigenous . . . that would strike the visitor from the East as a *different* kind of thing—instead of a not always successful imitation of the sort of thing that can only reach its highest perfection in a moist climate."[40]

In 1913 the park board retained Olmsted to develop plans for four parks, including City Park, and to draw up planting plans for four parkways. The Olmsted office also proposed a Platte River parkway and struggled with the problem of Kessler's plantings for the Cheesman Park pavilion, where tall trees between the rear of the pavilion and the park boundary blocked the mountain view of "influential citizens." Olmsted wrote numerous advisory letters to the president of the board and its superintendent on such subjects as park department administration, park lawn and tree watering, and the implementation of the Olmsted Brothers' park and boulevard plans.[41]

By the time Speer's second term ended in 1912, the park and boulevard system had matured and had grown to encompass the whole city. The southeastern section, where the mayor lived and held property, was still favored with beautification expenditures. The system, nevertheless, had become comprehensive, aided by the park board's extraordinary powers under the 1904 charter and by the practice of designating some residential streets as

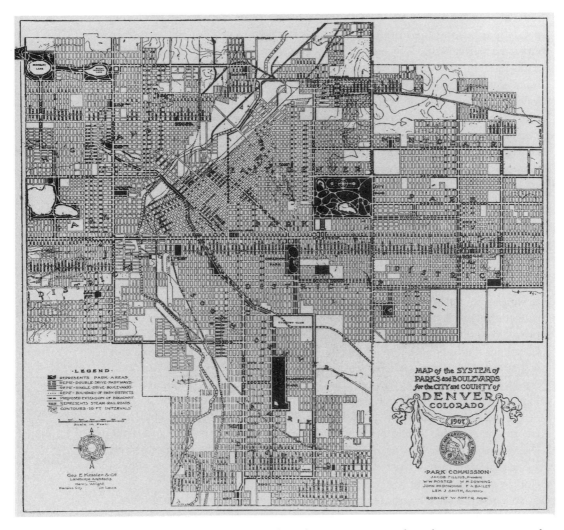

The general arrangement of the Denver park and boulevard system is apparent from this 1907 map prepared in George Kessler's office. The largest dark rectangle is City Park. Congress (later Cheesman) Park is southwest of City Park. Washington Park, with its long north-south axis, is the southernmost park. Boulevards beginning six blocks north of Washington Park flank Cherry Creek, which runs northwest to the South Platte River. The three parks and the Cherry Creek (later Speer) boulevards favored the fashionable residential areas in east and southeast Denver. The natural lakes within the city limits are surrounded by parks in northwest Denver. Rocky Mountain Lake Park is the easternmost park. West of it is Berkeley Park, with a western extension leading to Inspiration Point. Sloan's Lake Park is south of Berkeley Park. The drives and other features of the parks, as well as some later park and boulevard improvements, differed from many of those projected on this map. The formal entrance to City Park is in the southwest corner of the park. Broadway at the civic center site is twenty-six blocks west of the City Park entrance, and eight blocks east of Cherry Creek. The eastern edge of the site is identified by a three-block rectangle, the capitol grounds. (*American City* [May 1910]. Courtesy, Texas/Dallas History and Archives Division, Dallas Public Library.)

parkways. At the end of 1913 the parks contained 1,238.91 acres. City Park, with its zoo, natural history museum, lakes, electric fountain, varied land-scapes, and diversified recreational activities, was becoming an urban multi-purpose park. The boulevards and parkways united most of the parks and branched through many residential areas. From the Monaco Street Parkway and Syracuse Boulevard reaching the northeast corner, the tree-lined streets swung west to City and Cheesman parks and to Speer Boulevard flanking Cherry Creek. Speer, Federal, and other boulevards linked Rocky Mountain and Berkely parks and Inspiration Point. Only the lack of a northernmost east-west boulevard prevented the system from boxing the Denver rectangle. Ten playgrounds dotted the city.[42]

The developing Civic Center and the mountain parks added luster to Denver's fame as a city with significant amenities. Summer band concerts in the parks, the more formal concerts in the civic auditorium, an extensively remodeled Union Station, and the activities of the Art Commission—which would in 1914 release a devastating but carefully considered attack on Den-ver's smoke problem—further enhanced its reputation. Lilian Whiting's ec-static promotion of the scenic west, *The Land of Enchantment*, appeared in 1906 but even at that early date Whiting praised City Park, "a center of attraction," a focus "to Denver as is the Pinican Hill to Rome, or as Hyde Park to London,—the fashionable drive and rendezvous." In the residential area east of the capitol she found "spacious" lawns and tree-lined parkway streets giving "to this part of the city the appearance of an enormous park." In 1911 McFarland took note of Denver's many "agreeable and not over-elaborate homes. This means the settling of the city into grooves which promote civic virtue, or in short, patriotism." Denver, McFarland declared, "is doing the work that might be expected of a city of half a million people," and though the city lacked enough parks, they were expanding.[43]

All this was not without its price. No amount of City Beautiful activity could save Speer from a determined reform coalition and from political blunders so discreditable that he decided not to run for reelection in 1912. A disastrous Cherry Creek flood in July 1912 spread water for blocks around the confluence of the creek and the South Platte. It undermined the pilings supporting the walls along the creek. Portions of the walls, the proud symbols of Speer's regime of aesthetic and utilitarian construction, cracked, buckled, and fell into the creek bed. Speer's reform successors had a field day with the failure of the boss's flood control system. Their own flood commission, how-ever, pointed a finger at general conditions, not Speer. The uncompleted walls did not follow the creek along its entire urban length. Bridge pilings and dumping retarded water flow, as did weir dams built "for the purpose of forming ornamental pools." DeBoer later pointed out that nobody then understood how a roiling, raging torrent rushing down a mountain stream could churn its bed and undermine wall pilings. "The designs were correct," the landscape

Denver's Cherry Creek improvement combined beautification and flood control. (MacMechen, ed., *Robert W. Speer*. Courtesy, Colorado Historical Society.)

architect maintained, "but they were based on the slow water of other regions."[44]

Floods aside, the Speer improvements and level of city services were expensive. J. Paul Mitchell examined United States cities from 100,000 to 300,000 in population and found "that Denver's per capita rates of total payments, general governmental expenses, and property taxes were highest." In 1907 Denver's debt was relatively low, placing its per capita indebtedness twenty-first in a list of twenty-nine cities in its population range. By 1910 the debt was significantly higher, and although the city's swelling population had reduced

City Park, Denver, about 1930, showing its development into a multipurpose park containing an athletic field (*upper left*), and a zoo (*lower left*). (Western History Department, Denver Public Library. Reproduced by permission.)

per capita costs, Denver's expenses were "still by a wide margin the highest among nearly three dozen cities in the 100,000–300,000 population category." Speer was "touchy" about these realities and offered three defenses. First, he insisted, Denverites should consider the services and improvements they received. Second, he produced his own statistics in attempts to demonstrate moderate urban expenses. Third, he oversaw at least one financial retrenchment, during which he fired the city forester. In any case the reformers were unable to uncover gross malfeasance in the Speer administration or to curb spending significantly. Most importantly, Speer's beautification, recreational, and utilitarian improvements increased Denver's attractions as a residential and tourist city.[45]

III ◆

The Later City Beautiful

9 ◆ The Kansas City Union Station and the City Beautiful Ideal

THE NEED FOR A NEW UNION STATION

In 1914 Kansas City's Union Station opened and its park and boulevard system reached virtual maturity. Together they represented the attainment of a functional-aesthetic City Beautiful ideal. The Union Station was a private venture but its construction and the attendant reorganization of the city's rail network were matters of vital public concern that the voters had to approve. The station was no isolated monument but rested beside a broad plaza and boulevard. From the first it was knit into the park and boulevard system, and the bond strengthened with the years.

Like the park system, the station had a venerable past, for railroads traditionally were important to Kansas City's development. One of the city's most cherished myths concerns the acquisition of the Hannibal Bridge, the first railroad bridge across the Missouri River, completed in 1869. The myth overestimates the role local people played in fixing the bridge's location but not its importance in determining which of several well-sited riverport towns would triumph in their industrial and commercial rivalry. The bridge went to Kansas City and Kansas City became a major distribution center.[1]

An event almost as dramatic as gaining the bridge was the removal of Kansas City's terminal complex from its original river bottom location to a midtown site about a mile from the heart of the retail district. It was like the gaining of the bridge in another respect, for local people had relatively little to do with the move. The decision was a result of many factors: pressures of population growth, the limitations of the old station site, local newspaper publicity of adverse conditions at the old depot, the pleas of the Kansas City business community, the architect's vigorous presentation of his own plans, and the resolution of conflicts among the interested railroads.

A railroad terminal not only determined Kansas City's dominance, but its location within the city decided the placement of factories and wholesale houses and the speed and ease with which freight and passenger traffic could be handled. The clutter of industrial buildings around the terminal at the foot of the west bluffs grew through the 1870s. In less than a decade after the Hannibal Bridge opened, the railroads realized a second permanent station was necessary. The expanded facilities were needed because of the growing number of warehouses, wholesale houses, and industrial plants crowded along the wagon-filled streets. The city's increasing passenger traffic demanded something more than the makeshift structure built to replace the original depot, which burned shortly after completion.[2]

The second station opened in the spring of 1878. It was jammed into the northeast angle of the great triangle of land called the west bottoms, partly in Missouri and partly in Kansas, bounded on the north by the Missouri River, on the west and south by the Kansas (Kaw) River, and on the east and south by the steep, craggy west bluffs. The station itself was a three-story brick French Renaissance structure that looked more like a seventeenth-century chateau than a railroad depot. With its later additions it rambled for almost a block along Union Avenue.[3]

The station's surroundings made it even more anomalous. It looked out on Union Avenue, an east-west street that swung northeast on a sharp diagonal when it reached the railroad yards. Along the diagonal, opposite the depot, stood a packed row of pawnshops, saloons, hotels, and ticket offices. In 1913 Union Avenue boasted twenty-three saloons and a reputation as the city's "wettest block." In the previous year busy west bottoms police made almost one thousand arrests along the street on charges of drunkenness, vagrancy, and disturbing the peace. Behind the station the old-fashioned yards, with wood flooring between the rails, spread to the base of the west bluffs. The face of the bluffs, pocked by shacks and garish billboards, was slashed by the Ninth Street cable car incline and the Twelfth Street viaduct, two principal connections with the retail and residential city.[4]

If the station's surroundings were ugly and boisterous, the station itself became less and less serviceable as the passenger and freight traffic mounted decade after decade. A few population figures show why. The station was built to handle the railroad business of the twin Kansas Citys, which had an 1880 population, without their suburbs, of not quite 59,000. Ten years later the two cities almost had tripled in size and held over 171,000 souls. By 1900 their population was well above 200,000, and by 1910, it had reached 330,712, an increase of over 550 percent in thirty years. This was in an age when the railroads enjoyed a near monopoly on long-distance land transportation, yet the 1878 station served Kansas City until 1914. Scarcely ten years after it opened, the *Star* complained that it was too small.[5]

The questions of a new station and its location were questions about which the citizens could agitate and complain, but about which they could do relatively little. A private concern, the Union Depot Company, owned the depot and owned or controlled the land around it. The company was controlled in turn by a board of directors representing the railroads that used the terminal.

Few directors lived in Kansas City; local topographical conditions and land prices could and did influence them, but they were comparatively immune to newspaper criticisms, importunate delegations from the Commercial Club, petitions from indignant citizens, and other pressures that sometimes had a magical effect on popularly elected bodies. Indeed, it was not always possible for local delegations to reach the directors of the depot company, because they held many of their meetings in Chicago.[6]

Newspaper agitation helped keep the public interested through the years of planning and construction of the new facilities. The newspapers developed two themes: the cramped quarters and inadequate arrangements in the old station and the railroads' unreasonable delay in reaching their decision to build a new terminal. In 1897 the *Star* objected to the way rail passengers were exposed to the elements, to engine smoke on the platforms, and to toilet rooms without running water during part of the day. Later it turned its humor upon "the old contraption on Union Avenue" and "the old shack," which the railroads wished to preserve "in the pristine condition of the days when Kansas City was a village." It counseled the Union Depot Company directors to "buy a large quantity of 'preservaline' and spray the station with this powerful substance daily to perpetuate it." Caustic press comments mounted as delays of the final decision stretched out over almost a decade.[7]

The railroad did not need the newspapers to tell them the west bottoms rail yards were unsatisfactory, a fact the newspapers were willing to admit. The west bottoms location had one advantage. It was low and flat, so that trains could reach it along short, easy grades from the Missouri and Kansas river bridges and could travel around on it without difficulty. Otherwise, it was an outstanding example of bad site planning. The station could not readily be expanded. It was hemmed in by Union Avenue, the Ninth Street cable car station, and precious track space. There was room only to the south, so the station grew lengthwise until it reached the end of the diagonal on Union Avenue. The unalterable space between the depot and the soaring west bluffs fixed the amount of track room.[8]

Worse still was the "gooseneck," a sliver of land between the Missouri River and the point of the west bluffs, over which all trains going or coming from the east and north had to pass. Only six through tracks ran from the gooseneck past the station. Worst of all, the west bottoms, low-lying and bounded on two sides by rivers, was subject to floods.[9]

In 1896, 129 passenger trains each day crowded into the old depot's yards. By 1903 the same facilities were clogged with a daily 187 trains, besides freight hauling and transfer operations. As a result, 75 percent of all trains were late. If a passenger were on the one train in four that somehow ran the blockade of other engines and cars on time, he was not certain to alight near the depot, because there was room for only seven cars directly behind it. Longer trains overlapped other needed tracks, so the additional cars, with their hapless passengers, were detached and shunted to another part of the yard.[10]

The Search for a New Station

In 1897 the Union Depot Company directors admitted that "it is perhaps true, at times, that the present Union station is crowded and that the facilities are not in every way all that the railroads, the City and the traveling public would like." A year later they bowed to increasing pressure on the depot and commissioned the famous architectural firm of Van Brunt and Howe to re-design its interior, but the remodeling afforded only temporary relief. In 1901 the *Star* reported the main waiting room was so crowded that people stood or sat on the floor. In 1905 the directors capitulated. They resolved to search for an adequate site.[11]

The question in the directors' minds, then and before, was where should the new station be built? The directors seriously considered three sites. The first of these was the old west bottoms location. The second was in the "north end," near the Missouri River. The third was in the vicinity of the little Grand Avenue Station, which stood south of the retail district along the tracks of the Kansas City Belt Railway Company, which, like the Union Depot Company, was a representative firm for the lines using its tracks.

Despite its disadvantages, the west bottoms site nearly became the location for the new station. In 1902 the railroads studied the feasibility of condemning the saloons and other places on Union Avenue to make room for a large depot, but a lack of unanimity killed the plan. Some railroads continued to hold out for the west bottoms until the great flood of 1903.[12]

In June 1903 the Missouri and Kansas rivers leaped their banks, crushed iron bridges, snapped the city's main water pipe, surged over the livestock yards, streets, and railroad tracks in the bottoms, and lapped at the face of the west bluffs. Waters six feet deep swirled through the Union Depot, and when they fell back, left a foot of sand and silt piled on the platforms. No trains moved through the west bottoms for a week. The *Star* effectively made light of the railroad's embarrassment. The Union Depot became in its columns "that venerable and amphibious structure" and "the old ark." Railroad men viewed the situation more seriously. "The flood has forever settled the proposition against the location of the new Union depot in the West bottoms," said the president of the Santa Fe.[13]

The 1903 flood also dampened railroad enthusiasm for the north end site. Floodwaters did not reach the proposed station location itself but cut it off from both east and west. In February 1904 the executive committee of the Union Depot Company ordered the engineer "to examine and report upon plans for a depot upon line of the Kansas City Belt Railway near Grand Ave." In June the directors appointed a committee of five "to further develop the situation," which meant, one of the committee members told the *Star*, that "this committee is authorized to carry the matter to a finish." Early in 1905 the *Star* reported agreement of all interested railroads on the location and cost of a new depot, but by April there were signs of the more familiar bickering among the constituents of the Union Depot Company.[14]

The squabbling over location continued almost a year; then six railroads forced a dramatic decision. Despairing of ever achieving the unanimous vote needed to move the station, they broke with the Union Depot Company in February 1906 and announced their intention to build a new station south of the retail district, "costing approximately 4 millions of dollars." These railroads had secured options on forty-four acres of needed land and had begun preparing proposals to submit to the city council, covering "street vacation and other matters." By June other lines had joined the original dissidents and acted with them to merge, on 10 July, the Kansas City Belt Railway Company and the Union Depot Company into the Kansas City Terminal Railway Company. The new corporation thereafter conducted negotiations for the station.[15]

The site the railroads decided to favor with their new terminal was not ideal. The tracks running east from the proposed site were built on steep grades that long passenger trains could not climb without additional engines. Street and trolley crossings frequently were "at grade." Where viaducts over the tracks existed they were narrow iron structures unable to carry heavy traffic. The station site, at the intersection of Twenty-fourth and Main streets, was an ugly wasteland cut by a meandering open sewer, O.K. Creek. A few warehouses fed by the belt line stood nearby. To the south loomed a great hill, covered mostly with small, unkempt frame houses that reached south to Penn Valley Park. Main Street, a bumpy wagon rut over the belt line tracks, led nowhere.[16]

Yet the location had important advantages. The site itself was low and broad and could accommodate a large number of tracks. It was a natural location for a "through" station, in which trains simply pull up and start off again in the same direction, rather than a "back-in" or dead-end depot requiring complicated switching to enter. The site and its surroundings could not flood. It was far from Kansas City, Kansas, but downtown Kansas City, Missouri, could be seen from the wide business streets that ended abruptly at the belt line tracks. Some of the city's finest residential sections were only a few minutes' automobile or trolley ride distant. The Kansas City Terminal Railway Company already owned some of the necessary land. Problems of viaducts and grades could be solved, for a price. And the new location presented an opportunity for the railroads to build a giant structure symbolic of their wealth and power, flanked by parks and tied to the city's developing boulevard system.

By July 1906 the preliminary plans were completed, and the railroads had to secure the community's approval of those plans. A charter amendment, negotiated with the council and approved by the voters, would be necessary. There had to be consultations with the Board of Public Works and the park board on such matters as viaducts, rights of way, and the surroundings of the station itself. The negotiations between the railroads and a committee of the city council consumed almost three years. On 7 July 1909, the council approved a comprehensive ordinance that ran to 140 pages. The next step was approval by the people in a special election. Popular ratification was necessary because, among other reasons, the city could not sell boulevard or park land without voter approval, and the council and the railroads had found it necessary to take small strips of parkway for viaduct reconstruction and expansion.

The document the voters had to confirm granted the Kansas City Terminal Railway Company a 200-year franchise, authorized it to run six through tracks at a specified grade over the old belt line, charged it with liability for all land damages arising from condemnation and construction, and obligated it to build or reconstruct twenty-six viaducts and eleven subways in accord with plans approved by the Board of Public Works or the park board. All maintenance of the viaducts and subways would fall to the railroads, except that street railways that used them were required to pay one-half the construction and maintenance costs. The railroads were also to build an O.K. Creek sewer. More important to the City Beautiful movement were sections that required the company to acquire some eight and one-half acres directly south of the station site for a park (to prevent another Union Avenue from springing up just across the broad station plaza) and to build a station to cost "not less than Two Million Eight Hundred Thousand Dollars." The last requirement would appear quite unnecessary in the light of the final station cost of over $6,300,000.[17]

On September 9 the people voted. Seven hundred and eight citizens rejected the proposals. Their ballots were swamped by a tide of 24,522 votes cast in favor of a new union station. It was a "magnificent victory" and one more popular demonstration in favor of the City Beautiful. The victory was also notable because it doomed the old station and boisterous Union Avenue, the commercial heart of the old First Ward, with the acquiescence of James Pendergast, First Ward boss.[18]

Pendergast's career revealed remarkable parallels to the lives of the reformers and planners whose park and boulevard ordinances he backed in the council at decisive times. He came to Kansas City in the late 1870s, and like Kessler, Meyer, and Haff, he was a young man when he came. From the time he opened a saloon on St. Louis Avenue, not far from the old Union Depot, his political power grew. While Nelson built his *Star*, Meyer his smelting and mining operations, and Haff his legal work, Pendergast enlarged his personal following and extended his influence by a system of alliances with other Democratic ward leaders. By 1909 he had two saloons in the west bottoms and one on lower Main Street, across from the old city hall.[19]

Local patriotism contributed to Pendergast's decision not to oppose the ordinance in the council or at the polls. But, as with Boss Speer's civic loyalty, there were other considerations. By 1909 he was planning to retire. "It used to be exciting," he said of his political activity. "I thought it was great sport the first few times I was elected. . . . For the last two years I've been racing around and two doctors telling me to get out of politics or they would be forced to quit taking my money." All he wanted to do, he said, was remove to his farm in neighboring Johnson County, Kansas. In 1910 Pendergast retired and bestowed his aldermanic mantle upon his younger brother, Thomas, who would become the boss of Kansas City. In 1911 James Pendergast died of Bright's disease.[20]

DESIGNING AND BUILDING THE NEW STATION

The election victory had been magnificent, and the new station would be magnificent, too. Its architect, Jarvis Hunt, dynamic and outspoken to the point of flamboyance, would make sure of that. Hunt, a product of the City Beautiful tradition, was born in Wethersfield, Vermont, in 1859, the son of a prominent lawyer and the nephew of two distinguished men. One uncle was William Morris Hunt, the painter. The other was the man whose profession he followed: Richard Morris Hunt. R. M. Hunt was no ordinary architect. He was, Louis Sullivan admitted, the "acknowledged dean of his profession," an eclectic whose masterpieces included the William K. Vanderbilt chateau and the Metropolitan Museum in New York and the Administration Building at the Chicago World's Fair. "Uncle Dick" Hunt was as blunt of speech as he was successful in his occupation. When he came to Chicago to attend a planning session for the fair, he listened for a few minutes to Daniel H. Burnham's apology for the barbarity of western architects. When he could tolerate no more excuses, he exploded, "Hell, we haven't come out here on a missionary expedition. Let's get to work."[21]

Jarvis Hunt resembled his uncle professionally and temperamentally. He was capable, an associate recalled, of "the neatest kind of profanity artistically rendered." Like his uncle, the younger Hunt was drawn westward to design a building for the World's Columbian Exposition, the Vermont State building. Unlike his uncle, who returned to New York, he stayed in Chicago almost thirty-five years.[22]

As early as 1901 the railroads secretly commissioned Hunt and, either then or later, two other architects to draw plans for a Kansas City station and approaches. Hunt's competition was formidable: D. H. Burnham and Company and Howe, Hoit and Cutler, a Kansas City firm. While the railroads bickered and squabbled over the station site, Hunt drew and redrew his plans and even built a three-dimensional model, complete to the stained glass windows, of the station he hoped to build in Kansas City. On 18 June 1906, the railroad executives gathered in Chicago to choose their architect. Hunt's elaborate plans and effective presentation carried the day. His original plans showed a mammoth building, its vast ticket lobby flanked by office wings four stories high. A gigantic waiting room thrust northward over some twenty-five

tracks to form a big T. The vaulted roof of the ticket lobby arched 115 feet
above the floor. Outside, the triple arches of the carriage concourse rose
seventy feet above the pavement.[23]

The chairman of the Union Depot Company's board of directors was delighted. "The arrangements of . . . the hundred and one . . . things necessary
to a modern station are better than any that I have ever seen devised." Hunt
declared, "If I do say it myself, no city on this earth will have a finer station
than Kansas City." "I was prepared for something pretty big," another flab-
bergasted railroad official said, "but I confess . . . I wasn't looking for the
complete and adequate terminal which Mr. Hunt has devised." Neither were
he and his colleagues looking for the expense, which Hunt estimated at $3.5
million, so they resolved to hold the cost of a station and yards to approximately $3 million. They reckoned without Hunt's persuasive powers, for in
1909 he was back with plans for a station reduced in size but fitted with every
convenience. This time Hunt estimated the price at $5.7 million, and the
railroad directors, "after extended discussion," approved it.[24]

The station was to be more than simply another monumental building. The
ticket lobby and its wings would parallel the tracks, with the long waiting
room extending twenty-five feet above the rails. The waiting room would be
at right angles to and on the same level as the ticket lobby and built along the
station's north-south axis. Thus Hunt preserved his original T-shaped depot.
The ticket lobby provided lunchrooms, barbershops, a post office, a drug
store, and baggage and check rooms. The waiting room's walls were pierced
with gates leading down long concourses and stairs to the trains. Passengers
would go down to meet the trains; their baggage, handled on a below-tracks
level, would come up. The system was designed to reduce the collisions
between people attempting to reach trains, those using the building's services,
and baggage. A ventilation system would carry off engine smoke. Hunt summarized his plans in a characteristic manner: they would "give Kansas City a
station unexcelled."[25]

Meanwhile, a group of Main Street businessmen persuaded the railroads to
make a concession to purely local interests. The railroads consented to move
the station slightly west so it would unblock Main Street and allow the
businessmen to build a viaduct over the terminal company's tracks. The
businessmen, organized into the Central Improvement Association, were
careful not to rest their arguments on self-interest alone. "We told them . . .
how important it was to have two streets connecting to the depot from the
north." Grand Avenue, the next street east of the station site, "could hardly
take care of all the heavy traffic." The association was so anxious to ensure
Main Street's unbroken connection to the rapidly building residential sections south of the O.K. Creek valley that it undertook to build the viaduct
itself. Preliminary plans projected a 60–foot-wide roadway arching over the
tracks, to run 1,320 feet from Twentieth Street to Twenty-third Street at a
cost of between $120,000 and $125,000. The project was financed by levies

The Union Station, Kansas City, Missouri, under construction, winter 1913–14, looking west. The privately funded Main Street viaduct crosses over the train sheds from the right center to the center of the photograph. (Lyle W. Dorsett Papers. Courtesy, Joint Collection, Western Historical Manuscript Collection and State Historical Society of Missouri Manuscripts, University of Missouri—Kansas City.)

on business property in the downtown area. Contributions were voluntary, but the association was supported so well it could announce, 20 May 1908, that construction of the viaduct would begin within sixty days. Before June 1910, the structure was completed to the north line of Twenty-third Street. From there the terminal company extended it to the station plaza as a part of the construction of depot approaches.[26]

It was not surprising that a new station would inspire plans for a civic center. Several schemes were proposed. All of them became known collectively as the "Jarvis Hunt plan," though Hunt himself devised only two, a civic center arrangement and a boulevard plan for South Main Street. The civic center idea probably originated with Hunt. As early as April 1901, he wrote Kessler: "I will be ready with my drawings for the civic improvement in about ten days . . . and would suggest that we have a meeting of the Park Board and anybody else you may see fit to call in." Sixty years later a man who helped design the details of the station and its approaches wrote how "all of us identified with the terminal work became aware right from the very beginning, that the area to the South of the Station posed a challenging opportunity for the creation of a spacious plaza around which buildings of a public character could be grouped against a suitably landscaped Park."[27]

There were good reasons why the plans of Hunt and others rated so much popular consideration. People in and out of the city government wished to avoid a replica of notorious Union Avenue across from the proud new station. Their concerns inspired little Station Park, which the terminal company obligated itself to buy and deed to the city. The park would leave the ground immediately in front of the station plaza unsullied by beer halls and cheap hotels, but the flanks of the small reservation were exposed to all types of commercial building. A wider park, the *Journal* remarked, would be "out of the way of saloons and loafers." Hunt recognized that the uncontrolled land might invite "a lot of dinky 2–story buildings and bum saloons, and, oh, say, it's a crime. It's an outrage." On another occasion he said: "I found a 1–story building going up . . . this morning. Just a common red hot! And once you get a Union Avenue here you'll always have it. As for those buildings—oh, Lord!"28

The fact that Kansas City had no cultural center was another reason for designs that called for more than a small landscaped park. Its city hall and courthouse, both built in 1892 within the confines of the original town, were left in the backwash of the retail district's steady southward advance. Not only were the two buildings removed from the city's retail and residential centers, they were three blocks from each other. The library was six years newer, better designed, and much closer to downtown. The post office was three blocks closer still, but the organization of a civic center around it and the library would have involved condemnation of expensive business properties. Far on the other side of downtown, at Thirteenth and Central streets, stood Convention Hall, important to a civic center scheme but isolated from all the other component buildings. The plans received an added stimulus in 1911, when a wealthy woman bequeathed the city $300,000 for an art museum.29

A completed civic center, or at least a broad park on which civic buildings could rise as funds permitted, was further thought necessary because it would be a distinguished badge of municipal progress and proof of civic pride. "If the railroads are willing to spend 4 million dollars [sic] in an improvement that will be a lasting benefit the city should reciprocate by spending some money to make the surroundings attractive," said a city official shortly after the south side station site was announced. Hunt paused on an inspection tour of his terminal to ask what sort of impression Kansas City would make on the distinguished people who planned to attend the station's grand opening. "And what will they see? They'll see . . . Kansas City's front yard, eh? Yes, they'll see those clay banks, if Kansas City doesn't do something." When Hunt spoke to the public affairs committee of the Commercial Club he said sharply, "That park out in front is to be Kansas City's work, and if it's bad it's going to show you up."30

Civic center ideas began tumbling forth soon after the original station plans were announced. The *Journal* unveiled the first plan to be made public, a narrow park running south from the station to Penn Valley Park along an extension of Gillham Road. In the summer of 1907 Kessler presented a civic center plan based on conferences with Hunt and others. Public buildings were placed in groups from Broadway on the west side of the terminal to Grand Avenue on the east, a distance of six blocks. From an intersection at Twenty-fifth and Main streets that was decorated at its center with a tall monument on a circular base, short radial streets interspersed with small parks ran to the station plaza. Kessler's plan connected the civic center to Penn Valley Park and provided an entrance to the park in the shape of an ornamental traffic separation at the junction of Grand Avenue and Main Street. No trace of the bluff in front of the station would remain. Despite his devotion to naturalistic landscape architecture, Kessler believed the hill was too formidable for any designer to perch a civic center on top of it.[31]

More than two years passed before Hunt revealed part of his own plan. "That is," he said, "to widen Main Street to two hundred feet, or even more, . . . and cut it down to a 2 or 3 percent grade." Main Street would then carry northbound traffic into the station, or it could be diverted to other streets at Twenty-sixth Street and enter the station plaza after turning east around the base of the big hill south of the station.[32]

The *Star* gave generous if irregular support to Hunt's proposal for several years. The architect's blunt, colorful speech, his strong opinions, and his faith in Kansas City, "the best city in America," he called it, all attracted Editor Nelson to him. Nelson probably knew about Hunt's Main Street and civic center plans before the *Star* publicized and supported them. Hunt's associate of those years recalled that "the Colonel and Hunt met frequently and must have discussed the matter." At any rate the *Star* fell in behind the plans editorially on 25 November 1909, the same day that its morning edition carried Hunt's announcement of his plan. A month and a half later the plan was attacked in a letter to the *Star*. Among other things, its detractor claimed, the widening would result in steep grades for cross streets, wipe out business property as far back as the alleys, and be ruinously expensive.[33]

Undaunted, Hunt replied with a vast civic center plan that recalled the Court of Honor at the Chicago fair, except that Hunt arranged his buildings in a semicircle and designed them in the Italian Renaissance substyle. Opposite the station, at the deepest part of the curve, stood an enormous domed city hall, reminiscent of his uncle's Administration Building, and flanked by four identical but undomed buildings. The two on the east would serve as a post office and library–art museum, while the other group would house a county building and a hall of records or armory. The city hall sat astride a huge circular area that diverted Main Street's great double boulevard to Grand Avenue. Hunt's plan also provided an elaborate multilevel approach to the station for commercial, carriage, and trolley traffic. Whatever its aesthetic or fiscal merits, Hunt's design was spacious and well located on the rim of downtown, a convenient walk or trolley ride from retail and residential sections alike.[34]

No organized support for Hunt's scheme developed. Therefore, he and D. J. Haff, the park board's president, agreed to modest improvements to little Station Park. A preliminary plan for expensive grading was abandoned in favor of smoothing, terracing, and sodding.[35]

The civic center portion of Hunt's plan might languish, but the *Star* continued to press for adoption of his Main Street boulevard idea. It called "for a broad thoroughfare on South Main Street—250 feet wide—from the Union Station south." On 20 July 1912, the Thirty-first and Main Street Improvement Association, a businessmen's organization formed to consider the problems of a Main Street trafficway, met to pass on the "Jarvis Hunt plan." Its unanimous resolution demanded grading Main Street through the hill at its existing width and rejected Hunt's idea. When the chairman of the meeting asked, "Where are those that favor the Jarvis Hunt plan?" the audience shouted, "No one favors it." A former city engineer told the group that the "widening of Main Street to 250 feet would wipe out productive business territory and you cannot expect the owners of this property to attend your meeting and dance in jollification over the confiscation of their goods and chattels." Despite the *Star*'s rantings against "men of little faith," the street was lowered through the hill at its old width, about 100 feet.[36]

A variety of proposals for beautification of the station surroundings were made between 1911 and the date of the station's opening in 1914. The Commercial Club undertook the most promising action when it appointed a "committee of twelve on the station park project" to talk with city officials and make a formal report. Opinion within the committee divided over whether to adopt the "large park" idea, involving the land embraced in the Kessler and Hunt civic center schemes, or something more modest. The less pretentious and less expensive proposal, which was adopted, called for acquisition of a four-block front of land between Main and Central streets, extending south to Penn Valley Park, two blocks away at its nearest point. The committee also proposed a broad trafficway connecting Broadway on the west with Gillham Road on the east. The price tag for the two plans was $1.7 million. Both proposals became reality in the next decade, when they were adapted to the Liberty Memorial, the city's giant World War I monument, a great limestone terrace topped by a 217-foot stone shaft that towers above the Union Station.[37]

For the time being there would be no great monument, civic center, or park. Spasmodic newspaper agitation, some architect's sketches, and a Commercial Club report were inadequate in the face of the high cost of the proposed civic center and the organized opposition to the trafficway plan. The effective coalition of determined men that built the city's park system had disintegrated by the end of 1914. Meyer was dead. Nelson, seventy-three and almost blind, had but a few months to live. Haff's legal battles were a decade behind him, and he never became enthusiastic about the civic center plan during his presidency of the park board. Kessler, estranged from both Nelson and Kansas City, fulfilled the duties of his minor consulting job with the park board from his home in St. Louis. No local men of such diverse yet complementary talents and temperaments took their places.

The city was denied its civic center, but it still had its Union Station. After delays and postponements, the grand opening was announced for 30 October 1914, with an additional day of celebration to precede the scheduled train service, which began on 1 November. At 2:47 on the afternoon of 30 October the guns of Battery B, emplaced on the hill south of the station, roared the official opening salute. The crowd, estimated at 100,000, poured into the building. Those who could not get inside filled the plaza, the streets, and the viaducts over the tracks for blocks around.[38]

The station they saw was one of the largest in the United States. The marble walls of the ticket lobby rose ninety feet from the polychromatic marble floor to a flat plaster ceiling rich in ornamental relief of bright red, blue, and gold. The lobby, almost the size of a football field, was flanked by three-story wings that appeared low by comparison. The waiting room had a lower ceiling less rich in detail, but it stretched 450 feet north over the train yard and could hold ten thousand people at one time. Outside, the style was French Renaissance, severely modified, and finished in gray-white Bedford limestone and New England granite. Three great arched windows began above the second-story level of the ticket lobby and looked out over the plaza. The grading of little Station Park was, unfortunately, incomplete. As soon as the station filled, the band played "America" and the audience sang. The noise of the crowd and the acoustics in the vast lobby made it impossible for more than a few to hear the ceremonies on the speakers' platform.[39]

THE PARK AND BOULEVARD SYSTEM

Hunt's Union Station provided a climax to the waning City Beautiful movement. When the station opened, Kansas City's park and boulevard system was substantially complete. The story of its development from 1900 to 1914 is a story of technical success and increasing recognition. At the turn of the century the newly acquired parkland lay largely undeveloped. The park maintenance tax was still in litigation, and the receipts from those who paid it were used almost entirely for maintenance of existing facilities. Therefore basic improvements such as drives, curbs, artificial lakes, and shelter buildings had to be squeezed from small annual budgets or left undone for another year.

To speed this piecemeal building two private improvement associations began to agitate, early in 1903, for a park improvement bond issue. The two organizations, the Southeast Improvement Association and the Forestry and Artistic Improvement Association, met with Kessler, appointed study committees, and held joint meetings in members' homes to examine the bond questions. The president of the Southeast Improvement Association lived in Nelson's neighborhood and the editor himself may have been a member. At

The last of the falsework stands in the cavernous ticket lobby of the Union Station, late March 1914. (George A. Fuller Co. Photograph Collection. Courtesy, Joint Collection, Western Historical Manuscript Collection and State Historical Society of Missouri Manuscripts, University of Missouri—Kansas City.)

UNION STATION, KANSAS CITY, MISSOURI.   JARVIS HUNT, ARCHITECT.

The ticket lobby of the Union Station, ready for its grand opening on 30 October 1914. (George A. Fuller Co. Photograph Collection. Courtesy, Joint Collection, Western Historical Manuscript Collection and State Historical Society of Missouri Manuscripts, University of Missouri—Kansas City.)

any rate the association received a good press. In March these organizations were joined by improvement associations, professional groups, and business clubs, including the Commercial Club, which drew up a long list of needed bond improvements. Representatives of the organizations met with city officials and formed a bond commission to be divided into subcommittees to study the feasibility of each bond proposal and the amount of money it should receive. The commission chose the president of the park board as its chairman. The park subcommittee subsequently recommended half a million dollars for park and boulevard improvement.[40]

Then Nature intervened on the side of the bond commission. The same 1903 flood that poured into the old Union Depot snapped the big water pipe from Kansas, where the main reservoir was. Citizens of those districts deprived of water for two weeks turned out in September to register large majorities for the new waterworks bonds and other bond proposals. The *Star* was always anxious for park propositions to stand on their own merits, yet it recognized that the total vote, well over the two-thirds majority needed for the park bonds, was greater because the park issues rode the coattails of popular interest in a safe water supply. Somewhat more grudgingly it confessed that the propositions carried in the Pendergast wards, not so much because their inhabitants loved civic beauty, but because they were interested in the employment extensive public improvements would provide.[41]

There were disappointments, too, for City Beautiful advocates. The bond money transformed the parks slowly, after a long initial delay. A clause in the unsuccessful 1905 charter would have given the park board power to impose restrictions aimed at keeping the residential character of "any boulevard, parkway, road or avenue" under its control. A similar section passed in the charter of 1908, but with the crucial provision that it would not apply to parkways established prior to the charter's taking effect. In 1910 a park bond issue failed by 163 votes of the needed two-thirds majority.[42]

The vicissitudes of local politics decreed that the park boards that would superintend most of the impressive improvements would have no link with the boards that guided legal affairs to the point at which vigorous construction could begin. Despite several changes in board membership, Meyer, the greatly admired and respected businessman, remained its president until 1901. Then a new mayor wanted his own board as well as a counselor to replace Haff. Personnel changes paled beside the tremendous physical changes park improvements wrought in the city during the first fifteen years of the twentieth century. Kessler and his talented assistant Park Superintendent Wilbur H. Dunn forged chains of parkways and boulevards binding the city's most distant parks into a comprehensive and coherent development.[43]

Penn Valley Park was one of the gems of the system. For years its natural beauty was scarred by cheap houses and stores. When they were auctioned off, the land was pocked with old cellar excavations and defiled by rubbish heaps. Because it tilted steeply south to north into the bed of O.K. Creek along the belt line, runoff water from the south and from higher ground on the east and west gouged the hills, tearing away topsoil needed for newly planted trees, shrubs, and fields of grass. To enlist this damaging drainage in the cause of beauty Kessler threw an earth dam thirty feet high across the low northwest section, partly filled the basin thus created with earth and allowed the water to spread over the rest, forming a pretty artificial lake. Not all of the park drained into the lake, so a system of underground drains, "as complete as if it were to serve a similar area covered with houses," was built to catch the destructive little rivulets and funnel them harmlessly away. Drives with cement gutters to carry more water away from their macadam roadbeds wound for over three miles through the 130-acre park. In places where the roads had to be cut into limestone cliffs, the stone was prevented from sliding by specially constructed masonry foundations designed to blend with the rocky ledges above. A series

Beaux-Arts neoclassicism in the "middle landscape," the Colonnade in North Terrace (now Kessler) Park, about 1905. (George E. Kessler Collection, Missouri Historical Society, St. Louis. Reproduced by permission.)

of lookout points afforded a succession of shifting views of the city's business and industrial districts. By 1904 the traces of small houses and shops were gone and Penn Valley Park presented a finished appearance.[44]

Improvement in other parks was almost as dramatic. The slow work of improving West Terrace, last of the original triad of big parks to clear the courts, was not complete in 1906, but North Terrace Park had its long, winding Cliff Drive and Swope Park its streetcar connection with the city over a boulevard built by the county. Kessler recalled in his 1906 report that North Terrace was derided years earlier because it was a supposed "squirrel pasture," which was "too rugged for a goat to climb." The views over the Missouri River from the palisades along Cliff Drive are unmatched in any other Kansas City park. Spring Valley Park, an undeveloped tract once used as a quarry, just east of the Paseo extension at Twenty-eighth Street, was brought into the system in 1902 as a result of a campaign by area residents.[45]

Trees were the outstanding adornment in the parks and along the boulevards. Because Kessler always planted them close together, the boulevards' parkings became nurseries from which he took alternate trees for planting in newer parks and parkways. Trees numbered 35,000 by the summer of 1904, with elms predominating over European lindens, hard maples, and other varieties.[46]

Recreational facilities expanded with the system. On 4 July 1901, the first public bath, a swimming pool privately built from a fund begun by Nelson and others, opened in the Parade, a twenty-one-acre playground at the south end of the original Paseo. The park board established playgrounds in the Parade and West Terrace Park. Women's clubs donated play equipment for old Shelley Park, and in 1907 the board located additional playgrounds in the crowded north end. Though Kessler in 1909 scoffed at the "so-called play-ground having a lot of expensive directors and sociological workers," by 1911 he admitted the value of supervised playgrounds. Neighborhood playgrounds under the control of "trained attendants, directing the children's play," taught mutual respect and concern for public property. His qualified acceptance of organized play capitulated to public demand, but he was determined not to surrender his own conception of recreation without a fight. The trouble with the "average 'playground' enthusiast"—who thought in terms of "violent exercise"—was the disregard for "the value of natural beauty as an induce-ment to enjoy out-door recreation in surroundings that appeal to and educate the eye of a growing child."[47]

Kessler's objection has been characterized as merely his half of a light skirmish, an "intramural sniping" between people who argued over the most effective mechanism of social control. It was more than that for Kessler, because he believed profoundly in the elevating and improving effects of naturalistic landscape. The rising playground movement threatened deeply held convictions as well as traditional park budgets and acreage.[48]

By 1915 the Kansas City park and boulevard system had assumed the shape it would show, with minor additions, for half a century. The great North Terrace and Swope parks were linked with chains of connecting boulevards that passed through or near all the interior parks and some of the playgrounds. Swimming pools, tennis courts, play equipment, and other recreational facili-ties dotted the parks and parkways. The Paseo, built only to Eighteenth Street under Kessler's original plan, swept in an alternate series of formal and natu-ralistic roadways to Seventy-ninth Street, the city limits. Flanking the Paseo on the west, Gillham and Rockhill roads carried traffic to the junction with Meyer Boulevard, which ran eastward to Swope Park. Farther west another series of boulevards joined West Terrace, Penn Valley, and Roanoke parks before linking with Meyer Boulevard. East of the Paseo, Benton, Van Brunt, and Linwood boulevards could carry travelers from the most remote parts of North Terrace Park southward to broad Swope Parkway, the principal route to the gigantic park. These boulevards and their east-west links tied not just the parks but the entire city together. By April 1915 the cost of the system—including condemnation, maintenance, construction, expenses, salaries, and equipment—had climbed to over $14.7 million. In 1920, when the system had expanded very little from 1915, Kansas City enjoyed 1,992.25 acres of parks; 676 parkway acres, and almost 90 miles of boulevards and drives.[49]

The maturing system brought praise from local laymen. Real estate men commended it for opening up attractive residential areas and raising property values. The Board of Public Welfare's 1912 housing report, while it emphasized both the prevalence and effects of substandard housing, applauded the park board's slum clearance role. The park board's recreation report of the same year asserted that the recreational values of the system reached far beyond a simple statistical compilation of people using swings or baseball diamonds. "We should recognize that every pleasure ride on a boulevard, every stroll in Swope Park, and every ball game on school or park property is a part of public recreation, even if no records are kept of most of these forms."[50]

Parallel developments complemented the growth of the park and boulevard system. One of these was a movement for tree planting along residence streets, supported by private groups, including the Municipal Improvement Association. In March 1899 the city council approved and the mayor signed an ordinance providing for a city forester, and by August the city had let contracts for about 7,200 trees. By 1901 the *Journal* could assure its readers "that more progress is being made here along the line of arboriculture than in either Chicago or St. Louis."[51]

The *Star* campaigned for a time against industrial smoke pollution and installed a smoke abatement device for its own pressrooms. Private associations formed for the purpose of bringing lands into the park system, improving those already incorporated, or beautifying certain neighborhoods continued to flourish. In 1906 the council passed an ordinance establishing the Kansas City Art Commission, a body created to "approve all works of art before they are accepted by the city and decide upon their location" and to advise city departments on the aesthetic merits of various projected improvements. Although Kessler was a member, the commission was not notably effective.[52]

Indeed, Kessler grew increasingly alienated from Kansas City. Geographic circumstances were partly to blame. His work in St. Louis, first with the world's fair and then with the restoration of Forest Park, the exposition site, required his presence much of the time. His growing Eastern clientele could be reached easily by train from St. Louis, while a trip east from Kansas City required a change of trains. To be nearer the center of his activity, he moved to St. Louis in 1911 and returned to Kansas City only for brief stays. Geography aside, what Kessler believed were attempts to rob him of his rightful importance in the city's planning history hurt him deeply. He was greatly irritated by the confusion of Frederick Law Olmsted's single visit at the time of the World's Columbian Exposition with an original contribution to Kansas City's planning. Typical of this disproportionate emphasis on Olmsted was the *Star*'s comment that plans for part of Gladstone Boulevard were "prepared by George E. Kessler of this city and the late Frederick Law Olmstead [sic] of Boston." In 1902 Kessler wrote the secretary of the Lincoln Park, Chicago, commissioners, "Except in one way, I have been alone in the selections, outlining, and finally designing and in construction of the entire Kansas City park work." He warmly acknowledged Meyer's support and assistance, but he emphasized that Olmsted's contribution was confined to "a report . . . approving in general terms the selections made."[53]

More galling were the attempts of Nelson's admirers to credit the editor with the success of the park and boulevard system. To Haff, who had written him, "for after all your K. C. job will be your 'opus magnus,'" Kessler replied that "the Kansas City job is not an 'opus magnus' for me, but will be for, first, the owner of the *Star*, as per recent magazine stories to that effect, and next to any one whom he chooses to exploit in that field." Ridicule of his work may have hurt Kessler more than slights from Nelson. The fountain he designed at Fifteenth Street and the Paseo apparently suffered from a chronic lack of water pressure and was turned on only at intervals, when the water rippled gently over its tiers instead of gushing and spouting. The *Star* lampooned the fountain, describing it as a "something" which "resembled a cross between an Egyptian pyramid and pigs in clover," and with the water turned off, "the monument to a mistaken idea." Eventually the fountain was demolished and replaced with a flower garden. Possibly Kessler had that article in mind when he wrote that "Kansas City's papers and much of Kansas City's expression with reference to my affairs there, in recent years, has been so nasty in spirit and temper, that I have cared very little whether any of it . . . exists or not." On another occasion he confided that "it had been so repeatedly brought to me that Kansas City had treated me so very generously, that it in part accounts for my leaving the city, and I would not seriously object to a complete severance of relations."[54]

It was not the last time that Kessler's sensibilities would be shocked over what he believed was unfair treatment. Nonetheless his Kansas City work was the springboard for his successful career in consulting landscape architecture. Not only Denver and Dallas, but Memphis, Cincinnati, and Salt Lake City, among many others, employed him. Kansas City remained his "opus magnus" and the monument to a remarkable coalition of City Beautiful activists.

10 ◆ The Collapse of the Civic Center Dream in Seattle

The Bogue Plan and the Circumstances of Its Defeat

In the autumn of 1911, in the twilight of the City Beautiful movement, Virgil G. Bogue's magnificent *Plan of Seattle* was published in oversize book form. Its stunning designs encompassed the area from the Snohomish County line on the north to Orillia, twelve miles southeast of downtown, and from Puget Sound to Lake Washington's eastern shore. Bogue traced out extensions of the graceful boulevards created or planned by the Olmsted Brothers firm, as well as new highways, rail lines, and recreation areas. In the city itself he projected reorganized steam and electric railways while he thrust new traffic arteries through the clashing street grids. He planned an extensive harbor redevelopment. For the nearly vacant Denny regrade, north of downtown, he designed an elaborate civic center. Nearby, facing Queen Anne Hill, he located a union passenger station with a soaring tower. Bogue's vision was extravagant and comprehensive. His ambitious proposals were detailed, often including legal descriptions. His illustrations were instructive, while his prose was almost always lucid.[1]

For five months, Seattle citizens debated the "Bogue plans," as they were called, in neighborhood meetings, pamphlets, and the press. On 5 March 1912, the voters emphatically rejected the plan. The vote was 24,966 against, only 14,506 for. A look at the plan's genesis and development and at the debate over its acceptance will demonstrate that the defeat at the polls stemmed from three related problems.[2]

The first problem involved the efforts of Seattle's design professionals to override or ignore the legal and political basis of comprehensive city planning. Astute planners long had recognized the need for expert urban design and for flexibility in its application. A park board or other urban agency would adopt a professionally prepared plan as a guide that would permit both gradual construction as a city's funds allowed and changes compatible with the overall plan as growth required. Traditionally, the plan was legally nonbinding. Only

Bogue proposed a civic monument for a promontory overlooking Puget Sound. (Bogue, *Plan of Seattle*. Courtesy, Special Collections Division, University of Washington Libraries.)

the bond issues and contracts necessary to construct and maintain the planned improvements were matters of legal obligation. Under this arrangement, the plan would be sensitive to sociopolitical realities. It would include features such as a park or square widely desired for a particular location. It would contain nothing likely to offend or alienate a section of the city, significant blocs of voters, or important economic interests. It would obligate the tax-payers for reasonable amounts over the years of its development. The process was a familiar one in Seattle and in scores of other American cities.

The disadvantage of this arrangement was that a discretionary plan might be altered beyond recognition or remain unbuilt. In Seattle, the professionals proposed to eliminate such possibilities. They would impose a practically mandatory plan on the city, elevate the expert to a position of design control, and ensure the realization of a comprehensive plan despite the vicissitudes of electoral politics and the struggles among interest groups. Although the circumstances involving the adoption of mandatory language are not entirely clear, it is likely that only a minority of the design professionals and their allies consciously strove to overturn the accepted planning relationships. They all shared responsibility, however, for what proved to be a miscalculation fatal to the Bogue plan.

The other two problems were almost as serious as the first. The Bogue plan was a topographically insensitive design based on its author's premise that engineers could subdue landforms no matter what the cost or institutional dislocation. And the city's political leaders, while effective in some respects, were indifferent to comprehensive planning.

The drive for what later became the Bogue plan originated within the Washington State Chapter (WSC) of the American Institute of Architects, an organization concerned with professional advancement. The WSC worked to expand the role of the independent, apolitical expert in local government. During the first decade of the twentieth century, it lobbied for an improved design of the municipal building, for an art commission, and, citing greater efficiency, for a building department independent of the city engineer's office, replete with a building commission and a board of appeal. The WSC intended that some of the appointees to the new board be architects. It had an active civic improvement committee and, by the end of 1907, a general committee on a civic center.[3]

In May 1908 A. Warren Gould, a WSC member, stepped before the Commercial Club to present an elaborate plan for a civic center, plaza, esplanade, and other improvements radiating from the hill directly east of downtown. He had arrived at his sweeping scheme after consultation with the mayor and the Board of Public Works. The next month, he announced that he and his supporters would secure a state enabling act to create a commission "of representative men to formulate a comprehensive plan of civic improvement for Seattle." A charter amendment later became the chosen instrument. Other than that, Gould's proposal incorporated the basic idea for the commission that eventually oversaw Bogue's work. "Every commercial body in the city should be represented," Gould declared. "Business men, workingmen, architects, lawyers, clergy, bankers, as well as the various city departments, should be included." After a plan won commission endorsement, he said, "it should, of course, be submitted to the people for their consideration and approval." Once adopted, "this large plan would be followed." For under Gould's formula, implementation would be practically automatic, and the plan would be removed from any further involvement in electoral or administrative politics. The implications for professional control of the planning process were not lost on Gould.[4]

Six months after Gould's remarks, the planning movement had crystallized. At the end of January 1909 the WSC organized a meeting of almost a hundred architects, other professionals, and businessmen to establish the Municipal Plans League (MPL). The transition was quickly and smoothly worked. A WSC meeting adjourned, to be immediately reconvened with all those present as the first meeting of the MPL. In its already prepared constitution and bylaws the organization pledged itself to a comprehensive plan. The constitution included the "Gould formula" in somewhat different language.[5]

The MPL's executive committee spent most of 1909 publicizing the planning idea and developing a united front in favor of an authoritative planning commission with the chamber of commerce, the Commercial Club, and the WSC. In November, representatives of the four organizations formulated a proposed charter amendment and submitted it to the city council, which accepted it for inclusion on the March 1910 general election ballot. The proposed amendment provided for a municipal planning commission of twenty-one members drawn partly from the city council, county commissioners, and various city boards. Other representatives were to be nominated by commercial, professional, and labor groups and confirmed by the mayor. The amendment permitted the commission to employ up to three experts to devise a comprehensive plan, and it allowed a special tax to be levied for their salaries, staff assistance, and office space. The commission was to meet regularly and frequently, supervise and approve the work of the experts, and submit the completed plan to the city council no later than 30 September 1911. The "Gould formula" binding the city to the plan appeared in Section 8: "If a majority of the voters voting thereon shall favor the adoption of said City Plan . . . it shall be adopted and shall be the plan to be followed by all City officials in the growth, evolution and development of said City of Seattle, until modified, or amended at some subsequent election."[6]

Such wording was designed to ensure that the architects and planners would reshape the city unimpeded by politicians and the public. The decision to apply the Gould formula was the first of three decisions that would undermine the acceptance of a comprehensive plan for Seattle.

Support for the amendment and the planning idea came from traditional sources such as the chamber of commerce and from influential individuals, including the city engineer, Reginald H. Thomson. The Workingmen's League, an early-day political action committee, endorsed the amendment, as did the Seattle Central Labor Council. The MPL established a speaker's bureau to educate audiences in the benefits of city planning. The supporters of planning dealt in abstractions unconnected to the costs, removals, and disruptions required for a concrete plan. There was no serious challenge to the practically coercive language in Section 8, and no concerted opposition to planning. The amendment carried each of the fourteen wards, rolling up 13,852 votes in favor, 7,371 opposed—"the largest majority ever cast for an amendment to the charter of the City of Seattle." It was a resounding endorsement of the conception of comprehensive planning.[7]

By late spring the Municipal Plans Commission (MPC) was operating. During the summer of 1910 it further crippled the Bogue plan. "After considerable debate," the commission decided to plan for an area of 150 square miles and a projected population greater than a million. Realizing such a plan would be very expensive. The "considerable debate" may have come from the politicians on the MPC, who shared the public's concern for great tax obligations. The planning-oriented commissioners may have responded to the example of Daniel H. Burnham's *Plan of Chicago*, metropolitan in scope, published the year before. In any case, the city was now saddled with a virtually mandatory, metropolitan plan of enormous cost.[8]

Meanwhile a committee of the MPC was moving toward the second fateful circumstance, the decision to hire Bogue. Dominated by Thomson, one of its most prominent members, the committee was to pick a group of experts and then narrow the choice to the three that the planning amendment allowed. The three were Bogue, a civil engineer; Bion J. Arnold, a public transit engineer; and John C. Olmsted, park and boulevard designer and consultant to the park board. But Thomson recommended that Bogue alone be hired. To understand why, and why Bogue designed an unnecessarily costly and topographically disastrous plan, a brief reference to the careers and attitudes of both men is necessary.[9]

As city engineer from 1892, Thomson combined the breadth of vision and determination needed to produce water and sewer systems for a burgeoning city. He was a keen, tough-minded, transplanted Hoosier, whose power rested on his authority, granted by the city charter, to control utilities extensions. He refused to admit that his success resulted "from the fact that I was a politician, because of all things, I [am] that the least."[10] In reality, Thomson had an excellent political sense.

Thomson's sympathy with the natural environment was limited to allowing water to run downhill. He expanded the disruptive, expensive, but probably necessary regrades (sluicing and shoveling down Seattle's hills to provide gentler slopes and more buildable sites). Seattle, a few park reservations aside, was to him a vast field to be sluiced into Elliott Bay, paved over, or built upon. He lacked the landscape architect's sense of the landscape as an artifact to be preserved and enhanced for human enjoyment.

Bogue was cut from the same cloth. He built an impressive career on defeating natural barriers in the name of improved commerce. After a brief stint with the senior Olmsted, Bogue located a trans-Andean railroad in Peru. Next he drew the Northern Pacific Railway through Stampede Pass in the Cascade Mountains. These triumphs sent him, literally and metaphorically, to the summit of his profession. Sixty-four in 1910, he was eager for a challenging new responsibility.[11]

Bogue and Thomson enjoyed a long-standing personal and professional friendship. Thomson wanted Bogue to be the sole expert, but he had to convince the committee and turn aside Olmsted, who was also interested in the job.

There was no love lost between Thomson and Olmsted. The first meeting of the two men did not go well, at least from the landscape architect's point of view. "I felt obliged to accept Thompson's [sic] hospitality at lunch," he wrote, but Olmsted complained of feeling "decidedly chilly," refused the fried ham, and only sampled the vegetables. More than planning philosophies or dietary preferences separated the two men. To Thomson, Olmsted was an interloper, while to Olmsted, Thomson was a potential threat to the development of his plan. Further, the engineer's concerns for drainage and traffic relief clashed with Olmsted's naturalistic impulses. A sewer incident in Washington Park shocked Olmsted and the park commission into a realization of the sort of man Thomson was. In August 1904, James F. Dawson, an Olmsted assistant, reported that Thomson's crews had "brought in a sewer built of plank and with the sides not specially tight," a sewer emptying into the park stream, "thereby destroying the brook for all purposes and beauties we had anticipated." Thomson offered to rectify this visual and olfactory disaster with a septic tank. Dawson scoffed at the idea, declaring "that the brook would be of no further value to us for the park and in fact it would be a severe detriment to the enjoyment" of the park. The park commissioners were dismayed by the situation and were "trying to find some way in which to have it obviated." Eventually the stream was restored, but not before the park commissioners endured more of Thomson's interference in their domain.[12]

Olmsted was only indirectly involved in most of Thomson's intrusions into park matters, but the two went head to head over the city engineer's plan to extend Stone Avenue north through Woodland Park and away from the shores of Green Lake. Olmsted recognized the need for a traffic street but protested against carving it through the playground area of the park. Thomson was, as usual, determined to have his way. Olmsted dug in. "I have the greatest admiration for Mr. R. H. Thomson in his capacity of City Engineer," he wrote a park commissioner in September 1907, "yet it seems to me that he might welcome the suggestions of a competent landscape architect when it comes to plans affecting the development of the city's parks, without implying any doubt as to his ability as a civil engineer." At one point Thomson appeared to capitulate but later returned to his ideal solution, a street as straight and on as easy a grade as possible. The dispute simmered until February 1909, when the street committee of the city council reported a bill favoring Olmsted's solution—a street at the eastern edge of Woodland Park, then following the lake contours.[13]

Thomson lost that one but had an opportunity to even the score when, in 1909, informal discussion turned to the selection of the city planning experts. It was apparent that Olmsted was considered a foregone choice as one of the triumvirate. Olmsted spoke to the January 1909 organizational meeting of the MPL and so was identified with the movement from its public beginnings. The "understanding," he wrote his wife, was "that there will be three, Mr. R. H. Thomson the City Engineer being one of them and myself another & an eastern architect, Cass Gilbert or D. H. Burnham being the third." Although Olmsted doubted the willingness of someone like Gilbert or Burnham to give adequate time to the project and was skeptical of the desire of Seattle citizens to tax themselves for a comprehensive plan, he harbored no doubts about his selection. Given the tacit understanding that Olmsted would be retained, Thomson had to make an overture to him. In June 1910 he informed Olmsted of the MPL's desire to use the landscape architect "more as a 'buffer' to keep parks & parkway enthusiasts from running the thing 'wild' than to devise anything elaborate or costly." What would Olmsted charge for the estimated seven months' work? "I told him $4,000 and expenses. They may think . . . that high but I rather think they will accept it." Later Thomson assured Olmsted of his belief that he would "be elected as a member of the board of experts."[14]

But Thomson was playing a double game, courting Olmsted while hoping to maneuver the job for Bogue. Scarcely two weeks after his letter to Olmsted, Thomson wrote Bogue: "I think that if it could be so arranged, you and I could handle this matter together. . . . If it could be done, I would like to work a scheme by which we would go together to Hamburg, Antwerp and other European ports of prominence and to Buenos Ayres, and possibly other ports in South America." By 1 September, Thomson was able to telegraph Bogue of the MPC's "unanimous" decision to hire him at a salary of $1,500 per month. Thomson got the job for his friend, probably on the grounds that he could work with Bogue and that one expert was cheaper than three.[15]

Thus the commission hired a man whose ideas would defy economy and topography. To be fair to Bogue, Seattle's hills and ridges posed nearly unsolvable planning problems. It might have been better for the larger plan had Bogue resisted the temptation to exploit the Denny regrade area and instead drawn a modest civic center incorporating the existing public property in the south end of downtown. Perhaps then he would not have alienated a powerful interest group, the south-end property holders.

Bogue arrived in late September and set to work. Besides designing, he directed an office force of three principal assistants, as many as five engineers, nine draftsmen, an architect, clerical assistants, and two field survey parties. He met frequently with MPC committees and attended a round of banquets. He worked quickly. By April 1911 he had selected a civic center site. By the end of June his entire plan was practically complete and extensively publicized. On 24 August he presented his finished product to the MPC, which ratified and forwarded it to the city council a fortnight before the charter deadline of 30 September. Significantly for later attacks on Bogue's work, the three votes against the plan came from city and county representatives, who probably were concerned about costs.[16]

Bogue's Insensitive Civic Center Plan

The *Plan of Seattle* was comprehensive, but for good reasons the debate following its publication focused disproportionately on the civic center and the adjacent railroad nexus. Whatever his engineering proclivities, Bogue believed in a "Civic Idea" or "Civic Consciousness; a consciousness demanding recognition of organic unity and intelligent system; recognition of the fact that community life is not an aggregation of unrelated parts and functions, . . . but a growth, a product, whose many elements are virtually interwoven and inter-dependent." He intended the civic center to express this "civic consciousness," just as he borrowed the design and the defense of his center from the ideal conceptions of the City Beautiful. He used a standard City Beautiful argument, urging purchase of the entire site before a surge in growth sent land prices soaring. Then he presented the economic and social benefits of a civic center. The grouping of public buildings would invite "economy in the conduct of business in and between the several city departments," while citizens would enjoy "a saving in time and money . . . spent in transportation" to scattered public buildings. A civic center should be a public gathering place. Grouped, harmonious buildings, properly spaced, would induce civic pride. Bogue emphasized the need for equal accessibility from all parts of the community. No wonder, for he claimed to have located his civic group at the population center and arterial "conflux" of the future city of a million.[17]

Bogue's happy find was at Fourth Avenue and Blanchard Street, three to four blocks beyond the north edge of downtown. It was the site of Thomson's recent engineering marvel, the reduction of Denny Hill, then and now known as the Denny regrade. Bogue revealed that more than traffic convergence had influenced his decision. The land would be cheap because it was almost vacant. His cost estimate was $3.5 million, reducible by one-third if the city and county sold their property in the southern part of downtown. The area, claimed Bogue, was of "suitable amplitude" and enjoyed "practical grades," unlike the already crowded and expensive south end, where a civic center

would preempt needed commercial space and wreak havoc on traffic patterns.[18]

Bogue's civic center design grouped six public buildings in an oval closed at
the south and slightly tapered at the north. A new major traffic street,
"Central Avenue," entered the center's southeastern arc, then ran north
through the center plaza. Central Avenue continued seven blocks to the plaza
of the proposed railroad passenger station, which faced west toward Queen
Anne Hill. The street met the station plaza, jogged west around it, then
continued north. At the civic center oval, a cross axis ran west to a water gate
on Elliott Bay. Bogue carried an eastern extension of the cross axis two blocks
to a proposed market area.

Unfavorable auguries for the Bogue plan appeared early. When, in July, the
MPC asked the city attorney for an opinion on its options, he replied that the
charter amendment required that the entire plan as approved had to be submitted to the council and to the voters. Parts of the plan could not be proposed
and others withheld, nor could alternative plans be suggested. In late August,
before the plan's formal publication, the North End Improvement Club protested the heavy grading necessary for one of Bogue's projected arterials. The
MPC was by then worried about the obligatory character of the plan. "The
plan is elastic," the commission declared in its letter of transmittal to the
council; "its adoption does not require any expenditure whatsoever; nor does
[it] exclude changes. . . . Its adoption means simply, the acceptance of it as a
plan of action." As a later legal opinion pointed out, however, such dis-
claimers did not offset the language of the charter amendment.[19]

Publication of the plan and a WSC banquet for Bogue occasioned another
wave of publicity. Organizational support was nevertheless limited to the
WSC and the Municipal League, a group of middle-class professionals and
businessmen devoted to civic reform. Both organizations had played prominent roles in defeating bond issues for new public buildings proposed while
Bogue was laboring over his designs. The proposals enjoyed the support of
wealthy property owners in the southern downtown section. In September
1910 the council proposed a $1 million bond issue for a new city hall to be
located on city property in the south end. After that proposition was defeated,
an effort to have the question resubmitted failed in the council by one vote.
Next a committee of citizens persuaded the county commissioners to place on
the ballot a $1.5 million proposal for a new courthouse in the same area. An
independent effort to secure space for an art museum east of the central
downtown area also faced the voters. Both propositions failed. Whatever
their merits, these schemes, except perhaps the art museum idea, were pat-
ently designed to forestall selection of the northern civic center site. The
WSC and the league prevailed partly because they convinced voters to
postpone their decision until Bogue completed his work.[20]

The pro–Bogue plan organizations soon discovered that it was easier to

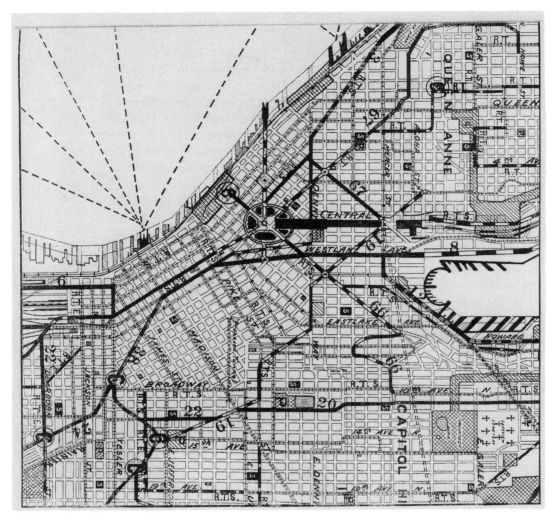

Virgil Bogue's proposed civic center and passenger rail complex, superimposed on a map of Seattle's existing streets. The proposed Central Avenue runs north to the future passenger station. A portion of Lake Union is visible in the center right, or north, portion of the map, while Volunteer Park lies east of the southern tip of Lake Union. (Bogue, *Plan of Seattle.* Courtesy, Special Collections Division, University of Washington Libraries.)

defeat the schemes of others than to advance their own. As early as 1 November, the WSC and Bogue decided against building a display model of the civic center. Possibly because a model would focus opposition as well as aspirations, "it would be better for the present not to urge that part of the plan." On 25 November the *Municipal League News* published an attack on the civic center as being "tinged too much with sentiment and the desire for an artistic show and not enough with economic reasoning." The author, Paul B. Phillips,

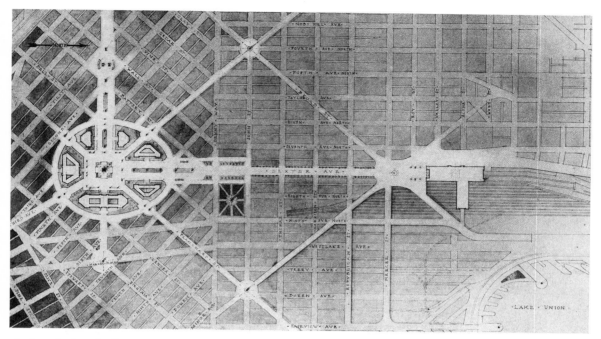

A closer look at the Bogue civic center, Central (Dexter) Avenue, plaza, and passenger station. This map clearly shows the east-west cross axis. (Bogue, *Plan of Seattle*. Courtesy, Special Collections Division, University of Washington Libraries.)

wrote for the southern downtown property owners, whether or not he was their direct spokesman. The owners opposed locating the center more than a mile away from their properties in the main business district of the city.[21]

Phillips's arguments against the Bogue plan and later dissents by the south-enders were self-interested but they were neither shallow nor unrefined. Phillips first protested running the proposed Central Avenue through the civic center, where heavy traffic was unnecessary. Then he turned to the twin matters of stability and specialized land use downtown. The financial district, he asserted, would remain in the south and south-central area of the business district. Most of the traffic to the post office, courthouse, city hall, and customs house came from this financial area, not from the developing retail section to the north or from the wholesale district farther south. Phillips was affirming the existence of an established functional subgrouping of downtown, which a civic center in Bogue's location would disrupt.

In late December the weekly *Argus* raised the issue of the deadening effect a compulsory plan would have on property in the path of proposed improvements. "The moment that this plan is adopted many acres of real estate will become unsalable." A property owner in the civic center with "nerve enough" might improve his holdings, but few others would do so, and all would confront extremely low resale prices and the vagaries of condemnation proceedings. The *Argus* criticized a plan that was binding once approved, yet subject—by the charter amendment's Section 8—to the vicissitudes of the ballot. "It would be possible to adopt the plan, hold up improvements for years on privately owned property and then change the plans so that the city would not take it after all." The action would leave the landowner with "a white elephant."[22]

Penetrating as these criticisms were, the Bogue plan's roughest going was yet to come. In February 1912 the Civic Plans Investigation Committee (CPIC) produced a thirty-one-page pamphlet analyzing the plan. It was a bombshell. Two legal opinions convincingly showed that at least parts of the plan would be binding, subject to future electoral uncertainties and, probably, to court decisions. There was little doubt that property in the path of the proposed improvements would have to be purchased, particularly the lands for the civic center, the arterial highways, and some parks and playgrounds.[23]

The CPIC scored some of its most telling hits against the civic center. The site, including the two axial streets, would cost, not Bogue's $3,500,000, but more than $5,500,000. Reconstruction would bring the total to more than $8,130,000, according to estimates of the CPIC's appraisers and engineer. Even if Bogue's figures were accurate, the city was within $2,928,130.17 of its bonded debt limit and thus unable to purchase the land, except through the adventitious sale of public property elsewhere. The center was so expensive because Bogue's elevations required topping much of the Denny regrade with fourteen to thirty feet of fresh fill. In other words, Bogue was proposing to rebuild a 100-foot hill only just knocked down and to bury all the newly created streets and other improvements. So much for the "slight change of grade" announced in the plan. And the cost of the "ornate" buildings Bogue envisioned was yet to be added![24]

Bogue's disregard for Seattle's regraded surface was matched by his indifference to its natural topography. His insensitive design was, after the bold strike for professional control, the second major deficiency of the planning process. Bogue's designs were acceptable in themselves, but he proposed moving too much earth to achieve them. The CPIC's pamphlet mercilessly revealed the drastic changes required to accommodate the new passenger station. The station was to face the east slope of Queen Anne Hill, an eminence graced on its upper elevations by spacious middle-class homes. On that slope Bogue planned cuts of up to eighty-one feet to route his proposed Central Avenue west and north of the station. "It is evident that this sort of scientific demolition . . . would produce a mile and a half of chaos, and make East Queen Anne Hill a scene of slides," the CPIC contended. The pamphlet estimated the plan's total costs at "well over $100,000,000," a staggering sum in an era when land prices and construction costs were many times less than those of the late twentieth century. The CPIC predicted that only "business depression and industrial stagnation" could follow the adoption of such a plan.[25]

Top, the Bogue civic center, looking south from a point above Central Avenue. The obvious expense of such an improvement, even if gradually developed, helped to defeat the Bogue plan in 1912. *Bottom*, Bogue sketched a view from his civic center looking north along Central Avenue toward the plaza and tower of the railroad passenger station. (Bogue, *Plan of Seattle*. Courtesy, Special Collections Division, University of Washington Libraries.)

The *Times*, which had already declared the civic center "a bit of ruinous folly," eagerly retailed the CPIC's conclusions on its editorial pages. Epithets such as "pall," "blight," and "inflexible" decorated these attacks. The Municipal League was an object of special scorn.[26]

Supporters of comprehensive planning fought back gamely, but they were on the defensive. Besides using the general City Beautiful arguments for efficiency, economy, and varied social benefits, they insisted upon the Bogue plan's flexibility and nonbinding character. A clever critic vitiated the last argument. If the people "are merely to vote" on the plan "just for the fun of voting," he replied, "there will be enough propositions submitted to them on the ballot . . . to furnish them all the amusement of that nature anyone could possibly ask for." The criticism was telling. A discretionary plan required no vote, yet Section 8 of the charter amendment called for electoral approval, after which the plan "shall be . . . followed." Section 8 also allowed for changes to the plan, but those who sought change had to organize a referendum. Problematic as the outcome might be, the fact that the plan could be overridden at all cast a shadow over Bogue's designs.[27]

Defenders of the plan extolled Bogue's qualifications, his expert study, and his critics' lack of comparable knowledge of, or immersion in, Seattle's problems. Thomson attacked "oratorical engineers" who believed they could improve on a year of Bogue's labors "in a few minutes of off hand talk." Such "advisory geniuses," he sneered, had failed to land jobs comparable to Bogue's. Thomson raised a central issue, that of the expert's relation to society, which a Bogue plan critic analyzed differently. "The people are in the position of a man whose architect has designed a dwelling for him," wrote Phillips. If the owner questioned elements of the plan, "the architect need not claim infallibility for himself [or] that the owner's judgment is at fault merely on the ground that the architect is an expert and the owner is not. It is up to the architect to defend the plans."[28]

The plan's defenders attacked the members of the CPIC, calling them a "Landlords' Trust" determined to maintain high rentals and property values in the southern business district. The argument was as effective as most ad hominem attacks usually are. The *Times* pointed out that three of the CPIC's leading lights also owned property in or near the area of Bogue's proposed civic center. Their motives were not as selfish, therefore, as the plan's advocates supposed. They wished to avoid the Bogue plan's "blighting effect" on property all over the city.[29]

How completely the plan's supporters were cornered became clear when the eminent engineer Hiram M. Chittenden wrote in defense of the plan: "There is perhaps a moral obligation to acquire the Civic Center tract at an early date because of the alleged cloud upon the development of the property." But he did not vouchsafe the source of the necessary funds in excess of the city's bonded debt limit. Another friend of the civic center asserted, without specific evidence, that piling sixteen feet of earth on top of the Denny regrade would save the cost of cutting elsewhere. As for the cuts on Queen Anne Hill he claimed, without mentioning any offers, that the railroads would bear the expense.[30]

Not only were the plan's defenders trapped by its inflexible and topographically insensitive nature, they could not overcome Seattle's unresponsive partisan politics. The two leading mayoral candidates of 1912 personified the problem. Hiram C. Gill cultivated a folksy manner, was hospitable to vice and graft, and was innocent of any civic vision. In 1910 he came out for a "'City Beautiful' . . . so long as it is a 'City Practical' and a 'City Economical,'" stock phrases obligating him to nothing. In 1912 he was noncommittal. His opponent and the victor, George F. Cotterill, was a reformer, a civil engineer, and a planner of single-system improvements. Cotterill's 1950 memoir revealed no understanding of comprehensive planning. He was an early opponent of Bogue's civic center. This third, partisan political barrier to the success of the Bogue plan might have been overcome had its friends been more attuned to the politics and economics of planning. But they had already made the decision to dissociate, as much as they could, the Bogue plan from traditional planning politics.[31]

WHY THE BOGUE PLAN FAILED

Several explanations have been advanced for the defeat of the Bogue plan, but most of them fail rudimentary analytical tests. One explanation is that the plan was submerged by other issues. It was not. The widely available *Plan of Seattle* and its summaries, the pamphlets broadcast by the CPIC and the Municipal League, the speakers dispatched by both sides to neighborhood meetings, and the tattoo of newspaper letters, editorials, and advertisements immediately preceding the vote force the conclusion that only a comatose or supremely indifferent citizen of Seattle would have been unaware of the Bogue plan, no matter how many inches of print were granted to other issues.[32]

Opposition from organized labor has been considered important to the voters' rejection of the plan. The Central Labor Council did recommend against the Bogue measure; it also opposed a $500,000 park bond issue that appeared on the same ballot. The park issue passed by nearly two to one. The park bonds carried every ward, matching their citywide margin in two of four wards supposedly containing the highest concentrations of workers who were likely to be union members. That these two propositions met opposite fates gainsays the influence of organized labor.[33]

A closely related assertion is that "it was the more prosperous workingmen who really torpedoed" the plan. The language implies that prosperous workingmen held the balance of power. Had they withheld their torpedoes or fired them at the plan's enemies, presumably the Bogue plan would have carried. The assertion is vulnerable on two grounds. First, its supporting analysis assumes upper-level blue-collar workers to have been concentrated in, and determining the vote of, four wards. But Janice L. Reiff's work on urbanization in Seattle suggests relatively low levels of residential segregation by occupation as late as 1910, casting doubt on the ability of any occupational group to control the vote in any ward.[34] Second, if the voters who actually voted on the issue in the wards identified as prosperous workingmen's had either refused to vote or voted yes, the result would have been the same: the other wards would have defeated the Bogue plan by a comfortable majority. Only if all the prosperous workingmen who had actually voted would have reversed their decisions and voted for the measure in the same numbers that they in fact voted against it and voted no as often as they had voted yes, would they have produced a change. The margin of victory would have been narrow: 21,974 for, 20,993 against. This hypothetical squeaker in favor of the Bogue plan is highly conjectural. To argue for this outcome is to argue for the plausibility of presenting the plan with a radical and convincing bias toward prosperous working people, while alienating no more than 980 voters in other socioeconomic categories. It is probably true that prosperous working people voted against the plan in a higher proportion than middle- and upper-income people. Such voting patterns may illustrate the class bias of early twentieth-century planning, class-consciousness, or class-based perceptions of civic responsibility, but they do not prove that prosperous working people "torpedoed" the plan.

Another line of reasoning credits elite businessmen—the southern downtown property owners—with defeating the Bogue plan. In this analysis the plan is the catalyst of a rupture between the elite, whose economic and political dominance was threatened, and the middle-class businessmen and professionals of the Municipal League, who saw planning as a means of asserting their control over a booming metropolis. This analysis is plausible insofar as it concerns the Municipal League, given the league's overwhelming endorsement of the plan on 13 January 1912, at a time when some opposition and little support had surfaced. But it does not explain why the arguments of a tiny elite were so compelling for the mass of voters, especially laboring men. The Municipal League assumed a connection between strident downtowners and deluded workingmen when it addressed a last, desperate advertisement to blue-collar workers. The League advised of the downtown property owners' anonymous ads featuring the decision by the Central Labor Council. "A vote for the plans is a vote against the landlords' trust," the League declared. The urging was unavailing. Working people would vote against the plan for their own reasons, regardless of the propaganda from other groups.[35]

Additional reasons for the failure of the Bogue plan have appeared under the rubric "tactical blunders." The charter amendment did not grant authority or funding for the MPC to continue after 30 September 1911. The commission disbanded, unable to carry on a fight for the plan it had approved. It is unclear, however, what even a vital MPC could have done to overcome an almost two-to-one negative vote. The Municipal League's speakers may have been uninspiring and poorly prepared, but that charge rests on only one account of a single meeting. Finally, the ballot was a lengthy and cluttered one, containing mayoral and council candidates, twenty-seven proposed charter amendments, two city propositions besides the Bogue plan, four bond issues, and eight Port of Seattle questions. Yet there is no proof that the voters were confused, either about the Bogue plan or about any other items.[36]

Thus far this review has followed the path of the partial explanations for the defeat of the Bogue plan: that voters rejected it for reasons inherent in their deference to certain types of leadership, their occupations, their places of residence, or their mental acuity. All of these explanations tend to obscure the fact that almost two-thirds of the voters, including a majority in each of fourteen wards, rejected the measure. Even in the University District—a bastion of the progressive, enlightened, proplanning middle class—the plan lost by 555 of the 3,071 votes cast. Under the circumstances, there must be broader, more inclusive reasons for the voters' decision. Two such reasons have been suggested. The first is blatantly antidemocratic, declaring voters incompetent to decide on the merits of the Bogue plan. The assertion is unacceptable, given the realities of political democracy and the need to analyze, not dismiss, electoral results. A second interpretation is that many Seattle voters had achieved a type of personal City Beautiful pastoralism and had turned inward, away from the city. But this view does not explain why they would vote for park bonds yet reject the Bogue plan. Nor does it explain why the pro-Bogue vote was proportionately higher in some outlying, pastoral wards than in others more urban.[37]

Better inclusive reasons for the negative vote exist. One of these is the new Port of Seattle, but it must be considered in the legal-political context of the Bogue plan. In 1911 the city and county voters created the port under state enabling legislation passed during the same year. The new entity made Bogue's elaborate harbor plans irrelevant unless the port commission independently adopted them. Further, the port commission could use its own bond funds to undertake specific projects directly related to the economic well-being of Seattle. In contrast to this carefully defined power, the Bogue plan obligated taxpayers to spend huge, if uncalculated, amounts on a myriad of improvements. The CPIC pamphlet made these points when it declared the Bogue plan "unnecessary" and the Port of Seattle bonds critically important. These arguments have been correctly credited with the plan's defeat; however, not enough emphasis has been given to their close relationship to the larger considerations of the binding nature of portions of the Bogue plan once adopted and the associated unacceptable costs.[38]

Another inclusive argument, that a voter might well approve of planning but object to some specifics of the Bogue plan, also is valid. But it, too, should be seen in the light of the more pervasive problem. The mandatory plan practically denied the city the freedom to pick and choose among projects and ensured large expenditures on improvements almost certain to displease some individuals or groups.[39]

Given modernist criticism of City Beautiful neoclassicism and formality, it is instructive to find aesthetic questions almost absent from the Bogue plan debates. Only Phillips condemned the civic center as an exercise in "artistic show" at the expense of the rational distribution of civic buildings, but he made no criticism of the design itself. The CPIC denounced the "ornate" buildings in the Bogue plan, but cost was the basis of its objection: "The ornate is extremely expensive both to build and to maintain."[40] Nor did the civic center's critics mount a charge against civic center theory or other City Beautiful planning ideas. Legal rigidity and incalculable costs, not aesthetics or sociology, concerned them.

EFFORTS TO REVIVE THE BOGUE PLAN

The Bogue plan, so soundly defeated, could not survive intact. But hope rose in the hearts of Bogue's partisans, for the site of the new courthouse was yet to be selected. If the county commissioners could be persuaded to locate the courthouse in the Denny regrade, then the county building would be the nucleus of a north-end civic center. J. M. Neil has skillfully related the ensuing struggle within the context of the battle over building height limitations and the contest between north-enders and south-enders. In summary, the former Bogue advocates organized into the Seattle Civic Center Association, designed to propagandize the benefits of the Fourth and Blanchard site. The Municipal League also entered the lists on the side of the northern location. The county commissioners were intent upon developing a county-owned block at Third Avenue and James Street on the south edge of downtown, and should they waver, the south-end property owners were on hand to firm up their resolve. City officials wished to rent space in a new south-end building to avoid scattered offices and high rentals. At a joint meeting of Mayor Cotterill, four councilmen, and the three commissioners, only one councilman argued for the Bogue site. His advocacy "brought out expressions from all the other conferees that there was no disposition to construct the start of a permanent civic center but that necessity demanded" a new public office building.[41]

The Civic Center Association nevertheless pressured the county commissioners to place the north-end proposal on the ballot. The Civic Center Association could not, however, control the dollar figures for each proposition, which the commissioners fixed at $950,000 for the building at Third and James and $1,400,000 for the land purchase near Fourth and Blanchard. The *Union Record* caught the spirit of the commissioners' decision when it declared that the choice was between King County voting "$950,000 for a county building . . . on a site in the heart of the business district . . . which it already owns and has paid for, or, . . . $1,400,000 for the purchase of a site for a county building, one mile from the center of the business district." On 5 November 1912 King County voters downed the "civic center" site almost as decisively as the Seattle voters had earlier defeated the Bogue plan. The vote against the north-end location was 31,206 to 18,123. Voters favored the south-end site 35,768 to 16,565.[42]

The vote settled nothing but instead precipitated a classic donnybrook. The rumbling of the opponents of the building proposed for the south end site burst into a roar. At issue was whether the county commissioners had fraudulently colluded or conspired to deceive the public about the type of building that could be built for the $950,000 bond funds. It was true that the commissioners' architect, A. Warren Gould, had drawn a skyscraper soaring twenty-three stories above the pavement, with a copper pyramid capping its impressive tower. The drawing was reproduced numerous times during the campaign, notably in advertisements promising "this building on this site" if the bond issue carried. It was true, too, that one commissioner confessed that the amount for the building had been reduced to $950,000 because the commissioners feared voter rejection of a larger figure. It was true that, after the bond issue, the worst fears of skeptical opponents were realized. Not even seven floors of the pictured building could be built for $950,000, a possibility bruited about during the campaign. Indeed, it was shown to be practically impossible to build any useful portion of the structure for $950,000.[43]

The Municipal League investigated, found fault with the commissioners, and took them to court to prevent the issuance of the bonds. In so doing, the league virtually sounded the death knell of the Bogue civic center. It dropped the issue of the site, asserting that it only wanted an honest appraisal of building costs, followed by a second, fully informed vote. Meanwhile the Council of the Washington State Chapter of the American Institute of Architects recommended Gould's expulsion from the WSC on the grounds of unprofessional conduct during the bond issue campaign. The man whose 1908 civic center idea had catalyzed the movement for the Bogue plan fell into professional disgrace. A few months later, in December 1913, the Washington Supreme Court decided against the Municipal League. In the absence of proven fraud or a ballot commitment to build a certain type of structure, the court held, the commissioners were free to do as they wished. The court could not inquire into the motives or assumptions of voters.[44]

The civic center plan was dead beyond revival. In 1914 plans for a municipal auditorium fizzled, but comprehensive planning was eclipsed in any event. Beautification and planning proposals were limited to such matters as vacant lot gardens, drinking fountains and flower baskets in the commercial district, or demands that the park board divert more funds to playgrounds. Meanwhile, the Bogue plan rested in limbo beside the comprehensive planning ideal. More than fifty years passed before journalists, planners, and historians wrote much about Bogue's ambitious designs. Then they praised his sweeping vi-

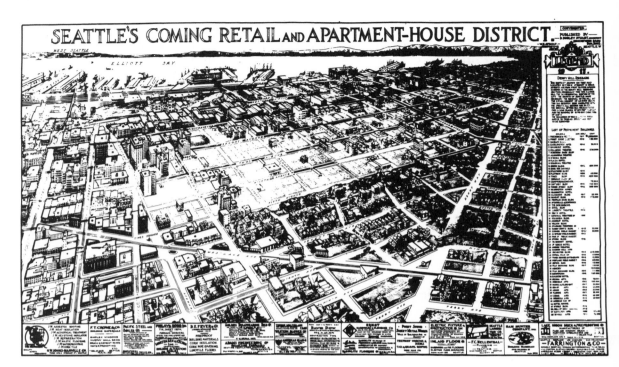

Despite its headline, this 1917 bird's eye view shows that five years after the defeat of the Bogue plan, the civic center area was little more than an urban wasteland. The Denny regrade itself was uncompleted east of Fifth Avenue, between Fifth, Westlake Avenue, and Denny Way. West of Fifth, it was almost entirely undeveloped. (Special Collections Division, University of Washington Libraries, negative UW 4115. Reproduced by permission.)

sion, questioned his class biases, or decried the obsolete features of his plans. Few carefully examined what he really had proposed. Bogue, tamer of the Andes and conqueror of Stampede Pass, planned to reshape Seattle's landscape as though it, too, were a wilderness. Public approval of his plans would have mandated their construction at enormous cost. To the voters of 1912, if not to later critics, the issue was palpable and concrete. Comprehensive planning, they had already decided, was a good idea. A specific plan drawn in the climate of a grasp for power, disregard for the urban landscape, and political hostility was a poor one.[45]

Park and Boulevard Successes

The Bogue plan failed, but Seattle citizens enjoyed a rapidly maturing park and boulevard system. From 1909 to 1916 the system embraced three significant additions: Ravenna Park, at the north edge of the university area residential district; Seward Park, almost two hundred acres jutting into Lake Washington from its southwestern shore; and Alki Beach in West Seattle. By 1916 there were thirty-one miles of boulevards, including a temporary link to

Seward Park. Active recreation areas included twenty-four playfields or athletic fields and a new golf course in Jefferson Park. The system's cost at the end
of 1916 stood at more than $6.5 million, including land acquisition, mainte-
nance, and improvement. The very topography that helped to undermine the
Bogue plan allowed Seattle a spectacular park and boulevard system.[46]

11 ◆ The Realization of the Civic Center Ideal in Denver

INTRODUCTION

Despite the varied interests of Denver's immensely practical and intensely idealistic Mayor Speer, his greatest ambition was a civic center. Speer succeeded while Seattle's parallel effort, the Bogue plan, was failing. The realization of the civic center had practically nothing to do with its aesthetics, just as Bogue's building designs had little to do with their rejection. The Denver center's success depended, instead, upon the persuasive presentation of a realistic plan for its construction within the context of effective political leadership. It depended upon a working relationship between Speer and the electorate as well as a collaboration between Speer and a designer, a collaboration enduring enough to translate an aesthetic yearning into a buildable design.

The early battle for a civic center taught Speer the hard political lesson that popular support did not automatically follow his lead. After the defeat of his proposal to fund the Robinson civic center, he learned the value of careful preparation. He meticulously secured the necessary backing from civic organizations for his subsequent center designs while at the same time he adroitly brought the leading opponent of the Robinson plan into his camp. When the center was presented to the public for approval, Speer's allies on the park board tied the plan to a variety of recreation and beautification projects. Their arrangement would force the public to reject much more than the center should it refuse to go along. The public went along.

THE FAILURE OF THE ROBINSON PLAN

Initial discussions of grouped public buildings in Denver were inspired by the Senate Park Commission plan of Washington. In May 1902 the Denver Municipal Art League, which was the city improvement society, met to see "illustrated views" of the Washington plan and to discuss "something similar on a smaller scale for Denver." The league's role as an umbrella organization and its successful agitation for an official Art Commission, have been related.[1]

The Art Commission's July 1905 report to Speer, urging the adoption of a city plan, could rely on a well-articulated ideology of the civic center emphasizing accessibility, utility, harmony, and celebration. The idea of grouped civic buildings appealed, too, because the first generation of permanent civic structures typically was scattered about the central city landscape to take advantage of cheap sites or to placate various downtown interests. Denver well illustrated the problem. In 1905 the forty-two-year-old city hall stood on a cramped triangle of land fifteen blocks northwest of the Colorado capitol. The courthouse was equally elderly but enjoyed a locational advantage. It lay at the other end of the central district, forming a rough isosceles triangle with the capitol at the apex and the United States Mint at the other base angle.[2]

The triangle formed by capitol, mint, and courthouse offered a site for the concrete affirmation of an ideal. But Denver's conflicting street grids were a complication. The downtown and some older residential sections were laid out "across the compass," with the named streets running southwest to northeast. Most other areas were developed on the directional grid, with named streets running south to north. The capitol grounds ran west and downhill to a major junction of the two plats at Broadway, Colfax Avenue and Fifteenth Street. When Robinson visited in 1905 and 1906, he thus confronted a situation familiar to planners.[3]

Many local minds had been made up concerning where the center would be and what it would contain. For example, Robinson had to accept the task of fitting formal civic center elements into the triangle formed by courthouse, mint, and capitol. The president of the Municipal Art League had spoken for that solution at a November 1904 conference organized by the Artist's Club. Both the league and the club were constituents of the Art Commission, a sponsor of Robinson's visits. The city had selected ground for a new library along the leg of the triangle between the mint and the capitol. Mayor Speer and the chamber of commerce wanted a civic auditorium in time for the Democratic National Convention of 1908. The chamber, another sponsor of Robinson's visits, wished for a new headquarters. Speer and the chamber apparently assumed that their buildings would grace the new center. Speer desired a memorial to the pioneers of Colorado, an ideal embellishment of a building group. Added to Robinson's difficulties were the necessity of reconciling the clashing street grids and the lack of reciprocity or facade alignment among the existing or proposed buildings. Lastly, any acceptable plan would involve converting seven or eight blocks of private property to public use. Little of it was prime commercial property, but it was expensive in the aggregate.[4]

Robinson ingeniously harmonized this visual cacophony. He joined the mint and the library site to the capitol grounds by a chain of small rectangular parks facing the south side of Colfax. He proposed to create a sight line

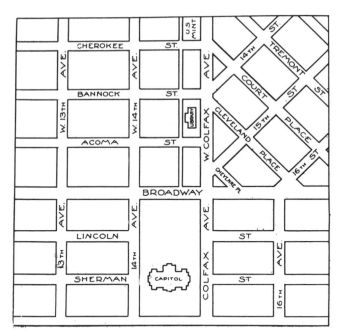

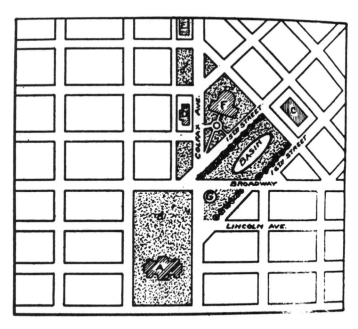

Top, a map of the civic center area as it existed for many years, with the Colorado capitol and the Denver Public Library in place. The capitol faces west. The clashing street grids created difficult design problems. *Bottom*, a crude sketch of the 1906 Robinson plan. It shows Charles M. Robinson's expensive solution to the discordant street plats, cutting Sixteenth Street through to Colfax Avenue. The auditorium building, "F" on this scheme, was not built at that location, a situation saving Denver from an automobile parking nightmare. (*Denver Municipal Facts*, 6 March 1909 and 14 May 1910. Courtesy, Colorado Historical Society.)

between the capitol and courthouse by leveling the two blocks between their grounds. He would convert the blocks into a parked basin reflecting both buildings and providing an axis from the courthouse to the capitol's southwest corner. To achieve a stunning capitol vista he would slice Sixteenth Street through the two blocks northwest of the capitol. The block farthest from the capitol was to be broken in two by Sixteenth. Robinson proposed to park its southern half, to help unify his plan and to provide space for a spectacular seventy-foot water jet. Between the courthouse-capitol axis and the mint-capitol axis he placed a combined auditorium and chamber of commerce headquarters, pivoted on its lot to create a sight line to the capitol's west front. For the pioneer monument he suggested a spot in front of the auditorium. The arrangement appears jumbled on a map, but mature trees and the small parks would have done much to unify it.[5]

Robinson had assembled the plan. The local press had given space to it. Now its realization devolved upon elements in Denver's business community. The Real Estate Exchange sponsored the major publicity effort, a "Taxpayers' Public Improvement Dinner" at the fabulous Brown Palace Hotel, early in February 1906. Though the exchange presented its gathering as an information meeting, the 350 to 400 guests soon realized otherwise, if they did not know it already. The banquet was, in fact, a typical City Beautiful promotional event. A large diagram of Robinson's plan loomed above the speaker's table, while miniature versions were printed on each menu card. No speaker opposed the plan. All of them displayed familiarity with the civic center idea.

Speer's speech met head on the grumblings about cost, which was said to be a million dollars or more above Robinson's estimate of $2 million. The mayor proposed extending the maximum maturity of park district bonds from fifteen to fifty years. If the voters approved, the burden would be lightened on property owners in the East Park District, in which the proposed taking lay. The owner of a $2,000 house would be charged but $30, with fifty years to pay. The beauty of the center would raise surrounding property values, while the center would anchor the business district and advertise the city. "But above all it will make people proud of Denver," Speer intoned. Applause often interrupted his remarks. "The hall rocked with the cheers of the guests" when he concluded. "A great majority rose to its feet and handkerchiefs, napkins and glasses were waved in the direction of the speaker's table. . . . Somebody cried, 'We have the city, we have the mayor!' and the cheers were redoubled. It was a stirring scene."[6]

Stirring, certainly, but convincing it was not. A Property Owners' Association organized against the fifty-year bond proposition. The association's most publicly active member was John S. Flower, a real estate man who denounced the Robinson plan in a fiery speech to the Real Estate Exchange. Flower sent out a circular opposing the plan and requesting an opinion to two hundred "heavy taxpayers." Of one hundred replies, only five favored the plan unequivocally. A scattering supported a scaled-down improvement or one financed by the entire city or county. The overwhelming majority of Flower's correspondents flatly rejected the plan.[7]

Shrewdly, Flower abandoned the field of aesthetics and utility to the civic center enthusiasts. He seized ground from which he could attack the plan's high cost. To Flower, high cost had four components. First, the plan would strike business property worth $4 million from the tax rolls, merely "to make hayfields" and "to plant grass seed instead!" Second, taxes were already high and destined to increase. Third, the price of the necessary property would be $5 million or more, not the $2 million estimated by Robinson. Fourth, the expense was too much for the East Park District to bear alone. The proposed fifty-year bonds, if approved and issued, would burden a piece of property for unknown amounts that would have to be paid before the property could be mortgaged or sold. Flower declared that he opposed neither improvements nor progress, only "wild and foolish and disastrous" schemes such as the Robinson plan.[8]

The attack of Flower and his association succeeded. At a 17 May election the fifty-year bond proposal failed decisively: 6,228 for and 8,042 against. Press opposition and the association's scare advertisements may have influenced the outcome. More to the point was Flower's confining his campaign to an issue on which it was difficult to challenge his expert knowledge of real estate values. Most important for the future, Speer and his allies never again relied upon one inspirational banquet and a few bland followup statements. Thenceforth they organized and propagandized.[9]

THE 1907 CIVIC CENTER PLAN

The land west of the capitol continued to be a focus for civic improvement. In January 1907 Speer appointed a committee of prominent business and professional men, Flower included, to plan a new center. Flower's inclusion suggests that Speer had co-opted an opponent. The functional elements of the new plan, essentially a reduced version of Robinson's, included cutting through Broadway north of the civic center area to relieve traffic and develop property. Another utilitarian proposal was the cutting of Fifteenth Street through the southwest corner of Broadway and Colfax to ease traffic congestion. The aesthetic recommendations included purchasing the Bates triangle facing and running east of the library site along Colfax. The Denver Gas and Electric Company had purchased the triangle to construct an eight-story office building, the back of which would face the library, but the company was willing to postpone construction for a time. Further, the report endorsed locating a monument to the pioneers at the northwest corner of Broadway and Colfax. Finally, it suggested the purchase of the rough trapezoid northeast of the Bates triangle and northwest of the monument site. The estimated cost was $1.1 million, to be borne by property in the East Park District.[10]

The second plan's street extensions later were implemented but its defi-

Top, a minimal local program of 1907 replaced the rejected Robinson plan but retained Robinson's orientation. *Bottom*, in 1907 sculptor Frederick MacMonnies suggested pivoting the civic center axis from Robinson's northwest orientation to due west. His idea was adopted in 1908. (*Denver Municipal Facts*, 14 May 1910 and 6 March 1909. Courtesy, Colorado Historical Society.)

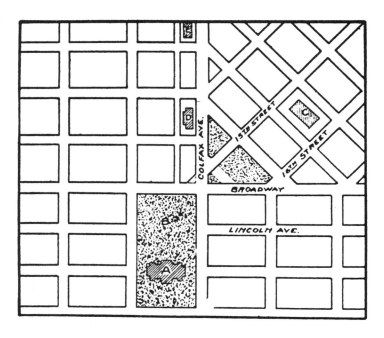

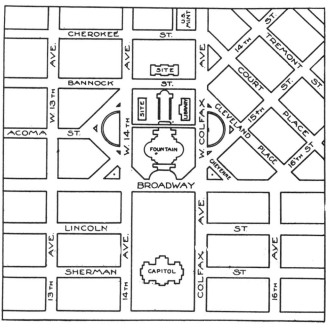

cient civic proposals doomed it. The scheme linked none of the existing or proposed buildings in Robinson's plan. Its three irregularly shaped blocks north and east of the library site could not be merged without closing major streets. They were too small, in any case, to be an effective civic focus. The plan cost less than Robinson's but its limitations set a high price in terms of planning benefits. Probably because it was cheap, it garnered endorsements from the Real Estate Exchange and the chamber of commerce.[11]

THE MacMONNIES SOLUTION

The basic solution to the civic center problem arrived with Frederick MacMonnies, sculptor of the *Pioneer Monument*, who came to Denver in 1907 to view the site and resolve a disagreement over the statue's design. The sculptor's discussions with the Art Commission included a review of the entire civic center program. MacMonnies suggested swinging the center from the capitol-courthouse axis south to the two blocks directly west of the capitol. A new courthouse could be built upon the third block, between the library site and the mint. After slightly revising MacMonnies' sketches and submitting them to Speer and to several planners and designers, the Art Commission prepared a plan in 1907. In January 1908 Speer's committee abandoned its truncated Robinson plan in favor of MacMonnies' inspiration. The ritual of endorsements followed. In August 1908 the Art Commission published a pamphlet depicting a cruciform civic center with the library balanced by a corresponding building to the south. A large ornamental fountain and reflecting pool appeared on the east, or Broadway, end of the center. A projected city-county building lay west of the center, across Bannock Street. The Bates triangle was reshaped into a semicircle with its chord running east and west along Colfax. A balancing semicircle faced the south edge of the center across Fourteenth Avenue. The Fifteenth Street cut to Broadway and the *Pioneer Monument* were balanced on the south by a similar cut and monument space. A small stadium, located south of the library, was inadequate to the center's celebratory role.[12]

MacMonnies' solution possessed the virtue of simplicity. Robinson's tour de force gave way to a straightforward east-west axis that unified the street grids through the *Pioneer Monument*, triangle purchases, and the Fifteenth Street extension. The new library displayed its partly unadorned back to the axis of the MacMonnies center, so the Art Commission proposed a neoclassical dress matching the library's street facade, a motif repeated in later plans. The new city-county building would make the county offices slightly less accessible to downtown. It would, however, replace two aging, inconveniently separate structures.

Other circumstances favored the plan. The auditorium had been built ten blocks northwest of the capitol in time for the Democratic convention of 1908. There was no longer any need for Robinson's auditorium site, which eased the abandonment of two other expensive features, the plaza between the courthouse and capitol and the cutting through of Sixteenth to Colfax. The estimated cost of MacMonnies' scheme, $1,500,000, and its final cost of about $1,815,000 were below Robinson's low estimate of $2,000,000. Further, the conception of cost had altered in the years between 1906 and 1909, when the park board completed its land selections for the civic center. By the summer of 1909, park and boulevard acquisitions required Denver's three other original park districts to bond $800,000 against property assessed at $32,000,000. The East Park District, with an assessed valuation of $60,000,000 and containing City and Cheesman parks, had spent nothing. Its eventual improvement burden was disproportionately high, but the East Park District included both the retail-financial section and the fine residential area east of the capitol. Wails from the owners of such property about tax burdens were unlikely to generate much sympathy.[13]

Speer's most recent biographer maintains that the shrewd mayor was willing to make concessions elsewhere to defuse opposition to the civic center idea. In December 1908 Speer worked to pass an ordinance raising building height limitations, the "Skyscraper Bill," at the same time he cooperated with the owners of low-grade business buildings on or near the civic center site in opposing toughened fire codes. He responded in both cases, so the argument goes, to threats of opposition to his pet project. The actions were typical of Speer and may have been made to save the center concept. If that were the case, he could have saved himself the trouble. Some opponents of the center were not to be deflected by legislative and administrative concessions.[14]

An Anti–Civic Center Association organized some time during the park board's land selection, benefit-assessment rule-making, and property owner notification, a process lasting from April through August 1909. The Anti–Civic Center Association was composed of some East Park District property owners, who were about the same socioeconomic status as the Civic Center proponents. Its members laid down a scattergun barrage. Speer and his friends, they said, had purchased property in the civic center area and stood to profit on the basis of inside information. The park board was abetting the fraud. The whole city, not the East Park District, should be taxed for the center, an improvement designed to benefit everybody. The center was principally an essay in beautification and as such was "a fake and pure buncombe," inferior to almost any imaginable utilitarian project. They solicited objections to the land takings, hoping to convince owners of the required 25 percent of the lots in the East Park District to protest the city's purchases within the ninety days allowed, thereby invalidating them. They fought the levies on the East Park District through the courts until 1920. Their charges, their protests, and their lawsuits came to nothing.[15]

One reason for their failure is that Speer and his cohorts responded with a full complement of City Beautiful campaign techniques. A Civic Center League opened offices downtown and began issuing propaganda for the center and against the Anti–Civic Center Association. It accused the "antis" of vilification and of hiring agents to exaggerate tax payments in hopes of securing more protests. It distributed forms by which citizens who had filed protests could withdraw them. A few did so. The official city newspaper, *Denver Municipal Facts*, reprinted speeches and editorials extolling the civic ideal. It ran reports and photographs of municipal improvements elsewhere. Speer and other local speakers drove home the City Beautiful rationale.[16]

The astute behavior of the park board also was important. The board had selected relatively cheap land to be purchased with the proceeds from bonds having a maturity well within existing law, ten years. Further, the board deliberately combined the civic center with other improvements. It included eight boulevard or parkway extensions and a small addition to Cheesman Park. Eight playgrounds and a street opening completed the package. Anyone who objected to the center was, therefore, protesting park and parkway expansion, recreation, and traffic relief. Finally, the board made no distinctions in ownership when it calculated the property subject to the 25 percent protest rule. All land not in streets, parks, and parkways, including federal, state, and school land, went into the area from which the Anti–Civic Center Association was required to compile its 25 percent of property owners objecting to the improvements. The "antis" would have reached 22.3 percent if the board had not included government property. As it was, the board declared valid the protests on 20 percent of the property at its 23 December meeting.[17]

The process of council approval, appraiser's awards, challenges to adjustments of the awards, and a comprehensive court suit occupied almost two years. On 22 November 1911, in a key decision, the Colorado Supreme Court upheld the Denver charter provisions related to land acquisitions and the city's procedure under the charter. Nineteen-twelve was a pivotal year for the civic center and for Denver politics. An earnest reform coalition succeeded Speer, completed the East Park District bond sale, and purchased the property. In September the new administration began clearing the site.[18]

The Lagging Implementation of the MacMonnies Plan

Civic center developments from 1912 to 1916 reflected the confused politics of the time. Speer's successor, Henry Arnold, was committed in principle to civic improvements but was torn by a conflicting desire for economy and moral reform. In 1913 his administration gave way to the commission form of government. The center and the park system continued under park board administration, supervised by the commissioner of property. In 1914 the park board resigned in protest over its lack of authority. Under the circumstances it was not surprising to find the MacMonnies plan scrapped in favor of a series of projects well illustrating Olmsted, Jr.'s dictum: "Any respectable plan consistently followed will give better results than can be obtained from successive conflicting plans, even though each of the latter be a work of extraordinary

Top, the civic center site, looking west from the Colorado capitol, before 1910. What once was developing into a middle class residential area had changed to mixed uses. *Bottom,* the civic center, about 1913, showing the library and the Bates triangle north across Colfax Avenue. (Western History Department, Denver Public Library. Reproduced by permission.)

genius in itself." Worse, none of the plans, including Olmsted's, displayed much genius or, indeed, the competence of the MacMonnies scheme.[19]

Mayor Arnold broached the first plan in June 1912. He proposed eight buildings: two near the library and three each on the semicircles north and south of the civic center. All administrative offices except the courts would be located there, he told a real-estate luncheon. Excluding the courts was a blow struck for aesthetics, because the courts would attract riffraff incompatible with the center. "We do not want the derelicts of humanity to detract from the beauty of the project," Arnold declared. The small buildings, he went on, would achieve both diversity and regularity on their crowded sites. Local architects would orchestrate the designs. Best of all, the buildings would cost nothing. Arnold proposed to sell the courthouse site (from 1904 the home rule City and County of Denver had controlled it) and use the funds for construction.[20]

If Arnold intended to detract from the impending visit of the junior Olmsted or limit Olmsted's design freedom, he failed. Olmsted arrived in July for a week's preliminary study of the proposed mountain park system, the park and boulevard system, and the civic center. Unfortunately, the hopes for a fresh center plan dwindled away in disagreements over design and ended more than three years later with a disputed claim for Olmsted's services. Neither Olmsted nor the Denverites who reviewed his designs could overcome three barriers to an acceptable plan.

First, there was the reform regime's conflict between its desires for embellishment on the one hand and for economy on the other. The park board reflected this indecision, failing to give Olmsted clear direction from the beginning.

Second, in the absence of unambiguous signals, Olmsted hewed to his own preference, to re-create the Washington Mall in miniature. It was understandable for Olmsted, a Senate park commissioner, to repeat his triumph. His wish for a mall conflicted, however, with the strong cross axis suggested by the Bates triangle and its twin to the south. He used the library to argue against the transverse axis. The library was already there; the axis was not. Development of the axis would bring it too close to the library for the design independence of either. Nor would he countenance suggestions that would modify the center's symmetry. He rejected the Fifteenth Street cut and the closing of Fourteenth Avenue, which would have joined the center to an unbalancing concert grove on the south.

Third, Olmsted gave relatively little time to the center; it was a semi-independent study done in collaboration with architect Arnold Brunner. He devoted most of his attention to the mountain parks and to the park and boulevard system.[21]

Olmsted prepared a preliminary center report and several designs both with and without Brunner's collaboration. All were either too spartan, too elaborate, or aesthetically dubious. His proposed municipal building immediately

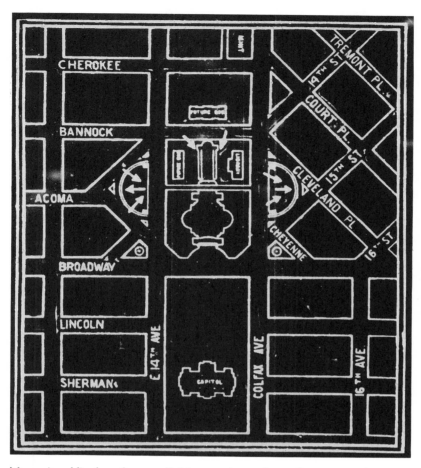

Mayor Arnold's plan of 1912 called for crowding eight small city-county buildings on the cleared and sodded civic center. The arrows designate the building locations. (This illustration is a negative print from the *Denver Republican*, 20 June 1912. Courtesy, Western History Department, Denver Public Library.)

west of the library fell victim to the park board's conviction that the city charter prohibited general public buildings on park land. Eventually Olmsted washed his hands of the project. His half-brother, John, and Brunner prepared a final report in April 1914, insubordinately calling for expensive acquisitions that the board had directed them to excise. Two months later the board resigned. The Olmsteds' work was ignored. Not until October 1915 did they wring a grudging monetary settlement from the commission administration. [22]

Consultations with outside experts having collapsed, Denver's commission government turned once more to local talent. In September 1915 the commissioner of property appointed six businessmen, including the ubiquitous Flower, to a Civic Center Commission. Their new scheme, published early in

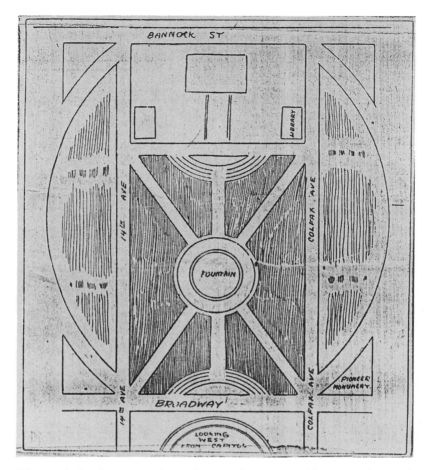

This rough sketch was one of several prepared or supervised by Frederick Law Olmsted, Jr., in the course of an unsuccessful attempt to arrive at a final design. With the exception of Mayor Arnold's suggestion, other plans showed a municipal building west of Bannock Street. Here Olmsted proposed a major building closing a foreshortened vista, east of Bannock and on the center itself. (From a clipping attributed to the *Rocky Mountain News* in the Records of the Olmsted Associates, Inc., Manuscript Division, Library of Congress. Courtesy, Library of Congress.)

1916 with the usual endorsements, deferred to the passion for economy and to the growing displeasure with the irresolute reform government. It solved the problem of cutting through Fifteenth on a diagonal by its one innovation, a parking and a second, western double lane for Broadway, which would meet Fifteenth across Colfax and avoid slicing off the center's northeast corner. It modified the MacMonnies idea to include more elaborate decoration, which was not, on the surface, a politically palatable solution.[23]

To justify their expensive design, the local planners reached back to a standard Olmstedian argument. They wrote of gradual improvement as funds

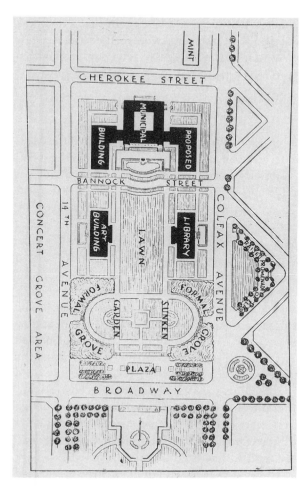

A variant of Olmsted's design, with the civic center dressed up as a longitudinal *tapis vert*. The park board rejected Olmsted's designs partly because of the expense involved in condemning the land and buildings on the "Concert Grove Area" to the south across Fourteenth Avenue. In these and other designs Olmsted refused to slice the northeast corner off the civic center and allow Fifteenth Street traffic direct access to Broadway. (*The City of Denver [Denver Municipal Facts]*, 12 Apr. 1913. Courtesy, Colorado Historical Society.)

allowed, using in part Speer-established revenues from public service corporation taxes and private donations. They urged the city to overcome its lethargy and act decisively. Property owners around the center were complaining about the inability to improve property that might or might not be purchased by a vacillating government and about heavy benefit taxation that had produced only a barren center and a collection of deteriorating buildings on the south triangle. Such deference to local opinion did not compensate for defective design, especially the double-lane Broadway. The commission failed to explain how the separated Broadway traffic would turn on the intersecting streets or how it would reenter the narrower Broadway north and south of the center.

The report was one of the last gasps of reform government. In May 1916 the voters swept aside the commission form and returned to the mayor-council system with Speer at its head. That summer, Speer and the park board called in Edward H. Bennett, a Chicago architect and planner. In Bennett, Speer found a man of independent and wise judgment who realized the mayor's vision while overriding his uninformed enthusiasms. The two worked together until the boss's death in May 1918.[24]

THE BENNETT PLAN

In February 1917 Bennett completed his plan. His adaptation of the Mac-Monnies idea harmonized the features of past designs. On the center's east end the *Pioneer Monument* and a similar site on the south set off a formal grove, a borrowing from Olmsted and Brunner. Bennett cut Fifteenth Street through the center, providing traffic relief while leaving a parked remnant at the northeastern tip. Next westward, a balustrade marked a drop in the grade. Bennett opened its concave portion toward the west, making it less conspicuous from the capitol vista. The large fountain appearing at the eastern end in the MacMonnies design, Bennett moved west of the balustrade, near the middle of the center, on a paved plaza. There crowds would surround, offset, and enjoy it, emphasizing the center's role as a gathering place. The plaza continued west to a proposed expanded library and a balancing art museum, enlarged for the needs of a burgeoning city. Four small parked rectangles containing statuary relieved the plaza's harshness and framed the restored transverse axis. On the west end a long, narrow reflecting pool placed between the library and its proposed companion building reinforced the dominant east-west axis while it contrasted with the fountain's elaborate design and soaring water jet. Bennett wanted the narrow pool surrounded by trees and statuary, "forming a sculpture garden in connection with the art gallery." As Speer wished, and as Olmsted had suggested, Bennett planned extensive lighting for night functions. The west vista across Bannock Street was closed by the proposed new city hall.[25]

On the south side of the transverse axis Bennett combined a small band concert amphitheater with a semicircular colonnade. His design blended the concert grove of the Olmsted plan with Speer's desire for a colonnade on which the names of distinguished donors to the city could be placed. Bennett adroitly solved the problem of placing the colonnade and amphitheater on the triangle south of Fourteenth Avenue. His plan adopted a previous suggestion to close Fourteenth, diverting traffic around a graceful semiellipse running the length of the center. In the arc of Fourteenth Avenue he placed the colonnade, facing north, its curving arms embracing the amphitheater and repeating the sweep of Fourteenth across a strip of buffer parking. At the north end of the transverse axis, the Bates triangle remained a severe equilateral in contrast to the ovoid to the south. Reflecting pools, entrance pylons, and a promenade repeated the motifs of earlier designs. Bennett solved the vexing problem of building rights around the center with the sensible suggestion that nearby building height limits be included in a city-wide height limitation ordinance.

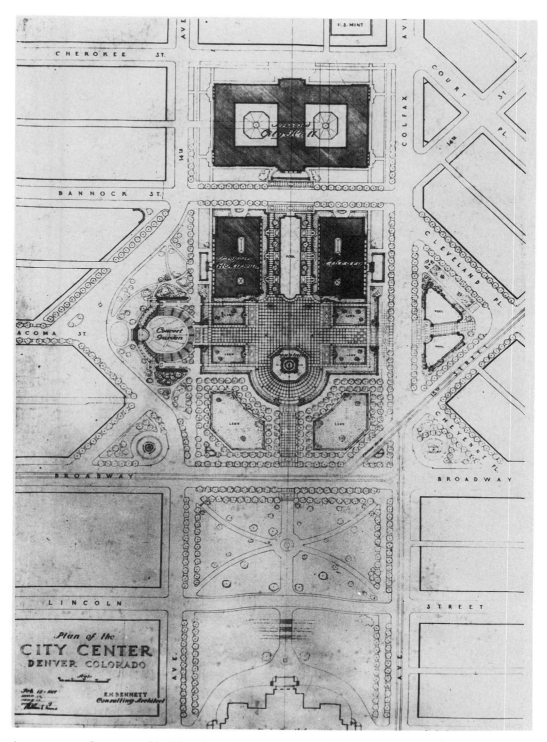

A civic center plan proposed by Edward H. Bennett in 1917, before he conceived the idea of routing Colfax Avenue around the Bates triangle on the north. (Western History Department, Denver Public Library. Reproduced by permission.)

Top, a rendering, probably prepared by Bennett's Denver associates, depicting the transverse axis of the civic center. It clearly shows Bennett's abandonment of the *tapis vert* in favor of a paved plaza useful for civic celebrations. (Courtesy, Colorado Historical Society.) *Bottom*, a perspective prepared by the architects of the Voorhies Memorial shows Fourteenth Avenue (*left*) and Colfax Avenue (*right*) taking sharper turns around the civic center than Bennett planned. Otherwise, it presents the completed civic center as Bennett and Mayor Speer intended it. A projected city-county building closes the vista. The perspective assumes the development of harmonious private construction around the civic center. ([*Denver*] *Municipal Facts*, Sept.–Oct. 1919. Courtesy, Colorado Historical Society.)

Top, the civic center, 1920–21. The Greek Theater is on the south (*left*), and the newly completed Voorhies Memorial colonnade is on the north (*right*), with Colfax Avenue diverted around it. *Bottom*, the civic center in 1933, with the new City and County Building facing the capitol. (Western History Department, Denver Public Library. Reproduced by permission.)

Normally, Bennett's association with Denver would have ended with the submission of his plan, but Speer retained him to advise on the civic center and other design matters. The association was both fruitful and volatile. Speer backed Bennett when the Chicagoan clashed with a member of a local advisory committee, but the paunchy, steely-eyed boss had his own disagreement with Bennett. In April 1918 Speer plumped hard for placing "Proctor's Bronco," an equestrian statue that he had worked to acquire, in the center of the plaza. The bronze rider and bucking steed were too small and incongruous to control the plaza, and Bennett knew it. He objected strenuously. The next day, as Bennett described it, "Mayor Speer rode a high horse (Proctors [sic] Bronco) and objected to severe criticisms of Monday." But Bennett won his point. "I convinced him of my interest in the work and desire to have the best results."[26]

The final shape of the Bates triangle was the most significant result of the Bennett-Speer collaboration. By April 1918 Speer had selected the triangle to be the site of the Voorhies Memorial, the result of a bequest for a park gate. A perspective of the center drawn in a local architectural office had shown Colfax Avenue closed and diverted around the triangle, somewhat as Fourteenth had been rerouted. Unlike Fourteenth, however, Colfax was a major traffic artery. The two proposals—the Voorhies Memorial and the Colfax diversion—set the stage for Bennett's clinching suggestion. During a meeting the day before the "Proctor's Bronco" argument, Bennett advised the "oval treatment" of the Bates triangle, a proposal designed to balance the south oval. Speer accepted Bennett's solution.[27]

Bennett's ultimate version of the Colfax closing provided a shallower half-ellipse than its mate to the south. The resulting gentler bend in Colfax than in Fourteenth was intended to ease the heavier traffic flow along Colfax. With the solution in hand the city built the center essentially as it has stood since. By the spring of 1919 the balustrade, the Colonnade of Civic Benefactors, and the amphitheater were in place. The Voorhies Memorial was completed in 1920. Fifteenth was cut through to Broadway the next year. Except for the addition of statues and plantings and the rearrangement of walks, the center's appearance remained unchanged until the neoclassical City and County Building, completed in 1932, closed the vista to the west.[28]

THE CENTER AND THE CITY BEAUTIFUL: AN ANALYSIS

Since then the Civic Center has become an oasis of City Beautiful design. A hodgepodge of state, city, and private buildings, most without any design or scale relationship to the center, has sprung up near the green lawns, but they increase an observer's awareness of the older structures. Despite all the construction, in some respects the center remains incomplete. Bennett's plaza, fountain, and reflecting pool never replaced the turf. In 1924 DeBoer proposed extending the center four and one-half blocks west to Speer Boulevard and Cherry Creek, a move that would have tied the center to the park and boulevard system and encouraged an open vista with flanking civic buildings. DeBoer's plan joined Bennett's unbuilt designs in limbo. The library, now a public office building, was not expanded nor was its companion building ever constructed. As it stands, however, the center is a pleasing contrast to its surroundings. Its invitation to relaxation and tranquillity belies the bitter struggles involved in its creation.[29]

While the Civic Center is inviting, in important respects it symbolizes failure. It did little to motivate enduring feelings of civic pride and community responsibility. Too many environmental influences pressed upon the Denver citizen for the center to wield much power over him. The center's role as an urban gathering place was limited largely to band concerts and other performances in the amphitheater. It could not focus Denver's spreading street, parkway, and boulevard systems. That the center would produce civic efficiency was problematical; in any event deconcentration has rendered the idea obsolete. Today the center's immediate surroundings are pleasant enough, but they are scarcely an affirmation of the belief that civic beauty inspires adjacent loveliness.

Yet the center's existence is a telling comment on urban realities. Its construction demonstrates the need for steadfast political courage. Speer's desire for the City Beautiful went beyond the demands of his political function, which was to serve as the broker among disparate groups. His quest for the Civic Center suffered from opposition and division within an essential constituency, the business community, but he persevered. The gentle topography and relatively low price of the center helped, too, in contrast to the difficult problems of the Denny regrade confronting Bogue in Seattle.

Together, Bennett and Speer demonstrated the importance of personal relationships and the possibility of harmonious urban design. Speer knew what he wanted; the Colonnade of Civic Benefactors on the south, the Voorhies Memorial on the north, and night lighting. Bennett supplied them all, with graceful design. His ovoids to the north and south, diverting streets with different traffic loads around different civic monuments, are separately shaped. Bennett's adaptability stopped short of subservience. When Speer mistakenly argued for placing "Proctor's Bronco" in the middle of the plaza, Bennett refused. The mayor had the grace to give way. Both men strove for the essence of the City Beautiful, rather than its perfect form. They exhibited the human spirit that the City Beautiful sought to celebrate and ennoble.

12 ◆ The Survival of the City Beautiful Technique in Dallas

INTRODUCTION: DALLAS AND ITS PROBLEMS

Founded in 1841 on a bend of the Trinity River, Dallas developed as had Seattle and Denver into a commercial and transportation center. Manufacturing concerns, eagerly sought, played a subordinate role. The site was not especially promising, except as farming country. Precipitation, though adequate by the annual measurement, bunched in the autumn, winter, and spring but was virtually nonexistent in the baking summers. There were practically no natural lakes. The Trinity was scarcely more than a rivulet, except when heavy downpours in its watershed transformed it into an implacable giant sweeping down its mile-wide floodplain.[1]

Dallas's growth repeated a familiar pattern. In 1880 its population was a little over 10,000, but by 1890 it was home to 38,067 and the dominant town in the north Texas region. Typically, growth slowed during the depression-wracked nineties, to surge again after 1900. In 1910 the population reached 92,104, exploded to 158,976 in 1920, and soared to 260,475 in 1930. Dallas's relatively late population boom created an automobile city, with subdivisions spreading out among the stands of gnarled post oaks, scraggly hackberries, and dwarfish blackjack oaks. The land thus consumed was gently rolling for the most part, with few ravines or picturesquely broken ground. There was little in the way of views or vistas, nothing to compare with those sublime scenes in Denver or Seattle or to match the riverscapes of Harrisburg or Kansas City.[2]

Nor had Dallas's citizens made any notable effort to compensate for the site, which imposed severe practical as well as aesthetic limits. By far the most menacing problem was the Trinity River, which meandered southeastward through Dallas, separating the original site and its extensions from neighborhoods on the south and west. Occasional high water on the Trinity immobilized the commercial and industrial development of its 10,000-acre floodplain. In May and June of 1908, a rampaging torrent drowned four people, drove four thousand residents from their homes, ripped out a high

This crowded, not to say chaotic, scene occurred about 1908 at the Houston and Texas Central Station, east of the downtown area. It typified the unsatisfactory conditions at Dallas's five passenger stations. (Courtesy, Texas/Dallas History and Archives Division, Dallas Public Library.)

railroad trestle, and inundated the southern edge of downtown. The swirling waters of the Trinity helped to catalyze city planning in Dallas. They raised the level of citizen awareness of the need for controlling the rambling, usually docile stream.[3]

In many more ways, Dallas in the first decade of the twentieth century desperately needed planned improvements. Dusty streets were paved—when they were paved—mostly with old style, water-bound macadam. They ran in a crazy quilt over the city, with three independently oriented grids jamming together in and around the central business district. Downtown streets sometimes varied in width, jogged through offsets and angles, or halted abruptly, perhaps to begin a few blocks beyond, possibly under another name. The city's railroads daily flirted with chaos as they shunted freight and passengers this way and that over a mishmash of tracks. Interline transfers of goods had to be made among widely separated storage and warehouse areas. Freight delays were sometimes so severe that the Texas customers of Dallas shippers were more quickly served by suppliers as far away as Boston. Nine railroads used five passenger stations scattered over the central business district. A mile of Pacific Avenue separated the Missouri-Kansas-Texas Station from the Houston and Texas Central Station. Passengers transferring from one rail line to another were forced to ride streetcars (where they existed), walk, or pay high hack fares. Pacific Avenue lay one block north of Elm Street, paralleling Elm,

This advertisement for the State Fair of Texas shows the entrance to Fair Park at about the time George E. Kessler completed his plan for Dallas. Fair Park, some 130 acres, was the largest in the city. (Hays Collection. Courtesy, Texas/Dallas History and Archives Division, Dallas Public Library.)

Main, and Commerce, the major downtown streets. Pacific, potentially a major commercial artery, was rendered sooty, dangerous, and frustrating to cross traffic by the trains chugging along the double tracks of the Texas and Pacific Railway.[4]

Dallas suffered from other deficiencies—bureaucratic, aesthetic, and recreational. Government buildings were spotted here and there around downtown. Most were picturesque but outgrown. None occupied a large open space or terminated an impressive street vista. Excluding the then-remote Bachman Lake Park, where acreage was mostly water, Dallas's parks and playgrounds occupied some 150 acres. All but about twenty acres were in Fair Park on the east side, the site of the annual State Fair of Texas and more an exposition and carnival ground than a landscape park. There was no boulevard system. Few residential streets or neighborhoods were designed for stability and long-term value. In short, the city was choking on its own growth.[5]

In 1910 some members of the Dallas elite began a sustained effort to beautify their city. Typically, the program rested upon a base of failed or partly successful ventures that provided the elite leadership with experience and the public with some awareness of problems. Unfortunately, the elite failed to unify its own community on behalf of comprehensive planning. When the plans at last appeared in 1912, the eclipse of the City Beautiful was virtually complete. The new focus on the city practical concerned itself with workable solutions to pressing problems in such areas as housing, utilities, and transportation. Comprehensive plans continued to be drawn but the emphasis shifted away from the gradual realization of ultimate goals to shorter term results,

bureaucratically achieved. Kessler was a busy man who spared little time for intramural debates or for dwelling upon change, but his *City Plan for Dallas* reflected the new reality. Nor were Kessler's recommendations completely integrated on the program level. In Harrisburg, J. Horace McFarland and his allies had been careful to fuse Manning's park plans with plans for paving, flood control, sewage, and water supply. The Dallas elite carried forward with the City Beautiful technique but, as in the Harrisburg of later years, without the inclusive City Beautiful spirit.

EARLY EFFORTS FOR CITY IMPROVEMENT

By 1910 a few prominent bankers, attorneys, merchants, and other businessmen had made fitful, piecemeal planning efforts. Organizationally and intellectually they moved from civic improvement plans to comprehensive City Beautiful planning and finally to the utilitarianism and specious inclusiveness of the city practical. At the beginning, newspaper agitation and a Cleaner Dallas League in 1899 produced a significant, if largely temporary, improvement in surface sanitation. Late in 1902 a similar effort created the Civic Improvement League (CIL) as a local branch of the American League for Civic Improvement. The CIL committed itself to making Dallas "a more beautiful place [in which] to live," a goal both remote and readily advanced. "Viewed from a civic point of view," the CIL president declared, "there is scarcely a more slovenly community in the United States than this city. Probably in the whole civilized world there is no more slovenly community than Dallas." He advised his fellows to attempt only a few projects but execute them well, for the "artistic side of Dallas, outside what the women make, is totally ignored and neglected." The CIL's program included park planning. The league campaigned during 1903 in the newspapers and at public rallies for enactment of a special park tax but saw the proposition narrowly defeated. The CIL remained active for a time, but was unable to seize any more planning opportunities.[6]

Through these efforts George B. Dealey, the operating head of the *Dallas Morning News*, emerged as a leader in the struggle for a better city. An English immigrant, son of a failed Galveston merchant, Dealey was early acquainted with work. An office boy job with the *Galveston News* in 1874 led to rapid promotions and the business managership of the new Dallas paper in 1885. A small, compact man given to irascibility when his routine was disturbed, Dealey was usually diplomatic and always ambitious, intelligent, and hardworking. He rose in the *News* management through talent, the too-overt ambitions of rivals, and the fortuitous deaths of superiors or potential superiors. After 1902 he practically controlled editorial policy, and in 1906 he became the vice-president of the *News*, the same year that the death of its founder's son left operating authority in Dealey's hands. The dedicated newspaperman regretted his lack of formal education and compensated partly by assiduous reading on city planning and other subjects. He was a moderate reformer who peppered his speeches to other businessmen with references to Lester F. Ward, Charles W. Eliot, James Bryce, and the socialist Scott Nearing.[7]

Some of his associates considered Dealey to be a self-interested enthusiast, but there was no doubt of his determination to advance comprehensive planning in his adopted city. Early in 1908, before the Trinity River flood, he wrote to McFarland's American Civic Association, requesting information on city planning. McFarland responded to Dealey's inquiry by sending twenty-five copies of his illustrated pamphlet *The Awakening of Harrisburg*, describing the origins of city planning in the Pennsylvania capital.[8]

McFarland's tract convinced Dealey of the inadequacy of his own civic improvement formula. He had conducted improvement crusades modeled on earlier efforts elsewhere and had helped to found improvement organizations but had refused to play a leading organizational role. The arrangement left him time and energy to devote to his newspaper and permitted him some independence from the citizen groups. The organizations and campaigns of Dealey and his cohorts collapsed, however, once their immediate goals were reached or denied. What had awakened Harrisburg and kept it from returning to sleep? Citizen awareness of the city's inadequacies, certainly, but an awareness stimulated and sustained by a permanent businessman's organization. Through business involvement in planning, the Harrisburg program had stimulated and regulated urban growth, generating "increasing enterprise" at a cost of lower-than-expected tax increases.[9]

Two men who made vital contributions to city planning in Dallas: George B. Dealey (*left*), chief executive of the *Dallas Morning News*, and his friend, George E. Kessler, exemplified the partnership of citizen activist and planning professional. (Dallas Historical Society. Reproduced by permission.)

Dealey realized that his approach to civic improvement lacked the continued commitment of the Harrisburg effort. The impetus behind the Harrisburg programs had been more than mere publicity or organizational activity, for behind publicity and organization lay the inspiration of a potential, and later actual, comprehensive plan. As McFarland explained in *The Awakening of Harrisburg*, success lay in "the method of engaging expert advice" for definite, related proposals, "so that all the needs of the town might be met through a coincidentally proceeding and harmoniously interlocking plan of improvements." Emulating Harrisburg in Dallas had to wait upon the Trinity River flood and the 1909 State Fair of Texas, both of which delayed efforts to secure a plan. Beginning in 1910, however, Dealey and his associates attempted to apply the Harrisburg formula. They received expert advice and scored some notable victories for beautification and utilitarian improvements, but for various reasons they achieved little comprehensive planning. [10]

Dealey was at the vortex of citizen involvement. In January 1910 he called a staff meeting to launch a civic improvement series in the *Morning News*. Reprints of articles from *American City* and *Survey* magazines supplemented stories by the newspaper's own urban specialists. The *Morning News* also publicized sermons on city developments and carried a pictorial review of civic beauty that ran almost daily into 1918. Before 1910 had passed Dealey estimated the combined length of improvement articles at 800 to 900 columns. Simultaneously the newspaperman opened his drive to build an effective private organization that would secure and sustain a comprehensive plan. Early in 1910, he persuaded President L. O. Daniel and Secretary John R. Babcock of the newly formed Dallas Chamber of Commerce to assume leadership of a civic improvement drive. The chamber's board of directors approved the idea and charged a steering committee with suggesting a plan of action. The committee recommended first of all that the chamber of commerce bring McFarland (whose ACA the chamber had just joined) to Dallas for a speech launching the city's improvement campaign. It also advised the creation of a broad-based organization to assist with developing a city plan.[11]

On 25 February McFarland addressed a luncheon audience in Dallas that included business leaders, the park board members, the city commissioners, and the mayor. In the evening he urged a general audience to join in the "Crusade Against Ugliness." The feisty little printer delivered a no-holds-barred, straight-from-the-shoulder speech designed to galvanize his listeners. He had seen both good and bad in Dallas, he said, but "Dallas is a city in the making." American cities should not be expected to achieve in a hundred years what it had taken European cities eight hundred years to accomplish. "We have the courage to retrieve our errors as we see them." McFarland found suggestions for Dallas in the Harrisburg campaign. Explanation and publicity of the Harrisburg type were beyond price. The Pennsylvania city's "rich men" were willing to have taxes raised to finance the improvements because they understood their value, but the masses also had to be roused. "Our idea was to get to the voters, and we gave them the information we had and they took it in homeopathic doses." It was all eminently worth it. "The change in the city has been more marvelous than that shown in any patent medicine 'before and after taking' advertisement I have seen."[12]

In the afterglow of McFarland's exhortation, Dealey and his associates organized the Dallas City Plan and Improvement League (CPIL) as an adjunct of the chamber of commerce. The CPIL was designed to work with city officials in securing "expert advice" to develop a plan. Dealey and his colleagues on the CPIL executive committee turned immediately to Kessler, who by 1910 enjoyed a national reputation. Kessler had lived with his family in Dallas during his youth and was well known in the city because of his design work in Fair Park. The CPIL executive committee wanted him to arrive on the heels of McFarland's speech, but the busy planner put them off until late May. Meanwhile, the committee lobbied with city officials to hire Kessler and adopt his concept of comprehensive planning. After he arrived, Kessler toured the city and then met with members of the municipal commission and the park board, who voted unanimously to retain him.[13]

THE KESSLER PLAN

Kessler did not complete his plan for another year and a half, and it was not published until February 1912. His proposals responded in the main to problems already identified by the city's business leaders, although the finished product reflected Kessler's deft, ingenious handling of planning issues. In a brief, trenchant introduction, he laid bare the city's problems and their origins. "In exaggerated form Dallas today presents the difficulties attendant upon the expansion into a great city of a village at a temporary railroad terminus, no apparent thought having been given in the interim to the needs of the increasing population." The Trinity River and the railroads, recklessly intersecting Dallas streets at grade, gave shape, but not shapeliness, to the city. Residence areas sprang up around the commercial, industrial, and warehouse areas, but as haphazardly as the core was developed. "Instead of having been planned," the residential growth of Dallas, "as in other cities," was "directed by the land speculator who, with rare exceptions, gives little or no attention to continuous or ample thoroughfares." Thus there was no easy communication between most residence areas and the business district. "Even with such thoroughfares existing in ample number and of ample width, nearly all residents living beyond the business district, with its encircling railroads, must daily pass over the dangerous grade crossings, which should be eliminated at the earliest possible time." Kessler discovered, despite the thoughtless development, a "natural selection" of land uses: railroads and industry on the lowest lands, retail and wholesale activities on higher ground, and residential sections on the highest elevations. "Regard for the interests of the people at large means that a city should be divided into areas and zones each devoted to its own particular purpose."[14]

To promote superior urban organization in the present and better opportunities for the future, Kessler listed the actions required in Dallas, including relieving the street congestion that blocked downtown expansion, zoning land according to function, maintaining or increasing land values, improving the Trinity floodplain, and making "Dallas an attractive residential city by the building of a comprehensive system of parks and boulevards." Kessler promised that implementing his suggestions would "immeasurably enhance the attractiveness of the city and will give impetus and stability to its commercial life."[15]

His first recommendation, for leveeing the Trinity, was dear to the hearts of Dealey and others who owned property in the bottomlands. Kessler called for extensive levees some 1200 feet apart and 25 feet high, dimensions expanded in the final plans of two decades later. Kessler envisioned an industrial area laced with railroad tracks, a canalized river, and a dam, a lock, and a barge-turning basin to accommodate river traffic along the eight miles of levees. The dam should be "collapsable . . . to retain water during low stages and at the same time provide a large discharging capacity during flood times." The Trin-

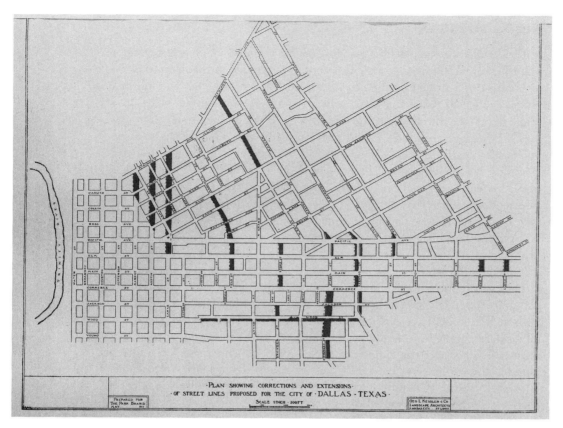

Kessler's suggestions for street improvements in central Dallas, many of which were carried out in later years. (Kessler, *City Plan for Dallas*. Courtesy, Dallas Historical Society.)

ity bottoms were worth "practically no more than farm values" but securing the land from flooding would cause "a great city" to "spring up immediately" along the former floodplain. Simultaneously Kessler scotched all talk of beautification, for this was to be a strictly utilitarian measure. "Much has been suggested toward so-called beautification of the Trinity River banks through the city." But flood protection, a turning basin, and the conversion of the floodplain to industrial use would mock all "temporary and puny efforts at minor improvements."[16]

Kessler next urged the reorganization of all rail lines and traffic into two belt loops, one around the Oak Cliff and West Dallas neighborhoods south and west of the Trinity and the other encircling the city proper. The encircling loop at its northernmost point would run through open country a few blocks north of Lover's Lane, the northern limit of Kessler's proposed boulevard network. The area would be considered old, settled, and close-in fewer than seventy years after Kessler wrote. Most tracks inside the loop, except those to

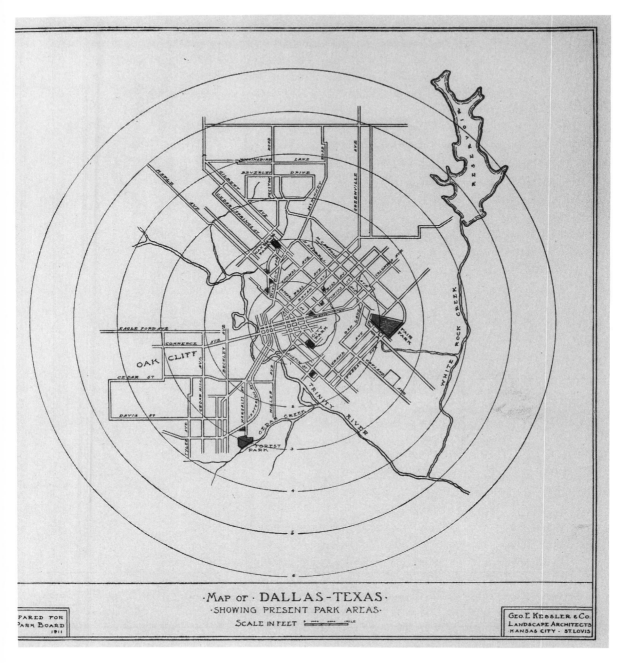

Kessler traced out existing park areas in 1911 Dallas. (Kessler, *City Plan for Dallas*. Courtesy, Dallas Historical Society.)

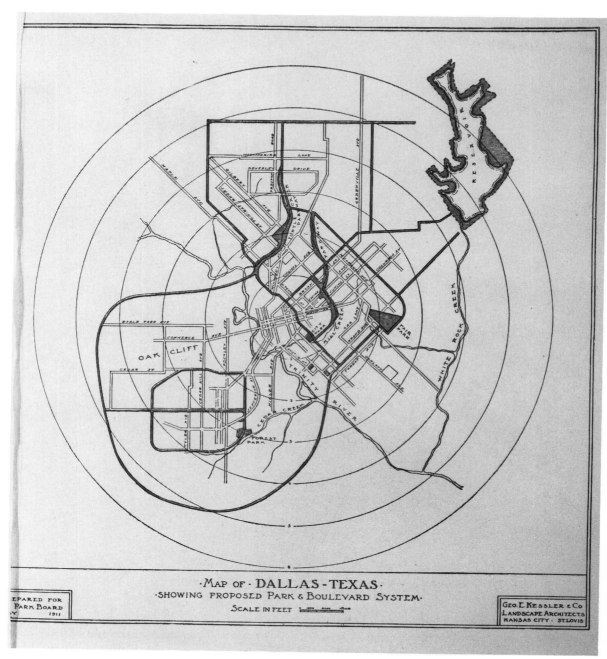

Kessler proposed an elaborate, inclusive park and boulevard system for Dallas. The city constructed only segments of his projected system. (Kessler, *City Plan for Dallas.* Courtesy, Dallas Historical Society.)

a new union station and freight terminal, would be taken up, beginning with the immediate removal of the Pacific Avenue tracks. Kessler urged the construction of a union station on the western edge of downtown to replace the scattered passenger depots each serving one or a few lines. He planned for the widening, opening, or realignment of several streets and offered new, uniform standards for street construction and improvement. He unveiled an ambitious park and boulevard program. Among his proposals were inner and outer boulevard loops for Oak Cliff and West Dallas, a boulevard network for Dallas north and east of the Trinity, and parkways along Turtle and Mill creeks.[17]

Kessler urged the city to acquire playgrounds within and outside the parks, which themselves would be tied together with parkways and boulevards. He brought the same contemporary view of playgrounds to his Dallas report as he exhibited in his later Kansas City documents. He wished no "contracted, barren spots called playgrounds, too often found in congested districts in cities," but developed tracts "within easy walking distance" of all homes. Kessler agreed with John Olmsted that the park board should not be responsible for playground administration. To this end he recommended expanded schoolyard playgrounds and separate playgrounds with shelter houses and extensive play apparatus. He called for gathering all "of this so-called playground work, which is really educational," under the "educational forces of the city" which could advance it "more successfully than . . . departments not organized for educational work." Kessler would not, however, surrender to the playground movement without an oblique reference to the recreational value of landscape. "Unfortunately," he wrote, "the term apparatus has alone in many cases come to represent playgrounds. Frequently the places where such grounds are most needed are such in which vacant property cannot be bought, but it is well worth the trouble and expense involved to clean out a slum in order to make room for a park." He held with a larger definition of the word playground, "as applicable to all forms of other recreation," thus "every area of park and parkway land in Dallas becomes a playground."[18]

Kessler recognized the desirability of grouping public buildings but was deliberately ambiguous about the composition or location of a civic center. Declaring it "essential that the approaches and first impressions of a city be as pleasing as possible," he urged the city to purchase a "plaza" in front of the union station "regardless of expenditure." Surrounding "this park there could be grouped public or semi-public buildings, such as a post office" or "a traction terminal building." Other public buildings might be erected "in the eastern sections" of downtown. This curious recommendation stemmed from Kessler's own caution and from his careful consultation with Dealey and other Dallas business leaders. Dealey's *News* had received letters opposing the construction of a new courthouse or city hall near the "dirt, smoke, filth and noise" of a union station. Locating such public buildings there would block commercial expansion, serve only "to impress a traveler" and force their occupants to work behind closed windows, the writers claimed. Moreover, some businessmen were raising funds to build a civic center in the middle of downtown. The railroads, on the other hand, were considering station sites in the southwest corner of the commercial-retail district, too remote for a full-fledged civic center. Kessler was not afraid to make bold and controversial recommendations, his call for the Pacific Avenue track removal being a case in point, but he realized that it would be foolhardy to appear overly contentious. [19]

The Pacific Avenue track removal was possibly "the most revolutionary change recommended in this report," when taken together with other proposed removals within the circumference of his projected belt line. Before reiterating his recommendations, the planner considered the circumstances involved in elevating or depressing the Texas and Pacific tracks. Elevating the Pacific Avenue tracks would have required a high viaduct over the Trinity to provide both a reasonable grade and headroom at intersecting streets. The viaduct would continue east to the crossing with the Houston and Texas Central Railroad (the present North Central Expressway), where the trains would begin a gradual descent to grade. The lengthy viaduct would eliminate grade crossings, Kessler conceded, but "it would undoubtedly be an injury to the abutting property and consequential damages might accrue to said property to such an extent as to make this form of relief exceedingly difficult." Depressing the tracks until they entered a tunnel at Ervay Street in east-central downtown would have required at least three impractically steep and costly intersecting street viaducts. The only practical solution was to tear up the tracks. "Analysis of the situation . . . will doubtless lead to the conclusion that even for the Texas and Pacific Railroad it would be better and cheaper to move them to eliminate the dangers on crossings." Indeed, all business property would benefit from the rational expansion of the downtown area. [20]

Kessler's report and recommendations were published and received in the era of the emerging city practical. The plan was comprehensive in the sense that it addressed citywide problems and offered citywide solutions, but Kessler presented his recommendations in series and confined an explanation of their interrelations to his brief introduction. Transportation issues dominated the report. Indeed, the Kessler and August Meyer 1893 Kansas City study emphasized the interdependent character of its proposed improvements more than did the Dallas plan. Nor were Dealey and his associates much concerned with comprehensiveness, except for their insistence on the widespread benefits of specific programs such as the Trinity levees or street improvements. They nonetheless continued to employ City Beautiful promotion techniques. Their improvement campaign included a businessmen's organization designed for an indefinite life, close ties between the organization and city officials, and plenty of publicity. [21]

Union Station

Dallas's Union Station, formally opened in October 1916, was the first product of this perfected technique. The campaign for a union station antedated the Kessler plan. From 1895 the railroads had given a union station some study, with the powerful state railroad commission looking on. In 1908 the vice-president and general manager of one line assured the commission chairman that his railroad had "done all we could to bring about the construction of a new union passenger station, and have been ready to join in such an arrangement for several years." During the next year the Texas legislature enhanced the authority of the railroad commission by granting it the power to compel the construction of union depots when public necessity required. The commission then ordered the railroad to build a union station and established a timetable leading to the beginning of construction in the autumn of 1910. The railroads replied with legal and extralegal delays. In September 1910 the commission, exasperated with the railroads' foot dragging, directed the state attorney general to sue them.[22]

Kessler and Dealey struggled with the rail transportation issue, the landscape architect mostly behind the scenes, the editor at the firing line. Dealey reacted after a major wholesale shipper apprised him of the desperate freight situation in Dallas. The *Morning News* responded with a three-pronged campaign in which the paper pointed out the city's rail deficiencies, discussed traffic solutions in other cities, and outlined Kessler's maturing plans. At Dealey's request, Kessler supplied the newspaper with information to use in the publicity campaign. Simultaneously the chamber of commerce put as much pressure as possible on the railroads. In January 1911 the railroad commission once more intervened, this time with an order to the railroads to build on an arbitrarily selected site. Dallas businessmen reacted quickly. Pleading the desirability of mutually agreeable land selection, they persuaded the commission to suspend its order until they could reach an agreement with the railroads. In February Kessler arrived in Dallas, where he and others addressed a convocation of local shippers and railroad executives. All sides agreed in principle to the need for a union station and joint freight terminals. Four Dallas businessmen were elected to work with the railroads and with city and county officials. In the course of 263 meetings the parties hammered out a complex agreement, which included a county-funded Trinity River overpass.[23]

After studying various sites Kessler recommended a station closing the west end of Main Street (the present triple underpass and Dealey Plaza). The railroads, however, selected a location more convenient for them three blocks farther south, on Houston Street between Wood and Young streets. In 1912 eight lines created the Union Terminal Company. Preliminary construction work began early in 1914, and the station opened for business 8 October 1916. The formal opening celebrations were held a few days later, during the annual

The Union Station was completed in 1916 at the west end of downtown. In this view, from about 1927, the station looks out on Ferris Plaza. (Courtesy, Texas/Dallas History and Archives Division, Dallas Public Library.)

State Fair of Texas. Some 75,000 people saw a Union Station designed by Jarvis Hunt in a recessive Renaissance style dominated by the planes and rectilinearity of the coming modernism. The structure could handle 50,000 passengers every twenty-four hours over ten through tracks, and yards comprising nineteen miles of tracks. The building itself cost about $1.5 million, with a total cost of some $6.5 million including land, new track, other installations, and supplementary buildings. The Union Station was a monument to the City Beautiful formula of publicity, private organization, and close working relationships between the private groups and public authorities.[24]

Pacific Avenue

A far more Byzantine process secured the removal of the Texas and Pacific Railway tracks from Pacific Avenue. The process carried out a recommendation of Kessler's that some locals desired and that was in keeping with the City Beautiful concern for transportation. Its resolution depended upon the mainstays of City Beautiful activity, including publicity, private group action, administrative politics, and the solution of difficult legal problems. The solutions in two instances were federal, involving the Woodrow Wilson administration and the United States Supreme Court. Kessler remained in the fight. He worked with August A. Busch, also of St. Louis, who owned commercial property in Dallas and favored the track removal. Not until 1921 could prominent Dallas citizens hold a spike-pulling ceremony at the corner of Pacific, Live Oak, and the present St. Paul Street. Reconstructing and resurfacing the street followed. An October 1923 celebration of the revivified avenue was designed to coincide with the State Fair of Texas. The gala included a parade featuring a mockup railroad locomotive, bands, fireworks, speeches, and motion pictures. It was an event of the city practical era, but the vanished City Beautiful could claim the spirit of civic celebration and the utilitarian improvement along Pacific Avenue.[25]

THE FRAGMENTATION OF THE CITY BEAUTIFUL IDEAL

In the midst of the Pacific Avenue fight Dealey and Charles L. Sanger of a prominent Dallas mercantile family were discussing three related problems in the west end of the retail-commercial district: unpaved streets, the "decaying process" of property uses, and the underdevelopment of potentially valuable land. They had reason for concern, for the area they designated—the major downtown east-west streets, Elm, Main, and Commerce from Broadway to Akard Street—included the Sanger Brothers Department Store and the offices of the Morning News. Dealey and Sanger solicited the property owners in the area for donations and urged Kessler to locate a capable young engineer for them.[26]

By March 1919 Sanger and Dealey had rented offices for a Dallas Property Owners' Association (DPOA) and had hired, on Kessler's advice, Lawrence V. Sheridan to be the organization's resident engineer. They charged Sheridan with devising improvement plans. The DPOA published information and improvement bulletins and formed a committee to continue wangling voluntary assessments from property owners. Dealey remarked that only one area property owner refused to join the organization, and "he is a 'mossback.'" The DPOA was further proof of Dealey's organizational skills, but it was a retrograde step. Instead of creating or revitalizing a citywide, comprehensive planning group, the newspaperman and his allies had developed a narrowly defined organization.[27]

Soon other businessmen founded the Central Improvement League of the eastern business district and the Metropolitan Development Association (MDA), a branch of the chamber of commerce. Like the DPOA, the MDA hired a resident engineer; it also published a planning periodical, the Dallas Metropolitan. In 1919 and 1920 the three groups brought Kessler back to Dallas to revise his traffic relief proposals. Kessler's new street improvement plan became a basis for a host of cooperative private and public redevelopment projects. Unfortunately, the DPOA, Central Improvement League, and MDA were too geographically or institutionally parochial to build a broad appeal or even to sustain interest among those most immediately affected. The property owners' contributions to the DPOA, for example, fell from $18,879 in 1919 to $7,650 in 1922.[28]

Pacific Avenue looks like an industrial or wholesaling street, despite its location one block north of the retail-commercial district. The photograph was taken about 1920. (Courtesy, Texas/Dallas History and Archives Division, Dallas Public Library.)

The members of the DPOA wrestled with the problem, finally falling back on the City Beautiful conception of a citywide planning organization. In a March 1924 memorandum to Dealey, John E. Surratt suggested replacing the DPOA with "an organization that will have the funds, the prestige, and the city-wide backing that will enable it to put over whatever feature of the Kessler Program it gets in behind." Besides tying the new organization to the Kessler plan, emphasis on the inclusive aspects of Kessler's work would encourage "the other fellow . . . to contribute his part of the funds, . . . to do his part of the work and voice in the management." Because many more people would be contributing, the "organization can be funded on a much lower scale of dues." Surratt also argued against the dangers of urban sectionalism: "There never was a greater fallacy than the idea that the development of one section would hurt another section. The carrying out of the Kessler Program will help every section of Dallas."[29]

Surratt had come to Dealey's attention with Surratt's co-founding of the Texas Town and City Planning Association. The newspaperman went to Sherman, Texas, early in 1917 to address a meeting of the association, of

About seven years later, the transformation of Pacific Avenue has begun in this scene looking west along Pacific from the intersection of Pacific, St. Paul, and Live Oak streets. (Frank Rogers photograph. Courtesy, Texas/Dallas History and Archives Division, Dallas Public Library.)

which Surratt was the secretary, as well as secretary of the Sherman Chamber of Commerce. The two men hit it off. Kessler was impressed with Surratt's efforts to inculcate planning in Sherman, efforts culminating in a Kessler plan for the small city. "I wonder how long Surratt will be permitted to remain in a town the size of Sherman," the planner wrote to Dealey. "He certainly seems to be alive." When he helped to found the DPOA, Dealey was looking for an effective secretary, "a mixer, a man of good address, who can persuade the people that we want to persuade of the need of action."[30] Dealey was unable to convince Surratt to relocate at once, although the younger man clearly wished to escape the confines of Sherman. By 1924 all that had been worked out, and Surratt became the secretary, first of the DPOA, then of the Kessler Plan Association (KPA). The KPA was a comprehensive organization designed to operate on the committee system and to advance the original Kessler plan, plus its revisions. Surratt at first worked well with Dealey and others who held the policy-making initiative in the KPA. In 1927, however, he edged into the policy area when he invited the renowned planner Thomas Adams to visit Dallas that summer, writing "Mr. Dealey joins us in this." Dealey rebuked

Surratt with "you used my name I think, without authority." Surratt carefully repaired the disaccord, but it was a portent for the future.[31]

Meanwhile, under Surratt's secretaryship the KPA issued a stream of pamphlets and brochures and coordinated neighborhood planning meetings. The new organization emphasized street widening, improved traffic flow, building levees along the Trinity, and, beyond these specific measures, the importance of effective planning in attracting desirable new businesses and residents to Dallas. The KPA's major publication was a 1927 grade-school text entitled *Our City—Dallas: A Community Civics* by former Dallas School Superintendent Justin F. Kimball. In 384 pages, this provocative book surveyed the founding and growth of Dallas, emphasized the need for planning, and pointed out successes under the Kessler plan. An enlightened chapter on housing and zoning introduced extensive discussion of municipal organization and government functions. The book was remarkable, too, as an expression of what adults in the 1920s expected seventh-graders to understand and retain.[32]

The KPA claimed that Walter D. Moody's *Wacker's Manual of the Plan of Chicago* (1911) inspired *Our City—Dallas*, but the claim was true only in the most general sense. Both authors wrote in a progressive tradition that emphasized education, expertise, and environmentalism to achieve a higher civicism and, through lofty civic patriotism, the attainment of a more refined and community-regarding human type. Both books were used in the public schools. But Moody's book was the product of the Chicago Plan Commission, not of a more widely ranging private group. Of large ($10\frac{1}{4}$ by $8\frac{1}{4}$ inch) size and lavishly illustrated, it hewed closely to Burnham's grand plan. Kimball's smaller book was visually and topographically more modest but its content was more sophisticated. It included eleven effective chapters on civic organization and functions.[33]

The KPA also supported the so-called Ulrickson plan, which was a 1927 bond program rather than an elaborate city plan. The Ulrickson plan included fifteen projects, among them park improvements, street opening and widening, water system extensions, public library expansion, drainage proposals, and an airport. The bond issue passed, and by 1938 the core of the Ulrickson program—flood control drainage systems long the Trinity River—was practically complete. The Ulrickson program and the leveeing of the Trinity under separate auspices cleared the way for the present massive commercial-industrial development of the former floodplain.[34]

Rapid population increases accompanied these planning programs, but the question is, did the programs effectively direct and accommodate growth? Judged on its own terms, the Dallas approach to planning reveals a number of weaknesses. The commitment of business leaders and city officials to comprehensive planning as a means of achieving quality growth was largely rhetorical. *Comprehensiveness* and *quality* were abstract terms; widening or unkinking Lamar or Pearl Street and the resulting rise in real estate values were concrete. The City Beautiful method without the City Beautiful idealism emphasized sheer growth, not its direction or control.[35]

Dallas businessmen, moreover, were sometimes provincial. The manager of the John Deere Plow Company declared in 1929 that he would no longer ask his firm to contribute to the KPA fund. The organization's activities, in his opinion, had become "so general . . . that they can be of very little benefit to the property owners in this end of town." Another prominent Dallas citizen complained that the KPA was too much the lengthened shadow of one man, Dealey, and that it supported only those projects approved in advance by the chief of the *Morning News*. The complainer protested that the KPA's "sole purpose is to develop the Trinity River and the west business district, that it was organized by G. B. Dealey, that it is Mr. Dealey's plaything, and . . . Mr. Dealey can go ahead and have it."[36]

Most Dallas businessmen equated healthy social progress with their own prosperity. It seldom occurred to them that planning and community expenditures for improvements could be justified unless they somehow promoted economic development. Thus, Dealey found few serious listeners when he harped on the low-income housing problem. Similarly, a boulevard system and Kessler's proposed Mill Creek parkway—an eastward companion of the Turtle Creek parkway—failed largely because their benefits were more aesthetic than utilitarian. Moreover, property along Mill Creek was divided into a myriad of parcels, and the owners had little incentive to support integrated development.[37]

Nor did the City Beautiful formula of organization, publicity, and close public and private cooperation work as smoothly as the claims for it suggested. Surface improvements and sewer expansion were never promoted and coordinated as effectively in Dallas as they had been in the city Dealey chose for his model, Harrisburg. The newspaperman helped to arrange for James H. Fuertes's contract to consult on sewage problems, but Fuertes's work was not linked with Kessler's in the planning or construction phases.[38]

Understandably, Dallas public officials sometimes resented such intrusion of private individuals or groups into planning. Following Kessler's initial visit to Dallas, local business organizations pressed the park board and the city to retain the renowned planner to direct the construction of his recommended improvements. In 1913 Dallas Chamber of Commerce Secretary J. R. Babcock suggested to Mayor W. M. Holland that the city employ Kessler to assist with a street-widening program. Holland, determined to control the project himself, resented proposals from self-appointed advisers outside his administration. "My suggestion," Babcock informed Dealey, ". . . brought out the statement on the part of the Mayor [that] 'when I was requested to take part in those affairs it was time enough for me to do so.'" Although the park board occasionally retained Kessler, it did so only fitfully and always on the cheap. Dealey and his staff hoped for Kessler's steady employment under the Lindsley administration, but Mayor Henry D. Lindsley was cool to the idea of retaining Kessler. In 1918 Kessler wrote to Dealey enclosing the board's latest request for advice. Noting that the letterhead listed him as a "consulting landscape architect," Kessler asked "whether this is on a per diem basis or the old consideration of zero per year and no expenses."[39]

Kessler himself must share the burden for Dallas's halting progress toward the City Beautiful ideal. The planner's first visit to Dallas came in May 1910; he did not submit his plan until late 1911. His mother's final illness and his work elsewhere understandably delayed the plan's completion, but a one-and-a-half year wait for a fairly brief, modestly illustrated, and often general report was too long. Kessler's laggard habits did not, by themselves, prejudice most park board members against him. When asked why they did not employ Kessler with regularity or place him on a permanent retainer, most city officials cited a shortage of funds, but there was some grumbling. One park commissioner charged in 1915 that "Mr. Kessler had made the Dallas plan merely a convenience in visiting other places," but even if he had not, "public opinion had been poisoned against" him, and in any event there was no money to retain him.[40]

Kessler had already responded to the city's failure to follow through by confiding to Dealey that he had decided "as a result of this experience to undertake no further municipal development without an obligation on the part of such municipality to continue services long enough to secure results within the lines of my own thoughts [about] the improvements so planned." Dealey's mind was more occupied with saving the situation in Dallas. Again and again he urged his close friend Kessler to confront city officials and explain the value of retaining him. Considering how little Dealey and some of his staff accomplished by pressuring the same city officials to retain Kessler, the tactic probably would not have worked. Kessler was unwilling to try it. "It is not my intention to attempt to suggest how I might serve the City of Dallas," he wrote to Dealey in 1915, "since its officers seem entirely unable to express their own desire for this. . . . You have repeatedly told me that I should teach these gentlemen how I could serve them best, what I can do for them, and all that sort of thing. My experience is against attempting to illustrate to people that or how they need any class of service. If they are not conscious of such needs and do not entirely understand their particular value, then it has always seemed to me an utterly hopeless thing to attempt to render such service."[41]

Dallas's public agencies were not always willing or able to keep their end of implied bargains. In 1917, for example, the park board was unable to finance parkway construction and unwilling to attempt a bond issue. It turned over construction of the Turtle Creek boulevard to the city and never developed a parkway and boulevard system. When the city built boulevards, they were usually wide traffic streets designed to move a mounting load of automobiles. Gone was the City Beautiful concept of boulevards as linking parks and defining the city. Finally, the Dallas businessmen's organizations enjoyed neither the continuity nor the broad influence with which their founders tried to invest them. The CPIL, created to bring Kessler to Dallas in 1910, was

Find the civic center. Dallas built a neoclassical Municipal Building in 1913 at the east end of the retail-commercial district. The busy, windy streetscape dates from about 1934. (Hays Collection. Courtesy, Texas/Dallas History and Archives Division, Dallas Public Library.)

declared "defunct" in 1918 by one of Dealey's city planning writers. The KPA in 1932 fragmented under the dual impact of the Great Depression and a bitter dispute over the disposition of storm sewer bond funds from the Ulrickson plan. The drainage issue was complex and sensitive. Surratt and the KPA urged the spending of some storm sewer monies in residential areas, while Dealey wanted no diversion from storm drainage construction in the Trinity River bottoms. It was the final break between the two men, even though Surratt sought a reconciliation with the newspaperman.[42]

The very growth that the Dallas business elite so desired helped to undermine its organizational effectiveness. Physical expansion quickly outstripped some of Kessler's proposals. By 1927 Dallas was almost too large to rely on the City Beautiful formula. Civic-minded businessmen could no longer depend upon the old assumption that a small, well-organized group could direct a leaderless, mentally dormant public toward preselected goals. An example of the new order could be found in J. Waddy Tate, a white populist politician who would later gain fame as Dallas's "hot dog mayor" and wear blue shirts to symbolize his identity with the working class. Tate turned some of the businessmen's techniques back on them. "They want us to borrow money and build a negro library," he shouted at a 1927 rally against the Ulrickson plan, "build a place for these black skunks to go read Shakespeare. Any time you take a spade and a hoe from the negroes you have ruined them." Tate lost, but his campaign was a portent. There would be many more challenges to business domination of Dallas politics, some of them successful.[43]

BENEFICIAL CITY PLANNING RESULTS

Granted the limitations of the City Beautiful formula, there were positive results from what Kessler in 1916 termed "the intimate connection between public and private development which is the real city planning." By 1928 eighteen major street widenings and improvements were complete. The Pacific Avenue tracks were removed. Union Station was open, and belt line tracks carried freight and passengers in and out of the city. All these improvements, together with many minor ones, greatly enhanced traffic flow in Dallas. Moreover, by 1923 the park board had boosted park acreage from 150 acres in 1908 to more than 650 acres. The Trinity River improvements did nothing for the appearance of Dallas—Kessler never claimed that they would help—but they did open roughly fifteen square miles to commercial development. It is difficult to imagine contemporary Dallas without its bustling Trinity bottoms, Marsalis and Reverchon parks, or Turtle Creek Boulevard. It is equally difficult to imagine the city functioning with the clogged downtown streets and helter-skelter rail layout of 1908.[44]

There were intangible benefits as well. Kimball, the author of *Our City— Dallas*, urged upon planners the need to deliver the message "that beauty costs no more than ugliness" during "the ideal-making days of youth." Because of his work, generations of schoolchildren learned something of civic responsibility from *Our City—Dallas*. As late as 1927 the KPA supported park improvements partly because they would contribute "to the welfare and happiness of the tired mothers and little children in the laboring districts." The statement was testimony to the endurance of Olmstedian humanitarianism.[45]

The upper-class merchants, bankers, and businessmen of Dallas employed the City Beautiful formula for more than a generation. Their belief in planning to control and direct growth was an idea whose time had come to southwestern cities by 1908. In Dallas, unfortunately, growth overwhelmed the comprehensive idea of the City Beautiful movement. Physical sprawl and the automobile soon rendered the Kessler plan obsolete. As civic leaders searched for specific remedies to problems created by rapid expansion, they

Pacific Avenue in 1951, thirty years after the tracks were removed. (Courtesy, Texas/Dallas History and Archives Division, Dallas Public Library.)

developed a justification for piecemeal improvements that verged on mere boosterism. All too often they glorified the growth that planning was supposed to accommodate. In the years after World War I—the heyday of the city practical—the richly varied City Beautiful ideal was all but discarded in favor of little more than traffic control, utilities regulation, and recreation management.

IV ◆

The National Level

13 ◆ The Glory, Destruction, and Meaning of the City Beautiful Movement

Daniel H. Burnham and the *Plan of Chicago*

Burnham's and Bennett's magnificent *Plan of Chicago* (1909) symbolized the maturation of the City Beautiful. Analyses of the plan accept the symbolism and divide its proposals into advanced elements looking forward to contemporary planning and atavistic schemes expressive of a City Beautiful already under attack when the plan appeared. [1]

Critics generally have approved of the plan's attention to the metropolitan region, which Burnham defined as a sixty-mile radius from the Loop (Chicago's downtown). They have admired the system of diagonal and circumferential roads designed to ease crowding and congestion. They have applauded Burnham's attention to the lakefront, a concern of his virtually from the time of the World's Columbian Exposition. Burnham's bold conception of a continuous green strip from Jackson Park to the north city limits and beyond would banish or suppress the railroad along Lake Michigan and open the vast water sheet to the citizens' recreational and aesthetic enjoyment. Burnham's plans for active recreation areas within the lakefront park strip have worn well with critics, as have his calls for expanded park and boulevard areas and for forest preserves.

The proposed cultural center in lakefront Grant Park, between Lake Michigan and the southern portion of the commercial core, has been less commented upon, but its merits have been recognized despite its dated neoclassical designs. The realization of Burnham's plan for widening Michigan Avenue north of the Chicago River has been hailed because it opened underdeveloped areas to retail-commercial expansion. The critics generally have approved his plans for reorganizing the city's passenger and freight rail traffic and for improving the Chicago River.

Burnham's other proposals, associated with the allegedly narrow social and aesthetic concerns of the City Beautiful, have fared less well. The commentators have been particularly antagonistic toward his grand—or grandiose—

civic center at the intersection of Congress and Halsted streets, on the southwestern fringe of the downtown commercial district. Here Burnham fashioned an overpowering centerpiece, a huge city hall with a soaring dome resting upon an elongated drum. Fernand Janin's sketches of the city hall, published with the plan, intended to flatter Burnham's conception but outlined instead a gargantuan parody of an administration building or a capitol. Three analysts of the plan, Carl Condit, Paul Boyer, and Mario Manieri-Elia, have understood the purpose behind the huge building and its vast plaza, which was to inspire the public to civic unity and adoration. But no one expressed the purpose better than Burnham himself, who wrote of the "central administration building, . . . surmounted by a dome of impressive height, to be seen and felt by the people, to whom it should stand as the symbol of civic order and unity. Rising from the plain upon which Chicago rests, its effect may be compared to that of the dome of St. Peter's at Rome."[2]

The other proposed government buildings, the city hall, and their accessories "would combine to unite the square into an harmonious whole." Further, the civic center, "when taken in connection with this plan of Chicago . . . becomes the keystone of the arch." After reviewing the plan's elements of practicality, beauty, and harmony, Burnham returned to "the center of all the varied activities of Chicago," where "will rise the towering dome of the civic center, vivifying and unifying the entire composition."[3]

The civic center had to bear so much heavy symbolic and ceremonial weight and was so obviously costly that there would be doubts about its feasibility. The center conformed in a general way to prevailing civic center theory but was without an existing anchor building such as the Colorado capitol in Denver. It was a mile or so from the northern and eastern areas of downtown and far from the northern expansion of the commercial city that the widening of Michigan Avenue was expected to produce. Burnham himself disclaimed any commitment to specific designs, writing that his were "suggestions of what may be done, for the report does not seek to impose any particular form." Manieri-Elia's reasonable conclusion is that the civic center buildings involved "a kind of ceremony," an "illusionistic" inspiration "persuasive in direct proportion to the improbability of their execution." In order to agree with his fundamental proposition, one need not accept Manieri-Elia's contention that Burnham was boosting real estate in the civic center area. Burnham himself knew very well how little relation to reality his huge hexagonal space could have. In the year of his plan's publication, the city and county broke ground for a new city hall and courthouse well away from his proposed site. There was virtually no possibility of his design becoming more than what it was, an awesome visual idealization of civic harmony.[4]

Commercial buildings of uniform, limited height appear in the Chicago plan, a second source for the criticism of Burnham's supposedly alien, aristocratic, Parisian solution. In the absence of a clarifying statement from Burnham, there are two possible responses to the criticism. One is that Burnham intended for his city to adopt height limitations corresponding approximately to the building heights in the perspectives accompanying his plan. Height limitations were hardly unknown in twentieth-century American cities. They dated from the municipally imposed cornice height limits around Boston's famous Copley Square and were inspired by desires for visual harmony, for abundant sunlight and air, which excessively tall buildings would block, and for public safety in case of serious fires or other disasters. Denver had height limitations, though Speer's "Skyscraper Bill" raised them late in 1908. So did Seattle. The Puget Sound city retained its 200-foot limit until 1912, when it permitted the Smith Tower to rise forty-two stories. As Thomas Hines, Burnham's biographer, has pointed out, Beaux-Arts buildings lining the architect's conception of Michigan Avenue were scarcely squat. Uniform ranks of huge, block-long structures rose eighteen stories, although the heights generally tapered off to the north, south, and west.[5]

For all the cohesion and rationality of the uniform facades and heights, and despite ample precedent, it is doubtful whether Burnham intended for Chicago to adopt building height limitations. He wrote nothing about height limits, even while he lavished analytical prose upon a civic center practically impossible to build in the shape or on the site projected. Thus it hardly seems likely that he seriously hoped for the adoption of a height-limit program that he did not bother to defend at all. Had he fought for building height limitations and facade uniformity, he would have added to the already formidable expenses of the plan with the huge costs of demolition, exterior remodeling, and possible purchase of unusable air rights. He would have, additionally, created an aesthetic controversy potentially inimical to his plan's success. Burnham's silence on the subject could be interpreted as indifference to height limits, but if that were so, why did he bother to introduce plate after plate of perspective paintings revealing buildings uniformly clad and corniced?[6]

The more plausible response to Burnham's critics identifies a valid role for his buildings. They served as the matrix for his proposals. Practically superfluous but visually vital, they framed the reconstructed Michigan Avenue and the new railroad stations and deferred without competition to the dominating dome of city hall. They were a pictorial representation of Burnham's hopes for a dynamic cultural and commercial city where mere individualism was subordinated to the harmony of the greater good.

Critics of the *Plan of Chicago* have decried Burnham's brief if trenchant references to the slum problem and his routine solutions, cutting boulevards through dilapidated housing and enforcing sanitation measures. Burnham and other City Beautiful planners were little concerned with housing, it is true. Whether their approach is open to criticism is another matter, to be considered later. For now it may be said that housing details were outside the purview of the comprehensive planning of the era. The planner's task, instead, was to provide the spatial opportunity for good housing at all income levels. Ensuring adequate housing for poor people was a matter for private initiative and for thoroughgoing housing code inspection and enforcement.[7]

Burnham paid little attention to the automobile, an omission costing him additional credibility with the critics. A more charitable approach would suggest how difficult it is to predict the future, especially without any particularly sophisticated tools and substantial data on trends in metropolitan areas. It is one thing to understand the American expectation of democratized technology—Burnham probably had some grasp of it—but quite another to gauge accurately when the inexpensive, durable mass car would arrive. It had not arrived by 1909. To judge beforehand the urban, spatial, social, and economic impact of the mass automobile was a still greater challenge. The planners of the city practical era might better be charged with dereliction. The compilers of *City Planning Progress in the United States: 1917* derided the City Beautiful, as it was fashionable to do, "but barely hinted at the congestion and parking problems the automobile was already causing," problems that only "emerged clearly in the 1920s" with soaring car registrations.[8] It is unreasonable to criticize Burnham for failing to incorporate the car into the city plan when his supposedly scientific successors did not, though the mass car and its developing consequences were right under their noses.

In fact most of the criticism of the *Plan of Chicago*, as well as much of the praise, arises from a misunderstanding of the City Beautiful movement. While the critics correctly acclaim the plan for its sumptuous, evocative craftsmanship and correctly attribute its quality to the extraordinary resources at Burnham's disposal, they do not see it for what it really is—a typical, if grand, City Beautiful plan. Burnham's regional sweep was one proof of his self-assessment as "a door opener"[9] who grasped the implications of tendencies a little in advance of the rest. Many cities grew fabulously after the turn of the century, projecting urban regionalism beyond the era of the big city into the age of the metropolis. Mayor Robert Speer and others in Denver already had under consideration some sort of regional relationship with recreation areas in the Rocky Mountains. Street traffic improvements similar to Burnham's were embedded in Kessler's 1893 Kansas City plan and the 1901 plan for Harrisburg, in various Denver proposals, and in many other plans of the City Beautiful era.

Burnham's lakefront park scheme was as sweeping in its way as his street plans were in theirs, but waterfront improvement ideas reached back at least as far as the senior Olmsted's Charlesbank in Boston, through Manning's River Front Park in Harrisburg, John Olmsted's plans for the Lake Washington boulevard in Seattle, and many more. Burnham's plans for active recreation in the park deferred to a movement whose time had come. His replanning of Chicago's rail traffic extended a City Beautiful tradition in which he and his firm were much involved. Burnham designed the monumental Union Station in Washington in conjunction with the massive rail reorganization in the capital city. He lost the Kansas City station job to Jarvis Hunt but was aware of the great rail relocation in the offing there. His firm's other union station designs testify to the rail transportation activity associated with the City Beautiful.

Nor was the *Plan of Chicago* the swan song of the movement. Continued development under existing comprehensive plans aside, Bogue's *Plan of Seattle* was yet to appear, as was Kessler's Dallas plan. In sum, the *Plan of Chicago* was most extraordinary because of its generous funding by Chicago's business elite, its comprehensiveness, and its evocative paintings and drawings of a sublime City Beautiful.[10]

CITY PRACTICAL CRITICISMS OF THE CITY BEAUTIFUL

By the time Burnham's plan appeared, the reaction against the City Beautiful had set in. The attack combined valid criticism with ridicule and misrepresentation, but it was effective. Opponents of the City Beautiful succeeded in stigmatizing it as excessively concerned with monumentality, empty aesthetics, grand effects for the well-to-do, and general impracticality. Most defenders of the City Beautiful offered little resistance to the onslaught and soon joined their attackers' ranks. The city practical carried the battle because it benefited from three interrelated developments: increasing specialization, rising professionalism, and burgeoning bureaucracy.

Specialization developed rapidly in the nineteenth and early twentieth centuries. The National Municipal League dated from 1894, and the American Society of Landscape Architects from 1899. They joined the revived American Institute of Architects and were joined in turn by the National Playground Association of America in 1906. Housing reformers and settlement house workers held conferences and organized the Committee on Congestion of Population. Professional awareness reinforced specialization. The hallmarks of both included university curricula, a growing body of literature, prerequisites for professional standing, and exclusivity. For a time professionals coexisted with enthusiastic laymen in such organizations as the APOAA and the ACA. But professional organizations and activities increasingly claimed the specialists' time and energy. Although laymen, not professionals, were the primary targets of the City Beautiful bulletins of the ALCI and the ACA, increasingly specialized publications appeared; the Pittsburgh Survey, launched in 1907, the city planning issue of *Charities and the Commons* in 1908, and the appearance of *American City* in 1909 were among several newer entrants in the field of urban problem writing.[11]

The bureaucratization and professionalization of the planning and other functions of city government were equally ominous for the City Beautiful. Beginning in the nineteenth century, municipal engineers deliberately preempted several planning areas, especially those involving sanitation, street grading and surfacing, drainage, and the oversight of improvement construction. The search for discipline, accountability, and professional service in city

government moved from "strong mayor" charter proposals, to the city commission form, and to reformers' advocacy of the council-manager system.
Simultaneously, the rise of the quasi-independent, specialized commission
heralded the increasing bureaucratization of urban government. Most significant for the City Beautiful movement was the establishment of the first city
planning commission at Hartford, Connecticut, in 1907. That body forecast a
new reality. City governments would assume planning responsibilities and
retain professional planners, usurping the catalytic role of the lay activists,
who were the backbone of such groups as the ACA.[12]

The planners welcomed the changes because they held out the hope of
divorcing professional planning not only from various lay enthusiasms but also
from sponsoring elites, who might advance their own ideas with proprietary
firmness. As Manning discovered in Harrisburg and John Olmsted learned in
Seattle, the experts' continuing supervision of a plan did not ensure harmonious relations with its sponsors. Increasingly, consulting planners worked
with city governments directly, with private developers, or with corporate
planning groups more remote from electoral politics than earlier organizations
such as the Harrisburg League for Municipal Improvements.[13]

All these developments were visible or were just below the horizon when
the First National Conference on City Planning convened in Washington,
D.C., during May 1909. Benjamin C. Marsh, a New York housing reform
enthusiast, organized the conference. Marsh was already on record against the
City Beautiful as too concerned with cosmetic display. Parks, civic centers,
and other great public works were attractive, he wrote, but the poor only
occasionally could afford to "escape from their squalid, confining surroundings
to view the architectural perfection and to experience the aesthetic delights of
the remote improvements." Marsh mixed practicality with his humanitarianism. He called for zoning, especially limits on factory location, for height
limits, efficient transportation, parks and playgrounds in crowded districts,
and excess condemnation.[14]

The conference attendees ranged from housing reformers through architects, planners, and engineers, to socially aware businessmen. Politically the
group found equilibrium in the moderate left. The sessions reflected Marsh's
efforts to condemn the City Beautiful and move planning toward practical
humanitarianism as defined by specialists. Robert Anderson Pope, a New
York landscape architect, took up the rhetorical cudgels against the City
Beautiful movement. The movement's great sin was masking the "true nature"
and "proper aim" of city planning, which was "to remedy congestion" of
population. Population "congestion" was, not surprisingly, the hobby of
Marsh, the guiding spirit of the Committee on Congestion of Population.
Pope attacked the City Beautiful for encouraging the assumption that "the
first duty of city planning is to beautify." The movement had "made the
aesthetic an objective in itself." Pope decried "the expenditure of huge sums
for extensive park systems, . . . inaccessible improvements . . . made avail-

able to but a small portion of the community—the wealthy and leisure classes, who of all society needs these advantages the least." Moreover, "we have rushed to plan showy civic centers of gigantic cost," inspired by "civic vanity, . . . when pressing hard-by, we see the almost unbelievable congestion with its hideous brood of evil; filth, disease, degeneracy, pauperism, and crime. What external adornment can make truly beautiful such a city?"[15]

Other speakers joined Pope in praising European, especially German, cities for improving housing and thereby raising the character and quality of their inhabitants. They asserted, with Pope, that a city planned for social benefit and economic efficiency would be beautiful. Marsh's speeches featured propositions for effective urban improvement: a survey of existing conditions bent on an "ascertaining of the facts," which would discredit "corporate interests"; dissemination of the facts through publicity campaigns; and the creation of powerful planning commissions able to enforce planned change. Marsh called on the federal government to conduct a civic census of American cities in conjunction with a nationwide city planning committee organized along the lines of other national organizations such as the Consumer's League and the Red Cross. At the end of the conference he proposed a "commission on land values in our great cities, similar to the Interstate Commerce Commission," which would determine a "fair profit on real estate," Marsh having already decided to his own satisfaction that "a profit of three or four fold in a few years is . . . unsafe and unnecessary and undemocratic." Marsh could hardly have better expressed the latter-day left-progressive faith in statistics, publicity, and the beneficence of drastic governmental intervention.[16]

Nor could he have more decisively repudiated the City Beautiful belief in the ability of uplifted, enlightened citizens to work through their private destinies harmoniously amid scenes of surpassing public beauty, in a city organized for utility and efficiency. But if any supporter of the City Beautiful believed that Marsh and his fellows represented merely a fad, a passing squall, he was soon disabused. In December 1909 architect Cass Gilbert flayed the City Beautiful at the annual meeting of the American Institute of Architects. "If I were disposed to delay, interrupt, or confuse the progress of city development I would publish the phrase 'city beautiful' in big head lines in every newspaper," Gilbert declared. "Let us have the city useful, the city practical, the city livable, the city sensible, the city anything but the city beautiful." Gilbert called for "a city that is done, completed, a city sane and sensible that can be lived in comfortably. If it is to be a city beautiful it will be one naturally." Gilbert's tirade was a hit. "The sentiment against the 'city beautiful' term was unanimous." According to one account, the AIA delegates issued a search warrant for "the originator of 'city beautiful'. The culprit had not been discovered at 3 o'clock this afternoon."[17]

Robinson fell into line. Reporting on the "unanimous and hearty applause" that greeted Gilbert's remarks, he insisted that the people who were "doing most to make cities beautiful, long ago gave up use of the phrase." They now understood the source of urban beauty: the "adaption to purpose and co-operative harmony of parts." Arnold Brunner echoed Gilbert's and Robin-son's themes at the ACA's 1910 convention. "To the average citizen the 'city beautiful' suggests the city impossible," he asserted. Brunner insisted that "boards of aldermen and city treasurers are apt to believe that it means an attempt to tie pink bows on the lamp posts." George B. Ford, a Columbia University planning instructor, took up the cry before the ACA in 1911. The City Beautiful, Ford charged, was too often concerned with "superficialities," with "frills and furbelows," and was "dazzling," but it was a mistake to advance the City Beautiful *before the problems of living, work and play have been solved.*"[18]

At last the leading lay apostle of the City Beautiful capitulated. Although McFarland did "not at all agree with his separation of what he called the aesthetic from the practical," Ford's attack shook the ACA president. The effect of Ford's charges was evident when McFarland stepped forward to ad-dress the 1912 convention of the ACA on "Not Only the City Beautiful." In a speech that surrendered to functionalist aesthetics, he ridiculed laymen who clung to the idea of the City Beautiful as "a tawdry soldier's monument, flanked by a monstrous flag-pole, several dismounted cannon . . . and four or five enormous telephone poles." When cities were made clean, practical, and efficient, then they would be beautiful. McFarland looked back to the World's Columbian Exposition, taken in his own time to be the starting point of city planning, but with an eye to its utility. Planners "properly" admired and emulated "that glorious 'White City' which the great Burnham gave to us in 1893," he said. Planners needed to recall, however, that the fair was "both convenient and beautiful, both sanitary and sightly, and therefore truly admi-rable."[19]

These assaults on the City Beautiful caricatured the movement as being as concerned with the wealthy as it was indifferent to the poor and as obsessed with surface aesthetics as it was disregardful of practicality. It was, further-more, outrageously expensive, an affront to responsible citizens and public officials. Attacks on the City Beautiful reflected the changing relationships among citizen activists, professional planners, and urban governments. Ideas not professionally or bureaucratically approved could be denounced as al-legedly expensive and impractical. Moreover, by 1909 there was some impa-tience with the optimism of early progressivism, when men of lofty purpose and good will would refashion American cities. Perhaps the panic of 1907, the portentous electoral successes of socialists, and the bureaucratic routinization of reform all made Robinson's and McFarland's hopeful urgings seem a little threadbare.[20]

Nor were the grand city plans all that successful. Some remained partly or wholly unbuilt, unable to confer their presumed psychic and material benefits on the citizenry. "Practically all the planning of cities and 'additions' to cities . . . has been done by Engineers," Olmsted, Jr., wrote in a candid, perceptive letter, "and while most of it has been very badly done their work has simply met the standards and demands of their communities." Landscape architects had planned, usually, better than engineers, with regard for aesthetics and for life's amenities, but their work was "a drop in the bucket" compared with the influence of municipal engineers in the lives of the people. For "real results" in planning "and not just a continuation of the interesting but ineffective talk and theorizing that has been going on for some years now upon this subject, it is essential that able and influential municipal engineers should take a more prominent part in the movement."[21]

Frederick's half-brother John addressed the related issue of taxpayer resistance to expensive grand plans at a time when he yet believed that he would be chosen to help design what became Seattle's Bogue plan. "It is going to be much harder to get the money for expensive schemes here than it was in the case of Cleveland. Grand schemes were devised for St. Louis, but I haven't heard how the execution is getting on," he wrote to his wife. "I think they wanted $30,000,000 to carry out the St. Louis scheme. . . . It's hard to persuade economical practical voters & taxpayers to spend that much in improving the plan of the city."[22]

Another problem involved the phrase *City Beautiful* itself. By 1909 it had been in service for a decade and was becoming a bit time-worn. It was a protean phrase, comprising activities as disparate as a women's club agitating for improved trash collection and Daniel Burnham superintending the corps of designers at work on the *Plan of Chicago*. Unfortunately, *City Beautiful* denoted aesthetic concerns, not necessarily an important consideration in housing surveys, recreation, or land use control. City Beautiful devotees such as Robinson, Kessler, and McFarland could embrace playgrounds, zoning, and improved housing without betraying the movement, but their eclecticism did not deflect the bureaucratic thrust toward utilitarianism.[23]

Finally, the City Beautiful was a victim of its own success. Citizen activists achieved or approximated their goals in Chicago, Denver, Harrisburg, Kansas City, and other places. Utility wires went underground. Graceful street furniture replaced crude utility poles or grotesque drinking fountains. Billboards were tamed by municipal regulation and the self-imposed restrictions of the bill posters.[24] Park, parkway, and boulevard systems expanded while their older segments were developed. Many civic centers were planned and some were built. Public and semipublic buildings usually improved in design and commodiousness, whether or not they were grouped along civic center malls. All this was expensive, however, and as the years of construction went by, there were fewer fresh victories to inscribe on the banners of the City Beautiful. It became easier for critics to attack the City Beautiful for aesthetic obsessions and to ignore the movement's long-standing concerns in such areas as recreation, traffic and smoke control, and urban efficiency. This city practical critique was a caricature but it was credible enough to be accepted for years, in the absence of careful studies of the City Beautiful movement. In 1962 an otherwise thoughtful analysis declared the City Beautiful to be "a narrow and pathetically fragile ideal, remote from business, commerce, industry, transportation, poverty, and similar mundane but integral features of urban life."[25] Few critics questioned, then or later, whether the presumably more realistic and more humane city practical could, or did, advance comprehensive planning with greater effectiveness.

The junior Olmsted was one who looked into the pit that the city practical planners were digging for themselves, and saw problems almost beyond imagination. Olmsted confessed to the Second National Conference on City Planning his dismay over "the appalling breadth and ramification" of planning and "the play of enormously complex forces which no one clearly understands and few pretend to." Olmsted's solution was to divide the planning task among specialists, from whom a comprehensive plan would somehow emerge. He glossed over the danger of lost or compromised comprehensiveness with the statement that anyone who fashioned "*any smallest element*" of the plan was responsible for the welfare of the entire city. Olmsted's rhetorical resolution of the city practical dilemma was as fatuous as any City Beautiful formulation. John Nolen and other city practical planners, far from abandoning the City Beautiful, appropriated the movement's emphasis on civic consciousness and utility as well as its naturalistic and formal designs. Axial, neoclassical City Beautiful war memorial proposals flourished in the wake of World War I. Mel Scott found that the application of the survey technique or other city practical mechanisms neither eliminated biases or assumptions nor guaranteed a plan's implementation.[26]

Later Attacks on the City Beautiful

Another, later critique censured the movement for its limited achievements. The analysis rests on a number of assumptions. The first assumption is the city practical belief in the impossibility of completing City Beautiful plans. It built on criticisms about unfulfilled plans; these criticisms were made in the early years of the city practical, before greater experience provided a better perspective. The second assumption failed to acknowledge the centrality of politics to the City Beautiful and reduced the movement partly or wholly to civic center design exercises. Then it declared the alleged design movement a failure because so few civic centers were built. Thirdly, the critics asserted a functionalist or "American" aesthetic against the neoclassicism of many City Beautiful designs, assuming that the designs were rejected because they were dated foreign imports false to American needs or ideals. Beyond these three assumptions, the critics believed that the city practical and subsequent planning eras enjoyed a significantly higher rate of implementation than did the City Beautiful. Almost the only positive value of the City Beautiful, in this view, was its success in stimulating public thought and discussion of planning.

This strident criticism dominated in the 1930s and 1940s and persisted much longer. Two examples will impart the flavor. Henry S. Churchill noted in 1945 how "scarcely a single city carried out, except in minor details, any plan that was drawn up. Of the 135 published reports, nearly every one was filed in the City Engineer's office and forgotten." The few exceptional cities "carried out only plans relating to large and spectacular public works," while they avoided "real replanning." To Churchill, the City Beautiful "plan generally meant the paper architectural development of a civic center," one with a domed building, fountains, and marble paving. "Fortunately, little of it came to pass, except in Washington and an occasional place that got out of control, like Harrisburg." James Marston Fitch found "a lot of Baron Haussmann and precious little democracy in these vast geometrics of befountained plazas and intersecting boulevards." For Fitch, their "vastly important role" was "introducing the concept of *planned* reconstruction into the popular mind. However pompous and autocratic the solutions, they were at least admissions that real problems did exist." The movement by and by "involved many well-intentioned souls" who eventually understood "that the problem was much more than one of simple face-lifting."[27]

Unfortunately, the critics of the 1930s and 1940s molded their social and aesthetic biases into a critical framework. It is doubtful whether any City Beautiful plan succeeded or failed because it was judged to be unworkable by city practical standards, included a civic center, or was neoclassical. As for the success rate of City Beautiful plans, comparing City Beautiful successes with later efforts would be a study in itself. In its absence, a present judgment is that the full implementation of comprehensive plans is modest in all eras.

A less biased examination of nationwide City Beautiful planning suggests that a variety of reasons lay behind the limited success of the City Beautiful. The low proportion of plans in the South (an even distribution by states, territories, and possessions should have produced about 50) indicates that conditions in the region and not the City Beautiful should explain the South's relatively weak planning impulse. Of the 233 planning activity reports in the 1917 compendium *City Planning Progress*, only 34 concerned cities in the states of the Old Confederacy. Of the 34, more than half involved cities in southwestern Texas and in the upper southern states of Virginia, North Carolina, and Tennessee.[28]

Some southern City Beautiful proponents seemed to exhaust themselves in the early stages of the planning struggles. The Woman's Club of Raleigh, North Carolina, hired Robinson in 1912, who submitted a typical Robinsonian effort the next year. The club printed and sold copies of the plan but failed to agitate for concomitant political or administrative reforms. It may have been that Robinson's suggestions were insufficient to gather popular support, but there is no way of knowing, for the Woman's Club conducted no further promotion of the plan, such as newspaper followup stories or reprinted excerpts. Greensboro, North Carolina, hired Robinson in 1917, but he died before completing a plan. The Greensboro movement died with the planner.

In Birmingham, Alabama, transplanted Yankees and native southerners worked for civic improvements under the leadership of the chamber of commerce. Warren Manning produced a civic center and park system plan in 1919, the late date indicative of cultural lag. Unfortunately Birmingham's inadequate parks were little improved and expanded, especially in black areas, and "Manning's plans came to naught." Labor spokesmen opposed spending municipal funds on civic improvements until free school textbooks and other services were provided. The Sloss-Sheffield Steel and Iron Company defeated the city's smoke abatement efforts in a series of maneuvers extending over several years. These and other problems frustrated the southern City Beautiful, but they were unrelated to aesthetics.[29]

The areas outside the Deep South, where the greater proportion of City Beautiful plans appeared, were those enjoying the most City Beautiful success. Again, however, design considerations played a negligible or modest role. City Beautiful planning succeeded most often in commercial cities similar to Kansas City, Denver, and Seattle, although manufacturing did not militate against the City Beautiful when it involved light industry and processing. Heavy-industry cities and single-industry towns fared less well, perhaps because they held a higher proportion of laborers likely to be skeptical of sweeping improvement plans. They may have lacked a large, powerful, dedicated middle class. Plans were prepared for eastern cities, but with some exceptions—the reconstruction of politically anomalous Washington, the earlier Boston metropolitan park system, Philadelphia's Fairmount Parkway—much less was done. Sheer size, high land values inhibiting large public works, diversity of interests, and fragmented leadership played negative roles. Smaller cities sometimes fared better, if, like Harrisburg, they were state capitals or for some other reason contained a significant middle class.[30]

New York's City Beautiful failed principally because, as its historian demonstrated, it suffered through a long gestation. When it finally emerged as the *Report of the New York City Improvement Commission* in 1907, it was an orphan without adequate media or community support, another reflection of the city's scattered interests and leadership. But its historian condemned the plan, instead, for its "static conception," its failure to "pay enough attention to the vast economic resources of the city and the way in which these resources could be better developed through planning," and its "overemphasis on aesthetic considerations" resulting in "slighted social concerns." All this criticism poured out upon a plan devoted to unifying the city through an expanded park and boulevard system, improved traffic circulation, and revitalized piers, including recreation piers, among many other proposals.[31]

If such ritualistic condemnation of the City Beautiful in the face of its social, economic, and utilitarian concerns does not advance the analysis of failure, what does, beyond naming New York's diversity and fragmentation? Herbert Croly, in his 1907 criticism of the plan, grasped another part of the problem when he cited the stupefyingly high land costs "in the central part of the older city," leading the city fathers to "inevitably adopt the cheapest plan which has any promise of being adequate." But the high costs of a comprehensive plan depended upon New York's size, density, and economic dynamism. New York had long since lost the plasticity allowing for a relatively inexpensive implementation. Charles F. McKim refused to have anything to do with New York planning for that very reason. Although willing to advise Mayor Seth Low of the need for an independent, well-salaried commission to pursue a comprehensive plan with expert, specialized advice, he would not become personally involved with "any but an ideal proposition, which is not very likely to be made. The difficulties to be overcome here, are, so far as the Borough of Manhattan are [sic] concerned, insuperable, and with but a few years of breath left to hope for, there are several ways in which I could put in my time more effectively."[32]

The critics of City Beautiful achievement have one more high card to play: San Francisco. In 1905 Burnham, with Bennett's collaboration, completed his excellent planning report for the bay city elite. On 18 April 1906, the great earthquake and fire destroyed most newly printed copies of the plan while they reduced some four square miles of San Francisco to a charred ruin. Within four years the city was rebuilt almost entirely as it had been, without reference to Burnham's plan. The failure allows the plan's most careful interpreter the pleasure of declaring San Francisco to be "better off" without the plan while condemning private property interests for preventing its realization. Many of Judd Kahn's observations about Burnham's plan and the City Beautiful movement in general are intelligent and sympathetic, but his point that the plan required an imperial power lacking in the American system is not well taken. The point is, instead, that existing cities may be replanned through politics, but cities destroyed are almost always reconstructed on the old street pattern, and their damaged areas are rationalized with commercial considerations in mind. Baron Haussmann possessed imperial authority, true, but he worked with an existing city.[33]

Kahn surveyed post–World War II reconstruction and found the "overall pattern" to be "one of continuity"—in other words, rebuilding on the preexisting lines. There were "a number of cities in which street plans were modified and a few in which more extensive changes were accomplished," yet Kahn admitted that "disaster seems more likely to beget substantial continuity in urban form, rather than radical innovation." The post–World War II reconstruction is all the more remarkable when the international growth of planning lore and planning consciousness from Burnham's time is considered. Human beings confront urban destruction with a powerful urge to rebuild. Across time, cultures, and systems of land ownership, existing cities may be more or less replanned and modified. Destroyed cities, including San Francisco, usually are restored.[34]

The civic center problem raises issues similar to those already discussed. Beginning two or three years after the publication of the 1902 plan for Washington, civic center designs were important, if not central, to the City Beautiful. The failure of civic center plans, while not synonymous with an unsuccessful City Beautiful movement, calls into question its methods and goals. For the plans did fail. Joan E. Draper has identified seventy-two civic center plans. Perhaps a tenth of them were begun during the City Beautiful era, and very few after that time. Draper isolated five circumstances affecting a center's fate: "1) the quality of project leadership; 2) the financial situation of the city and funding methods for the project; 3) the city's legal powers; 4) the degree of cooperation from potential tenants (city, state, federal, and semi-public agencies); and 5) the feasibility of the plan in physical terms." Her induction is sound and, excepting her point 4, could be applied to almost any public improvement project, including the park and boulevard systems identified with the City Beautiful.[35]

A full response to the issue of civic center failure involves two additional considerations. First, cost is an independent variable in the civic center case. Civic centers, apart from the other features of their accompanying plans, were necessarily expensive. Unlike parks, boulevards, street furniture, or other elements of the City Beautiful ensemble, they could not, usually, be gradually acquired. Government functions depended upon the immediate acquisition of adequate land and the timely construction of at least some essential buildings. Necessity and civic center theory both dictated a center near the commercial-retail core, where land was expensive. Neoclassicial buildings finished to the standards of the day were costly as well. After World War I construction costs rose to double and more above those of the City Beautiful era, inhibiting late starts on civic centers during the 1920s.[36]

Second, too many people perceived civic centers to be, in themselves, impractical solutions to problems of poor government organization and inadequate civic idealism. This does not mean that they opposed neoclassical aesthetics. Rather, as in Kansas City and Seattle, they weighed high costs, extreme centralization of government activity, loss of private revenue- and tax-producing property, and the impact on the immediate area of the civic center against the presumed benefits. Not surprisingly, they found the monetary and other costs overwhelming. The realities of civic center politics caution against reading later aesthetic norms, advanced by the architectural and critical avant-garde, into the struggles over realizing the City Beautiful. They also caution against arguing that civic centers and related improvements were meant to increase centralization. City Beautiful advocates saw civic centers as enhancing efficiency, not centralization. They may have subconsciously promoted centralization, but if they did, their unstated agenda left many downtown businessmen unimpressed. Moreover, the street widenings, radial streets, boulevards, and outlying parks associated with the City Beautiful could be interpreted as assisting decentralization.[37]

Design-oriented detractors of the City Beautiful have attacked its architectural handmaiden, neoclassicism. The argument runs essentially as follows:

The World's Columbian Exposition imposed a derivative, passé style upon America. Neoclassicism had no proper relation to American aspirations, ideals, or building needs, yet City Beautiful planners adopted neoclassicism from the exposition, just as they did its formality and axiality. The critics expressly or implicitly follow the convictions of the embittered Louis Sullivan, who declared that the Chicago fair foisted neoclassical architecture on the country. Burnham unwittingly lent strength to Sullivan's charge with his assertions that the exposition inspired civic centers.[38]

Despite Burnham's inadvertent support, there is a false ring to Sullivan's charge that the fair clouded the public mind with the neoclassic and throttled the development of native American architecture. Thomas E. Tallmadge challenged Sullivan in 1927, three years after the architect's celebrated autobiography appeared. The challenges have continued and may be summarized as follows. The fair did not end Sullivan's career or Frank Lloyd Wright's or any other advanced architect's. Sullivan continued with his designing, and Wright built Prairie-style houses into the twentieth century. Chicago school buildings and Prairie school residences appeared until the eve of World War I. Moreover, Sullivan's Transportation Building at the Chicago fair hardly qualified him to be an architectural seer. Its structure, beneath a mediocre exterior, was less advanced than some others at the exposition. Sullivan himself developed a repugnantly toplofty personality, while Wright reveled in his role of feisty maverick. Neither man conceived of city-planning ideas congenial to the local elites who retained planners. Shifts in emphasis of Chicago school architects from commercial to residential design and public infatuation with arts other than architecture also explain the expiration of the Chicago school style.[39]

These challenges may be expanded in several directions. Taking Sullivan first, for all his daring innovation, he was not a high-quality planner. He entertained few notions of the city as ensemble, and the Burnham firm excelled him in interior building design. In his lyrical-to-bombastic *Kindergarten Chats* Sullivan did not ask the capitalist to shut up shop but rather to develop a social conscience in architecture. It is difficult to imagine a building more congenial to private enterprise than the skyscraper, the style of which Sullivan did so much to advance, or an institution more representative than the bank, small examples of which he designed in the declining years of his practice. As for Wright, nothing save his personal lapses stayed his work. He was in full career as America's reigning architectural genius when he died, nearing ninety-two, in 1959. Wright's city plans, when they did come, were unrealistic. No antidote for pressing urban problems, Broadacres instead visualized a suburbanized middle-class utopia held together by ubiquitous automobiles, telephones, and televisions.[40]

So far as the Chicago school goes, its demise has as much to do with its own design sclerosis as with anything else. William H. Jordy remarked on the inability of Chicago architects to develop new wall and window treatments after 1900. Sullivan, though he continued his innovation in detail, achieved his final breakthrough, the Schlesinger, Mayer department store, in 1899. These failures of vision and imagination are as serious as any of those charged against the architects of the City Beautiful. As for the Prairie school, some of its practitioners fed upon City Beautiful ideas. Mark L. Peisch's sensible study notes the positive impact of the Columbian Exposition upon several Chicago architects and how Walter Burley Griffin used City Beautiful devices such as axes, groupings, and waterscapes in his 1913 plan of Canberra.[41]

The Chicago fair and the City Beautiful hardly impeded the rise of the skyscraper. City Beautiful planners usually left commercial-retail cores to their own devices, except for individual building designs and schemes for functional definition and traffic relief. City Beautiful architects created low public buildings more useful to the governments of their day than skyscrapers. When they designed commercial buildings, they sometimes employed neo-classical detailing on the lower floors. Above five or six stories, however, the motif became attenuated or lost in mass and silhouette as the buildings rose. Talbot F. Hamlin's straightforward, popular discussion of the "American style" argued convincingly that the "American" quality of the skyscraper lay in its proportions, not in its ornamental detail. As Lewis Mumford deftly phrased it, tall commercial architecture is for "angels and aviators," not for the ter-restrial critic. The City Beautiful influenced the main run of skyscraper design much less than technology, ground rent, labor costs, land use controls, and tax policy. Sullivan's statement condemning neoclassicism reflects the pain of a picturesque secessionist whose designs and ideas failed to conquer. Nor had the neoclassic conquered. Both styles continued, before and after 1893, bor-rowing from one another as well as battling. Both helped to prepare the path for the International style and its successors.[42]

More recently the City Beautiful has come under the critical scrutiny of Marxist historians. They argue that the City Beautiful movement, responding to imperialistic impulses and economic cycles, strove to create spatial order and unity in the city. The effort epitomized new governmental efforts to rationalize the urban chaos produced by capitalism and to allow private enter-prise to function more efficiently. The movement attempted to impose disci-pline and control upon the masses through visual and spatial manipulation. It tried to provide a noble idealism and the symbolism of a purified city in neoclassic design. Consultant-planners such as Robinson were bound to fail, or achieve limited success, partly because of their fake aestheticism and al-truistic rhetoric. Worse, they could not or would not understand that private enterprise itself was the cause of urban malformations. Therefore they could only arrange, at best, a somewhat brighter facade behind which capitalism continued its dirty work of exploitation. The limits of the City Beautiful were no more evident than in its failure to deal with housing, for an effective housing program would have challenged exploitative, speculative land values. Americans, in contrast to Europeans, would not assent to significant land use controls until planners could demonstrate the capitalist utility of zoning.[43]

A one-paragraph summary cannot do justice to the Marxist analysis, nor can a non-Marxist rebuttal hope to satisfy Marxists. With those caveats entered, the way is open for some observations. First, most of the Marxist critique of the City Beautiful has been advanced by non-Marxists: the relationship to imperialism; the thrust toward utilitarianism, improvement, social control, and civic idealism; and the lack of detailed concern for housing. The critique, in other words, does not necessarily spring from the Marxist beliefs in the depravity of private enterprise, the class struggle, or the inevitable dictatorship of the proletariat. The Marxists themselves, beyond their dialectical conclusions, disagree on such matters as the application of the business cycle to planning and the definition of the City Beautiful movement. A word about housing: given popular attitudes that place "adequate" housing well down on the list of desirable goods, an ever-expanding definition of adequate housing responding to the rising level of prosperity and to suburbanization, and poor housing in countries having a less potent ideology of private property or none at all, it does not seem so strange for the City Beautiful movement to place housing beyond the scope of its full treatment. Settlement house workers and others were studying the housing question without, at the same time, dealing effectively with many of the other problems engaging the City Beautiful planners. It was a sensible division of labor.[44]

The origin and spirit of the City Beautiful idea refute the Marxist belief in beautification as the willing tool of capitalism. The phrase *City Beautiful* had been around at least from the time Frances Hodgson Burnett, in her 1895 formula novel, applied it to the Chicago fair. But the inspiration for its widespread use derived from the lecture series of the Arts and Crafts Exhibition Society in England, published in 1897. Two years later Robinson and *Municipal Affairs* applied its arguments to American cities, and the gathering movement had a slogan. The English lecturers had emphasized two themes: the city, the home of all citizens, should be beautiful, and its beautification involved a substantial restraint on private enterprise. The problem, in their view, was not the inadequacy of individual housing but the pathetic state of humanity's common room, the city. T. J. Cobden-Sanderson declared that "Art must be controlled and directed" toward "the creation of the City Beautiful, the beautiful house of Mankind." Halsey Ricardo spoke for the psychic benefits of a beautiful, polychromatic city. "Strong and brave," he urged, "let us go out to our fight clothed with the distinction that colour can give us, and cheered by the *camaraderie* . . . the day's work done, there is the city beautiful—firm, stable, our home."[45]

The curbs on capitalist activity involved more than those necessary to secure public land and construct various improvements. W. R. Lethaby denounced the "sticky slime of soot" falling from the London sky. Walter Crane attacked advertising posters, "often vulgar, coarse, and debased." Ricardo referred to the struggle "against want and disease, dirt and disorder." Capitalism might survive a cleanup of London soot, strict advertising regulation, and the controls necessary to defeat "want and disease, dirt and disorder." If it survived, it would be as an economic arrangement much modified from the late nineteenth century's. In any case the issue was not the destruction or survival of capitalism. It was the creation of the City Beautiful.[46]

Nor is it correct to claim that the struggle for the City Beautiful involved the more insightful, progressive capitalists versus the retrograde industrial capitalists, who wanted to keep their chimney soot. No such neat vocational divisions existed, as examinations of Kansas City, Harrisburg, and Seattle have demonstrated. Appeals to economic self-interest accompanied improvement campaigns in those cities and others, to be sure. But they rested on a belief in human rationality, a realistic assessment of existing socioeconomic arrangements, and a conviction that the private enterprise system was generally beneficial. They were not born of a blind trust in capitalism or capitalists.

THE SURVIVAL OF THE CITY BEAUTIFUL

The ideals of the City Beautiful survived in spite of the critics' best efforts. The phrase *City Beautiful* continued popular for years with laymen, who applied it to a variety of planning and improvement concerns. In 1928 the magazine of the Dallas Chamber of Commerce urged each homeowner to adapt an exterior lighting plan and "develop our residential sections into veritable fairylands after sundown." The use of outdoor lighting would demonstrate how the "quest of the 'City Beautiful' proceeds continuously in America." Two years later the president of the Dallas Chamber told his organization's annual meeting that "the love of beauty prompts and motivates most of our individual desires." Urban beauty in architecture, landscaping, and other arts "differentiates grandeur from mere size" and "leaves its imprint upon the very soul of citizenship." A beautification program would mean "that Dallas might be known throughout the land not only as the 'City of the Hour,' but also as the 'City Beautiful.'" McFarland, inveigh as he might against the use of *City Beautiful*, could not keep the phrase out of circulation.[47]

Critics and planners could censure or ignore the City Beautiful but they did not rule out urban beautification altogether, nor did most of them completely condemn the movement. Thomas Adams's 1915 statement of city practical planning "factors" would not have caused a quarrel with a City Beautiful advocate. Nelson P. Lewis, a New York engineer and bureaucrat, took a city practical view of planning in 1916 and breathed a sigh of relief over the declining use of *City Beautiful*, but he did not discourage beauty. Indeed, he stressed the need for park development and the intelligent placement of public buildings. The publication, in 1922, of Werner Hegemann and Elbert Peets's *The American Vitruvius: An Architects' Handbook of Civic Art* testified to the survival of traditional civic design. The 1922 National Conference on City Planning heard two papers on beautification as an integral part of planning.

Two years later Lewis Mumford let fly a scathing criticism of the City Beautiful in his now-famous *Sticks and Stones*. But he was far too perceptive to dismiss the movement outright. "The civic center and the parkway represented the better and more constructive side of" it, as did railroad stations. In the next decade, when Mumford the critic metamorphosed into Mumford the planner, he proposed many City Beautiful concepts and designs for Honolulu: vistas, formal parks in town and wilder ones in remoter areas, and a comprehensive view of the organic city ranged against the special claims of neighborhoods. The Hubbard and Hubbard's text of 1929 praised contemporary city planning, located its origins in the late nineteenth century, and defused "the bugbear of the 'City Beautiful.' "[48]

Perhaps the most amazing restatement of the City Beautiful ideal was George B. Ford's, delivered to the 1929 National Conference on City Planning. "Yes, most of our towns are colorless and anything but inspiring and so perhaps a wistful longing comes over us to recapture some of the beauty of life," declared a man who led the charge against the City Beautiful. Saying that "the demand for beauty is innate," Ford called for more than making "our towns merely safe, healthy and convenient." He reminded his listeners that beauty "is not a cosmetic" but "is fundamental and basic to the design of any object." He lamented how "our towns, so well planned for safety, health and efficiency have failed to inspire our enthusiasm." Ford called for new efforts at tree planting. Of street fixtures and furniture, he said, "We may not be conscious of them, but subconsciously they give us a sense of well being and satisfaction and a certain unconscious pride in the street." His praise of beauty and of " 'The City Beautiful' " was so fulsome, it is tempting to interpret it as the recantation of a dubious devotion to the city practical. It is evidence, certainly, that City Beautiful positions were defended for a generation after they first came under siege.[49]

In 1943 Harland Bartholomew praised the practicality of City Beautiful plans. "Unfortunately," he wrote, "most of these first comprehensive city plans were considered too visionary or impractical or were misconstrued to be schemes intended chiefly for beautification of the city. Their more fundamental objectives, intended to correct mistakes and bring about a more orderly growth, were seldom appreciated." Bartholomew's appreciation was unusual in a depression and wartime America not so hostile to the City Beautiful as it was forgetful.[50]

In the late 1940s and 1950s professional planners and architectural modernists held the field, but two books forecast a reawakening to the classical heritage. Christopher Tunnard's *The City of Man* (1953) was at once urban and community history, a celebration of the humane environment, a condemnation of modernist self-indulgence, and a recovery of neoclassical civic design. Henry Hope Reed, Jr.'s paean to the grace, proportion, utility, and humanity of neoclassicism and to City Beautiful planning appeared in 1959. Mainstream architectural historians ridiculed *The Golden City* and its author, but Reed's book foretold a resurgence of neoclassical appreciation.[51]

The ferment of the 1960s focused fresh attention on American cities. A rejuvenated search for the urban past arose from nostalgia, preservationism, fresh scholarship, a yearning for individual and neighborhood stability amid a whirligig of change, dissatisfaction with "modern" commercial and domestic architecture, and disaffection from contemporary city planning. The 1962 protest against the demolition of the magnificent, neoclassical Pennsylvania Station drew attention to the emerging attitudes. Lewis Mumford, who forty years before declared railroad stations to be among the great artifacts of the City Beautiful, walked a picket line in front of the vast building. The protesters failed to halt the great monument's demise, but they helped to spark the preservation movement. Vincent Scully, no uncritical friend of the City Beautiful, was not alone when, in 1969, he published second thoughts: "A later generation was to deride [Penn Station's] formal dependence upon the Baths of Caracalla. One is less sure than one used to be that such was a very relevant criticism. . . . It was academic building at its best, rational and ordered according to a pattern of use and a blessed sense of civic excess." Nor were the contributions of landscape architects forgotten, as when in 1964 Leonard K. Eaton published his appreciation of Jens Jensen.[52]

The momentum gathered. Ada Louise Huxtable forcefully criticized contemporary architecture and lovingly evoked Beaux-Arts tradition for New Yorkers and the nation. In 1974 August Heckscher published *Alive in the City: Memoir of an Ex-Commissioner*, a sympathetic appraisal of the New York City parks from his commissioner's perspective. Three years later, in *Open Spaces: The Life of American Cities*, he performed the same service for the rest of the country, praising half-forgotten City Beautiful plans and suggesting how their built features could be recaptured for contemporary use. George E. Condon detailed the beginnings of the revival of Cleveland's mall area, and the Da Capo Press republished Burnham's *Plan of Chicago*. Walter C. Kidney's *The Architecture of Choice* (1974) assayed the substyles of the neoclassical. A preservationist and architecture buff could better comprehend styles through such books as John J.-G. Blumenson's *Identifying American Architecture* (1977). In 1979 the Brooklyn Museum published the sumptuous *The American Renaissance, 1876–1917*, which contained Richard Guy Wilson's thoughtful essay on "Architecture, Landscape, and City Planning." Historical scholarship on the City Beautiful era and its artifacts, designs, and planning politics continued into the 1980s. Reinforcement of the City Beautiful belief in the psychological and economic value of urban plants came when the first International Symposium on Urban Horticulture, held in 1983, devoted several papers to the subject.[53]

Simultaneously local planning staffs, planning consultants, commissions, city councils, and critics sought to recapture their legacy of urban beauty. In 1956 a Dallas master planning committee compared the Turtle Creek improvement, finished along the lines of Kessler's recommendations, with the ragtag Mill Creek area. Along Turtle, read a photograph underline, "residential values enhanced and stabilized as the direct result of following a Kessler recommendation." On Mill, cheap construction "necessitated installation of a storm sewer at cost of over $4,000,000. . . . Residential decay is prevalent here today." In the 1970s and 1980s other Dallas authors bemoaned the loss of Mill Creek, revived Kessler's idea of a lake in the Trinity River bottoms, and praised Lake Cliff Park in the Oak Cliff section. In Denver in 1971 and again in 1973, the city council imposed building height limitations around the Civic Center area, responding partly to pressure from the private Civic Center Association. The actions were intended to preserve the Rocky Mountain views and prevent skyscraper encroachments on the center. In 1976 the council designated the Civic Center area a historic district.[54]

Harrisburg's Susquehanna riverfront area has become dowdy with age but still graciously hosts civic celebrations such as Fourth of July fireworks displays. In the early 1960s the Kansas City Board of Park Commissioners published an illustrated historical booklet, *Cowtown 1890 Becomes City Beautiful 1962*, proudly reviving the once-ridiculed phrase. Kansas City's public fountains spout and splash, and its Civic Center, built far away from the Union Station during the Boss Pendergast era, is attractively maintained. Seattle's city government has been especially sensitive to its civic areas and to the Olmsted legacy. The city's neighborhood associations have demonstrated a remarkable vitality and success in improving the quality and integrity of their communities. The parks and boulevards continue to be attractive.[55]

The City Beautiful revival continued despite the publication, in 1961, of Jane Jacobs's *The Death and Life of Great American Cities*. Her landmark work condemned the professional planners' macroscale mentality and stimulated a neighborhood revival movement already well under way. The book was trenchant and close-grained in argument but it also contained a condemnation of the City Beautiful movement written from ignorance of its purposes and achievements, as well as special pleading and faulty logic. Fortunately for the survival of City Beautiful artifacts, Jacobs's many adherents read her book selectively.[56]

There is, of course, some validity to the critics' comments, however limited it might be. The City Beautiful movement attempted too much. America's fragmented politics was a formidable barrier to the coordinated physical overhauling of widely varying sizes and types of cities ranged across a continent. Enthusiastic organizing, speechmaking, and writing were no substitute for determined and intelligent action in each and every city. Too often a published plan and citizen idealism passed for purposefulness.

The movement was too naive and hopeful, socially and architecturally. McFarland's writings are a case in point. "It is well known that environment very greatly influences human beings," the hyperactive, diminutive printer wrote in 1908. That was well enough, but the moralistic McFarland had a corollary to deliver. "The education in ugliness that is constantly proceeding through the special privilege assaults of the billboards is not an education which tends toward the production of good citizens." It is easy to imagine, behind the charming simplicity and directness of McFarland's statements, a chilling assumption of an adroit environmental manipulation that would produce "good citizens." McFarland could not have achieved such a drastic physical reshaping of cities and, anyway, such a reformation almost certainly would not have created McFarland's "good citizens." Later generations inherited McFarland's environmentalism, but they are also the legatees of totalitarianism's horrible brutalities. It is understandable if nonsensical for them to read into environmentalist statements an ignorance of the complexity of urban life and an overweening desire for close control of the citizen.[57]

Moreover, the architectonic visions of the movement's civic design phase invited the ridicule and reductionist critiques of the city practical. Changes in architectural taste and in society invite us to depreciate outmoded styles. Nothing else earns a certificate of critical acuity as rapidly and easily as an attack on the architecture of the immediate past from the perspective of the present. It is equally facile if as intellectually slipshod to compare architecture in the mode of the good-natured City Beautiful with that of a repressive totalitarianism.[58]

The Contributions of the City Beautiful

The limitations of the City Beautiful movement and of its critics aside, the movement achieved much. It spoke to yearnings for an ideal community and to the potential for good in all citizens. Therein lies its most important but least remarked contribution. For all its idealistic rhetoric the movement was imbued with the courage of practicality, for it undertook the most difficult task of all, to accept its urban human material where found, to take the city as it was, and to refashion both into something better. Contrast its realism with the contemporaneous anti-urban Garden City movement, which proposed radical deconcentration and the destruction of the great cities. The Garden City movement and its heirs have thrilled academics with their altruistic systems involving significant restrictions on private ownership and enterprise. The fact is, however, that the Garden Cities and their successors have at best become suburbs with fairly typical suburban dynamics.[59]

The City Beautiful movement was fundamentally an urban political reform movement. It left a legacy of civic activism and flexibility in the urban political structure. The professional planning expert advanced to the fore during the era, but the network of concerned, politically aware laymen was equally important to City Beautiful success. The network survived in the ACA and found outlets in general and specialized periodicals, conventions, and speeches. Women, usually middle-class women, learned how to make their communities aware of problems of sanitation, cleanliness, and public beauty. The physical legacy—tree-shaded boulevards, undulating parks, and graceful neoclassic buildings rich in ornament and craftsmanship—remain to remind later generations of ancestors who built for their own times, to be sure, but who consciously tried to create a future city of order, system, and beauty. We must, therefore, consider not only what City Beautiful planners designed and wrote, but also what they did. The City Beautiful mode of civic scale was for a time so pervasive that even the architects of skyscrapers respected it. As Thomas Bender and William R. Taylor have written, the design and detailing of the first five or six stories of the early skyscrapers responded to sidewalk and street viewing.[60]

The movement generated a large and continuing interest in the improvement and preservation of beauty in Washington, D.C. While acknowledging Washington's "undemocratic and arbitrary form of government," McFarland appealed to "the opportunity Washington affords for working out the physical details of city improvement in a broader fashion than is likely to be practicable under the ordinary conditions." McFarland understood Washington's oxymoronic quality. It was politically anomalous and therefore of no practical use to the citizen activist in the midst of a struggle over a bond issue, but its inspirational possibilities were potentially unbounded.[61]

The City Beautiful movement also illuminates some issues of continuity and change in urban America. The City Beautiful assumed, without acknowledgment, much of the Olmstedian rhetoric about the value of urban beautification. City practical planners embraced beauty in the cityscape despite their denunciations of the City Beautiful. The spirit of each era differed one from the other, underlining the simultaneity of continuity and change.[62]

Its development of the comprehensive plan marked the City Beautiful era's great departure from the past. The adjective *comprehensive* has so often modified the noun *plan* as to rob *comprehensive* of all meaning. Restoring content to *comprehensive* assumes that a truly comprehensive plan is pervasive, reaching into all or almost all parts of the city; that it attempts to deal with a broad range of urban problems; and that, consequently, it is multifunctional.

By such a definition few of the senior Olmsted's plans were comprehensive, although the later ones addressed the issues of recreation, controlled urban growth, and residential area development, among others. They were multifunctional but they left important central areas untouched. Andrew Green's 1865 plan for Manhattan Island above Fifty-ninth Street was all-embracing but geographically limited. A single-function plan, a sewage disposal system for example, meets only one urban need, albeit an essential one. It cannot be comprehensive, no matter how elegantly designed, no matter what insights into urban structure and form its designer gains while developing it. Nor does deciding where certain buildings or institutions should be scattered about make one "a comprehensive city planner" unless the placing is done with reference to a comprehensive city plan. Partial plans were often intelligently designed, carefully integrated with other activities, and systematically carried out, but none of that makes them comprehensive.[63]

The City Beautiful movement produced the first comprehensive plans based on a theory of the organic city. The park and boulevard systems would provide varied recreational and educational opportunities, help shape cities while they directed their growth, open up new residential developments, divide urban areas into functionally separate subdistricts, and assist in the development of transportation and other utilities. Civic centers adjacent to retail-commercial cores would rationalize and centralize governmental functions, enhance civic pride through inspirational scenes, and build civic patriotism by providing a place of democratic mingling and celebration. The civic center and the park and boulevard system, together with playgrounds, would pervade the city with their positive influences. Later planners would decry the City Beautiful as much as they wished but they owed it a heavy debt—their own concept of comprehensiveness.

Despite the City Beautiful's contributions, its legacy is not always appreciated or preserved. The realities of urban budget constraints, the pressures of the private automobile, and changes in citizen interest and use combine with public indifference to wreak havoc with some City Beautiful survivals. Harrisburg's boulevard system is a shambles of neglect, obliterated in places by trafficways. Wildwood Park is a ruin, its lake silted, its pathways overgrown and befouled with trash illegally dumped, its meadow the site of a freeway interchange—in all a mockery of McFarland's praise for the reclaimed Harrisburg of the 1910s and 1920s. White Rock Lake Park in Dallas, City and Washington parks in Denver, and Green Lake Park in Seattle attract crowds far beyond their capacity, creating maintenance headaches and, in some cases, heartburn in nearby residents. David Dillon, Dallas's insightful architectural critic, warned of the high-rise buildings, many of indifferent-to-ghastly design, crowding the margins of Turtle Creek. Denver's *Pioneer Monument* stands deserted in a tiny, uninviting triangle reduced to accommodate noisy automobile traffic, its basin empty, its fountain jets turned off. In Kansas City, Jarvis Hunt's grand Union Station, now disused, molders away.[64]

The shabby treatment of some City Beautiful artifacts underscores the reality: however much it may be praised or fondly recalled, the City Beautiful movement is over and cannot be revived in the megalopolitan era. Even sympathetic critics find City Beautiful sumptuousness a little too much. As Joan Draper remarked, when the San Francisco Civic Center was placed on the National Register of Historic Places in 1978, the revived interest in neoclassic design did not lead anyone to propose creating new neoclassical monuments.[65]

Still, a neoclassical revival might not be a bad idea. A look around the later public architecture of Denver's Civic Center area does little to inspire faith in the individuality of architects restrained only by "funding," "the site," and "the problem." The Denver Art Museum appears to be thrown up by a Mesa Verde chieftain to keep his treasures safe from the hordes. Its slabby bulk, too close to the City and County Building, dominates the older structure's tower.

Wildwood Park in the late 1970s, its silted lake a wetland of aquatic plants and grasses. (Photograph by the author.)

The Colorado State Judicial Building stands on two legs at either end of a giant cutout first floor. The four floors above threaten to press down upon the void and bow the building in the middle. It is an unsettling experience either to view this strange white concoction or to walk underneath it, through the cutout. Next to the judicial building is the dark brown Colorado Heritage Center, looking like nothing so much as a wedge of chocolate cake badly cut and indifferently dropped on a plate by a Brobdingnagian hostess. The site and design make the structure practically incapable of expansion, an unfortunate circumstance in a building dedicated to the perpetual collection and preservation of Colorado's past. Only the 1950s brick-and-glass public library fits comfortably into its corner of the Civic Center and blends well with its surroundings.

It was not just the City Beautiful era in which reach exceeded grasp. So it becomes all the more important to remember what the City Beautiful advocates were reaching for, an ordered society in which dignified, cooperative citizens of whatever station or calling moved through scenes suffused with beauty. It was a glorious ideal, incapable of realization, but eternally beckoning. No one captured the spirit of the ceaseless quest better than Jules Guerin in a painting for the *Plan of Chicago*. In it, the viewer is suspended above Lake Michigan, near the yacht harbor, looking west over the city. It is dusk. A thin band of fading vermilion lingers above the western horizon. The city lights long since should have been turned on, but it is as though the citizens by common agreement have kept them off. There is purpose in their unity. How else could the viewer focus upon the dome of the great city hall, as the sun's last rays light it in glowing gold?

Notes

Introduction

1. For example, Mel Scott, *American City Planning since 1890* (Berkeley and Los Angeles: University of California Press, 1969), 1–182.

2. John Burchard and Albert Bush-Brown, *The Architecture of America: A Social and Cultural History* (Boston: Little, Brown & Co., 1961), 275–76; Jane Jacobs, *The Death and Life of Great American Cities* (New York: Vintage Books, 1961), 24–25, 171–72; Thomas S. Hines, *Burnham of Chicago: Architect and Planner* (New York: Oxford University Press, 1974), 195–96; and Judd Kahn, *Imperial San Francisco: Politics and Planning in an American City, 1897–1906* (Lincoln: University of Nebraska Press, 1979), 2–4.

3. Hines, *Burnham*, 74; and Jon A. Peterson, "The City Beautiful Movement: Forgotten Origins and Lost Meanings," *Journal of Urban History* 2 (August 1976): 426.

Chapter 1. Frederick Law Olmsted and the City Beautiful Movement

1. For a well-crafted example, see David Schuyler, *The New Urban Landscape: The Redefinition of City Form in Nineteenth-Century America* (Baltimore: Johns Hopkins University Press, 1986), 180–95. See also Francis R. Kowsky, "The Central Park Gateways: Harbingers of French Urbanism Confront the American Landscape Tradition," in *The Architecture of Richard Morris Hunt*, ed. Susan R. Stein (Chicago: University of Chicago Press, 1986), 78–89.

2. For Downing, see J. Stewart Johnson, "Introduction," in *The Architecture of Country Houses*, Andrew Jackson Downing (D. Appleton & Co., 1850; reprint, New York: Dover Publications, 1969), v–xv; John O. Simonds, "An Appreciation," in *A Treatise on the Theory and Practice of Landscape Gardening*, Andrew Jackson Downing (New York: A. O. Moore & Co., 1859; reprint, New York: Funk & Wagnalls, 1967), iv–ivD; John William Ward, "The Politics of Design," in *Who Designs America?* ed. Laurence B. Holland (Garden City, N.Y.: Doubleday & Co., 1966), 51–85; and W. G. Jackson, "First Interpreter of American Beauty: A. J. Downing and the Planned Landscape," *Landscape* 1 (Winter 1952): 11–18. For Cleveland, see Roy Lubove, "Introduction: H. W. S. Cleveland and the Urban-Rural Continuum in American Landscape Architecture," in *Landscape Architecture as Applied to the Wants of the West*, H. W. S. Cleveland (Chicago: Jansen, McClurg & Co., 1873; reprint, Pittsburgh: University of Pittsburgh Press, 1965), vii–xxi. For Eliot, see Charles W. Eliot, Sr., *Charles Eliot, Landscape Architect* (Boston: Houghton Mifflin Co., 1902); and Ian R. Stewart, "Parks, Progressivism, and Planning: Charles Eliot in Metropolitan Context," *Landscape Architecture* 58 (April 1968): 201–4. The voluminous writing on Olmsted includes Laura Wood Roper, *FLO: A Biography of Frederick Law Olmsted*

(Baltimore: Johns Hopkins University Press, 1973); and Elizabeth Stevenson, *Park Maker: A Life of Frederick Law Olmsted* (New York: Macmillan Co., 1977). Compelling interpretations of Olmsted may be found in Thomas Bender, *Toward an Urban Vision: Ideas and Institutions in Nineteenth-Century America* (Baltimore: Johns Hopkins University Press, 1982); Schuyler, *New Urban Landscape*; and Cynthia Zaitzevsky, *Frederick Law Olmsted and the Boston Park System* (Cambridge: Belknap Press of Harvard University Press, 1982). Charles Capen McLaughlin and Charles Beveridge are the editors in chief of *The Papers of Frederick Law Olmsted* (Baltimore: Johns Hopkins University Press, 1977–).

3. Schuyler, *New Urban Landscape*, 75.

4. Irving David Fisher, *Frederick Law Olmsted and the Philosophic Background to the City Planning Movement in the United States* (Ann Arbor: University Microfilms, 1978), 99–100, 112–18 (quotation, 120); and McLaughlin and Beveridge, eds., *The Papers of Frederick Law Olmsted* (Baltimore: Johns Hopkins University Press, 1977), vol. 1, *The Formative Years, 1822 to 1852*, 100–104, 313–16 (hereafter cited as FLO Papers). For Brace, see Bender, *Toward an Urban Vision*, 131–57; and Paul Boyer, *Urban Masses and Moral Order in America, 1820–1920* (Cambridge: Harvard University Press, 1978), 94–107.

5. Charles N. Glaab and A. Theodore Brown, *A History of Urban America*, 3d ed. (New York: Macmillan Co., 1983), 65–66, 76–86, 98–100, 163–66, 251–58; and Albert Fein, *Frederick Law Olmsted and the American Environmental Tradition* (New York: George Braziller, 1972), 18–29.

6. Fisher, *Olmsted and the City Planning Movement*, 52–54, 64–111. For a refutation of nineteenth-century fears of the consequences of village decline, see Hal S. Barron, *Those Who Stayed Behind: Rural Society in Nineteenth-Century New England* (Cambridge: Cambridge University Press, 1984).

7. Charles Beveridge, Charles Capen McLaughlin, and David Schuyler, *FLO Papers* (Baltimore: Johns Hopkins University Press, 1981), vol. 2, *Slavery and the South, 1852 to 1857*, 244.

8. Bender, *Toward an Urban Vision*, 38–51, 55–69, 73–93, 97–128 (quotations, 88). See also Leo Marx, *The Machine in the Garden: Technology and the Pastoral Ideal in America* (New York: Oxford University Press, 1964).

9. McLaughlin and Beveridge, *FLO Papers*, 1:99–100, 110, 114–17 (quotation, 100).

10. Downing, *Landscape Gardening*; Edward Hyams, *Capability Brown and Humphry Repton* (New York: Charles Scribner's Sons, 1971), 137–46, 213; and figs. 33–49.

11. Downing, *Landscape Gardening*, 46–68, (quotation, 51). See also Frederick Law Olmsted, Jr.'s assessment of Downing's influence on his father in a letter to George Dudley Seymour, 11 Aug. 1910, folder 2919, box 174, Records of the Olmsted Associates, Manuscript Division, Library of Congress (hereafter cited as Olmsted Records).

12. Downing is quoted in, in order, his own *Horticulturist and Journal of Rural Art and Rural Taste* 3 (October 1848): 154, 156; and Edward K. Spann, *The New Metropolis: New York City, 1840–1857* (New York: Columbia University Press, 1981), 167.

13. Frederick Law Olmsted, Jr., and Theodora Kimball briefly discuss the relationship in *Frederick Law Olmsted: Landscape Architect, 1822–1903* (1922; reprint, New York: Benjamin Blom, 1970), 1:88. For Vaux, see Charles Beveridge and David Schuyler, *FLO Papers* (Baltimore: Johns Hopkins University Press, 1983), vol. 3, *Creating Central Park, 1857 to 1861*, 63–68.

14. Frederick Law Olmsted, *Walks and Talks of an American Farmer in England* (Ann Arbor: University of Michigan Press, 1967), 52. Olmsted's references to European developments dated from this first trip to Europe. He ascribed to Birkenhead Park some of the social and economic advantages he later credited American parks with creating. See *Walks and Talks*, 54–55.

15. Quoted in Bender, *Toward an Urban Vision*, 169.

16. Stevenson, *Park Maker*, 143–45; Olmsted and Kimball, *Olmsted: Landscape Architect*, 1:68–74; and McLaughlin and Beveridge, *FLO Papers*, 1:117.

17. Roderick Nash, *Wilderness and the American Mind*, rev. ed. (New Haven: Yale University Press, 1973), vii–xii, 1–121.

18. Cecilia Tichi, *New World, New Earth: Environmental Reform in American Literature from the Puritans through Whitman* (New Haven: Yale University Press, 1979), 2, 68–71,

75, 90, 148, 181–84, 197–200, 214–18; Fisher, *Olmsted and the City Planning Movement*, 121–37; Nash, *Wilderness and the American Mind*, 78–83; and Downing, *Landscape Gardening*, 49–50. For Emerson's problems with the city, see Michael H. Cowan, *City of the West: Emerson, America, and the Urban Metaphor* (New Haven: Yale University Press, 1967). For Ruskin's influence, see Roger B. Stein, *John Ruskin and Aesthetic Thought in America, 1840–1900* (Cambridge: Harvard University Press, 1967), especially 46–73.

19. Downing, *Landscape Gardening*, 48–49, in which Downing discusses landscapes that are not cultivated although they could be pastoral. Thomas Bender does not make this point but he well illustrates how Americans were, by 1850, including farm scenes in the concepts of "nature" and "wilderness" (*Toward an Urban Vision*, 75–93). See also Hans Huth, *Nature and the American: Three Centuries of Changing Attitudes* (Berkeley and Los Angeles: University of California Press, 1957), 30–53, 57–86, 108–26, 135–36, 148–77; and James L. Machor, *Pastoral Cities: Urban Ideals and the Symbolic Landscape of America* (Madison: University of Wisconsin Press, 1987), 88–99, 122–44.

20. Downing, *Landscape Gardening*, 58, 59.

21. Beveridge and Schuyler, *FLO Papers*, 3:347, 348 (see the entire Olmsted 1861 article "Park," 346–60); and Albert Fein, "The American City: The Ideal and the Real," in *The Rise of an American Architecture*, ed. Edgar Kaufman, Jr. (New York: Praeger Publishers, in association with the Metropolitan Museum of Art, 1970), 79–84; and Olmsted and Kimball, *Olmsted: Landscape Architect*, 2:4–12.

22. Bender, *Toward an Urban Vision*, 79–88; and Beveridge and Schuyler, *FLO Papers*, 3:357.

23. Downing, *Horticulturist and Journal of Rural Art and Rural Taste* 3 (October 1848): 154; and Spann, *New Metropolis*, 163.

24. Spann, *New Metropolis*, 115; and Downing, *Landscape Gardening*, 70–71.

25. Norman T. Newton, *Design on the Land: The Development of Landscape Architecture* (Cambridge: Belknap Press of Harvard University Press, 1971), 182–232, and see figs. 140, 142, 144, 146, 152, 156–59, 165, 167, 170.

26. William H. Wilson, "Ideology, Aesthetics and Politics of the City Beautiful Movement," in *The Rise of Modern Urban Planning, 1800–1914*, ed. Anthony Sutcliffe (New York: St. Martin's Press, 1980), 167–68.

27. See, e.g., Bruce Kelly, "Art of the Olmsted Landscape," 5–71; James Marston Fitch, "Design and Designer: Nineteenth-Century Innovation," 73–77; Stephen Rettig, "Influences across the Water: Olmsted and England," 79–85, in *Art of the Olmsted Landscape*, ed. Bruce Kelly, Gail Travis Guillet, and Mary Ellen W. Hern (New York: New York City Landmarks Preservation Commission and Arts Publisher, 1981).

28. Beveridge and Schuyler, *FLO Papers*, 3:121, 124, 151.

29. Frederick Law Olmsted and Calvert Vaux, "Report of the Landscape Architects and Superintendents to the President of the Board of Commissioners of Prospect Park, Brooklyn (1868)," *Landscape into Cityscape: Frederick Law Olmsted's Plans for a Greater New York City*, ed. Albert Fein (Ithaca, N.Y.: Cornell University Press, 1967), 135–53.

30. Frederick Law Olmsted, *Public Parks and the Enlargement of Towns: Read before the American Social Science Association at the Lowell Institute, Boston, Feb. 25, 1870* (Cambridge: American Social Science Association, 1870; reprint, New York: Arno Press, and *New York Times*, 1970), 1–5 (quotation, 2).

31. Ibid., 5–10 (quotations, 5, 10). For parallels between Olmsted's work and thought and mass entertainment, see Gunther Barth, *City People: The Rise of Modern City Culture in Nineteenth-Century America* (New York: Oxford University Press, 1980), especially 177–91.

32. Olmsted, *Public Parks and Enlargement of Towns*, 23.

33. Ibid., 10, 11. Machor, (*Pastoral Cities*, 167–73) suggests that Olmsted believed cities to become "organic" with the introduction of natural areas into them, a suggestion at variance with Olmsted's repeated characterizations of urban areas.

34. Olmsted's statement on suburbs is from his 1868 report on Riverside, Illinois, partly reprinted in *Civilizing American Cities: A Selection of Frederick Law Olmsted's Writings on City Landscapes*, ed. S. B. Sutton, (Cambridge: MIT Press, 1971), 294.

35. Olmsted, *Public Parks and Enlargement of Towns*, 9 (quotations, 10, 12).

36. Olmsted, *Public Parks and Enlargement of Towns*, 16 (quotation, 20). For New York, see Frederick Law Olmsted and Calvert Vaux, "Preliminary Report of the Landscape Architect and the Civil and Topographical Engineer, upon the Laying Out of the Twenty-third and Twenty-fourth Wards," in Fein, *Landscape into Cityscape*, 353–36.

37. Olmsted, *Public Parks and Enlargement of Towns*, 13–16.

38. Beveridge and Schuyler, *FLO Papers*, 3:303–5; and Frederick Law Olmsted, "The Spoils of the Park: With a Few Leaves from the Deep-laden Note-books of 'A Wholly Unpractical Man,'" in Fein, *Landscape into Cityscape*, 389–99, 417–23.

39. For the exposition, see Roper, *FLO*, 432, 448, 450. For the park entrance, see Jon Alvah Peterson, "The Origins of the Comprehensive City Planning Ideal in the United States, 1840–1911" (Ph.D. diss., Harvard University, 1967), 182.

40. Stevenson, *Park Maker*, 422–27.

41. The relationship between Olmsted's work and the City Beautiful has been grasped, but not developed, by others. See, for instance, Olmsted and Kimball, *Olmsted: Landscape Architect*, 2:182; and Fisher, *Olmsted and the City Planning Movement*, 400.

42. For Olmsted's estimate, see Olmsted and Kimball, *Olmsted: Landscape Architect*, 2:95. For the engraving, see Fein, *Landscape into Cityscape*, facing 129. For Franklin Park, see Zaitzevsky, *FLO and Boston*, 149–50. For a pro-Olmsted argument which accepts Olmsted's contention that he should have been the arbiter on questions of park use and aesthetics, see Elizabeth Barlow, *Frederick Law Olmsted's New York* (New York: Praeger Publishers, 1972), 6–29, 49–51.

43. Leonard J. Simutis, "Frederick Law Olmsted, Sr.: A Reassessment," *American Institute of Planners Journal* 38 (September 1972): 282–83 (quotation, 282).

44. Roper, *FLO*, 426–30, 444–50; and Glen E. Holt, "Private Plans for Public Spaces: The Origins of Chicago's Park System, 1850–1875," *Chicago History* 8 (Fall 1979): 173–84.

45. Olmsted and Kimball, *Olmsted: Landscape Architect*, 2:95; and Beveridge and Schuyler, *FLO Papers*, 3:39.

46. Kelly, Guillet, and Hern, *Olmsted Landscape*, 66–69, 82; Beveridge and Schuyler, *FLO Papers*, 3:11–13; Olmsted and Vaux, "Report of the Landscape Architects," 148; Frederick Law Olmsted et al., "Report to the Staten Island Improvement Commission of a Preliminary Scheme of Improvements (1871)," in Fein, *Landscape into Cityscape*, 212–13; and Jon A. Peterson, "The Impact of Sanitary Reform upon American Urban Planning, 1840–1890," *Journal of Social History* 13 (Fall 1979): 92–94.

47. Beveridge and Schuyler, *FLO Papers*, 3:12–13.

48. Ibid., 420; and Zaitzevsky, *FLO and Boston*, 184–201.

49. Kelly, Guillet, and Hern, *Olmsted Landscape*, 16, 26–27, 38, 52, 108, 131; Roper, *FLO*, 296–97; and Zaitzevsky, *FLO and Boston*, 69, 73.

50. Kelly, Guillet, and Hern, *Olmsted Landscape*, 34, 38. For quotation, see Olmsted and Vaux, "Preliminary Report," in Fein, *Landscape into Cityscape*, 98.

51. Leonard J. Simutis, in *Frederick Law Olmsted's Later Years: Landscape Architecture and the Spirit of Place* (Ann Arbor: University Microfilms, 1972), 147, makes this point but argues that Olmsted did not adopt the crowd control technique until 1872. For Prospect Park, see Olmsted and Vaux, "Preliminary Report," in Fein, *Landscape into Cityscape*, 111–14 (quotations, 101); and idem, "Report of the Landscape Architects," in ibid., 130.

52. Simutis, *FLO: A Reassessment*, 137–46; Zaitzevsky, *FLO and Boston*, 68, 97–99.

53. Olmsted, "Preliminary Report in Regard to a Plan of Public Pleasure Grounds for the City of San Francisco," in Sutton, *Civilizing American Cities*, 122–24.

54. Ibid., 123–27 (quotation, 124); and Roper, *FLO*, 306–7.

55. Olmsted and Vaux, "Preliminary Report," in Fein, *Landscape into Cityscape*, 126–27.

56. Ibid., 127; Olmsted and Vaux, "Report of the Landscape Architects," in Fein, *Landscape into Cityscape*, 158–59.

57. Olmsted and Vaux, "Report of the Landscape Architects," in Fein, *Landscape into Cityscape*, 159. See also idem, "Preliminary Report," in ibid., 99.

58. Olmsted and Vaux, "Report of the Landscape Architects," in Fein, *Landscape into Cityscape*, 161.

59. Olmsted, Vaux & Co., "Report Accompanying Plan for Laying Out the South Park," in Sutton, *Civilizing American Cities*, 158, 178–79; and Frederick Law Olmsted and J. C. Olmsted, "The Projected Park and Parkways on the South Side of Buffalo," in ibid., 130–55.

60. Hines, *Burnham* (see intro., n. 2), 316.

61. Olmsted, "Preliminary Report," in Sutton, *Civilizing American Cities*, 111–12, 115; Olmsted and Vaux, "Report of the Landscape Architects," in Fein, *Landscape into Cityscape*, 163.

62. Olmsted and Kimball, *Olmsted: Landscape Architect*, 2:46; Olmsted, *Public Parks and Enlargement of Towns*, 34–35.

63. Olmsted, *Public Parks and Enlargement of Towns*, 19–22 (quotation, 22). A critical view of Olmsted and Central Park is in Seymour J. Mandelbaum, *Boss Tweed's New York* (New York: John Wiley & Sons, 1965), 74–76; and Jacob A. Riis, *How the Other Half Lives* (New York: Charles Scribner's Sons, 1890; reprint, New York: Dover Publications, 1971), 138–39.

64. Olmsted, Vaux & Co., "Report [on] the South Park," in Sutton, *Civilizing American Cities*, 171; Olmsted and Vaux, "Report of the Landscape Architects," in Fein, *Landscape into Cityscape*, 156–57; and Olmsted, *Public Parks and Enlargement of Towns*, 35.

65. 1874 report quoted in Peterson, "Origins of the Comprehensive City Planning Ideal," 104. For the 1886 report, see Olmsted, "Notes on the Plan of Franklin Park and Related Matters," in Sutton, *Civilizing American Cities*, 259.

66. Olmsted, *Public Parks and Enlargement of Towns*, 35; and Olmsted, "Notes on Franklin Park," in Sutton, *Civilizing American Cities*, 255.

67. Olmsted, *Public Parks and Enlargement of Towns*, 18; and Olmsted, "Notes on Franklin Park," in Sutton, *Civilizing American Cities*, 255.

68. Olmsted, "Preliminary Report," in Sutton, *Civilizing American Cities*, 105; and Olmsted and Olmsted, "Park and Parkways of Buffalo," in ibid., 130, 151.

69. Olmsted, *Public Parks and Enlargement of Towns*, 26.

70. For quotation, see Olmsted, Vaux & Co., "Report [on] the South Park," in Sutton, *Civilizing American Cities*, 179–80. For insights, see Olmsted, "Notes on Franklin Park," in ibid., 261. For European precedent, see Olmsted, "Preliminary Report," in ibid., 105–6, 120–21; and Olmsted and Olmsted, "Park and Parkways of Buffalo," in ibid., 141; and Olmsted and Vaux, "Report of the Landscape Architects," in Fein, *Landscape into Cityscape*, 157–58. For comprehensiveness, see Olmsted, *Public Parks and Enlargement of Towns*, 5–7, 28–34; Olmsted and Vaux, "Preliminary Report," in Fein, *Landscape into Cityscape*, 123–26; and Olmsted and Vaux, "Report of the Landscape Architects," in ibid., 144.

71. Quoted in Stevenson, *Park Maker*, 402.

72. Olmsted, "Preliminary Report," in Sutton, *Civilizing American Cities*, 119–20; Olmsted and Olmsted, "Park and Parkways of Buffalo," in ibid., 133, 135, 155; and Olmsted, "Notes on Franklin Park," in ibid., 236–37, 239 (quotation, 236). Gourlay's plan is discussed in Paul Boyer, *Urban Masses and Moral Order*, 266–67; and Zaitzevsky, *FLO and Boston*, 41, 96. For Copeland's plan, see Peterson, "Origins of the Comprehensive City Planning Ideal," 123–25; John W. Reps, *The Making of Urban America: A History of City Planning in the United States* (Princeton: Princeton University Press, 1965), 290, 292–93; Zaitzevsky, *FLO and Boston*, 37–41; and John Brinckerhoff Jackson, *American Space: The Centennial Years, 1865–1876* (New York: W. W. Norton & Co., 1972), 32, 131–34.

73. Charles Moore, *Daniel H. Burnham: Architect, Planner of Cities* (Boston: Houghton Mifflin Co., 1921; reprint, New York: Da Capo Press, 1968), 1:74.

CHAPTER 2. MUNICIPAL IMPROVEMENT AND BEAUTIFYING THE ENTIRE COMMUNITY

1. This discussion of municipal improvement and its important figures, including Robinson and Zueblin, is in debt to the work of Park Dixon Goist, Jon A. Peterson, and Mel Scott, cited elsewhere. At the same time the chapter presents a systematic review of

the relationships between municipal improvement and other elements of the City Beautiful movement and a review of the work of Robinson and Zueblin, not elsewhere available.

2. Roper, *FLO* (see chap. 1, n. 2), 404–5, 460–61; Peterson, "Origins of the Comprehensive City Planning Ideal" (see chap. 1, n. 39), 182–83; and M. L. Dock, "The Dauphin Chestnut," *Garden and Forest* 9 (18 March 1896): 114–16. Robert H. Wiebe, *The Search for Order, 1877–1920* (New York: Hill & Wang, 1967), 111–32, is the classic general statement on professional organization, while Jon C. Teaford, *The Unheralded Triumph: City Government in America, 1870–1900* (Baltimore: Johns Hopkins University Press, 1984), 132–73, is specific to urban government. For the founding date of the NML, see Scott, *American City Planning* (see intro., n. 1), 41. For the ASMI, see Stanley K. Schultz and Clay McShane, "To Engineer the Metropolis: Sewers, Sanitation, and City Planning in Late-Nineteenth-Century America," *Journal of American History* 65 (September 1978): 401; and Nelson P. Lewis, "The Work and Aims of the American Society of Municipal Improvements," in *Proceedings of the Rochester Conference for Good City Government and Seventh Annual Meeting of the National Municipal League*, ed. Charles M. Robinson (Philadelphia, 1901), 179–83. For the larger social implications of municipal engineering see the entire Schultz and McShane article, 389–411; and Martin V. Melosi, *Garbage in the Cities: Refuse, Reform, and the Environment, 1880–1980* (College Station: Texas A&M University Press, 1981), 79–104.

3. Newton, *Design on the Land* (see chap. 1, n. 25), 185–86; and American Park and Outdoor Art Association (APOAA), *First Report* (Louisville, 1897), 68–71. Manning to Messrs. Olmsted, Olmsted, and Eliot, 3 Feb. 1897, and to Charles Eliot, 5 Mar. 1897, folder 2922, American Civic Association, box 185, Olmsted Records (see chap. 1, n. 11).

4. APOAA, *First Report*, 5–7.

5. Ibid., 5 (quotation, 68). Mrs. Schuyler (Marianna Griswold) Van Rensselaer, *Art Out-Of-Doors: Hints on Good Taste in Gardening* (New York: Charles Scribner's Sons, 1893). For rearguard actions, see APOAA, *Second Report of the [APOAA]: Minneapolis, Minnesota, June 22, 23, and 24, 1898* (Boston, 1898), 26–29.

6. APOAA, *First Report*, 11–17 (quotations, 15, 16, 17).

7. Ibid., 19–24, 50–54, 56–62, 42–50.

8. For quotation, see APOAA, *First Report*, 5. For engineers, see Schultz and McShane, "To Engineer the Metropolis," 389–411; and idem, "Pollution and Political Reform in Urban America: The Role of Municipal Engineers, 1840–1920," in *Pollution and Reform in American Cities, 1870–1930*, ed. Martin V. Melosi (Austin: University of Texas Press, 1980), 155–72.

9. Horace W. S. Cleveland, "Influence of Parks on the Character of Children," in APOAA, *Second Report*, 105–8; O. C. Simonds, "Appreciation of Natural Beauty," in ibid., 75–80. For differing views, see APOAA, *Second Report*, 65–66, 108–11, and 132–36. Edwin L. Shuey, "Outdoor Art and Workingmen's Homes," in ibid., 112–23.

10. Mrs. Robert Pratt, "Improvement of School Surroundings and the Work of the Minneapolis Improvement League," in APOAA, *Second Report*, 100–104.

11. APOAA, *Second report*, 54.

12. APOAA, "Report of the Committee on Park Census, 1903," *Reports of the Standing Committees at the Seventh Annual Meeting* [Buffalo, 7–9 July 1903], vol. 7, pt. 2 (Rochester: Office of the Secretary, 1903), 14.

13. Ibid., 15.

14. Frederick Law Olmsted, Jr., "Public Advertising," in APOAA, *Proceedings of the Fourth Annual Meeting held at the Art Institute, Chicago, Ill., June 5, 6, and 7, 1900*, vol. 4, pt. 1 (Boston: Rockwell & Churchill Press, 1900), 3–11; George Kriehn, "The Abuses of Advertising and Their Correction," in ibid., pt. 2, 46 (quotation, 53). For expansions of the phrase *outdoor art*, see ibid., pt. 3, 28–35, 35–40, 42–45, 85–93, and 93–95. For forestry, see APOAA, *Second Report*, 144–52. See also APOAA, *Report of the Special School Garden Session of the Seventh Annual Meeting, Buffalo, July 8, 1903*, vol. 7, pt. 3 (Rochester: Office of the Secretary, 1904).

15. APOAA, *First Report*, 4, 6–7; idem, *[Proceedings] Detroit, Michigan, June 27, 28, and 29, 1899* (Boston, 1899), 29–39; and idem, *Year Book and Record of the Seventh Annual*

Meeting [Buffalo, 7–9 July 1903], vol. 7, pt. 1 (Rochester: Office of the Secretary, 1903), 12–22, 41–49, 51.

16. APOAA, *Proceedings of the Fourth Annual Meeting*, vol. 4, pt. 2, 13. Manning to Edward C. Van Leyen, 2 Mar. 1901, folder 2922, American Civic Association, box 185, Olmsted Records.

17. Charles Mulford Robinson, "Report of the Committee on the Federation of Societies," in APOAA, *Year Book*, 67–68; and J. Horace McFarland, "The Federation of Civic Forces—City, State and National," in *National Conference for Good City Government* (Philadelphia: National Municipal League, 1903), 202–10 (quotation, 208).

18. APOAA, *Year Book*, 5.

19. For an excellent introduction to progressivism, see Boyer, *Urban Masses and Moral Order* (see chap. 1, n. 4), 175–283. See also J. Horace McFarland, "The Great Civic Awakening," *Outlook* 73 (18 April 1903): 917–20; J. Horace McFarland and Clinton Rogers Woodruff, "The Uplift in American Cities," *World's Work* 8 (July 1904): 4963–79; and Charles Zueblin, "The Civic Renascence: The Harrisburg Plan," *Chautauquan* 39 (March 1904): 60–67.

20. Birdsey G. Northrup, "The Work of Village Improvement Societies," *Forum* 19 (March 1895): 95–105. For a discussion of the development of village improvement and small-scale landscaping into city planning, see David P. Handlin, *The American Home: Architecture and Society, 1815–1915* (Boston: Little, Brown and Company), 89–231. For the population of Minneapolis, see U.S. Department of Commerce, Bureau of the Census, *A Report on the Seventeenth Decennial Census of the United States: Census of Population, 1950* (Washington: GPO, 1952), 1:23-11.

21. For quotation about Hopkins, see League for Social Service, *Village Improvement: Advantages, Scope and Suggested Constitution* (New York: n.d.), 5. For Downing, see *Horticulturalist and Journal of Rural Art and Rural Taste* 1 (March 1847): 394. For village dwellers, see Mary Caroline Robbins, "Village Improvement Societies," *Atlantic Monthly* 79 (February 1897): 213. For suburbs, see Northrup, "Village Improvement," 99–100 (for Stockbridge quotation, see 96, and for New Milford, 97).

22. Northrup, "Village Improvement," 104. For a later publication containing examples of village improvement organizations from earlier times, see Frederick Law Olmsted, Jr., *Village Improvement*, leaflet no. 5 (Boston: Massachusetts Civic League, 1905).

23. Northrup, "Village Improvement," 104. For the Honesdale association, see League for Social Service, *Village Improvement*, 6, and for children, 9–10. For Stockbridge, see Northrup, "Village Improvement," 95–96; and League for Social Service, *Village Improvement*, 5.

24. For Wyoming, see Northrup, "Village Improvement," 97; and for Pasadena, 103. For Aiken, see Robbins, "Village Improvement," 221. For Springfield, see Northrup, "Village Improvement," 102; and U.S. Bureau of the Census, *Census of Population, 1950*, 1:21-8. For the early strength of Massachusetts village improvement, see *American Architect and Building News* 8 (11 December 1880): 278. For an excellent analysis of Springfield, see *Let Us Make a Beautiful City of Springfield, Mass.: A Series of Sixteen Articles Reprinted from the Springfield Republican with Illustrations* (Springfield: Republican Co., 1901).

25. Robbins, "Village Improvement," 213; and Northrup, "Village Improvement," 97–98, 102.

26. [Jessie M. Good], "The National League of Improvement Associations," *Home Florist* 4 (January 1901): 44; American League for Civic Improvement (ALCI), *The Twentieth Century City: A Record of Work Accomplished for Civic Betterment [Home Florist]* 4 (October 1901): 65; and idem, *Nation-wide Civic Betterment: A Report of the Third Annual Convention of the American League for Civic Improvement* (Chicago, 1903), 7 (quotation, 1).

27. For town improvement, see ALCI *Twentieth Century City*, 1–4; and idem, *Nation-wide Civic Betterment*, inside front cover. For the urban emphasis, see ALCI, *Twentieth Century City*, 1, 4–5, and 16–20. For urban concerns related to the City Beautiful, see David Glassberg, "The Design of Reform: The Public Bath Movement in America," *American Studies* 20 (Fall 1979): 5–21; James H. Potts, "The Evolution of Municipal Accounting in the United States: 1900–1935," *Business History Review* 52 (Winter 1978):

518–36; Raymond W. Smilor, "Cacophony at Thirty-fourth and Sixth: The Noise Problem in America, 1900–1930," *American Studies* 18 (Summer 1977): 23–38; Mark J. Tierno, "The Search for Pure Water in Pittsburgh: The Urban Response to Water Pollution, 1893–1914," *Western Pennsylvania Historical Magazine* 60 (January 1977): 23–36; and Marilyn Thornton Williams, "Philanthropy in the Progressive Era: The Public Baths of Baltimore," *Maryland Historical Magazine* 72 (Spring 1977): 118–31.

28. ALCI, *Twentieth Century City*, 62–65.

29. Ibid., 66–67. See also William S. Crandall, "The Model City: A Suggestion for the St. Louis Exposition," *Municipal Affairs* 5 (Fall 1901): 670–74.

30. "American Society of Landscape Architects Minute on the Life and Services of Charles Mulford Robinson, Associate Member," *Landscape Architecture* 9 (July 1919): 180–89 (quotation, 181); and "Bibliography of Writings on Civic and Kindred Topics," ibid., 189–93. For an example of a Robinson plan, see Robert D. Parker, "Fort Wayne with Might and Main," *Old Fort News* 37, no. 2 (1974): 3–14.

31. "Minute," portrait; and "Bibliography."

32. "Minute," 180–81; "Bibliography," 190. Charles Mulford Robinson, "Improvement in City Life" series, *Atlantic Monthly* 83 (1899), "Philanthropic Progress" (April), 524–37; "Educational Progress" (May), 654–64; and "Aesthetic Progress" (June), 771–85. The *Harper's* series included "Municipal Art in Paris," 103 (July 1901): 200–207; "Belgium's Art Crusade," 104 (February 1902): 443–52; and "Art Effort in British Cities," 105 (October 1902): 787–96.

33. Charles Mulford Robinson, *Improvement of Towns and Cities*, ix–xii, 52 ("city building"), 200 ("civic art's transforming touch"), 211 ("scenic picturesqueness"), 34 ("best planned city"), 35 ("monumental a structure"), 56 ("clear as is the menace").

34. Ibid., vii-viii; 1 ("city beauty"); 63 ("city beautiful"); and 71 ("urban beauty").

35. Ibid., for the Society for Checking the Abuses of Public Advertising, see 78–79; for L'œuvre national belge, see 100–104; for New York, see 47–48; and for Cleveland, see 109.

36. Ibid., for heights quotations, see 4; for shorelines quotations, see 17; for parks, see 155 (quotation, 165); and for architect quotation, see 264–65.

37. Ibid., 170.

38. ALCI, *Nation-wide Civic Betterment*, 13–18 (quotations, 16, 18).

39. Ibid., 2, 58–69, 96–103; and APOAA, *Year Book*, 12.

40. ALCI, *Nation-wide Civic Betterment*, for Addams, see 29–32; for Ohage, see 40–42; for McCall, see 50–56. For St. Louis, see "Work of the League: General News of Civic Improvement Progress," *Home and Flowers* 12 (September 1902): 134–35; Stephen J. Raiche, "The World's Fair and the New St. Louis," *Missouri Historical Review* 68 (October 1972), 98–121. For Kelsey, see ALCI, *Nation-wide Civic Betterment*, 70–71.

41. ALCI, *Nation-wide Civic Betterment*, 2.

42. For the merger of APOAA and ALCI and structuring of ACA, see McFarland to Mira Lloyd Dock, 28 Sept. 1903, box 6, Dock Family Papers, Manuscript Group 43, Pennsylvania State Archives (hereafter cited as Dock Family Papers); APOAA, *Year Book*, 5; minutes of the meeting of the executive board of the ALCI, 26 October [1903], and notice to the members of the APOAA and the ALCI, April 1904, bulletin 1, box 14, J. Horace McFarland Papers, Manuscript Group 85, Pennsylvania State Archives (hereafter cited as McFarland Papers). For McFarland's support of feminism, see McFarland to Mrs. J. Q. Adams, 10 April 1913, box 1, McFarland Papers. McFarland summarized the ACA's activities in a letter to Lawrence F. Abbott, 23 Mar. 1915, box 1, McFarland Papers. For quotations in sequence, see McFarland to members of the ACA, 1 Nov. 1905, folder 2922, box 185, Olmsted Records; to Abbott; and to Thomas Adams, 14 Nov. 1919, box 1, McFarland Papers. For ACA pamphlets, see Frederick Law Olmsted and Harlan Page Kelsey, *The Smoke Nuisance*, Department of Nuisances, ser. 2, no. 1 (Philadelphia, 1908); Joseph Lee, *Play and Playgrounds*, Department of Public Recreation, leaflet no. 11 (Philadelphia, 1906); and McFarland, "The American Civic Association's Work," *Park and Cemetery and Landscape Gardening* 18 (January 1909): 483.

43. For Woodruff's resignation, see McFarland to the members of the ACA, 6 Jan. 1909, vertical files, Frances Loeb Library, Graduate School of Design, Harvard University.

For McFarland's work and domination of the ACA, see McFarland to Eleanor E. Marshall, 30 Nov. 1917, box 6; to H. J. Heinz, 8 June 1915, box 4; to Archibald Johnson, 12 July 1917, box 5; to John Nolen, 30 June 1914, box 7; and to Morton D. Hull, 17 Sept. 1914, box 5, McFarland Papers.

44. For McFarland's quotations and arguments in sequence, see McFarland to Clinton Rogers Woodruff, 17 Dec. 1914, box 13; Richard B. Watrous to McFarland, 22 Jan. 1913, box 10; McFarland to Woodruff, 31 Dec. 1913, box 12; and McFarland to George T. Fox, 5 Nov. 1914, box 4, McFarland Papers. See also Zona Gale, *Civic Improvement in the Little Towns*, ser. 2, bulletin 7 (Washington, D.C.: American Civic Association, 1913).

45. McFarland's presidential letters compose the bulk of the McFarland Papers. For slides, see McFarland to J. Louis Breitinger, 21 May 1914, box 1; for pamphlets, see McFarland to Watrous, 16 Dec. 1912, box 10; for fees, McFarland to Orlando Harrison, 23 Feb. 1916, and to C. L. Harmonson, 22 June 1916, box 4; and for remission, McFarland to George W. Cliffe, 9 Dec. 1915, box 2, McFarland Papers. For lectures, see McFarland to Charles E. Fay, 17 Nov. 1911, box 15, McFarland Papers; Newton C. Blanchard, ed., *Proceedings of a Conference of Governors in the White House, Washington, D.C., May 13–15, 1908* (Washington, D.C., 1908), 152–57; "The Value of Beauty in Waterways," notes of illustrated address to Rivers and Harbors Congress, Washington, 10 Nov. 1908, and other manuscripts in box 14, McFarland Papers. For "Beautiful America" series, see Edward W. Bok, *The Americanization of Edward Bok: The Autobiography of a Dutch Boy Fifty Years After* (New York: Charles Scribner's Sons, 1920), 236–58; and Salme Harju Steinberg, *Reformer in the Marketplace: Edward W. Bok and the "Ladies' Home Journal"* (Baton Rouge: Louisiana State University Press, 1979), 90–95.

46. For quotation, see Edmund G. Hill to McFarland, 20 Oct. 1913, box 4, McFarland Papers.

47. For membership, see ACA, *A Year's Work for Civic Improvement*, bulletin 3 (Philadelphia, 1905), 3; ACA, *Another Year's Work for Civic Improvement* (Philadelphia, 1906), 3; and Marie Demitt to Barry C. Smith, 2 Dec. 1921, box 31, McFarland Papers. For professional, organizational, and publications changes, see Peterson, "Origins of the Comprehensive City Planning Ideal," (see chap. 1, n. 39), 373–425; Scott, *American City Planning*, 71–100; and John L. Hancock, "John Nolen and the American City Planning Movement: A History of Culture Change and Community Response, 1900–1940," (Ph.D. diss., University of Pennsylvania, 1964), 137–42.

Chapter 3. The Columbian Exposition and the City Beautiful Movement

1. The historiographical cliché dies hard: see Lewis I. Sharp, "Richard Morris Hunt and His Influence on American Beaux-Arts Sculpture," in Stein, *Architecture of Richard Morris Hunt* (see chap. 1, n. 1), 45.

2. For the fair, see David F. Burg, *Chicago's White City of 1893* (Lexington: University Press of Kentucky, 1976); Reid Badger, *The Great American Fair: The World's Columbian Exposition and American Culture* (Chicago: Nelson Hall, 1979); Stanley Appelbaum, *The Chicago World's Fair of 1893: A Photographic Record* (New York: Dover Publications, 1980); and Maurice Frank Neufeld, "The Contributions of the World's Columbian Exposition of 1893 to the Idea of a Planned Society in the United States" (Ph.D. diss., University of Wisconsin, 1935). Several books contain chapters or sections on the fair. I was most influenced by Donald Hoffman, *The Architecture of John Wellborn Root* (Baltimore: Johns Hopkins University Press, 1973), 220–45. See also two books by Charles Moore, *Burnham* (see chap. 1, n. 73), 1:31–81; and *The Life and Times of Charles Follen McKim* (Boston: Houghton Mifflin Co., 1929), 113–27; Hines, *Burnham* (see intro., n. 2), 73–124; Newton, *Design on the Land* (see chap. 1, n. 25), 353–71; and Robert W. Rydell, *All the World's a Fair: Visions of Empire at American International Expositions, 1876–1916* (Chicago: University of Chicago Press, 1984), 38–71. Two articles in *Journal of the Illinois State Historical Society* 55 (Winter 1972) recount the interurban struggle for the exposition site: Francis L. Lederer II, "Competition for the World's Columbian Exposition: The Chicago Cam-

paign," 382–94; and Robert D. Parmet, "Competition for the World's Columbian Exposition: The New York Campaign," 365–81.

3. Hines, *Burnham*, 3–72, 234–36; Moore, *Burnham*, 1:1–30, 35.

4. Hoffman, *Root*, 229–33. Quotations from Moore, *Burnham*, 1:41.

5. Hines, *Burnham*, 81–83, 92–106, 119–20 (quotation, 120); Hoffman, *Root*, 233–25, 244; Moore, *Burnham*, 42–48.

6. For reactions to contemporary warnings, see Hoffman, *Root*, 244; and William H. Jordy and Ralph Coe, "Editors' Introduction," in *American Architecture and Other Writings*, Montgomery Schuyler (Cambridge: Belknap Press of Harvard University Press, 1961), 1:78–79. For Burnham and contemporary accounts of the fair, see Hines, *Burnham*, 113–23.

7. Quotation from Thomas Adams, *Outline of Town and City Planning: A Review of Past Efforts and Modern Aims* (New York: Russell Sage Foundation, 1935), 173.

8. Badger, *Great American Fair*, 90–92; and Burg, *Chicago's White City*, 137, 337–38, 344–47. For sanitary reform, see Peterson, "Impact of Sanitary Reform upon American Urban Planning" (see chap. 1, n. 46), 83–103.

9. Badger, *Great American Fair*, 79, 101–2, 120–22; and Burg, *Chicago's White City*, 105–6, 163–68, 207–9, 262–65, 279–80, 321–25.

10. For examples of built and surviving nineteenth-century classical buildings, see John W. Reps, *Monumental Washington: The Planning and Development of the Capital Center* (Princeton: Princeton University Press, 1967), 37–38, 45, 47–49; Burchard and Bush-Brown, *Architecture of America* (see intro., n. 2), 92–96; and Walter Muir Whitehill, *Boston: A Topographical History*, 2d ed., enl. (Cambridge: Belknap Press of Harvard University Press, 1968), 133–34, 169. For the Library of Congress, see Helen-Anne Hilker, *Ten First Street, Southeast: Congress Builds a Library, 1886–1897* (Washington: Library of Congress, 1980); and Herbert Small, *The Library of Congress: Its Architecture and Decoration*, ed. Henry Hope Reed (New York: W. W. Norton & Co., 1982). For the Boston Public Library, see William H. Jordy, *American Buildings and Their Architects*, vol. 3, *Progressive and Academic Ideals at the Turn of the Century*, ed. William Harvey Pierson (Garden City, N.Y.: Doubleday & Co., 1972), 314–75; and Moore, *McKim*, 62–94. For the Washington Memorial Arch and White, see Charles C. Baldwin, *Stanford White* (New York: Dodd, Mead, 1931; reprint, New York: Da Capo Press, 1976), 194–207, 218–20. For the neocolonial, see Walter C. Kidney, *The Architecture of Choice: Eclecticism in America, 1880–1930* (New York: George Braziller, 1974), 7, 31–33. For stylistic debates within the neoclassical movement, see Mardges Bacon, *Ernest Flagg: Beaux-Arts Architect and Urban Reformer* (New York: Architectural History Foundation; Cambridge: MIT Press, 1986), 55–62, 193.

11. Jordy, *American Buildings: Progressive and Academic Ideals*, 314–75; Moore, *McKim*, 62–94; Richard Guy Wilson, *McKim, Mead & White, Architects* (New York: Rizzoli, 1983), 134–44; and especially the excellent discussion by Leland M. Roth, *McKim, Mead & White, Architects* (New York: Harper & Row, 1983), 116–30, which includes a version of the fountain on 118. Another view of the fountain is in *A Monograph of the Works of McKim, Mead & White, 1879–1915*, new ed., 4 vols. in 1 (1915; New York: Benjamin Blom, 1973), 48, with sketches suggesting some compromise between traffic needs and the retention of a small park around the fountain. See also Paul Zucker, *Town and Square: From the Agora to the Village Green* (New York: Columbia University Press, 1959; reprint, Cambridge: MIT Press, 1970), 1–2, 5–6, 11, 99–101, 189–90.

12. Paul R. Baker, *Richard Morris Hunt* (Cambridge: MIT Press, 1980), 27–36, 110–11, 326; Bacon, *Ernest Flagg*, 17–48; and Richard Chafee, "Hunt in Paris," in Stein, *Architecture of Richard Morris Hunt*, 13–45.

13. For the Statue of Liberty, see Baker, *Hunt*, 317–21. For Richardson, see Henry Russell Hitchcock, *The Architecture of H. H. Richardson and His Times*, 1st MIT paperbound ed. (Cambridge: MIT Press, 1966), 110–17, 136–44; and Mrs. Schuyler Van Rensselaer, *Henry Hobson Richardson and His Works* (Boston: Houghton, Mifflin & Co., 1888; reprint, Park Forest, Ill.: Prairie School Press, 1967), 51–53, 59–66. For quotation, see Burg, *Chicago's White City*, 346. For the Boston Public Library and the Library of Congress, see references cited in notes 10 and 11.

14. For architects' goals, see Baker, *Hunt*, 436–38; H. K. Bush-Brown, "Municipal Art Society of New York," in APOAA, *Proceedings of the Sixth Annual Meeting, Boston, 1902*, vol. 4, pt. 1 (Rochester, 1902), 67–68; *Year Book of The Municipal Art Society of New York* (New York, 1910), 7–8; and Homer Saint-Gaudens, ed., *The Reminiscences of Augustus Saint-Gaudens* (New York: Century Co., 1913), 2:209–10.

15. Helen Lefkowitz Horowitz, *Culture and the City: Cultural Philanthropy in Chicago from the 1880s to 1917* (Lexington: University Press of Kentucky, 1976), 27–48; Harold M. Mayer and Richard C. Wade, *Chicago: Growth of a Metropolis* (Chicago: University of Chicago Press, 1969), 100, 102; Lederer, "Competition: The Chicago Campaign"; and Parmet, "Competition: The New York Campaign."

16. Adams, *Outline of Town and City Planning*, 173; and Robinson, "Aesthetic Progress," 771.

17. Detailed discussions of the artists' contributions are in Badger, *Great American Fair*; and Burg, *Chicago's White City*. See also H. Wayne Morgan, *New Muses: Art in American Culture 1865–1920* (Norman: University of Oklahoma Press, 1978), 50–56, and passim for general developments in American painting.

18. Quotation, *Municipal Art Society of New York* (New York, [1910?]), 1. Bush-Brown, "Municipal Art Society of New York," 67–68; Baker, *Hunt*, 436; and, for the Municipal Art Conference, *Municipal Affairs* 3 (December 1899): 579–746. For an overview of the municipal art movement, see Scott, *American City Planning* (see chap. 2, n. 2), 43–46. For painters' society, see Burg, *Chicago's White City*, 318; and for sculptors', Baker, *Hunt*, 436. For competitions, see *American Architect and Building News* 51 (15 February 1896): 78–79; ibid., 52 (25 April 1896): 39; and ibid., 68 (13 January 1900): 13.

19. Thomas E. Tallmadge, *The Story of Architecture in America* (New York: W. W. Norton & Co., 1927), 211–12. Carroll L. V. Meeks, *The Railroad Station: An Architectural History* (New Haven: Yale University Press, 1956), 128. Compare the photograph of the Omaha Court of Honor, 381, with the 1893 court, 374, in Charles Zueblin, "The Civic Renascence: 'The White City' and After," *Chautauquan* 38 (December 1903): 373–84. For the Cleveland competition, see Hines, *Burnham*, 159–60. For the Dewey Arch, sponsored by the National Sculpture Society, see Barr Ferree, "The Dewey Arch—I," *American Architect and Building News* 68 (13 January 1900): 19–20.

20. Burg, *Chicago's White City*, 121–22, 123–24, 132.

21. Ibid., 337–47.

22. For Burnham's strictures against the bizarre, see Hines, *Burnham*, 95–97.

23. Robinson, *Improvement of Towns and Cities*, 145.

24. Christopher Tunnard, *The Modern American City* (New York: Van Nostrand Reinhold Co., 1968), 47.

25. Moore, *McKim*, 117–18. George Kriehn, "The City Beautiful," *Municipal Affairs* 3 (December 1899): 597.

26. Mrs. Edwin D. Mead, "Municipal Improvement," in APOAA, *Proceedings of the Fourth Annual Meeting* (see chap. 2, n. 14), 93.

27. Badger, *Great American Fair*, 190.

28. *Municipal Affairs* 3 (December 1899): cover and elsewhere; and Robinson, "Aesthetic Progress," 785.

29. APOAA, *First Report* (see chap. 2, n. 3); Frederick S. Lamb, "Municipal Art," *Municipal Affairs* 1 (December 1897): 674–88; and Charles Rollinson Lamb, "Civic Architecture from its Constructive Side," *Municipal Affairs* 2 (March 1898): 46–72.

30. Peterson, "Origins of the Comprehensive City Planning Ideal" (see chap. 1, n. 39), 417–20; and Hines, *Burnham*, 142. For Burnham's lakeshore development, see Hines, *Burnham*, 313–17. For parks and boulevards, August Heckscher, *Open Spaces: The Life of American Cities* (New York: Harper & Row, 1974), 162, 199–203, 206; Mayer and Wade, *Chicago*, 200; Newton, *Design on the Land*, 318–36; and Robinson, *Improvement of Towns and Cities* (see chap. 2, n. 33), 166.

31. Hines, *Burnham*, 156. For fair references, Kriehn, "City Beautiful," 597; Mead, "Municipal Improvement," 93; and Robinson, *Improvement of Towns and Cities*, 145.

32. Wilson, "Ideology, Aesthetics and Politics of the City Beautiful Movement" (see chap. 1, n. 26), 173–74.

33. For the Architectural League, a professional organization, see Albert Kelsey, ed., *The Architectural Annual*, 2d ed. (Philadelphia, 1900), 279. For the parkway, Parkway Association, *The Philadelphia Parkway Project: A Plea for the Success of the Present Movement in Favor of a Diagonal Boulevard from the City Hall to Fairmount Park* (Philadelphia, 1902).

34. For the background of the McMillan Plan see Reps, *Monumental Washington*, 44–45, 51–53, 66; Hines, *Burnham*, 132–42; and Moore, *Burnham*, 1:129–34.

35. Reps, *Monumental Washington*, 70–92; Moore, *Burnham*, 1:135–36; and Charles Moore, ed., *Park Improvement Papers; A Series of Twenty Papers Relating to the Improvement of the Park System of the District of Columbia; Printed for the Use of the Senate Committee on the District of Columbia; . . .* (Washington: GPO, 1903).

36. Jon A. Peterson, "The Hidden Origins of the McMillan Plan for Washington, D.C., 1900–1902," in *Historical Perspectives on Urban Design: Washington, D.C., 1890–1910*, ed. Antoinette J. Lee, Center for Washington Area Studies, Occasional Paper no. 1 (Washington, D.C.: George Washington University, 1984), 7. For another version of the paper, see "The Nation's First Comprehensive City Plan: A Political Analysis of the McMillan Plan for Washington, D.C., 1900–1902," *Journal of the American Planning Association* 51 (Spring 1985): 134–50. For Burnham and the Tarsney Act, see Hines, *Burnham*, 126–33.

37. Reps, *Monumental Washington*, 92–108; Peterson, "Hidden Origins of the McMillan Plan," 10–11; Moore, *Burnham*, 1:136–77; and Hines, *Burnham*, 142–57.

38. Paul D. Spreiregen, ed., *On the Art of Designing Cities: Selected Essays of Elbert Peets* (Cambridge: MIT Press, 1968), 61–64, 70–71, 79–87, 89–97, 105–6; and Reps, *Monumental Washington*, 137.

39. For the problem of street vista termination, see Anthony Sutcliffe, "Architecture and Civic Design in Nineteenth Century Paris," in *Growth and Transformation of the Modern City* (Stockholm: Swedish Council for Building Research, 1979), 92–95. For the plan, see Thomas Michael Walton, *The 1901 McMillan Commission: Beaux Arts Plan for the National Capital* (Ann Arbor: University Microfilms, 1980).

40. For quotation, see Montgomery Schuyler, "The Art of City-Making," *Architectural Record* 12 (May 1902): 5. For reaction to the plan, see Reps, *Monumental Washington*, 139–44; and Peterson, "Origins of the Comprehensive Planning Ideal," 290–302.

41. Daniel H. Burnham, "White City and Capital City," *Century Magazine* 63 (February 1902): 619–20.

42. Robinson, *Improvement of Towns and Cities*, 265.

43. Olmsted to Charles Moore, 14 June 1904, folder 2828-4, box 134, Olmsted Records. ALCI, *Nation-wide Civic Betterment* (see chap. 2, n. 26), 16–18.

44. Zueblin, "'The White City' and After," 373–78.

45. Ibid., 383–84.

46. Charles Mulford, Robinson, *Modern Civic Art, or, the City Made Beautiful*, 4th ed. (New York: G. P. Putnam's Sons, 1918; reprint, New York: Arno Press and *New York Times*, 1970). Quotations are from this, the most widely available of the editions. The book was only lightly revised through the years; for instance the 1918 edition makes but one brief reference to what may be the 1909 Burnham plan for Chicago (p. 98).

47. Ibid., v–vii, 236–41 (civic groups), 26–30 (quotations).

48. Ibid., 21, 271–79.

49. Ibid., 280–82.

50. Ibid., 101–22, 187–90, (quotation, 85).

51. Ibid., 245 (first quotation), 170 (second quotation), 205 (third quotation).

52. Ibid., 121; for first quotation, see 245–57; and for slum mobility quotations, see 254. For Ebenezer Howard and the Garden City idea, see Robert Fishman, *Urban Utopias in the Twentieth Century: Ebenezer Howard, Frank Lloyd Wright, Le Corbusier* (New York: Basic Books, 1977), 23–88.

53. Robinson, *Modern Civic Art*, 258–62 (quotation, 258), 323–25.

Chapter 4. The Ideology and Aesthetics of the City Beautiful Movement

1. For women, see Suellen M. Hoy, "'Municipal Housekeeping': The Role of Women in Improving Urban Sanitation Practices, 1880–1917," in Melosi (see chap. 2, n. 8), *Pollution and Reform*, 173–98.

2. Excellent determinist statements are Samuel P. Hays, "The Politics of Reform in Municipal Government in the Progressive Era," *Pacific Northwest Quarterly* 55 (October 1964): 157–69; and Wiebe, *Search for Order* (see chap. 2, n. 2), especially 111–85. See also Boyer, *Urban Masses and Moral Order* (see chap. 1, n. 4), especially 220–42, 252–83; Michael H. Ebner and Eugene M. Tobin, eds., *The Age of Urban Reform: New Perspectives on the Progressive Era* (Port Washington, N.Y.: Kennikat Press, 1977); Peter Marcuse, "Housing in Early City Planning," *Journal of Urban History* 6 (February 1980): 153–76; Bradley Robert Rice, *Progressive Cities: The Commission Government Movement in America, 1901–1920* (Austin: University of Texas Press, 1977); and Martin J. Schiesl, *The Politics of Efficiency: Municipal Administration and Reform in America, 1880–1920* (Berkeley and Los Angeles: University of California Press, 1977). The classification "determinist" is for convenience and does not suggest either the range and subtlety of each study or the differences between them. Kenneth Fox, in *Better City Government: Innovations in American Urban Politics, 1850–1937* (Philadelphia: Temple University Press, 1977), 87–88, critically examines determinist assumptions.

3. Roy Rosenzweig, "Middle-Class Parks and Working-Class Play: The Struggle over Recreational Space in Worchester, Massachusetts, 1870–1910," *Radical History Review* 21 (Fall 1979): 31–46; and Stephen Hardy, *How Boston Played: Sport, Recreation, and Community, 1865–1915* (Boston: Northeastern University Press, 1982), 65–84. See also Gregory E. Montes, "San Diego's City Park, 1868–1902, An Early Debate on Environment and Profit," *Journal of San Diego History* 23 (Spring 1977): 40–59.

4. See the analysis in chap. 9.

5. Samuel M. Kipp III, "Old Notables and Newcomers: The Economic and Political Elite of Greensboro, North Carolina, 1880–1920," *Journal of Southern History* 43 (August 1977): 373–94. See also the analysis in chaps. 9 and 11. For a review of the writings on collective biography, see Jerome M. Clubb and Howard W. Allen, "Collective Biography and the Progressive Movement: The 'Status Revolution' Revisited," *Social Science History* 1 (Summer 1977): 518–34.

6. For a study of one optimistic reformer, see William H. Wilson, "J. Horace McFarland and the City Beautiful Movement," *Journal of Urban History* 7 (May 1981): 315–34. For parallels in writings on urban problems, see Howard R. Weiner, "The Response to the American City (1885–1915) as Reflected in Writings Dealing with the City in Scholarly and Professional Serial Publications" (Ph.D. diss., New York University, 1972). For an essay in optimism, see the treatment of Dana Bartlett's *The Better City* in *Inventing the Dream: California through the Progressive Era*, Kevin Starr (New York: Oxford University Press, 1985), 246–48.

7. For McFarland quotation, see Wilson, "J. Horace McFarland," 317–18. For Bailey quotation, see "The Forward Movement in Outdoor Art," in APOAA, *General Addresses at the Seventh Annual Meeting, Buffalo, July 7, 8, 9*, vol. 7, pt. 4 (Rochester, 1904) (see chap. 2, n. 12), 7–8. For Parker quotation, "Cleveland's Civic Center," in *The Grouping of Public Buildings*, comp. Frederick L. Ford, Publications of the Municipal Art Society of Hartford, Connecticut, bulletin no. 2 (Hartford, 1904), 61. For Kirkham quotation, see "The Importance and Value of Civic Centers," in ibid., 50.

8. J. H. Patterson and E. L. Shuey, "The Improvement of Grounds about Factories and Employees' Homes," in APOAA, *Proceedings of the Fourth Annual Meeting* (see chap. 2, n. 14), 42–45; and discussion in ibid., 45–46. For Patterson and his welfare programs, see Samuel Crowther, *John H. Patterson: Pioneer in Industrial Welfare* (Garden City, N.Y.: Doubleday, Page & Co., 1923), 302–48; and Isaac F. Marcosson, *Wherever Men Trade: The Romance of the Cash Register* (New York: Dodd, Mead & Co., 1945), 222–40. See also James E. Cebula, "The New City and the New Journalism: The Case of Dayton, Ohio," *Ohio History* 88 (Summer 1979): 277–90. For the relationship between the City Beautiful

and Country Life movements, see William L. Bowers, *The Country Life Movement in America, 1900–1920* (Port Washington, N.Y.: Kennikat Press, 1974), 7–14, 21, 35–36, 38, 39, 41–42, 49–52.

9. McFarland to Charles H. Kilborn, 28 May 1908, box 15, and speech, "The Crusade Against Ugliness," box 14, McFarland Papers (see chap. 2, n. 42). For downtown changes, see Scott, *American City Planning* (see intro., n. 1), 154; and Seymour I. Toll, *Zoned American* (New York: Grossman Publishers, 1969), 74–116, 159–63, 172–87. For smoke, see R. Dale Grinder, "The Battle for Clean Air: The Smoke Problem in Post–Civil War America," in Melosi, *Pollution and Reform*, 83–103. For rivers, see William H. Wilson, "'More Almost than the Men,' Mira Lloyd Dock and the Beautification of Harrisburg," *Pennsylvania Magazine of History and Biography* (October 1975): 491; and Ray Ginger, *Altgeld's America: The Lincoln Ideal versus Changing Realities* (Chicago: Quadrangle Books, 1965), 23–24. For park statistics, see U.S. Department of the Interior, Census Office, *Report on the Social Statistics of Cities in the United States at the Eleventh Census: 1890* (Washington, D.C.: GPO, 1895), 35. Teaford argues for the success of American *versus* European cities' park development, but his case rests on gross acreage, a selective description of a few large parks, early-day elite park management, and a projection of developments only begun or agitated for during the 1890s; see his *Unheralded Triumph* (see chap. 2, n. 2), 68–72, 252–58. A shrewd look behind park statistics is in Charles Zueblin, *American Municipal Progress: Chapters in Municipal Sociology* (New York: Macmillan Co., 1903), 242–45.

10. U.S. Department of the Interior, Census Office, *Social Statistics of Cities: 1890*, 19; W. M. Slabaugh, "Civic Improvement in the City of Omaha and Its Environs," in ALCI, *Nation-wide Civic Betterment*, 36–39.

11. For harmonious relationships, see Robinson, *Modern Civic Art* (see chap. 3, n. 46), 355–75. For quotation, see Albert Kelsey, "Report of the Municipal Art Section Council," in ALCI, *Nation-wide Civic Betterment* (see chap. 2, n. 26), 2. For the bacchante statue, see Charles Moore, *McKim* (see chap. 3, n. 2), 90–94.

12. E. L. Shuey, "Commercial Bodies and Civic Improvement," *Home Florist* 4 (January 1901): 35; J. Horace McFarland, "Beautiful America," *Ladies Home Journal* 21 (January 1904): 15; Robinson, *Modern Civic Art*, 346; see also Charles Zueblin, *A Decade of Civic Development* (Chicago: University of Chicago Press, 1905), 41–57.

13. Darwinism is used here in the meaning developed in John C. Greene, *Science, Ideology, and World View: Essays in the History of Evolutionary Ideas* (Berkeley and Los Angeles: University of California Press, 1981), 128–51.

14. Dominick Cavallo, *Muscles and Morals: Organized Playgrounds and Urban Reform, 1880–1920* (Philadelphia: University of Pennsylvania Press, 1981), 8–9; Boyer, *Urban Masses and Moral Order*, passim. For insightful comments on progressivism, planning, playgrounds, and social control, see David B. Danborn, *"The World of Hope": Progressives and the Struggle for an Ethical Public Life* (Philadelphia: Temple University Press, 1987), 66–76, 104–7; and Don S. Kirschner, "The Ambiguous Legacy: Social Justice and Social Control in the Progressive Era," *Historical Reflections* 2 (Summer 1975): 69–88. See also Kirschner's *Paradox of Professionalism: Reform and Public Service in Urban America, 1900–1940* (New York: Greenwood Press, 1986), 179–82.

15. See Boyer, *Urban Masses and Moral Order*, 277–83, for an analysis less friendly to the progressive spirit. For an attack on progressive-style environmentalism, see William Michelson, *Man and His Urban Environment: A Sociological Approach* (Reading, Mass.: Addison-Wesley Publishing Co., 1970), 117.

16. Edward A. Ross, *Social Control: A Survey of the Foundations of Order* (New York: Macmillan Co., 1901), 196–217, 429. See also Josiah Royce, *Race Questions, Provincialism, and Other American Problems* (New York: Macmillan Co., 1908), 57–108, especially 107–8. For the analysis and application of social control, see Jack P. Gibbs, ed., *Social Control: Views from the Social Sciences* (Beverly Hills: Sage Publications, 1982), especially Lewis A. Coser, "The Notion of Control in Sociological Theory," 13–22. An interpretation of the civic ideal is in Boyer, *Urban Masses and Moral Order*, 252–60. For the concept of cultural hegemony, see T. J. Jackson Lears, *No Place of Grace: Anti-modernism and the Transformation of American Culture, 1880–1920* (New York: Pantheon Books, 1981), 10.

17. Ross, *Social Control*, 337, 428–31, 435–42 (quotation, 435).

18. The following discussion is based on Cavallo, *Muscles and Morals*, and Boyer, *Urban Masses and Moral Order*, 242–51.

19. For conflicts between the organized play movement and park advocates, see Hardy, *How Boston Played*, 85–106; Lawrence Finfer, "Leisure as Social Work in the Urban Community: The Progressive Recreation Movement, 1890–1920" (Ph.D. diss., Michigan State University, East Lansing, 1974), 121–26, 132; George Burnap, *Parks: Their Design, Equipment, and Use* (Philadelphia: J. B. Lippincott Co., 1916), 168; and Henry S. Curtis, *The Play Movement and Its Significance* (1917; reprint, Washington, D.C.: McGrath Publishing Co. and National Recreation and Park Association, n.d.), 126–27, 129–30, 315.

20. For Burnham quotation, see Moore, *Burnham*, 2:102.

21. Jessie Good, "The How of Improvement Work," *Home Florist* 4 (January 1901): 33. For the Harrisburg plan, see chap. 6. For Burnham's plans, see Hines, *Burnham*, (see intro. n. 2), 139–96, 312–60. For Brunner quotation, see American Civic Association, *Program of the Seventh Annual Convention* (n.p., n.d.), 7. A good review of Brunner's ideas and achievements is Robert I. Aitken et al., *Arnold W. Brunner and His Work* (New York: Press of the American Institute of Architects, 1926).

22. For smoke quotation, see "Abstract of an Illustrated Address on 'The Crusade against Ugliness,'" box 14, McFarland Papers. For "efficient" quotation, see McFarland, *How to Plant the Home Grounds* (Philadelphia, 1904), 4.

23. James Weinstein, *The Corporate Ideal in the Liberal State: 1900–1918* (Boston: Beacon Press, 1968), ix–x, 94–95; and Wiebe, *Search for Order*, 149–55, 160–61, 169–76.

24. Olmsted and Kimball, *Olmsted: Landscape Architect* (see chap. 1, n. 13), 2:45–47, 214–37. For the Kansas City plan, see *Report of the Board of Park and Boulevard Commissioners of Kansas City, Mo.: Embracing Recommendations for the Establishment of a Park and Boulevard System for Kansas City, Resolution of October 12, 1893* (Kansas City: Hudson-Kimberly Publishing Co., 1893), 3. For Harrisburg, see *The Plain Truth about the Improvements: Pure Water, Protection from Typhoid Fever, Modern Sewerage, Parks, and Playgrounds*, 2d ed. (Harrisburg: Harrisburg League for Municipal Improvements, 1901), 10. For AP-OAA, see *Reports of the Standing Committees at the Seventh Annual Meeting*, 20. For Robinson, see *Modern Civic Art*, 280–91. For Burnham quotation, see Moore, *Burnham*, 2:147.

25. Hines, *Burnham*, 317–19, 321, 324, 352; and Peterson, "Origins of the Comprehensive City Planning Ideal" (see chap. 1, n. 39), 342–47.

26. Olmsted and Kimball, *Olmsted: Landscape Architect*, 2:46; Olmsted, *Public Parks* (see chap. 1, n. 30), 18–36; *Harrisburg Telegraph*, 6 June 1901; and Moore, *Burnham*, 2:101. For recreation, see Wilson, , "'More Almost than the Men,'" 494; and J. Horace McFarland, "Chicago's Answer," *Outlook* 22 (October 1910): 443–52. For criticisms of Olmsted's position on recreation, see Jackson, *American Space*, 215–19; and Spreiregen, ed., *Art of Designing Cities* (see chap. 3, n. 38), 187–88.

27. Robinson, *Modern Civic Art*, 246; and Rhodri Jeffreys-Jones, "Violence in American History: Plug Uglies in the Progressive Era," *Perspectives in American History*, vol. 8 (Cambridge: Charles Warren Center for Studies in American History, Harvard University, 1974), 486–89. For progressives and community, see Park Dixon Goist, *From Main Street to State Street: Town, City and Community in America* (Port Washington, N.Y.: Kennikat Press, 1977), especially 121–30; Jean B. Quandt, *From the Small Town to the Great Society: The Social Thought of Progressive Intellectuals* (New Brunswick, N.J.: Rutgers University Press, 1970); and R. Jackson Wilson, *In Quest of Community: Social Philosophy in the United States, 1860–1920* (New York: John Wiley & Sons, 1968). For the general problem of community, see Thomas Bender, *Community and Social Change in America* (New Brunswick, N.J.: Rutgers University Press, 1978); and Glenn Tinder, *Community: Reflections on a Tragic Ideal* (Baton Rouge: Louisiana State University Press, 1980).

28. Robinson, *Modern Civic Art*, 3. For impact of Chicago, see chap. 5. For impact of European cities, see Moore, *Burnham*, 2:100–103. For faith in progressive leader, see Lincoln Steffens, *The Autobiography of Lincoln Steffens* (New York: Literary Guild, 1931), 470–81.

29. Albert Shaw, *Municipal Government in Continental Europe* (New York: Macmillan

Co., republished 1901), 6–13, 290–91, 401 (quotations, 410–11).

30. Frederick C. Howe, *European Cities at Work* (New York: Charles Scribner's Sons, 1913), ix, 7, 219–42, 253; McFarland to Richard B. Watrous, 5 June 1913, box 10, McFarland Papers. For American interest in European reform, see Howard Mumford Jones, *The Age of Energy: Varieties of American Experience, 1865–1915* (New York: Viking Press, 1971), 245–53; Justin Kaplan, *Lincoln Steffens, A Biography* (New York: Simon and Schuster, 1974), 38–39; Arthur Mann, "British Social Thought and American Reformers of the Progressive Era," *Mississippi Valley Historical Review* 42 (March 1956): 672–92; Roy Lubove, "Frederick C. Howe and the Quest for Community in America," *Historian* 39 (February 1977): 270–91; and Arthur A. Ekrich, *Progressivism in America: A Study of the Era from Theodore Roosevelt to Woodrow Wilson* (New York: New Viewpoints, 1974), 3–15, 19–33, 96–98.

31. McFarland, "The Great Civic Awakening," *Outlook* 73 (18 April 1903): 917–20; idem, "The Nationalization of Civic Improvement," *Charities and the Commons* 17 (3 November 1906): 229–34; Frederick C. Howe, *The City: The Hope of Democracy* (New York: Charles Scribner's Sons, 1905), 239–48. For progressive change and planning, see Scott, *American City Planning*, 47–109; Senate Committee on the District of Columbia, *Hearing . . . on . . . City Planning*, 61st Cong., 1st sess., 11 March 1910; and Benjamin C. Marsh, *An Introduction to City Planning* (New York: published by the author, 1909). See also Roy Lubove, "The Twentieth Century City: The Progressive as Municipal Reformer," *Mid-America* 41 (October 1959): 195–209.

32. Henry Hope Reed, Jr., *The Golden City* (Garden City, N.Y.: Doubleday & Co., 1959), 100; Huth, *Nature and the American* (see chap. 1, n. 19), 183–84; Downing, *Landscape Gardening* (see chap. 1, n. 2); and idem, *Architecture of Country Houses* (New York: Dover Publications, 1969). For rural amenities, see Bender, *Toward an Urban Vision* (see chap. 1, n. 2), 80–85; and Neil Harris, *The Artist in American Society: The Formative Years, 1790–1860* (New York: George Braziller, 1966), 201. For Olmsted, see the biographies and other works listed in the notes to chap. 1. For environmental role of trees, see Fein, *Landscape into Cityscape* (see chap. 1, n. 29), 234, 266, 273. For the nineteenth-century effort to save Niagara Falls, see Alfred Runte, "Beyond the Spectacular: The Niagara Falls Preservation Campaign," *The New-York Historical Society Quarterly* 58 (January 1973): 30–50. For the battle between active recreation versus contemplative restoration extended to the nineteenth-century wilderness, see Philip G. Terrie, "Urban Man Confronts the Wilderness: The Nineteenth-Century Sportsman in the Adirondacks," *Journal of Sport History* 6 (Winter 1979): 7–20. For naturalistic constructivism and the creation of the middle landscape in natural areas during the Progressive Era, see Peter J. Schmitt, *Back to Nature: The Arcadian Myth in Urban America* (New York: Oxford University Press, 1969), 28.

33. For Boston, see Scott, *American City Planning*, 17–23; and Zaitzevsky, *FLO and Boston* (see chap. 1, n. 2), 33–80. For Raleigh, see Kay Haire Huggins, "City Planning in North Carolina, 1900–1920, pt. I," *North Carolina Historical Review* 46 (October 1969): 381–87. For Dallas, see chap. 12. For McFarland, see Huth, *Nature and the American*, 184, 186–88, 189–91; Nash, *Wilderness and the American Mind* (see chap. 1, n. 17), 165–66, 180; and *Harrisburg Patriot*, 4 October 1948. For White, see Baldwin, *Stanford White* (see chap. 3, n. 10), 5. Patterson and Shuey, "Improvement of Grounds about Factories and Employees' Homes," 42–45; J. Horace McFarland, "How to Improve Railroad Stations and Their Surroundings," *American City* 9 (November 1913): 440–44; and John R. Stilgoe, *Metropolitan Corridor: Railroads and the American Scene* (New Haven: Yale University Press, 1983), 227–43.

34. For Burnham, see Hines *Burnham*, 153–54, 168, 182–88, 332–33; Burnham and Edward H. Bennett, *Plan of Chicago* (Chicago: Commercial Club, 1909), 43–60; and Reps, *Monumental Washington* (see chap. 3, n. 10), 109–38. For Robinson, see Tunnard, *Modern American City* (see chap. 3, n. 24), 49, 159; and Peterson, "Origins of the Comprehensive City Planning Ideal," 342–45. For Nolen, see Hancock, "John Nolen" (see chap. 2, n. 47), 323–33, 508–16.

35. Meeks, *Railroad Station* (see chap. 3, n. 19), 1–2, 24; and idem, "Picturesque Eclecticism," *Art Bulletin* 32 (September 1950): 229, 234. For the Romanesque, see Hitch-

cock, *Richardson* (see chap. 3, n. 13); Tallmadge, *Architecture in America* (see chap. 3, n. 19), 197; Donald Hoffmann, *The Meanings of Architecture: Buildings and Writings by John Wellborn Root* (New York: Horizon Press, 1967); and James F. O'Gorman, *H. H. Richardson: Architectural Forms for an American Society* (Chicago: University of Chicago Press, 1987), especially 67–69.

36. For quotation, see Tunnard, *Modern American City*, 47–48. Cf. Vincent Scully, *American Architecture and Urbanism* (New York: Praeger Publishers, 1969), 140–43.

37. William H. Jordy, *American Buildings: Progressive and Academic Ideals*, 3:333–42; Wilson, *McKim, Mead & White* (see chap. 3, n. 11), 134–44; Roth, *McKim, Mead & White* (see chap. 3, n. 11), 116–30; Alfred Hoyt Granger, *Charles Follen McKim: A Study of His Life and Work* (1913; reprint, New York: Benjamin Blom, 1972), 23–25; and Burchard and Bush-Brown, *Architecture of America* (see intro., n. 2), 280. For an appreciation of McKim's architecture, see Moore, *McKim*, 308–9. For criticism of McKim, see Oliver W. Larkin, *Art and Life in America*, rev. and enl. ed. (New York: Holt, Rinehart & Winston, 1960), 337–38. For Atwood quotation, see Hoffman, *Root* (see chap. 3, n. 2), 221.

38. For quotation, see Joseph Hudnut, "Architecture and the Spirit of Man," in *Architecture in America: A Battle of Styles*, ed. William A. Coles and Henry Hope Reed, Jr. (New York: Appleton-Century-Crofts, 1961), 245.

39. James E. Vance, Jr., "The Classical Revival and Rural-Urban Conflict in Nineteenth Century North America," *Canadian Review of American Studies* 4 (Fall 1973): 148–68; Baldwin, *Stanford White*, 222; James Early, *Romanticism and American Architecture* (New York: A. S. Barnes & Co., 1965), 27–49, 157–58; Harris, *Artist in American Society*, 44–45, 284–98; and George Heard Hamilton, *19th and 20th Century Art: Painting, Sculpture, Architecture* (New York: Harry N. Abrams, Publishers, 1970), 11–45, 47, 150–58. For Burnham's romantic view of Greece and Rome, see Moore, *Burnham*, 1:126–28, 150.

40. Newton, *Design on the Land* (see chap. 1, n. 25), 353–71; Hoffman, *Root*, 225–26; Fein, "American City" (see chap. 1, n. 21), 102, 104; Scully, *American Architecture and Urbanism*, 136–37; Barlow, *Frederick Law Olmsted's New York* (see chap. 1, n. 42), 8, 49–50; Spreiregen, ed., *Art of Designing Cities*, 68–69; and Peterson, "Origins of the Comprehensive City Planning Ideal," 178–80, 197–98, 356–59.

41. Harris, *Artist in American Society*, illus. 4, 5; Samuel Bing, *Artistic America, Tiffany Glass, and Art Nouveau* (Cambridge: MIT Press, 1970), 135; Wendell D. Garrett et al., *The Arts in America: The Nineteenth Century* (New York: Scribner, 1969), illus. 153, p. 213; and Newton, *Design on the Land*, 182–232, 273, illus. 141, 142, 144, 146, 148–49, 152, 154, 158–60, 169–70. For the exposition, Hoffman, *Root*, 222–29, illus. 163–67.

42. Montgomery Schuyler, "Last Words about the World's Fair," in Jordy and Coe, eds., *American Architecture and Other Writings* (see chap. 3, n. 6), 289, 290. For the traditional role of the square or civic center, see Zucker, *Town and Square* (see chap. 3, n. 11); and Werner Hegemann and Elbert Peets, *The American Vitruvius: An Architect's Handbook of Civic Art* (1922; reprint, New York: Benjamin Blom, 1972). For the Dewey and other celebrations, see Peterson, "Origins of the Comprehensive City Planning Ideal," 187–89. Kelsey was paraphrased in George Kriehn, "The Baltimore Conference on Municipal Art," in *The Architectural Annual*, 2d ed., ed. Albert Kelsey (Philadelphia, 1900), 47. For the Pan-American Exposition, see Mark Goldman, *High Hopes: The Rise and Decline of Buffalo, New York* (Albany: State University of New York Press, 1983), 3–20; Walter H. Page, "The Pan-American Exposition," *World's Work* 2 (August 1901): 1023; and (quotation) Charles H. Caffin, "The Pan-American Exposition as a Work of Art," *World's Work* 2 (August 1901): 1050.

43. Walter Hines Page, "Pan-American Exposition," 1048; Robinson, *Improvement of Towns and Cities* (see chap. 2, n. 33), 26–28.

44. John DeWitt Warner, "Civic Centers," *Municipal Affairs* 6 (March 1902): 1–23.

45. Citations for works not previously cited are Daniel H. Burnham, John M. Carrère, and Arnold W. Brunner, *The Group Plan of the Public Buildings of the City of Cleveland: Report Made to the Honorable Tom L. Johnson, Mayor, and to the Honorable Board of Public Service* (Cleveland, 1903); Albert Kelsey, "The City Possible: Utility—Beauty—Economy," *Booklover's Magazine* 2 (August 1903): 162–73; Zueblin, "'The White City' and After" (see chap. 3, n. 19), 373–84; and Frederick L. Ford, comp., *The Grouping of Public*

Buildings, Publications of the Municipal Art Society of Hartford, Connecticut, bulletin no. 2 (Hartford: Municipal Art Society, 1904).

46. Robinson, *Modern Civic Art*, 89–90; Parker, "Cleveland's Civic Center," in Ford, *Grouping of Public Buildings*, 62.

47. Robinson, *Modern Civic Art*, 92–93 (quotations, 82, 89, 95); Parker, "Cleveland's Civic Center," 61–62; Burnham, Carrère, and Brunner, *Group Plan of Cleveland*, 5.

48. Burnham, Carrère, and Brunner, 6; Zueblin, "'White City' and After," 374, 378, 381.

49. Robinson, *Modern Civic Art*, 41, 82, 91. J. G. Phelps Stokes, "Advantages to be Gained by Appropriate Grouping," in Ford, *Grouping of Public Buildings*, 23.

50. Stokes, "Advantages to be Gained by Appropriate Grouping," 23. Cf. Robinson's chapter, "The Administrative Centre," in Ford, *Grouping of Public Buildings*, 81–98. Kelsey, "City Possible," 171; Warner, "Civic Centers," 17, 23; Ford, "Connecticut's Opportunity: The State Capitol at Hartford to be the Center of a Conspicuous Group of Public Buildings," in Ford, *Grouping of Public Buildings*, 13, 18–19.

51. Burnham, Carrère, and Brunner, *Group Plan of Cleveland*, 4, 5. See also Carl Abbott, "Norfolk in the New Century: The Jamestown Exposition and Urban Boosterism," *Virginia Magazine of History and Biography* 85 (January 1977): 86–96.

52. Milo R. Maltbie, "Berlin's Civic Center," in Ford, *Grouping of Public Buildings*, 25–31; idem, "Paris—The City Beautiful," in ibid., 36–41 (quotation, 36); Burnham, Carrère, and Brunner, *Group Plan of Cleveland*, 5.

53. Robinson, *Improvement of Towns and Cities*, 16–17; idem, *Modern Civic Art*, 283; Arthur A. Shurtleff, "The College Yard—Harvard University," in Ford, *Grouping of Public Buildings*, 68–73; Irene Sargent, "Municipal Art: A Lesson from Foreign Towns," *Craftsman* 4 (July 1904): 321–28.

CHAPTER 5. THE STRUGGLE FOR AN URBAN PARK AND BOULEVARD SYSTEM IN KANSAS CITY

1. The best history of Kansas City is A. Theodore Brown and Lyle W. Dorsett, *K.C.: A History of Kansas City, Missouri* (Boulder, Colo.: Pruett Publishing Co., 1978).

2. *Kansas City Times*, 10 June 1877, 8 Sept. 1877, and 25 Apr. 1880; *Kansas City Journal*, 24 June 1877. For the old cemetery, see *Times*, 7 Dec. 1878.

3. Biographies of Nelson include Icie F. Johnson, *William Rockhill Nelson and the Kansas City Star: Their Relation to the Development of the Beauty and Culture of Kansas City and the Middle West* (Kansas City: Burton Publishing Co., 1935); Members of the Staff of the *Kansas City Star*, *William Rockhill Nelson* (Cambridge: Riverside Press, 1915); and Charles E. Rogers, "William Rockhill Nelson: Independent Editor and Crusading Liberal" (Ph.D. diss., University of Minnesota, 1948). For Fort Wayne, see Paul Fatout, *Indiana Canals* (West Lafayette, Ind.: Purdue Research Foundation, 1972); and Charles R. Poinsatte, *Fort Wayne during the Canal Era: A Study of a Western Community in the Middle Period of American History* (Indianapolis: Indiana Historical Bureau, 1969).

4. For Nelson's personal and managerial characteristics, see Rogers, "Nelson," 37–38, 84. William Allen White's *Autobiography* (New York: Macmillan Co., 1946), 230–31, 237–39, has appealing, if not entirely accurate, characterizations of Nelson.

5. For Nelson's real estate developments, see *Times*, 20 Jan. 1891; *Star* Staff, *Nelson*, 39–40, 87–89; and *Star*, 22 Apr. 1900, 23 June 1901, and 10 Sept. 1901.

6. *Star* Staff, *Nelson*, 119–21; Rogers, "Nelson," 315; and *Star*, 30 July 1887, 5 Jan. 1889, 2 Oct. 1890, 29 June 1891, and 19 Feb. 1892. For "Jack Bestovit," see *Star*, 30 Dec. 1890.

7. *Star*, 17 Apr. 1888, 19 Sept. 1889, 28 July 1891. For progress elsewhere, see *Star*, 8 Sept. 1887, 17 Apr. 1888, 10 Jan. 1889, 6 Feb. 1889, and 17 Nov. 1893.

8. *Star*, 25 May 1885.

9. *Star*, 11 Sept. 1886, and 26 Feb. 1890.

10. For quotations see *Star*, 4 Jan. 1889. See also *Star*, 28 Sept. 1882, 28 Nov. 1885, and 11 Sept. 1888.

11. *Laws of Missouri*, 1875, Art. vii, especially Secs. 1 and 7, pp. 244–50. For brief

discussions of legal problems, see Brown and Dorsett, *K.C.*, 125, 165–66; *Star* Staff, *Nelson*, 37; and Henry C. Haskell, Jr., and Richard B. Fowler, *City of the Future: The Story of Kansas City, 1850–1950* (Kansas City: Frank Glenn Publishing Co., 1950), 73.

12. For drafts and commentary on Cravens's work, see *Star*, 5 Mar. 1887, 26 Mar. 1887, 30 Jan. 1889, and 4 Feb. 1889.

13. For passage, see *Times*, 18 May 1889. For the court suit, see *Star*, 13 Jan. 1890, 28 Apr. 1890, 13 May 1890, 1 May 1891; and *The State ex rel. The Kansas City Park District v. The County Court of Jackson County*, 102 Brown (Mo.), 531, 537–39 (1891).

14. For the amendment campaign, see the February 1892 *Star*. For the board and its composition, see *Star*, 5 Mar. 1892, 14 Mar. 1892, 21 Apr. 1892, and 22 June 1903.

15. *The National Cyclopedia of American Biography* (New York: James T. White & Co., 1937), 16:172–73; *Star*, 17 Feb. 1892, 23 Feb. 1892, 5 Mar. 1892, 14 Mar. 1892, and Meyer's obituary, 1 Dec. 1905. See also Robert McE. Schauffler, untitled typewritten sketch of August R. Meyer based on personal acquaintance, in black binder titled "Municipal Government: Parks and Boulevards, Aviation and Airfields," Native Sons Archives, Missouri Valley Collection, Kansas City Public Library (hereafter cited as Native Sons Archives).

16. For quotation, see Meyer to Board of Park and Boulevard Commissioners, 5 May 1892; see also Jno. J. Sexby, Chief Officer, Parks Department, London County Council, to Meyer, 12 Dec. 1897; and Meyer to Kessler, 5 Jan. 1898, Board of Park Commissioners, Archives, letter file Reports from 1892 to 1897 (hereafter cited as Park Board Archives).

17. For budget, see *Star*, 22 Apr. 1893. For assessment districts, tax, and Board of Public Works actions, see Resolution of 27 June 1893, letter file Reports from 1892 to 1897, Park Board Archives; and *Star*, 4 Oct. 1892, 15 Oct. 1892, 11 Feb. 1893, 17 Apr. 1893, and 20 Oct. 1894. For the scenic park, see Council Proceedings, Lower House, binder 24, regular session, 23 May 1893, Office of the City Clerk, Kansas City; and *Star*, 1 June 1893, 6 June 1893. For the new park, see *Star*, 17 Dec. 1890, 23 Dec. 1890, and 1 Sept. 1892; and Kessler to Meyer, 24 Aug. 1892, letter file Reports from 1892 to 1897, Park Board Archives.

18. Except as otherwise noted, the information on Kessler's early life is found in *The National Cyclopedia of American Biography* (New York: James T. White & Co., 1929), 20:296–97; "Personalities: The Man Who Made 'That Pretty Kansas City,'" *Hampton's Magazine* 25 (September 1910): 411–12; George Creel and John Slavens, eds., *Men Who Are Making Kansas City: A Biographical Dictionary* (Kansas City: Hudson-Kimberly Publishing Co., 1902), 78; and obituary articles in the *Star*, 20 Mar. 1923. Other information is taken from an interview with G. E. Kessler, Kessler's son, 14 Oct. 1961.

19. *Star*, 22 May 1886, first quotation. For other railroad activities, see W. W. Fagan to Kessler, 15 Mar. 1894, box 1, George E. Kessler Collection, Missouri Historical Society, St. Louis (hereafter cited as Kessler Collection); and *Star*, 5 Oct. 1886, 15 Oct. 1886. Board of Park and Boulevard Commissioners, Official Record of the Proceedings, binder 2, 13 June 1895, p. 1, a date indicating Kessler's reappointment.

20. *Report of the Board of Park and Boulevard Commissioners* (1893) (see chap. 4, n. 24). For authorship of the sections, see D. J. Haff to Henry D. Ashley, 10 May 1917, box 9, Kessler Collection.

21. *Report of the Board of Park and Boulevard Commissioners* (1893), 3, 4, 11, 15.

22. Ibid., 9, 12.

23. Ibid., 8, 9.

24. Ibid., 46. For the description of the west bluffs, see *Times*, 27 Sept. 1896. For some early improvement efforts, see Council Proceedings, Upper House, binder 19, regular session, 1 Dec. 1890, 37; Council Proceedings, Lower House, binder 20, special session, 26 Oct. 1891, 584; *Star*, 1 May 1891, 28 Sept. 1891; and *Journal*, 27 Oct. 1891.

25. *Report of the Board of Park and Boulevard Commissioners* (1893), 13, 14–15.

26. Ibid., 34–35, 37–38, 41–42, 43–44, 47–48 (quotation, 77).

27. *Star*, 13, 14, 15, 16, 17 Oct. 1893; 15, 22 Nov. 1893; and 6 Dec. 1893 (Commercial Club quotation); *Journal*, 6 Dec. 1892; Council Proceedings, Upper House, binder 23, special session, 20 Oct. 1893, 417; and Council Proceedings, Lower House, binder 24, special session, 2 Nov. 1893, 261.

28. Adriance Van Brunt to Thomas H. Shirley, 21 May 1895, letter file K and L from 1891 to 1902, Park Board Archives; and statement by Kessler, *Star*, 26 Feb. 1895.

29. For the law, see *Star*, 8 Feb. 1893, 20 Mar. 1893. For Haff, see Walter Williams and Floyd Calvin Shoemaker, *Missouri: Mother of the West* (Chicago: American Historical Society, 1930), 5:235–36; *Star*, 10 June 1890; and *Times*, 11 Aug. 1943.

30. *Kansas City ex rel. North Park District v. Scarritt et al., Appellants*, 127 Brown (Mo.), 642, 648–51 (1895). For quotation, see *Star*, 17 Mar. 1895.

31. *Parks and Boulevards: Proposed Amendment to the City Charter of Kansas City Submitted to the Voters of Kansas City, Mo., on June 6, 1895* (Kansas City, 1895). Kessler to Stuart & Young, 16 Nov. 1897, and Kessler to Spitzer & Co., 13 Oct. 1900, letter file S and T from 1892 to April 1905, Park Board Archives; and Kessler to Messrs. W. J. Hayes & Sons, 27 June 1901, letter file M from — to April 1905, Park Board Archives.

32. *Star*, 21 May 1895, 23 May 1895.

33. Ibid., 24, 26, 28, 29, 30 May 1895; and 4, 5, 6 June 1895.

34. Ibid., 7 June 1895.

35. Ibid.

36. *Kansas City v. Ward et al.*, 134 Brown (Mo.), 172, 176–80, 187 (1879); and *Star*, 5 May 1896.

37. The best account of Swope's action is in W. I. Ayers, comp., historical binder "Q–Y," Office of the Superintendent of Parks, Board of Park Commissioners, Kansas City. For Swope's previous gift efforts, see *Times*, 15 Feb. 1890.

38. The best contemporary description of Swope Park is in *Star*, 24 June 1896. See also Council Proceedings, Upper House, binder 27, special session, 10 June 1896, 482; *Star*, 11, 14, 16, 17, 21 June 1896.

39. *Star*, 25 June 1896, 26 June 1896; and *Journal*, 26 June 1896.

40. *Star*, 12, 25 May 1896; 3, 6, 7, 12, 26 June 1896; and 19 Sept. 1896; and Council Proceedings, Upper House, binder 27, special session, 6 June 1896, 476.

41. For construction, see *Star*, 7 June 1896. For private parks, see advertisements in the *Star*, 11 July 1896, 23 Aug. 1896, 1 Sept. 1896.

42. *Star Staff, Nelson*, 38. Hoye's *Kansas City, Mo., Directory and Kansas City, Kan., Directory for 1895* (Kansas City: Hoye Publishing Co., 1894) and succeeding volumes (titles vary) listed Salathial C. Fancher, William S. Woods, D'Estaing Dickerson, Francis M. Black, James G. Minnear, Langston Bacon, Henry N. Ess, Bernard Corrigan, William H. Knotts, Joseph C. Ford, and Frank H. Kumpf. The *Star* identified Philip S. Brown, Sr., John Conover, Henry C. Morrison, Richard H. Field, Harry Brown, and Thomas H. Swope.

43. *Star*, 13 Aug. 1896; 24 Sept. 1896; 16, 17, 22 Oct. 1896; 13 Nov. 1896. *Journal*, 14 Nov. 1896.

44. *Star*, 12 Mar. 1891, 28 May 1891, 5 Aug. 1892, 21 May 1895. For the attack on Swope, *Star*, 24 Mar. 1897.

45. *Star*, 24 Mar. 1897, 13 July 1897.

46. Ibid., 31 Mar. 1897.

47. Ibid., 24 Apr. 1897.

48. Ibid., 26, 28 Apr. 1897; 12, 13, 20 May 1897; and 2 July 1897. For Nelson, see H. J. Haskell, "Interesting People: W. R. Nelson," *American Magazine* 69 (February 1910): 452.

49. Meyer to the Board of Park Commissioners, 29 Aug. 1898; and Campbell to the members of the park board, 4 Oct. 1898, letter file Reports from 1892 to 1897, Park Board Archives. Council Proceedings, Upper House, binder 25, special session, 25 Sept. 1898, 37–47, and binder 37, regular session, 3 Apr. 1899, 64. *Star*, 18 Aug. 1898; 16, 24, 28 Sept. 1898; and 4 Apr. 1899.

50. *Kansas City v. Marsh Oil Company, Appellant*, 140 Rader (Mo.) 458, 471 (1898); and *Kansas City v. Bacon et al., Appellants*, 147 Rader (Mo.), 259 (1899). The *Star* reprinted the text of the Bonfils decision, 14 Mar. 1900. See also Johnson, *Nelson*, 116–17; and Gene Flower, *Timber Line: A Story of Bonfils and Tammen* (reprint ed., Garden City, N.Y.: Garden City Books, 1951), 146–52. *Kansas City v. Bacon et al., Appellants*, 157 Rader (Mo.), 450, 473 (1900); *Kansas City v. Mulkey et al., Appellants*, 176 Rader (Mo.),

229 (1904); and *Bernard Corrigan et al., Appellants v. Kansas City and J. Scott Harrison*, 211 Rader (Mo.), 608 (1908).

51. Drawing, "The Paseo," in Board of Park Commissioners, Kansas City, Mo., *Report . . . for the Fiscal Year Ending April 19, 1909* (Kansas City, 1909).

52. *Star*, 15 June 1899, 3 Jan. 1900, 25 Jan. 1900, 4 May 1900, and 10 Aug. 1900; Kessler to the Board of Park Commissioners, letter file marked "Secretary," Park Board Archives.

CHAPTER 6. AN ELITE CAMPAIGN FOR BEAUTY AND UTILITY IN HARRISBURG

1. George P. Donehoo, *Harrisburg and Dauphin County: A Sketch of the History for the Past Twenty-Five Years, 1900–1925*, 2 vols. (Dayton, Ohio: National Historical Association, 1925); and idem. *Harrisburg: The City Beautiful, Romantic and Historic* (Harrisburg: Telegraph Press, 1927).

2. U.S. Bureau of the Census, *Census of Population*, 1950 (see chap. 2, n. 20), 1:38–11.

3. For urban conditions and park and planning history, see photographs and lantern slides, Dock Family Papers (see chap. 2, n. 42); *Harrisburg Telegraph*, 5 Nov. 1900; 27 Apr. 1901; 4 May 1901; 27, 29 July 1901; 8, 9, 15 Jan. 1902; 8 Feb. 1902; Harrisburg Park Commission, *Report for the Year Ending December 31, 1908* (Harrisburg, 1909), 7–9, 81–82; Harrisburg League for Municipal Improvements, (HLMI), *The Plain Truth about the Improvements*, 11–13, 17–22, 27–34, 50–55; and Capitol Grounds Extension Planning Committee, *The Proposed Extension of the State Capitol Grounds at Harrisburg, Pennsylvania* (Harrisburg, 1941), 7.

4. Biographical information and clipping photographs are in Dock Family Papers. See also L. C. Clemson to Dock, 1 June 1899; F. R. Wilkinson to Dock, 18 July 1901; and George P. Ahern to Dock, 24 Aug. 1901, Mira Lloyd Dock Papers, Manuscript Division, Library of Congress (hereafter cited as Dock Papers); and *Telegraph*, 17 Dec. 1900.

5. Mary Channing Wister to Dock, 29 Oct. 1896; John Hoffer to Dock, 12 Apr. 1898; and manuscript, "Report of the Department of Forestry and Town Improvement, year ending July, 1899," Dock Papers; and Donehoo, *Harrisburg and Dauphin County*, 1:138.

6. Mira Lloyd Dock, *A Summer's Work Abroad, in School Grounds, Home Grounds, Play Grounds, Parks and Forests*, Commonwealth of Pennsylvania, Department of Agriculture Bulletin no. 62 (1900).

7. McFarland to Dock, 26 June 1899; and Manning to Dock, 20 Nov. 1899, Dock Papers.

8. For the "graces" quotation, see *Wilkes-Barre Record*, 18 Apr. 1901. For the Harrisburg speech, see *Telegraph*, 21 Dec. 1900.

9. *Telegraph*, 21 Dec. 1900.

10. For quotation, see ibid., 9 Jan. 1901. For the April 1901 proposal, see ibid., 27 April 1901. The origins of the beautification campaign may be reconstituted from ibid., 21 Dec. 1900–21 Feb. 1902, and are summarized in Donehoo, *Harrisburg and Dauphin County*, 1:179–82; J. Horace McFarland, "The Awakening of a City," *World's Work* 3 (April 1902): 1930; and idem, "The Harrisburg Achievement," *Chautauquan* 36 (January 1903): 402.

11. Active involvement in the bond campaign is defined as contributing to the fund to employ planning experts and playing an active role in the campaign, such as speaking or serving on the experts fund executive committee. Sources of the biographical information include clippings and files of the *Patriot* and *Telegraph*; Dock Papers; Dock Family Papers; McFarland Papers (see chap. 2, n. 42); John W. Jordan, *Encyclopedia of Pennsylvania Biography* (New York: Lewis Historical Publishing Co., 1914); Thomas Lynch Montgomery, ibid. (1924); Ernest Spofford, ibid. (1928); Frederick A. Goodcharles, ibid. (1930); Donehoo, *Harrisburg and Dauphin County*; Luther Reily Kelker, *History of Dauphin County, Pennsylvania, with Genealogical Memoirs*, vol. 3 (New York: Lewis Publishing Co., 1907); *Commemorative Biographical Encyclopedia of Dauphin County, Pennsylvania, Containing*

Sketches of Prominent and Representative Citizens, and Many of the Early Scotch-Irish and German Settlers (Chambersburg, Pa.: J. M. Runk & Co., Publishers, 1896); *American Biography: A New Cyclopedia*, vol. 20 (New York: American Historical Society, 1924); *The National Cyclopedia of American Biography*, vol. 35 (New York: James T. White & Co., 1949); and W. Minster Kunkel to author, 26 Jan. 1979. The City Beautiful leadership did not directly represent the foreign-born 5 percent of Harrisburg's population, the black 8.2 percent, or the 15.2 percent of natives with foreign parentage. U.S. Census Office, *Twelfth Census of the United States Taken in the Year 1900* (Washington, D.C.: GPO, 1901), 1:cx, cxxii, clxxxix. That the population groups were ignored does not necessarily follow. For high school graduates, see U.S. Department of Commerce, Bureau of the Census, *Historical Statistics of the United States, Colonial Times to 1970*, Bicentennial ed. (Washington, D.C.: GPO, 1975), 1:379.

12. These conclusions are in concert with findings in Ebner and Tobin, eds., *Age of Urban Reform* (see chap. 4, n. 2; Rice, *Progressive Cities* (see chap. 4, n. 2; Schiesl, *Politics of Efficiency* (see chap. 4, n. 2); Teaford, *Unheralded Triumph* (see chap. 2, n. 2); and Fox, *Better City Government* (see chap. 4, n. 2).

13. For McFarland on property values and rights, see McFarland to John Nolen, 18 Dec. 1912, box 7; and to Dean Hoffman, 28 Oct. 1915, box 4, McFarland Papers.

14. *Telegraph*, 3, 4, 13 May 1901, McFarland to J. Kennard Johnson, 9 Nov. 1915, box 5, McFarland Papers.

15. *Telegraph*, 18 May 1901, 28 May 1901; 8 June 1901, 5 July 1901; and J. Horace McFarland, *The Awakening of Harrisburg: Some Account of the Improvement Movement Begun in 1902; With the Progress of the Work to the End of 1906* (Philadelphia: National Municipal League, 1907), 2–3. For Manning, see Manning to Dock, 25 Feb. 1901 and 27 May 1901, Dock Papers.

16. HLMI, *Plain Truth about the Improvements*, 7–15.

17. *Telegraph*, 22 Nov. 1901; 12, 20 Dec. 1901; 6, 7, 10 Jan. 1902; and McFarland, *Awakening of Harrisburg*, 3–5.

18. The final phase of the campaign may be followed in the *Telegraph* from 6 Dec. 1901 through 17 Feb. 1902. Examples include press release, 1 Feb. 1902; meeting, 21 Jan. 1902; comparable cities, 22 Apr. 1901; prominent locals, 30 Apr. 1901; other cities, 8 June 1901; sectionalism, 19 Dec. 1901; rents and taxes, 14 and 15 Feb. 1902; answering attacks, 19 Dec. 1901, 28 and 29 Jan. 1902.

19. For the "epidemic," see McFarland, "Harrisburg's Advance: A Lesson to Smaller Municipalities," in *Proceedings of the Boston Conference for Good City Government and Eighth Annual Meeting of the National Municipal League* (Philadelphia, 1902), 124; *Annual Reports of the City Controller . . . of the City of Harrisburg, Penna. for the Year 1900* (Harrisburg, 1901), 191; *Message of the Mayor and the Annual Reports . . . of the City of Harrisburg, Pa. for the Year 1902* (Harrisburg, 1903), 196. Harrisburg's typhoid fever death rate was relatively high for cities of its size and water supply origins, George M. Kober, M.D., "Conservation of Life and Health by Improved Water Supply," *Conference on Conservation of Natural Resources, Washington, 1908* (Washington, D.C.: GPO, 1909), 268–69.

20. For the HLMI, see *Telegraph*, 7 Jan. 1902; distribution, McFarland, "Awakening of a City," 1932; "clams," *Telegraph*, 1 Feb. 1902, 17 Feb. 1902. For board, see *Telegraph*, 12 Dec. 1901, 22 Feb. 1902; McFarland, *Awakening of Harrisburg*, 3–4.

21. For Dock, see *Telegraph*, 4 May 1901, 8 June 1901, and 17 Feb. 1902. For the Civic Club, see *The Twentieth Century City* (*Home Florist* 4 [October 1901]), 4–5. For Manning's talk, see *Telegraph*, 19 Oct. 1901. See also ibid., 26 Nov. 1901 and 18 Dec. 1901.

22. *Telegraph*, 26 Nov. 1901; 16, 21, 25 Jan. 1902; 1, 4 Feb. 1902.

23. Ibid., 22 Jan. 1902, 1 Feb. 1902. McFarland to Dock, 21 Feb. 1902, Dock Papers.

24. For the canal, see *Telegraph*, 11 Apr. 1901, 22 June 1901, 25 June 1901, 5 July 1901, and 15 Oct. 1901. For the effort to move the capital, see *Telegraph*, 27 Apr. 1901, 30 April 1901, and 8 May 1901. For floods, see *Telegraph*, 16 Dec. 1901, 22 Jan. 1902, and 23 Jan. 1902.

25. *Telegraph*, 21 Feb. 1902.

26. *Telegraph*, 23 Feb. 1899, 21 Feb. 1900, 20 Feb. 1901, 18 Feb. 1903, 22 Feb. 1905; *Patriot*, 20 Feb. 1902, 17 Feb. 1904.

27. McFarland to Richard B. Watrous, 27 Sept. 1915, box 11, and to Arnold Brunner, 15 Nov. 1915, box 2, McFarland Papers; Harrisburg Park Commission, *Report of the Harrisburg Park Commission for the Ten Years Ending October 31, 1912* (Harrisburg, n.d.), 2–3, 4; and Bureau of the Census, *Thirteenth Census of the United States, 1910* (Washington, D.C.: GPO, 1913), 3:586.

28. McFarland to Richard B. Watrous, 27 Sept. 1915, box 11, McFarland Papers. For McFarland's insistence that all phases of the improvement proceed as one, see *Telegraph*, 30 Apr. 1901; and McFarland, *Awakening of Harrisburg*, 10.

29. Donehoo, *Harrisburg*, 181. McFarland to Richard B. Watrous, 27 Sept. 1915, box 11, McFarland Papers.

30. Harrisburg Park Commission, *Report for the Year Ending December 31, 1908, Including Summary of Work Done since the Organization of the Commission in 1902* (Harrisburg, 1909), 7; McFarland to Henry Bruere, 18 Dec. 1913, box 1, McFarland Papers. For quotation, see McFarland to Dock, 26 Sept. 1905, box 1, McFarland Papers. For various activities, see McFarland to Dock, 17 Mar. 1905 and 26 Sept. 1905, box 1, and McFarland to Dock, 11 Mar. 1910, box 3, McFarland Papers. For shade tree law, see *Laws of the General Assembly of the Commonwealth of Pennsylvania Passed at the Session of 1907* (Harrisburg, 1907), 349–51; McFarland to M. Harvey Taylor, 16 Sept. 1914, box 9, McFarland Papers. For tree cutting, see McFarland to Dock, 11 June 1912, box 3, McFarland Papers.

31. For signs, see McFarland to Ezra S. Meals, 7 Oct. 1908, box 15, and to Vance C. McCormick, 19 May 1914, box 6, McFarland Papers. For the municipal league, see McFarland to Mrs. H. S. Artieda, 21 Sept. 1915, box 1, McFarland Papers. For 1908 donations, see Harrisburg Park Commission, *Report for the Year Ending December 31, 1908*, 32, 36, 39. For visitors, see McFarland to G. M. Steinmetz, 24 Apr. 1919, box 9, McFarland Papers.

32. For land acquisition, see McFarland to Dock, 11 Mar. 1910, box 3, McFarland Papers. For billboards, see McFarland to Charles A. Disbrow, 30 June 1908, box 14, McFarland Papers. For trolley line, McFarland to Richard B. Watrous, 13 Apr. 1914, box 10, McFarland Papers.

33. McFarland to Dock, 19 Feb. 1910 and 26 Feb. 1914, box 3; McFarland to M. Harvey Taylor, 16 Sept. 1914 and 2 Oct. 1914, box 9, McFarland Papers.

34. McFarland to Richard B. Watrous, 20 Sept. 1915, box 10; McFarland to Watrous, 27 Sept. 1915, box 11, McFarland Papers; and *Patriot*, 24 Sept. 1915. For the city planning commission, see *Patriot*, 22 Apr. 1914; McFarland to R. Nelson Bennett, 14 May 1914 and 22 Jan. 1920, box 1, McFarland Papers.

35. Manning, autobiographical writings, folder, personal copy, misc. typed estate work, etc., Manning Collection, Special Collections, Alumni/Lydon Library, University of Lowell; Stephen Conant, "Democracy by Design: Warren H. Manning's Contribution to Planning History" (M.A. thesis, Tufts University, 1984), 20–37, 68–69, 83–89, 106.

36. Anna S. Cubbison, "Harrisburg's Playgrounds and Their Romper Day," *American City* 15 (July 1916): 34–37; Irma A. Watts, "Kipona—The Annual Water Fete in Harrisburg," *American City* 17 (July 1917): 4–5; and "Ten-Story Penn-Harris Hotel Built by the Community," *American City* 21 (August 1919): 169.

Chapter 7. John C. Olmsted's Plan for Seattle

1. Murray Morgan, *Skid Road: An Informal Portrait of Seattle*, rev. ed. (New York: Viking Press, 1962); Roger Sale, *Seattle: Past to Present* (Seattle: University of Washington Press, 1976); and Constance McLaughlin Green, *American Cities in the Growth of the Nation* (London: University of London, Athlone Press, 1957; New York: Harper & Row, Publishers, Harper Colophon Books, 1965), 167–92.

2. U.S. Bureau of the Census, *Census of Population, 1950* (see chap. 2, n. 20), 1:47–48. For the economic and ecological development of Seattle, see Janice L. Reiff, "Urbanization and the Social Structure: Seattle, Washington, 1852–1910" (Ph.D. diss., University of Washington, 1981).

3. Olmsted to Sophia White Olmsted, 27 May 1903, folder 37, box 5A, John Charles Olmsted–Sophia White Olmsted Correspondence, Frances Loeb Library, Graduate

School of Design, Harvard University (hereafter cited as Olmsted Correspondence).

4. *Seattle Post-Intelligencer*, 16 Sept. 1892 (quotations) (hereafter cited as *P-I*); Donald Rex Roberts, "A Study of the Growth and Expansion of the Seattle Municipal Government" (M.A. thesis, University of Washington, 1942), 161–62; and Schwagerl's obituary, *Seattle Times*, 28 Jan. 1910.

5. Seattle Board of Park Commissioners, *Second Annual Report to the Honorable Mayor and City Council of Seattle for the Year Ending Nov. 30, 1892* (Seattle, 1892), 4–19; and idem, "Report of Park Commissioners," in *Seattle Municipal Reports: Fiscal Year Ending December 31, 1893, Published by Order of Mayor and City Council* (Seattle, 1894), 259–66.

6. *Argus*, 10 Nov. 1900, and 22 Dec. 1900; Clarence B. Bagley, *History of Seattle: From the Earliest Settlement to the Present Time* (Chicago: S. J. Clarke Publishing Co., 1916), 3:27.

7. *Argus*, 6 May 1899, 14 Oct. 1899, 21 Oct. 1899, and 11 Nov. 1899; *P-I*, 5 Feb. 1902; Seattle Board of Park Commissioners, *First Annual Report, 1884–1904* (Seattle: Lowman & Hanford Stationery and Printing Co., 1905), 7–18. The reports were renumbered beginning with this report. Olmsted to Olmsted, 4 May 1903, folder 36, box 5A, Olmsted Correspondence.

8. For the University of Washington, see Norman J. Johnston, "The Olmsted Brothers and the Alaska-Yukon-Pacific Exposition: 'Eternal Loveliness,'" *Pacific Northwest Quarterly* 75 (April 1984): 50–51; see also Charles W. Saunders to Frederick Law Olmsted, Jr., 16 Dec. 1902, file 2690, box 130, Olmsted Records (see chap. 1, n. 11). For Olmsted Brothers' work in Portland, see Carl Abbott, *Portland: Planning, Politics, and Growth in a Twentieth-Century City* (Lincoln: University of Nebraska Press, 1983), 41, 59–61; and Mansel G. Blackford, "The Lost Dream: Businessmen and City Planning in Portland, Oregon, 1903–1914," *Western Historical Quarterly* 15 (January 1984): 41–45. For quotation, see Olmsted to Olmsted, 16 May 1903, folder 37, box 5A, Olmsted Correspondence.

9. *P-I*, 3 Feb. 1902, 4 Feb. 1902 (quotation), and 5 Feb. 1902.

10. J. D. Blackwell to Percy R. Jones, 21 Mar. 1902; and Olmsted Brothers to Charles W. Saunders, 24 Dec. 1902, file 2690, box 130, Olmsted Records.

11. Charles W. Saunders to Olmsted, Jr., 16 Dec. 1902; Olmsted Brothers to Saunders, 23 Dec. 1902, and 24 Dec. 1902 (first quotation); and Saunders to Olmsted Brothers, 14 Jan. 1903 (second quotation), file 2690, box 130, Olmsted Records.

12. For a summary of Olmsted's career, see Newton, *Design on the Land* (see chap. 1, n. 25), 294–95 (quotation, 289). For "the lead" quotation, see Olmsted Brothers to Charles W. Saunders, 23 Dec. 1902, file 2690, box 130, Olmsted Records.

13. In order of quotation, Olmsted to Olmsted, 29 Nov. 1903, folder 47, box 6A; 31 Oct. 1906; and 15 Oct. 1906, folder 91, box 12A, Olmsted Correspondence.

14. Olmsted to Olmsted, 16 June 1903, folder 39, box 6A, Olmsted Correspondence; and Seattle Board of Park Commissioners, *First Annual Report, 1884–1904*, 44–85 (the printed version of Olmsted's 1903 report, Olmsted Brothers to E. F. Blaine, Chairman, Board of Park Commissioners). A brief survey of the plan is Rae Tufts, "Seattle's Double Legacy: The City Beautiful Movement and the Olmsted Park Plan," *Portage* 5 (Summer 1984): 11–12.

15. Seattle Board of Park Commissioners, *First Annual Report, 1884–1904*, 44–45 (quotation, 44).

16. Ibid., 45–48.

17. Ibid., 53–54, 55.

18. Ibid., 65, 66, 69 (roadway quotations), and 78 (Volunteer Park quotations).

19. Ibid., 48–51; and memorandum, Seattle Parks, J. C. Olmsted, 29 May 1903, folder 2690, box 130, Olmsted Records.

20. *The Charter of the City of Seattle, Adopted March 6, 1900* (Seattle: Lowman & Hanford Stationery and Printing Co., 1900), 78–81.

21. For a description of the board's struggle, and quotations, see Charles W. Saunders to Olmsted Brothers, 5 Feb. 1904, file 2690, box 130, Olmsted Records. For number of improvement clubs, see *Argus*, 9 Jan. 1904. For press support, see *Times*, 22 Feb. 1904; and *P-I*, 17 Jan. 1904. For the new charter article, see *The Charter of the City of Seattle, Adopted*

March 6, 1900, with Amendments 1902 and 1904 (Seattle: Metropolitan Press, 1905), 49–51.

22. For opposition, see Charles W. Saunders to J. C. Olmsted, 7 Mar. 1904, file 2690, box 130, Olmsted Records. For Thomson's letter, see *P-I*, 6 Mar. 1904.

23. The ward analysis here and in subsequent paragraphs follows that in Mansell Griffiths Blackford, "Sources of Support for Reform Candidates and Issues in Seattle Politics, 1902–1916" (M.A. thesis, University of Washington, 1967), 10–20. For official election returns, see *Journal of the Proceedings of the City Council of Seattle*, 11 Mar. 1904 (hereafter cited as *Council Proceedings*). For quotation, see *Times*, 7 Mar. 1904.

24. Mansell G. Blackford, "Civic Groups, Political Action, and City Planning in Seattle, 1892–1915," *Pacific Historical Review* 49 (November 1980): 561. For endorsements, see *P-I*, 4 Mar. 1906. For votes, see *Council Proceedings*, 29 Dec. 1905, and 9 Mar. 1906.

25. *Council Proceedings*, 29 Dec. 1908, 11 Mar. 1910.

26. For improvement clubs, see *Argus*, 4 Nov. 1905. For the press, see *P-I*, 6 Dec. 1908. For the association, see Seattle Playgrounds Association, *The Playground Movement in Seattle* (Seattle, 1909). For Griffiths, see Austin Edwards Griffiths, "Great Faith: Autobiography of an English Immigrant Boy in America, 1863–1950" (Seattle, 1950), unpublished, copy in Pacific Northwest Collection, Suzzallo Library, University of Washington, quotation, 160; and Charles Byler, "Austin E. Griffiths: Seattle Progressive Reformer," *Pacific Northwest Quarterly* 76 (January 1985): 22–32.

27. Olmsted to J. E. Shrewsbury, 28 Nov. 1906, 1–2, 3–6, 7–26 (quotations, 6, 7), file 2690, box 130, Olmsted Records.

28. Olmsted Brothers to J. M. Frink, 25 Jan. 1908, 9–10, ibid.

29. Ibid., 14–17. See also "Description of Parks, Recommended by Olmsted Brothers, January 25, 1908," file 2690, box 130, Olmsted Records.

30. Olmsted Brothers to J. T. Heffernan, 4 Oct. 1910 (quotations, 4–6), file 2690-1, box 130, Olmsted Records.

31. Ibid., 6–7, 9–23 (quotations, 6, 7).

32. For public buildings, see *Argus*, 7 Oct. 1899, and 1 Feb. 1902. For conference committee, see *Argus*, 4 June 1904, and 14 Oct. 1905; and *P-I*, 29 Mar. 1904. For prominent individuals, see *P-I*, 4 Aug. 1908, and 10 Dec. 1908. For architects, see *P-I*, 22 and 29 Dec. 1907, and 19 and 20 May 1908. For cleanup campaigns, *P-I*, 24, 25, 29 Apr. 1904; 22 Mar. 1905; and 3 Apr. 1905. For billboards, see *P-I*, 25 May 1904, 1 Apr. 1908, 22 Nov. 1908, and 26 Apr. 1909. For Franklin High School, *P-I*, 15 Feb. 1909.

33. Olmsted to Olmsted, 17 Jan. 1909, folder 146, box 19A, Olmsted Correspondence. For 1904 initiative, Olmsted Brothers to Charles W. Saunders, 11 Dec. 1903; and Saunders to Olmsted, 11 Mar. 1904, folder 2690, box 130, Olmsted Records. For Thompson recommendation, see Olmsted Brothers to Board of Park Commissioners, 24 Mar. 1904; and for Thompson characterization, J. F. Dawson to Saunders, 29 Nov. 1920, folder 2690, box 130, Olmsted Records. For private work, see folder 3353, box 233, Olmsted Records. For Volunteer Park, see *Times*, 17, 18, and 23 Oct. 1910; *P-I*, 16, 18, and 25 Oct. 1910; and Saunders to Dawson, 19 Oct. 1910, folder 2694, box 131, Olmsted Records.

34. Olmsted to Olmsted, 6 Jan. 1910 ("I wish"), folder 165, box 21A; 28 Oct. 1905, folder 92, box 13A; and 19 Dec. 1907 ("views"), folder 121, box 16A; 6 Nov. 1906 ("The total"), Olmsted Correspondence.

35. Olmsted to Olmsted, 4 Nov. 1906, folder 93, box 13A, Olmsted Correspondence. Olmsted to Charles W. Saunders, 22 Sept. 1904 (partial designs); notes, "Seattle Parks, Boulevards, Visit by J. C. Olmsted," 11 June 1909 ("What between"); and Olmsted to Edward C. Cheasty, 14 June 1909 ("a stiff" and "the lines"), folder 2690, box 130, Olmsted Records.

36. Olmsted to Olmsted, 16 May 1907 ("The landowners"), folder 107, box 15A, Olmsted Correspondence.

37. Notes, "Seattle Parks, Conferences by J.C.O., 10 December 1907" ("did not"), folder 2690, box 130, Olmsted Records; Olmsted to Olmsted, 6 Jan. 1910 ("Lots of"), folder 165, box 21A, Olmsted Correspondence.

38. *Argus*, 16 May 1903.

39. *Argus*, 6 July 1907. For the Central Park, see *P-I*, 16 Jan. 1910; *Times*, 23 Feb. 1910, and 2 Mar. 1910; and *Council Proceedings*, 11 Mar. 1910. For disputes, see Notes, Seattle Parks, J. F. Dawson, August 1904, folder 2690, box 130, Olmsted Records; and below.

40. For Ravenna, see *P-I*, 2 Feb. 1908, and 10 Sept. 1908; and E. F. Blaine to J. C. Olmsted, 21 Apr. 1908, folder 2690, box 130, Olmsted Records. For antisectionalism, see *P-I*, 26 Jan. 1906.

41. For quotation about Way, see *P-I*, 8 Apr. 1909. For Way's outburst at the meeting, see *P-I*, 29 Sept. 1909. For Way's extension of embargo and park board reaction, see *P-I*, 8 Apr. 1909. For the resolution of the issue, see *P-I*, 29 Apr. 1909, and 4 May 1909.

42. Seattle Board of Park Commissioners, *Sixth Annual Report, 1909* (Seattle, 1910), 17–62, 73–90, 107, 119.

43. For the Alaska-Yukon-Pacific park movement, see Johnston, "Olmsted Brothers and the Exposition," 60–61. For the comprehensive plan, see chap. 10.

CHAPTER 8. BOSSISM AS CIVIC IDEALISM, PLANNING, AND REFORM IN DENVER

1. The best history of Denver is Lyle W. Dorsett, *The Queen City: A History of Denver* (Boulder, Colo.: Pruett Publishing Co., 1977). For overviews of beautification improvements, see Thomas J. Noel and Barbara S. Norgren, *Denver: The City Beautiful and Its Architects, 1893–1941* (Denver: Historic Denver, 1987), 1–27, 139–83; and two studies by Don D. Etter, *The Denver Park and Parkway System* (Denver: Colorado Historical Society, 1986), and "A Legacy of Green: Denver's Park and Parkway System," *Colorado Heritage* 3 (1986): 9–16.

2. U. S. Bureau of the Census, *Census of Population, 1950* (see chap. 2, n. 20), 1:6-8.

3. Dorsett, *Queen City*, 43–44; and A. Allison, "Co-Operation: The Secret of Successful Bill Posting," *Agricultural Advertising* 18 (March 1908): 472.

4. For the rivers and lakes, see U.S. Geological Survey maps Arvada, Fort Logan, Commerce City, Englewood, Sable, and Fitzsimons, Colo.; and Ben Draper, "A History of Denver's Parks," 1934, typescript, Document Division, Denver Museum Collection, Western History Department, Denver Public Library, 12.

5. For quotation, see Charles A. Johnson, *Denver's Mayor Speer* (Denver: Green Mountain Press, 1969), 1. See also Edgar C. MacMechen, ed., *Robert W. Speer: A City Builder* (Denver: Robert W. Speer Memorial Association, 1919); John Richard Pickering, "Blueprint of Power: The Public Career of Robert Speer in Denver, 1878–1918" (Ph.D. diss., University of Denver, 1978); and Dorsett, *Queen City*, 121–58.

6. For "beautification" quotation, see Robert L. Perkin, *The First Hundred Years: An Informal History of Denver and the Rocky Mountain News* (Garden City, N.Y.: Doubleday & Co., 1959), 410. For "deep sense" quotation, see J. Paul Mitchell, "Progressivism in Denver: The Municipal Reform Movement, 1904–1916" (Ph.D. diss., University of Denver, 1966), 2. For an example of the regard for Speer, see George Cranmer, 24 June 1958, interview 0-44, Documentary Resources Department, Colorado Historical Society, Denver.

7. Board of Park Commissioners, *Annual Report for the Year 1913 of the Board of Park Commissioners of the City and County of Denver, with a Story of the Parks* (Denver, [1914?]), 5, 7–10; and Jerome C. Smiley, ed., *History of Denver: With Outlines of the Earlier History of the Rocky Mountain Country* (Denver: Denver Times, Times-Sun Publishing Co., 1901; reprint, Evansville, Ind.: Unigraphic, 1971), 645–47. The City Park acquisition data are given in Etter, *Denver Park and Parkway System*, 16.

8. "Concerning City Parks," signed W.G.E., folio 36, Private Papers of Governor John Evans, collection 226, Documentary Resources Department, Colorado Historical Society; and Allen duPont Breck, *William Gray Evans, 1855–1924: Portrait of a Western Executive* (Denver: University of Denver, 1964), 77–78.

9. Minute Book, Civic Federation of Denver, 1:44, 49, 145; 2:163, 173, collection 116, Documentary Resources Department, Colorado Historical Society.

10. For the Woman's Club, see Woman's Club of Denver, *Eighth Annual Announce-*

ment, 1901–1902 (Denver, n.d.), iii; and *Denver Times,* 9 Mar. 1899. For Bates, see *Times,* 5 Feb. 1903. For the CIS, see *Times,* 24 Dec. 1898.

11. CIS, *Cleanliness and Beauty Demanded: Second Annual Meeting of the City Improvement Society* (Denver, n.d.); and *City Improvement Society: The Third Annual Meeting of the City Improvement Society of Denver, Was Held at Unity Church on March 8th 1899* (Denver, n.d.) (quotations, 2, 3). For cooperation, see *Times,* 27 July 1899. For special meetings, see *Times,* 19 Mar. 1899, and 4 June 1899.

12. *Times,* 15 Apr. 1900, 24 Apr. 1900, and 25 May 1902.

13. *Times,* 30 Mar. 1903; Smiley, *History of Denver,* 975–76. For a beautification proposal, see *Times,* 19 Mar. 1902.

14. Dorsett, *Queen City,* 130–37; and Pickering, "Blueprint of Power," 65–82.

15. *Rocky Mountain News,* 24 July 1903 (hereafter cited as *RMN*); *Republican,* 10 Feb. 1904; and Art Commission of the City and County of Denver, *General Report* (Denver, 1911), 1–2.

16. Max Hayutin, 27 Dec. 1966, interview o-77, Documentary Resources Department, Colorado Historical Society.

17. Alex Stanbery, "Denver Floods and Urban Development," unpublished seminar paper, University of Denver, n.d., 5–6; and Pickering, "Blueprint of Power," 40–42.

18. Pickering, "Blueprint of Power," 42–43, 46–47; and Mitchell, "Progressivism in Denver," 172–73.

19. Pickering, "Blueprint of Power," 40–41, 43–44.

20. S. R. DeBoer, 22 Nov. 1963, interview o-46, Documentary Resources Department, Colorado Historical Society; and idem, "Plans, Parks and People," *Green Thumb* 29 (December 1972): 156.

21. Olmsted to John S. Macbeth, 22 June 1913, folder 5580, box 305, Olmsted Records; and Speer, "Address before the Commercial Club of Colorado Springs, 29 March 1917," quoted in MacMechen, *Speer,* 79.

22. For Evans, see Breck, *William Gray Evans,* passim; and *Denver Post,* 6 Jan. 1941. For Read, see James H. Baker and Le Roy R. Hafen, eds., *History of Colorado* (Denver: State Historical and Natural History Society of Colorado, 1927), 3:1268–69. For activities of the commission, see Art Commission, *General Report,* 4–7.

23. Art Commission of the City of New York, *Annual Report . . . for the Year 1912, Containing the Proceedings of the First National Conference of Art Commissions* (New York, 1913), 50 (quotation); Charles Mulford Robinson, *Proposed Plans for the Improvement of the City of Denver* (Denver: Art Commission, City and County of Denver, 1906), 12. For Denver's municipal art, see Phil Goodstein, "Monumental Denver: A Look at the City's Significant Public Art," *Colorado Heritage* 3 (1987): 34–43.

24. For the Welcome Arch, see Art Commission, *General Report,* 4; Lilian Whiting, *The Land of Enchantment: From Pike's Peak to the Pacific* (Boston: Little, Brown & Co., 1906), 41; Johnson, *Speer,* 50 (quotation, 137); and Charles Mulford Robinson, "The Development of Denver," *American City* 2 (May 1910): 199. For its demolition, see *RMN,* 16 Sept. 1931, 1 Dec. 1931.

25. *Post,* 17 Nov. 1904.

26. Ibid.

27. Ibid.

28. Ibid.

29. Robinson, *Plans for the Improvement of Denver,* 9–22 (quotations, 12, 14).

30. R. W. Speer, *Address of Mayor R. W. Speer, to Councilmen and Business Men, Delivered January Seven, Nineteen Hundred Seven, at a Testimonial Banquet Tendered by the Business Men of Denver* (Denver, 1907), 4–22.

31. Breck, *John Evans,* 78; and for quotations, "Between You and Me," *RMN,* 13 June 1907.

32. For Kessler, see letters in the Kessler Collection, boxes 2, 10, and 11 (see chap. 5, n. 19). For quotation, see Henry Wright to Kessler, 31 Jan. 1908, box 11, Kessler Collection. See also *Denver Municipal Facts* 1 (29 May 1909): 3–4 (hereafter cited as *DMF*).

33. MacMechen, *Speer,* 22; and DeBoer, "Plans, Parks and People," 162.

34. Johnson, *Speer,* 54, 226–44; and *DMF* 1 (20 February 1909): 10.

35. Dorsett, *Queen City*, 138; DMF 4 (27 April 1912): 3–6; and MacMechen, *Speer*, 18.

36. DeBoer, "Plans, Parks and People," 153, 158–59 (quotations, 153, 159); and MacMechen, *Speer*, "And . . . plunk!" quotation, 56.

37. For Speer's trip, see Johnson, *Speer*, 151–63.

38. Steffens, *Autobiography* (see chap. 4, n. 28), 649–53; and *Post*, 31 Aug. 1911 (quotation).

39. MacMechen, *Speer*, 71–72; Speer, *Address of R. W. Speer*, 21; Warwick M. Downing, "How Denver Acquired Her Celebrated Mountain Parks: A Condensed History of the Building of America's Most Unique Park System," *Municipal Facts* (continuation of *DMF*) 14 (March–April 1931): 12; and Seth B. Bradley, "The Origin of the Denver Mountain Parks System," *Colorado Magazine* 9 (January 1932): 26. For quotations, see Denver Chamber of Commerce, *News Bulletin* 2 (May 1912): 1.

40. Olmsted to Board of Park Commissioners, 17 July 1912, 16–24, folder 5582, box 305, Olmsted Records.

41. John S. Macbeth to Olmsted Brothers, 15 Nov. 1913, 27:462, Macbeth and May Collection, Documentary Resources Department, Colorado Historical Society (hereafter cited as Macbeth and May Collection). For the Platte River parkway, see George Gibbs, Jr., to Denver Park Commissioners, 28 Jan. 1914; and for Cheesman Park, see S. R. DeBoer to Olmsted Brothers, 11 May 1915, folder 5587, box 305, Olmsted Records. For administration, see Olmsted to Macbeth, 22 June 1913, folder 5580, box 305, Olmsted Records. For irrigation, see ibid., 21 July 1913. For implementation, see Olmsted to Fred C. Steinhauer, 29 July 1913, folder 5583, ibid.

42. For an account of the park board's power, see chap. 11. Board of Park Commissioners, *Annual Report for the Year 1913*, 7–16, 23.

43. Whiting, *Land of Enchantment*, 17–19; McFarland, DMF 3 (18 February 1911): 4. For park concerts, see MacMechen, *Speer*, 38. For civic auditorium concerts, see Johnson, *Speer*, 36. For the Union Station, see *Times*, 17 July 1915. For the Art Commission, see *City of Denver* (continuation of *DMF*) 2 (9 May 1914): 6–7.

44. For Speer's problems, see Dorsett, *Queen City*, 149–56. For the Cherry Creek flood, see Denver Board of Public Works and Cherry Creek Flood Commission, *Report of the Cherry Creek Flood Commission* (Denver: Smith-Brooks Press, 1913), 33–34 (quotation, 37); DeBoer, "Plans, Parks and People," 154–55 (quotation, 154); and idem, "A History of the Denver Parks: Cherry Creek Parkways," *Green Thumb* 16 (October 1959): 308–9.

45. Mitchell, "Progressivism in Denver," 127, 221–22 (quotations, 127, 221). For Speer's defenses, see DMF 1 (4 December 1909): 6; DMF 3 (23 December 1911): 5; DMF 4 (13 January 1912): 16; "What Has Been Done in Denver during the Eight Years from 1904 to 1912, under a Democratic Administration," folder 15, Robert W. Speer Papers, Western History Collection, Denver Public Library; and DMF 3 (4 November 1911): 11. For the reformers, see Mitchell, "Progressivism in Denver," 407–8; and Dorsett, *Queen City*, 158. For railroad passenger traffic increases in Denver, see *Colorado Factory Facts* 2 (November 1915): 46.

CHAPTER 9. THE KANSAS CITY UNION STATION AND THE CITY BEAUTIFUL IDEAL

1. Charles N. Glaab, *Kansas City and the Railroads: Community Policy in the Growth of a Regional Metropolis* (Madison: State Historical Society of Wisconsin, 1962), 1–9.

2. For complaints about the temporary station, see *Times*, 23, 28, 29 Sept. 1875.

3. Photograph, "Union Avenue Looking Southwest from St. Louis Avenue," and others in the photograph files of the Kansas City Terminal Railway Company, Kansas City, Missouri (hereafter cited as KCTRC).

4. Research Bureau, Board of Public Welfare, *Social Prospectus of Kansas City, Missouri*, in *Fourth Annual Report of the Board of Public Welfare of Kansas City, Mo.* (Kansas City, 1913), 44.

5. U.S. Bureau of the Census, *Census of Population, 1950* (see chap. 2, n. 20), 1:16-10, and 25-10; *Star*, 22 Feb. 1888.

6. For the corporate arrangements of the Union Depot Company, see *Charter and By-Laws of the Union Depot Company of Kansas City, Missouri, With Documents Relating to Its Organization and Management* (Kansas City, 1905). See also *Star*, 23 Jan. 1906; and Haskell and Fowler, *City of the Future* (see chap. 5, n. 11), 108.

7. *Star*, 17 Oct. 1897, 2 Apr. 1901, 12 Apr. 1901, and 17 Aug. 1904; and *Journal*, 7 May 1902.

8. *Star*, 14 Jan. 1902.

9. *Star*, 10 Dec. 1902.

10. See speech of Nat H. Parker to the Commercial Club, *Star*, 19 Feb. 1896; and statement by E. J. Sanford, president of the Union Depot Company, *Star*, 28 Nov. 1903.

11. Union Depot Company (hereafter cited as UDC), Minute Book, special meeting of the board of directors, 4 Nov. 1897, 203; ibid., 31 May 1898, 218–19; and ibid., meeting of the board of directors, Chicago, 26 Jan. 1905, 317. For the architects, see *Star*, 31 May 1898, and 1 May 1901.

12. UDC, Minute Book, meeting at St. Louis, 14 July 1902, 290–96; and ibid., meeting at Kansas City, 12 May 1903, 303–4. See also *Star*, 15 Jan. 1902, 12 Mar. 1902, and 22 Apr. 1902, 1 Feb. 1903, 19 Apr. 1903; and *Journal*, 7 May 1903.

13. For quotations, see *Star*, 7 June 1903, 18 July 1903, and 17 Sept. 1903. For other west bottoms developments, see *Star*, 3, 4, 7, and 12 June 1903; and 5, 19 Jan. 1904.

14. *Star*, 12 June 1903, 24 Aug. 1903; UDC, Minute Book, meeting of the executive committee, 5 Feb. 1904, 311; ibid., meeting of the board of directors, Chicago, 2 June 1904, 312; *Star*, 24 Aug. 1904 (quotation), 26 Jan. 1905, and 1, 7 Apr. 1905.

15. For quotations, see *Star*, 18 Feb. 1906. For background, see *Star*, 26 Jan. 1905, 1 Apr. 1905, 7 Apr. 1905, and 1 May 1905. See also UDC, Minute Book, meeting of the board of directors, Chicago, 23 May 1905, 319–20; ibid., 10 Jan. 1906, 325; KCTRC, "Corporate History, Diagrammatic Chart, 30 June 1916"; and idem, *By-Laws* (as amended to 1 Apr. 1928), 9.

16. KCTRC, Signed Minutes Meetings, 1 June 1906 to 20 Jan. 1913, "Report of President to Board of Directors," 10 Feb. 1911, 136; map, "Missouri 1" = 60', 25-3252"; map, "25-3256, Right of Way Map of the Kansas City Belt Ry. in Kansas & Missouri, Scale 1 inch = 400 ft."; map, "12-14936, K.C. Terminal Ry. Co. Profile of Main Line—Clark Junction to Rock Creek Junction," Office of the Chief Engineer, 30 Mar. 1937; and photographs in the possession of the KCTRC.

17. *Union Station Ordinance No. 2336, Approved July 7, 1909*, 71. Some provisions were changed by *Ordinance No. 9701, Approved August 19, 1911, Modifying and Amending Union Station Ordinance No. 2336*. For the estimated final cost of $6,352,942 for the "building and approaches," on 21 Feb. 1914, see transfer file no. 166, pt. 3, Office of the President, KCTRC.

18. *Star*, 10 Sept. 1909. For quotation, see *Journal*, 10 Sept. 1909.

19. Lyle W. Dorsett, *The Pendergast Machine* (New York: Oxford University Press, 1968), 3–49.

20. For Pendergast's health and future plans, see Dorsett, *Pendergast Machine*, 42, 46–48; and *Star*, 4 Mar. 1910 (quotation). Other biographical information is in *Political History of Jackson County* (Kansas City: Marshall & Morrison, 1902), 183; and Pendergast's obituary, *Star*, 11 Nov. 1911. For local patriotism, see Henry H. Crittenden, comp., *The Crittenden Memoirs* (New York: G. P. Putnam's Sons, 1936), 404.

21. Louis H. Sullivan, *The Autobiography of an Idea* (1924; reprint, New York: Dover Publications, 1956), 320.

22. Charles Bohasseck to the author, 10 Nov. 1961 (quotation); and Henry F. Withey and Elsie Rathburn Withey, eds., *Biographical Dictionary of American Architects (Deceased)* (Los Angeles: New Age Publishing Co., 1956), 308.

23. KCTRC, Secretary's Record, meeting of representatives of the terminal lines, Chicago, 18 June 1906, 12–13; ibid., meeting of the board of directors, Chicago, 22 Nov. 1907, 52–53; and *Star*, 21 June 1906.

24. *Star*, 21 June 1906 (chairman's quotation); *Times*, 22 June 1906 (Hunt's quotation); and *Star*, 17 July 1906 (railroad official's quotation). KCTRC, Secretary's Record, meeting of the board of directors, Chicago, 22 Nov. 1907, 52; ibid., 11 Feb. 1908, 57; ibid., Kansas

City, 22 Nov. 1909, quotation, 80; file no. 166, pt. 1, "Report of the Building Committee to H. L. Harmon, President," 5 Oct. 1909, Office of the President, KCTRC; and *Star*, 15 June 1907.

25. *Times*, 23 Nov. 1909.

26. *Star*, 19 June 1906, 30 Sept. 1906, and 20 May 1908; and photograph album no. 1, "Station Site Miscellaneous," photograph dated "6-29-10, 28," KCTRC.

27. Hunt to Kessler, 16 Apr. 1901, box 3, Kessler Collection (see chap. 5, n. 19); and Charles Bohasseck to the author, 10 Nov. 1961.

28. Ordinance No. 2336, 98–100. *Journal*, 23 Mar. 1906; and *Star*, 27 Feb. 1914, and 11 Mar. 1914.

29. *Star*, 17 Oct. 1911.

30. *Times*, 19 Feb. 1906 (city official's quotation); and *Star*, 27 Feb. 1914, and 11 Mar. 1914.

31. *Journal*, 26 Mar. 1906. A later park department plan was similar, *Star*, 16 Apr. 1906. There were at least five plans, George B. Ford, ed., *City Planning Progress in the United States, 1917* (Washington, D.C.: American Institute of Architects, 1917), 82. For Kessler's plan and attitude, see *Star*, 23 June 1907; and Kessler to Miles Bulger, 14 Jan. 1909, box 1, Kessler Collection.

32. *Times*, 25 Nov. 1909.

33. For "best city" quotation, see *Star*, 29 Apr. 1909. See also Charles Bohasseck to the author, 10 Nov. 1961; and *Star*, 25 Nov. 1909, and 9 Jan. 1910.

34. *Star*, 3 Aug. 1910 and 8 Aug. 1910.

35. *Star*, 23 Apr. 1911. See also Hunt to W. S. Kinnear, 27 Apr. 1911, file no. 166, pt. 1, Office of the President, KCTRC; "Memorandum of conversation in Jarvis Hunt's office, Thursday, March 30, 1911," transfer file no. 339-A, pt. 1, Office of the Chief Engineer, KCTRC; and *Star*, 19 May 1912.

36. *Star*, 16 June 1912, 17 July 1912 (quotation). For meeting quotations, see *Journal*, 20 July 1912.

37. *Star*, 3 Mar. 1914, 5 Mar. 1914, and 22 Mar. 1914.

38. *Times*, 31 Oct. 1914.

39. H. H. Adams, "Kansas City's New Union Station," *Rotarian* 4 (May 1914), 31; Board of Park Commissioners, *Report for the Fiscal Year Ending April 19, 1915* (Kansas City, 1915), 93–94; and *Times*, 31 Oct. 1914.

40. *Star*, 12, 16, 23 Jan. 1903; 4, 5, 25, 26 Mar. 1903; and 29 Apr. 1903.

41. *Star*, 23 Sept. 1903. The ward returns were ambiguous concerning a division of the vote along socioeconomic lines. In 1913 the *Social Prospectus of Kansas City* identified all or parts of the 1903 Wards 1 through 10 as social problem districts (see map, 25). Imposing the findings of 1913 upon the Kansas City of 1903 is problematic at best, because of the redrawing and redesignation of wards and because of substantial shifts in population. However, it is almost certain that in 1903 Wards 1, 2, and 3 were low-income, while Wards 10 through 14 were outlying, commuter wards with relatively low populations composed of mostly working people and small-business people depending upon the working people's trade. The total park bond vote in the first three wards was 1,494 yes, 314 no, or a 4.75 to 1 majority, compared with a vote of 1,490 yes, 288 no, on the popular waterworks proposition. The five outlying wards passed the park bonds by a total of 2,163 yes, 1,052 no, or slightly more than a 2 to 1 majority. The outlying wards passed the waterworks bonds 2,466 to 753 (*Times*, 23 Sept. 1903).

42. For park improvements, see *Star*, 27 Apr. 1904. For the 1905 charter, see *New Charter, Kansas City, Missouri, Framed by . . . a Board of Freeholders Elected for That Purpose at a General Election Held November 8th, 1904* (Kansas City, 1905), Art. 14, Sec. 41, 194; and *Star*, 8 Mar. 1905. For the 1908 charter, see *Parks and Boulevards, Article XIII of the Charter of Kansas City, Missouri, Adopted August 4th, 1908* (Kansas City, 1908), Sec. 40, 26–28; and *Star*, 5 Aug. 1908. For the 1910 park bonds, see the certified returns, 19 July 1910, Office of the City Clerk, Kansas City; and *Star*, 20 July 1910, and 22 July 1910. The bonds received a two-thirds vote of all votes cast yes or no, but not two-thirds of the total vote, which included valid ballots that did not declare for or against the parks issue. The *Social Prospectus of Kansas City* problem districts roughly coincided with Wards 1–12,

excepting 4. These wards contained pockets of upper-class residences but in the main were home to those judged to oppose bond issues of the type presented. Voters in those wards voted 8,933 yes, 4,579 no, or 1.95 to 1 in favor. Wards 4, 5, 13, and 14, outlying wards having little or no industrial population, voted 4,762 yes, 1,876 no, or more than 2.5 to 1, a high ratio largely attributable to a large yes vote in Ward 4. This instance vindicates the determinist argument.

43. *Star*, 20 May 1901, and 1 June 1901. A biographical sketch of Dunn is in W. I. Ayers, comp., historical binder "A–M," Office of the Director of Parks and Recreation, Kansas City, Missouri.

44. *Star*, 17 July 1904, second section.

45. Board of Park Commissioners, *Report . . . for the Fiscal Year Ending April 16, 1906*, 23–26.

46. *Star*, 22 Aug. 1901, 6 Sept. 1901; and 26 June 1904, second section.

47. For the growth of the system, see *Star*, 9 June 1902; *Journal*, 11 Apr. 1907; and the *Reports* of the park board for the years 1907, 14; 1910, 55; and 1911, 38–46. For the "so-called" quotation, see Kessler to W. H. Dunn, 29 July 1909, letter file, carbon copies from 1 Jan. 1909 to 1 Jan. 1910, W. H. Dunn, Park Board Archives (see chap. 5, n. 16). For the other quotations, see "Report of the Landscape Architect, K.C. Mo, 1911," box 2, Kessler Collection. For an instance of the fascination with the arrangement and appointments of public toilets in parks, see "Public Comfort Stations at Kansas City, Mo.: The Public Conveniences of a City That Has Recently Begun to Find Itself," *Domestic Engineering* 62 (4 January 1914): 2–7.

48. Boyer, *Urban Masses and Moral Order* (see chap. 1, n. 4), 245.

49. Board of Park Commissioners, *Report* (1915), 156; idem, *Park System of Kansas City* (Kansas City, 1920), 7.

50. For favorable comments, see E. M. Clendening to W. L. Day, 1 Dec. 1909, box "Personal, 1908–1909," Clendening Papers, Native Sons Archives; and *Star*, 9 Aug. 1911. Board of Public Welfare, Kansas City, Mo., *Report on Housing Conditions in Kansas City, Missouri: Showing Defects in Present Laws and Suggesting Form of Code Needed* (Kansas City, 1912), 5; and *Second Annual Report of the Recreation Department of the Board of Public Welfare* (Kansas City, 1912), 34. Public recreation remained heavily commercialized. See Alan Havig, "Mass Commercial Amusements in Kansas City before World War I," *Missouri Historical Review* 75 (April 1981): 316–45.

51. *Star*, 13 Feb. 1894, 20 Mar. 1894, 28 Mar. 1899, and 18 Aug. 1899. For quotation, see *Journal*, 7 Oct. 1901.

52. For smoke pollution and abatement, see *Star*, 17 Dec. 1896, 28 Feb. 1897, and 14 Mar. 1897. For improvement associations, see *Star*, 28 Jan. 1899, 9 Feb. 1899, 23 Apr. 1902, and 14 Jan. 1906. For the art commission, see *Star*, 21 Aug. 1906, 1 Oct. 1906.

53. Interview with G. E. Kessler; *Star*, 20 Mar. 1904; and Kessler to R. H. Warner, 23 Aug. 1902, box 2, Kessler Collection.

54. Kessler to Haff, 29 Aug. 1911, box 9, Kessler Collection; *Star*, 31 May 1908; and Kessler to J. C. Nichols, 29 May 1914 ("Kansas City's"), and 23 May 1914 ("it had"), box 7, Kessler Collection.

CHAPTER 10. THE COLLAPSE OF THE CIVIC CENTER DREAM IN SEATTLE

1. *Plan of Seattle: Report of the Municipal Plans Commission Submitting Report of Virgil G. Bogue, Engineer, 1911* (Seattle: Lowman & Hanford Co., 1911), 16–20. A superior account of the Bogue plan in the context of Seattle's growth and politics is Blackford, "Civic Groups, Political Action, and City Planning" (see chap. 7, n. 24). Another thoughtful analysis is J. M. Neil, "Paris or New York? The Shaping of Downtown Seattle, 1903–1914," *Pacific Northwest Quarterly* 75 (January 1984): 22–33. See also Padraic Burke, "The City Beautiful Movement in Seattle" (Master's of urban planning thesis, University of Washington, 1973), 71–118; Lee Forrest Pendergrass, "Urban Reform and Voluntary Association: A Case Study of the Seattle Municipal League, 1910–1929" (Ph.D. diss., University of Washington, 1972), 40–49; and Sale, *Seattle* (see chap. 7, n. 1), 94–104. These studies are informed, directly or indirectly, by two important works,

Neil Clifford Kimmons, "The Historical Development of Seattle as a Metropolitan Area" (M.A. thesis, University of Washington, 1942); and Alexander Norbert MacDonald, "Seattle's Economic Development, 1880–1910" (Ph.D. diss., University of Washington, 1959).

2. *Council Proceedings* (see chap. 7, n. 23), 11 Mar. 1912.

3. Washington State Chapter minutes, 6 July 1904 (municipal building), 5 Dec. 1906 (civic improvement committee), 12 Dec. 1907 (art commission and building department), and 19 Dec. 1907 (civic center committee), Washington State Chapter, American Institute of Architects Papers, Manuscripts Division, University of Washington Libraries (hereafter cited as WSC minutes). For the art commission and building department see also *P-I*, 29 Dec. 1907.

4. *P-I* (see chap. 7, n. 4), 13 May 1908, 21 June 1908.

5. WSC minutes, 28 Jan. 1909, with accompanying letter, Charles H. Bebb to A. J. Russell, n.d.; and for quotation, copy of constitution and bylaws. See also *P-I*, 29 Jan. 1909; and *Seattle Times*, 29 Jan. 1909.

6. For the work of the MPL, see *P-I*, 23 Feb. 1909, 2 Dec. 1909; "Seattle City Plan," report of J.C.O. [John C. Olmsted], 27 Nov. 1909, folder 2690, box 130, Olmsted Records (see chap. 1, n. 11); and WSC minutes, 26 Nov. 1909, 1 Dec. 1909, and 13 Dec. 1909. For the charter amendment, see *Plan of Seattle*, 9–12 (quotation, 11).

7. For Thomson, see *P-I*, 15 Dec. 1909. For his work and influence in Seattle, see Sale, *Seattle*, 72–78; and Grant H. Redford, ed., *That Man Thomson* (Seattle: University of Washington Press, 1950). For the chamber of commerce, see *P-I*, 22 Dec. 1909. For labor endorsements, see *Seattle Union Record* 19, 26 Feb. 1910 (hereafter cited as *SUR*). For speaker's bureau, see *P-I*, 14 Feb. 1910. For the vote, see *Council Proceedings*, 11 Mar. 1910. For quotation, see *Plan of Seattle*, 9.

8. For quotation, see D. W. McMorris, "The Organization and Work of the Municipal Plans Commission of the City of Seattle," *Proceedings of the Pacific Northwest Society of Engineers* 11 (January 1912): 4. Commercial Club of Chicago, *Plan of Chicago by Daniel H. Burnham and Edward H. Bennett* (Chicago, 1909; reprint, New York, Da Capo Press, 1970). For examples of references to the Chicago plan, see Reginald H. Thomson to A. H. Albertson, 25 Oct. 1909, folder 7, box 3, pt. 1, Reginald Thomson Papers, Manuscripts Division, University of Washington Libraries (hereafter cited as Thomson Papers); and *Times*, 14 Feb. 1910.

9. *P-I*, 17 June 1910.

10. Thomson to Rev. W. T. Hall, 5 Oct. 1910, folder 9, box 3, pt. 1, Thomson Papers; see also references in n 7.

11. Blackford, "Civic Groups, Political Action, and City Planning," 565; Burke, "City Beautiful Movement in Seattle," 76–82; and *Plan of Seattle*, 13. For engineers and topography, see Schultz and McShane, "To Engineer the Metropolis" (see chap. 2, n. 2), 398.

12. For "I felt" quotation, see Olmsted to Olmsted, 30 Apr. 1902, folder 23, box 4A, Olmsted Correspondence (see chap. 7, n. 3), almost certainly a misdating. For the sewer dispute and quotations, see J. F. Dawson, report on Seattle parks, Aug. 1904, folder 2690, box 130, Olmsted Records; and for Thomson's continuing intrusions, J. C. Olmsted, Seattle Parks, 28 Mar. 1905, ibid.

13. For "I have" quotation, see Olmsted to A. B. Ernst, 12 Sept. 1907, folder 2694, box 130, Olmsted Records. For Thomson's shifting attitudes, see Conferences by J. C. O., 18, 19 Nov. 1907, folder 2690, box 130; and Olmsted to J. M. Frink, 8 Jan. 1908, folder 2694, box 131, Olmsted Records. For the resolution of the controversy, see *P-I*, 19 Feb. 1909, 24 Feb. 1909.

14. For "understanding" quotation, see Olmsted to Olmsted, 12 Dec. 1909, folder 163, box 20A, Olmsted Correspondence. For "buffer" quotation, see Olmsted to Olmsted, 16 June 1910, folder 176, box 22A, Olmsted Correspondence. For "you will" quotation, see Thomson to Olmsted, 25 June 1910, folder 8, box 3, pt. 1, Thomson Papers. For Olmsted's presence at the MPC meeting, see *P-I*, 29 Jan. 1909; and *Times*, 29 Jan. 1909.

15. Thomson to Bogue, 7 July 1910 (first quotation); and Thomson to Bogue, 1 Sept. 1910 (second quotation), folder 8, box 3, pt. 1, Thomson Papers.

16. *Plan of Seattle*, 8–9, 12–15; and McMorris, "Municipal Plans Commission," 4–5.

For banquets, see WSC minutes, 5 Oct. 1910; folder 9, box 6, pt. 1, Thomson Papers; and *Times*, 20 Nov. 1910, sec. 1. For the civic center, see *Argus* 17 (28 January 1911): 1. For the plan and publicity, see *Pacific Northwest Commerce* (official publication of Seattle Chamber of Commerce, hereafter cited as *PNC*) 4 (May 1911): 17.

17. *Plan of Seattle*, 16–20, 34–36 (quotations, 16, 17, 34); and *Municipal League News* (hereafter cited as *MLN*) 1 (2 December 1911): 2. For somewhat different views of Bogue, see Scott, *American City Planning* (see intro., n. 1), 126–27; and Joan Elaine Draper, *The San Francisco Civic Center: Architecture, Planning, and Politics* (Ann Arbor: University Microfilms, 1979), 11, 21, 27–29.

18. *Plan of Seattle*, 36–40 (quotation, 39).

19. *P-I*, 14 July 1911; and *Times*, 30 Aug. 1911. For quotation, see *Plan of Seattle*, 14–15.

20. *Times*, 3 Sept. 1911; WSC minutes, 3 Jan. 1912; 31 Jan. 1912; and pp. 61–69 and 79 of minutes, vol. 2; and *MLN* 1 (20 Jan. 1912): 2. For opposition to new buildings, see ibid. (1 July 1911): 4; and ibid. (19 August 1911): 3. For a civic center plan, see *P-I*, 9 Oct. 1911, classified section. For the loss of the various proposals, see *MLN* 1 (15 July 1911): 2; ibid. (9 September 1911): 1; and *Council Proceedings*, 8 Sept. 1911.

21. For first quotation, see WSC minutes, 1 Nov. 1911. *MLN* 1 (25 November 1911): 3.

22. *Argus* 18 (23 December 1911): 4.

23. Civic Plans Investigation Committee, *The Bogue Plan Question* (Seattle: R. L. Davis, 1911), 27–31.

24. Ibid., 5–6, 11–13.

25. Ibid., 5, 14–20 (quotations, in order, 20, 5, 14).

26. *Times*, 4, 7, 8, 11 Feb. 1912; and 3 Mar. 1912.

27. Ibid., 25 Feb. 1912; for quotation from Sec. 8, see *Plan of Seattle*, 11.

28. For Thomson, see *MLN* 1 (3 February 1912): 2. For Phillips, see ibid. (9 December 1911): 2.

29. Ibid. (10 February 1912): 1, 4; and *Times*, 11 Feb. 1912.

30. For quotation, see *MLN* 1 (24 February 1912): 1. *P-I*, 29 Jan. 1912.

31. For Gill, see Morgan, *Skid Road* (see chap. 1), 169–98; and his quotation in *PNC* 2 (April 1910): 21. For Cotterill, see his memoir, Mary McWilliams, ed., folder 6, box 27, George F. Cotterill Papers, Manuscripts Division, University of Washington Libraries; and *MLN* 1 (25 November 1911): 4.

32. Burke, "City Beautiful Movement in Seattle," 106, 115. Forms of publicity, except advertisements, are cited in previous and subsequent notes. For advertisements, see *Seattle Star*, 1 Mar. 1912, 4 Mar. 1912.

33. *SUR*, 2 Mar. 1912; *Council Proceedings*, 11 Mar. 1912; Blackford, "Civic Groups, Political Action, and City Planning," 574. Wards 9, 12, 13, and 14 were the prosperous working-class wards according to Blackford, "Sources of Support for Reform Candidates and Issues," 11–20. A ward map is in *P-I*, 15 Feb. 1906. The park bonds carried almost 2 to 1 in Wards 12 and 14.

34. For quotation, see Blackford, "Civic Groups, Political Action, and City Planning," 575. Cf. Reiff, "Urbanization and the Social Structure" (see chap. 7, n. 2), 213–18, and Blackford, "Sources of Support for Reform Candidates and Issues" (see chap. 7, n. 23).

35. Pendergrass, "Urban Reform and Voluntary Association," 42–49. For the advertisement, see *Star*, 4 Mar. 1912.

36. Blackford, "Civic Groups, Political Action, and City Planning" (see chap. 7, n. 24), 575.

37. *Council Proceedings*, 11 Mar. 1912. The University District was in the Tenth Ward. For voter incompetence, see Cornelius H. Hanford, *Seattle and Environs, 1852–1924*, 3 vols. (Chicago: Pioneer Historical Publishing Co., 1924), 1:232. For pastoralism, see Sale, *Seattle*, 102–4.

38. Padraic Burke, "Struggle for Public Ownership: The Early History of the Port of Seattle," *Pacific Northwest Quarterly* 68 (April 1977): 60–71; CPIC, *Bogue Plan Question*, 10; and Neil, "Paris or New York?" 27.

39. Blackford, "Civic Groups, Political Action, and City Planning," 575–76.

Dallas, 1900–1960 (Ann Arbor: University Microfilms International, 1984).

2. U.S. Bureau of the Census, *Census of Population, 1950* (see chap. 2, n. 20), 2:43–11.

3. Ernest Sharpe, *G. B. Dealey of the Dallas News* (New York: Henry Holt & Co., 1955), 142–44; and Dallas Chamber of Commerce, *Dallas* 7 (June 1928): 16–17 (author hereafter cited as DCC).

4. *Dallas Morning News*, 1 Oct. 1935, sec. 7 (hereafter cited as *DMN*); and George E. Kessler, *A City Plan for Dallas* (Dallas: Dallas Park Board, 1912), 7–10, 15–16.

5. Kessler, *City Plan*, 7, 13–14, 21, 25, 35; and Dallas Park Board, *Report for the Years 1921–23, With a Sketch of the Park and Playground System* (Dallas, 1923), 71 (author hereafter cited as DPB).

6. G. B. Dealey, "Getting into Action for a City Plan," read before the Convention of the American Civic Association, Washington, D.C., 14, 15, and 16 Dec. 1910 (pamphlet), 1; miscellaneous typewritten sheets [1902], ("beautiful place" quotation); and typewritten article, 17 Dec. 1902 (CIL president's quotations), Early City Planning Data folder, George B. Dealey Collection, A6667, Dallas Historical Society (folder hereafter cited as ECPD, and collection as Dealey Collection).

7. Sharpe, *Dealey*, 4–64, 89–113, and for Dealey's learned references, typewritten speech, "Social Unrest," read before the Critic Club, Dallas, 30 Dec. 1912, folder 1, Dr. Herbert Pickens Gambrell Collection, A7650, Dallas Historical Society.

8. Dealey, "Getting into Action," 1, ECPD folder, Dealey Collection; and Sharpe, *Dealey*, 74, 119–21.

9. Dealey, "Getting into Action," 1, ECPD folder, Dealey Collection; Sharpe, *Dealey*, 140–42; and McFarland, *Awakening of Harrisburg*, (see chap. 6, n. 15), 20.

10. McFarland, *Awakening of Harrisburg*, 14; and Sharpe, *Dealey*, 144–54.

11. Dealey, "Getting into Action," 2–7, ECPD folder, and George E. Kessler to Dealey, 19 Mar. 1912, folder 18, Dealey Collection; Sharpe, *Dealey*, 155–56.

12. Dealey, "Getting into Action," 3–5, and, for quotations, *DMN*, 26 Feb. 1910.

13. DCC, *Reports of Officers and Committees of the Dallas Chamber of Commerce for the Year 1911* (Dallas, 1912), 33–37; Kessler to J. R. Babcock, 14 Mar. 1910, and 24 Dec. 1910, to William C. Scarff, 13 Dec. 1910, to Dealey, 21 May 1910, and S. J. Hay to Kessler, 23 Apr. 1910, box 13, Kessler Collection (see chap. 5, n. 19); and DPB, "Minutes," 14 Sept. 1910, Park and Recreation Department, Dallas City Hall.

14. DPB, "Minutes," 28 Feb. 1912; Kessler, *City Plan*, 7–8.

15. Kessler, *City Plan*, 8 (quotation), 9.

16. Ibid., 10–12.

17. Ibid., 12–14, 16–25, 31–40.

18. Ibid., 25–26.

19. Ibid., 13 (Kessler quotations). Kessler to Dealey, 5 June 1911, ECPD folder; John S. Aldehoff to *DMN*, 6 Jan. 1911; and O. K. Harry to *DMN*, 6 Jan. 1911 (quotation), Dealey Collection. Kessler to Alex Sanger and Henry D. Lindsley, 16 June 1910; Kessler to S. J. Hay, 22 June 1910; James A. Dorsey to *DMN*, 3 Aug. 1910, box 13, Kessler Collection. For Kessler's design and political problems with the union station and civic center, Kessler to R. C. Barnett, 30 Jan. 1911; Miss E. A. Sutermeister to Kessler, 17 Apr. 1911; and R. C. Barnett to Kessler, 12 May 1911, box 3, Kessler Collection.

20. Kessler, *City Plan*, 14–15.

21. For the shift to the city practical, see Scott, *American City Planning* (see intro., n. 1), 110–50.

22. An excellent review of the union station matter is in *DMN*, 1 Oct. 1935, sec. 7. All references not otherwise cited are to this summary. For quotation, see A. A. Allen to Allison Mayfield, 24 Oct. 1908, folder R R Comm 1909, box 2-10/518, Records of the Railroad Commission of Texas, Texas State Archives.

23. For the work of Kessler and Dealey, see Kessler to Dealey, 19 Aug. 1910 and 29 Sept. 1910, and for Kessler's assistance to *DMN*, 8 Dec. 1910, box 13, Kessler Collection.

24. Kessler, *City Plan*, maps and elevations titled "Viaducts Across Trinity River Bottoms"; Office of the City Manager, City of Dallas, *Dallas Union Terminal: Preliminary Application for a Capital Assistance Grant* (Dallas, 1975), 5; and Louis P. Head, *The Kessler*

City Plan for Dallas: Genesis and Development of the Plan 1910, the Supplement Plan of 1920, Progress in Fifteen Years (Dallas, 1925), 7–8.

25. *DMN*, 1 Oct. 1935, sec. 6, contains a good review of the Pacific Avenue situation.

26. Dealey to Kessler, 7 Jan. 1919; and C. L. Sanger to Kessler, 15 February 1919; Sanger to Miss Kate Fitzpatrick ("decaying" quotation); folder 26, Dealey Collection.

27. Dealey to Sanger, 10 Mar. 1919; Kessler to Dealey, 2 Mar. 1919; and Dealey to A. G. Wood, 6 Mar. 1919 ("mossback" quotation), folder 26, Dealey Collection. For west-end problems, see Dallas Property Owners' Association (DPOA), *The Union Station District: Its Present Condition and Its Possibilities*, bulletin no. 2 (Dallas, 1919). See also DPOA, *The Dallas Property Owners' Association: What It Stands For and What It Hopes to Accomplish*, bulletin no. 1 (Dallas, 1919).

28. *DMN*, 1 Oct. 1935, sec. 6; Dallas Metropolitan Development Association, *Dallas Metropolitan* 1 (April 1920): 1–2; *Kessler Map Showing Streets to be Widened and Extended* (Dallas: Kessler Plan Association, [1924]); and Head, *Kessler City Plan*, 12–13. For contributions, see J. E. Surratt to Dealey, 7 Mar. 1924, folder 21, Dealey Collection.

29. J. E. Surratt to Dealey, 7 Mar. 1924, folder 21, Dealey Collection; and DPOA Executive Committee, "Report," [1924], vertical files, Frances Loeb Library, Graduate School of Design, Harvard University.

30. Sarah Elizabeth Campbell, "George E. Kessler, Landscape Architect to City Planner: His Work in Texas Cities" (M.S. thesis, University of Texas at Austin, 1978), 79–80; Kessler to Dealey, 1 May 1917, folder 19; and Dealey to Kessler, 27 Feb. 1919, Dealey Collection.

31. For Surratt and the DPOA, see Dealey to DPOA, 12 Feb. 1924, folder 26, Dealey Collection. For Surratt's ability to work with others, see Surratt to Dealey, 16 Jan. 1924; Dealey to Surratt, 18 Jan. 1924; and Kessler to Surratt, 12 Feb. 1924, folder 26, Dealey Collection. Surratt to Thomas Adams, n.d. folder 27; Dealey to Surratt, 18 June 1927, folder 27; and Surratt to Dealey, 3 Oct. 1927, folder 203, Dealey Collection.

32. See, for example, KPA, "Kessler Plan Salesman," which appeared in various forms, including a pamphlet, vol. 1 (Autumn 1926). Justin F. Kimball, *Our City—Dallas: A Community Civics* (Dallas: Kessler Plan Association, 1927). For the origins of the textbook, see KPA, *Prospects Bright for Kessler Program: Cary Report Urges Action* (30 January 1926) [pamphlet].

33. Walter D. Moody, *Wacker's Manual of the Plan of Chicago: Municipal Economy* (Chicago: Chicago Plan Commission, 1911). For an analysis of the Chicago volume, see Thomas J. Schlereth, "Planning and Progressivism: *Wacker's Manual of the Plan of Chicago*," in *Ideas in America's Cultures: From Republic to Mass Society*, ed. Hamilton Cravens (Ames: Iowa State University Press, 1982), 125–77.

34. Sharpe, *Dealey*, 297; John E. Surratt, "City Planning in Dallas," *City Planning* 4 (January 1928): 17; "The Ulrickson Committee Report," *Dallas* 6 (November 1927): 7–9, 26–27; and memorandum, 21 Apr. 1938 accompanying Fred F. Florence to George B. Dealey, 27 Apr. 1938, folder 398, Dealey Collection.

35. KPA, *The Kessler Plan for Greater Dallas* (January 1925) [pamphlet].

36. W. T. Davis to Simon Linz, 12 Jan. 1929; and Surratt memorandum to Dealey, 15 Jan. 1929, folder 21, Dealey Collection.

37. For Dealey on housing, see "Social Unrest"; and "The Well-Planned City," *Texas Municipalities* 3 (July 1916): 78. For Mill Creek, see Head, *Kessler City Plan*, 32–34.

38. McFarland to Dealey, 10 Oct. 1911, ECPD folder; and undated petition from CPIL, folder 18, Dealey Collection; and DCC, *Reports of Officers and Committees*, 36.

39. J. R. Babcock to Dealey, 9 Aug. 1913, folder 25, Dealey Collection. DPB, "Minutes," 3 No. 1913, 28 Nov. 1913, 13 Dec. 1917, and 2 Apr. 1918. For Lindsley, see K. K. Hooper to Kessler, 13 Apr. 1915; and Hooper memorandum to Dealey, 16 June 1915, folder 25, Dealey Collection. Kessler to Dealey, 16 Feb. 1918, folder 19, Dealey Collection.

40. For Kessler's distractions, see Kessler to Dealey, 24 Mar. 1911, folder 167; Kessler to Dealey, 25 Aug. 1911, folder 167; and Kessler to Dealey, 7 Apr. 1911, ECPD folder, Dealey Collection. For park commissioner's attacks, see K. K. Hooper memorandum,

undated, to Dealey, folder 18; and Hooper memorandum to Dealey, 16 June 1915 (quotation), folder 25, Dealey Collection.

41. Kessler to Dealey, 13 Aug. 1912, ECPD folder; and 9 June 1915, folder 25, Dealey Collection.

42. For Turtle Creek, see Harry Jebson, Jr., et al., *Centennial History of the Dallas, Texas, Park System, 1876–1976* (Lubbock: Texas Tech University Press, 1976), 336–37. For the CPIL, see K. K. Hooper memorandum to Dealey, 11 Feb. 1918, folder 19, Dealey Collection. For the Ulrickson plan issue, see Sharpe, *Dealey*, 251–53; Surratt to Dealey, 30 Dec. 1932, and attached financial statement; and Dealey memorandum to Sam Acheson, 31 Dec. 1932, folder 22, Dealey Collection.

43. "Opposition Meeting," memorandum, 5 Dec. 1927, folder 21, Dealey Collection. For opposition to the business domination of Dallas politics, see Ann Prather Hollingsworth, "Reform Government in Dallas, 1927–1940" (M.A. thesis, North Texas State University, 1971).

44. Kessler to Hooper, 7 Nov. 1916, folder 19, Dealey Collection; *$75,000,000 Accomplishments under the Kessler Program* (Dallas: Kessler Plan Association, 1928) [pamphlet]. DPB, *Report for the Years 1921–23*, 7.

45. Justin F. Kimball, "Youth and City Planning," *City Planning* 4 (January 1928): 4; *A Big United Program for Dallas City and Dallas County for the Year 1927* (Dallas: Kessler Plan Association, 1927) [pamphlet].

Chapter 13. The Glory, Destruction, and Meaning of the City Beautiful Movement

1. Commentaries on the *Plan of Chicago* include Boyer, *Urban Masses and Moral Order* (see chap. 1, n. 4), 270–76; Carl W. Condit, *Chicago, 1910–29: Building, Planning, and Urban Technology* (Chicago: University of Chicago Press, 1973), 59–85; Wilbert R. Hasbrouck, "Introduction" to the reprinted *Plan of Chicago* (see chap. 4, n. 34), v–viii; Hines, *Burnham* (see intro., n. 2), 312–45; Horowitz, *Culture and the City* (see chap. 3, n. 15), 220–25; Mario Manieri-Elia, "Toward an 'Imperial City': Daniel H. Burnham and the City Beautiful Movement," in *The American City: From the Civil War to the New Deal*, Giorgio Ciucci et al. (Cambridge: MIT Press, 1979), 89–112; Reps, *Making of Urban America* (see chap. 1, n. 72), 517–24; Scott, *American City Planning* (see intro., n. 1), 100–109; and Paul Barrett, *The Automobile and Urban Transit: The Formation of Public Policy in Chicago, 1900–1930* (Philadelphia: Temple University Press, 1983), 73–81.

2. Burnham and Bennett, *Plan of Chicago* (see chap. 4, n. 34), 116.

3. Ibid., 117, 118.

4. Ibid., 116; and Manieri-Elia, "Toward an 'Imperial City,'" 95. For the city-county building, see Condit, *Chicago, 1910–29*, 178–82; and Joan E. Draper, "Paris by the Lake: Sources of Burnham's Plan of Chicago," in *Chicago Architecture, 1872–1922: Birth of a Metropolis*, ed. John Zukowsky (Munich: Prestel-Verlag, in association with the Art Institute of Chicago, 1987), 107–19.

5. For height limitations in Denver, see Pickering, "Blueprint of Power" (see chap. 8, n. 5), 134–35; and in Seattle, see Neil, "Paris or New York?" (see chap. 10, n. 1), 22–23. Hines, *Burnham*, 334–35.

6. Burnham and Bennett, *Plan of Chicago* (see chap. 4, n. 34), plates cxii, cxv, cvxi, cxxi, and cxxii.

7. Ibid., 108–9.

8. Ford, ed., *City Planning Progress* (see chap. 9, n. 31), iii; Scott, *American City Planning*, 167–68, 187.

9. Quoted in Hines, *Burnham*, 369.

10. A list of buildings completed by Burnham's firms is in Hines, *Burnham*, 371–83.

11. Hancock, "John Nolen" (see chap. 2, n. 47), 137–42; Newton, *Design on the Land* (see chap. 1, n. 25), 385–87; Peterson, "Origins of the Comprehensive City Planning Ideal" (see chap. 1, n. 39), 373–425; and Scott, *American City Planning*, 71–100. For the emergence of city planning professionalism and specialized publications, see Kirschner, *Paradox of Professionalism* (see chap. 4, n. 14), 4–10.

12. Schultz and McShane, "To Engineer the Metropolis" (see chap. 2, n. 2), 398–402; Clay McShane, "Transforming the Use of Urban Space: A Look at the Revolution in Street Pavements, 1880–1924," *Journal of Urban History* 5 (May 1979): 295–300; and Scott, *American City Planning*, 80–81.

13. For Manning and Harrisburg, see McFarland to Woodruff, 26 Nov. 1915, box 13, McFarland Papers (see chap. 2, n. 42). For expert planners' changing relationships, see Scott, *American City Planning*, 110–269, especially 227–37.

14. Benjamin C. Marsh, "City Planning in Justice to the Working Population," *Charities and the Commons* 19 (1 February 1908): 1514–18.

15. Robert Anderson Pope, "Some of the Needs of City Planning in America," in U.S. Congress, Senate, *City Planning*, including *Program of First National Conference on City Planning, Washington, D.C., May 21 and 22, 1909* (Washington, 1910), 75.

16. Ibid., 76–79; John Nolen, "What Is Needed in American City Planning," in U.S. Senate, *City Planning*, 74–75; Frederick Law Olmsted, Jr., "The Scope and Results of City Planning in Europe," in ibid., 63–70; Marsh, "A National Constructive Programme for City Planning," in ibid., 61–62; and idem, "Economic Aspects of City Planning," in ibid., 104–5.

17. The report from the delegate of the Washington State Chapter incorporated a newspaper clipping describing Gilbert's speech, WSC Papers, Records, 1894–1910 (see chap. 10, n. 3), 173–74. An interpretive biography of Gilbert is Geoffrey Blodgett, "Cass Gilbert, Architect: Conservative at Bay," *Journal of American History* 72 (December 1985): 615–36. Despite Blodgett's title, Gilbert's attack on the City Beautiful identified him with the planning and architectural avant-garde. See also an account of a Gilbert speech in *P-I*, 28 Nov. 1909 (see chap. 7, n. 4).

18. [Charles Mulford Robinson], "Notes and Comments: A Protest That Is Timely," *Architectural Record* 27 (February 1910): 202–3; Arnold Brunner, *Washington Star*, 16 Dec. 1910; and George B. Ford, "Digging Deeper into City Planning," *American City* 6 (March 1912): 557–62. See also Robinson's review of Ford's article in "A Broader and Saner City Planning," ibid., 555–56.

19. "The Convention of the American Civic Association," 21 Dec. 1911, box 14, McFarland Papers; and ACA, Department of City Making, *Not Only the City Beautiful*, no. 8, ser. 2 (Washington, D.C., 1913), 3, 10.

20. For McFarland's analysis of his role, see McFarland to John Nolen, 15 Feb. 1909, John Nolen Papers, Collection 2903, Department of Manuscripts and University Archives, Cornell University.

21. Olmsted to Benjamin C. Marsh, 21 Apr. 1909, folder 2921–1, box 183, Olmsted Records (see chap. 1, n. 11).

22. Olmsted to Olmsted, 12 Dec. 1909, folder 163, box 20A, Olmsted Correspondence (see chap. 7, n. 3).

23. McFarland's concern for the creation of new slums by failing to provide for the dispossessed from cleared slums is in his letter to Graham Romeyn Taylor, 14 Dec. 1912, box 9, McFarland Papers.

24. For billboards, see Kristin Szylvian Bailey, "'Fighting Civic Smallpox': The Civic Club of Allegheny County's Campaign for Billboard Regulation, 1896–1917," *Western Pennsylvania Historical Magazine* 70 (January 1987): 3–28; and William H. Wilson, "The Billboard: Bane of the City Beautiful," *Journal of Urban History* 13 (August 1987): 394–425.

25. Roy Lubove, *The Progressives and the Slums: Tenement House Reform in New York City, 1890–1917* (Pittsburgh: University of Pittsburgh Press, 1962), 220.

26. For "appalling" and "play" quotations, see Olmsted, "Introductory Address on City Planning," in *Proceedings of the Second National Conference on City Planning and the Problems of Congestion* (Boston, 1912), 15, 16; for "any" quotation, "How to Organize a City Planning Campaign," in ibid., 304. For Nolen, see Hancock, "John Nolen," 324–33, 508–16. See also Nolen, *Replanning Small Cities: Six Typical Cities* (New York: B. W. Huebsch, 1912); and idem, *New Ideals in the Planning of Cities, Towns and Villages* (New York: American City Bureau, 1919), 5–7, 10–11, 25–30, 78–83. For war memorials, see the following articles in *American City*: "The Proposed Liberty Memorial Square and Civic

Center for Berkeley, California," vol. 20 (May 1919): 428–29; and "Grand Rapids Considering a Memorial Building," ibid.: 429; O. B. McClintock, "Minnesota Proposes a Memorial Hall," vol. 21 (September 1919): 252; and "Civic Centers as War Memorials," vol. 21 (October 1919): 330–34. Scott, *American City Planning*, 120–22.

27. Henry S. Churchill, *The City Is the People* (New York: Harcourt, Brace & World, 1945; reprint, New York: W. W. Norton & Co., 1962), 82, for "scarcely" and "carried" quotations; and 69, for "plan" quotation. James Marston Fitch, *American Building: The Historical Forces That Shaped It*, 2d ed., rev. and enl. (Boston: Houghton Mifflin Co., 1972), 239–40. Fitch's book was first published in 1947.

28. Ford, ed., *City Planning Progress*, v–vi. Most of the plans dated from the City Beautiful era.

29. Huggins, "City Planning in North Carolina" (see chap. 4, n. 33), 383–87, 390. Carl V. Harris, *Political Power in Birmingham, 1871–1921* (Knoxville: University of Tennessee Press, 1977), 164–67 (quotation, 166), 229–31.

30. See Ford, ed., *City Planning Progress*, 5–193; and Hancock, "John Nolen," 334–44.

31. Harvey A. Kantor, "The City Beautiful in New York," *New-York Historical Quarterly* 57 (April 1973): 149–67 (quotations, 170, 171). See also Robert A. M. Stern, Gregory Gilmartin, and John Montague Massengale, *New York 1900: Metropolitan Architecture and Urbanism, 1890–1915* (New York: Rizzoli, 1983), 7–143.

32. Herbert Croly, "'Civic Improvements': The Case of New York," *Architectural Record* 21 (May 1907): 350. McKim to Charles Moore, 8 Jan. 1903, Scrapbook: Park Commission Correspondence, Mr. McKim, 1901–1903, Charles Moore Papers, Manuscript Division, Library of Congress.

33. Judd Kahn, *Imperial San Francisco*, 4 ("better off" quotation), and for Kahn's discussion of the influence of property and statement of his belief in the efficacy of centralized government in replanning, see 177–216. See also William Issel and Robert W. Cherny, *San Francisco, 1865–1932: Politics, Power, and Urban Development* (Berkeley and Los Angeles: University of California Press, 1986): 109–16, 170–72. For rebuilding after devastating fires in Chicago, Boston, and Baltimore, see Christine Meisner Rosen, *The Limits of Power: Great Fires and the Process of City Growth in America* (Cambridge: Cambridge University Press, 1986).

34. Kahn, *Imperial San Francisco*, 200, 201. Other examinations of Burnham's plan are in Hines, *Burnham*, 174–96; and Mellier G. Scott, *The San Francisco Bay Area: A Metropolis in Perspective* (Berkeley and Los Angeles: University of California Press, 1959), 79–121.

35. Draper, *San Francisco Civic Center* (see chap. 10, n. 17), 12 (quotation, 19). The one-tenth of centers begun is my estimate, not Draper's.

36. For comparative construction costs, see Hines, *Burnham*, 386.

37. For the centralization-decentralization dichotomy, see Samuel P. Hays, "The Changing Political Structure of the City in Industrial America," *Journal of Urban History* 1 (November 1974): 6–38. See also William W. Cutler III, "The Persistent Dualism: Centralization and Decentralization in Philadelphia, 1854–1975," in *The Divided Metropolis: Social and Spatial Dimensions of Philadelphia, 1800–1975*, ed. William W. Cutler III and Howard Gillette (Westport, Conn.: Greenwood Press, 1980), 257, 260, 262, 263.

38. Sullivan, *Autobiography of an Idea* (see chap. 9, n. 21), 321–25. The most recent biography of Sullivan is Robert Twombly, *Louis Sullivan: His Life and Work* (New York: Viking Penguin, 1986).

39. Tallmadge, *Architecture in America* (see chap. 3, n. 19), 196–97; David H. Crook, "Louis Sullivan and the Golden Doorway," *Journal of the Society of Architectural Historians* 26 (December 1967): 250–58; Dimitri Tselos, "The Chicago Fair and the Myth of the 'Lost Cause,'" ibid., 259–68; Hines, *Burnham*, 98–100; Burg, *Chicago's White City* (see chap. 3, n. 2), 303–9; and David S. Andrew, *Louis Sullivan and the Polemics of Modern Architecture: The Present against the Past* (Urbana: University of Illinois Press, 1985), 136–39. For Wright, see Scully, *American Architecture and Urbanism* (see chap. 4, n. 36), 138; and Thomas S. Hines, "The Paradox of 'Progressive' Architecture: Urban Planning and Public Building in Tom Johnson's Cleveland," *American Quarterly* 25 (October 1973): 445, 447. American architects attacked neoclassicism and the civic center concept at least as early as 1911, but their ideas were neither dominant among their colleagues nor very popular. See

Ernest Flagg, "Public Buildings," 42–55; and Irving K. Pond, "Discussion," in *Proceedings of the Third National Conference on City Planning* (Boston, 1911), 74–77.

40. Louis Sullivan, *Kindergarten Chats* (New York: George Wittenborn, 1947). For Sullivan as planner and businessman, see Andrew, *Sullivan*, 75–112, 128–34. Wright's planning ideas are in his *The Living City* (New York: Horizon Press, 1958). Colin Rowe, *The Mathematics of the Ideal Villa and Other Essays* (Cambridge: MIT Press, 1976), contrasts Sullivan's lack of interior planning with Wright's concern for the plan, 96, 98–99. Fishman, *Urban Utopias* (see chap. 3, n. 52), 122–60.

41. Jordy, *American Buildings: Progressive and Academic Ideals* (see chap. 3, n. 10), 3:63–70, 83–179; Mark L. Peisch, *The Chicago School of Architecture: Early Followers of Sullivan and Wright* (New York: Random House, 1964), 4, 13–15, 18, 32–33, 70, 105–24, 144–45, illus. 28.

42. For discussions of the parallelism of neoclassical and other styles, see Christopher Tunnard and Henry Hope Reed, *American Skyline: The Growth and Form of Our Cities and Towns* (Boston: Houghton Mifflin Co., 1955), 179–215; and Tunnard, *Modern American City* (see chap. 3, n. 24), 89–92. Talbot F. Hamlin, *The Enjoyment of Architecture* (New York: Charles Scribner's Sons, 1929), 266–97. Lewis Mumford, *Sticks and Stones: A Study of American Architecture and Civilization*, 2d rev. ed. (Boni and Liveright, 1924; reprint, New York: Dover Publications, 1955), 174. For the impact of neoclassicism on federal government construction, see Lois A. Craig et al., *The Federal Presence: Architecture, Politics, and Symbols in United States Government Building* (Cambridge: MIT Press, 1978). A different interpretation of the neoclassical impact on commercial architecture is Jack Tager, "Partners in Design: Chicago Architects, Entrepreneurs, and the Evolution of Urban Commercial Architecture," *South Atlantic Quarterly* 76 (Spring 1977): 212–18. For a discussion of "civic horizontalism and corporate verticality," in the New York context, see Thomas Bender and William R. Taylor, "Culture and Architecture: Some Aesthetic Tensions in the Shaping of Modern New York City," in *Visions of the Modern City: Essays in History, Art, and Literature*, ed. William Sharpe and Leonard Wallock (Baltimore: Johns Hopkins University Press, 1987), 189–219.

43. Manieri-Elia, "Toward an 'Imperial City,'" 1–121; and Francesco Dal Co, "From Parks to the Region: Progressive Ideology and the Reform of the American City," in Ciucci et al., *American City*, 143–221; M. Christine Boyer, *Dreaming the Rational City: The Myth of American City Planning* (Cambridge: MIT Press, 1983), 3–82, 114–36; Marcuse, "Housing in Early City Planning" (see chap. 4, n. 1), 153–76; and Richard E. Foglesong, *Planning the Capitalist City: The Colonial Era to the 1920s* (Princeton: Princeton University Press, 1986), 163–66, 206–10, 216.

44. For imperialism, see Burchard and Bush-Brown, *Architecture of America* (see intro., n. 2), 295. For social control and related issues not cited or discussed elsewhere, see Francoise Choay, *The Modern City: Planning in the Nineteenth Century* (New York: George Braziller, Publisher, 1970), 7–32, 97–110; Stephen Kern, *The Culture of Time and Space, 1880–1918* (Cambridge: Harvard University Press, 1983), 39–40, 56, 99–100, 139, 209–10; Weinstein, *Corporate Ideal* (see chap. 4, n. 23), ix–x, 94–96; and Wiebe, *Search for Order* (see chap. 2, n. 2), xiii–xiv, 149. For Marxist disagreements, see Manieri-Elia, "Toward an 'Imperial City,'" 49–52, 91; Boyer, *Dreaming the Rational City*, 5; Dal Co, "From Parks to the Region," 176–78; and Fogelsong, *Planning the Capitalist City*, 89–166. For housing problems, see Boyer, *Dreaming the Rational City*, 100; and Robert B. Fairbanks, "From Better Dwellings to Better Community: Changing Approaches to the Low-Cost Housing Problem, 1890–1925," *Journal of Urban History* 11 (May 1985): 314–34. For settlement house workers, see Allen F. Davis, *Spearheads for Reform: The Social Settlements and the Progressive Movement, 1890–1914* (New York: Oxford University Press, 1967), 73–74.

45. For the novel, see Burg, *Chicago's White City*, 290–92. For quotations, see Cobden-Sanderson, "Of Art and Life," in *Art and Life, and the Building and Decoration of Cities: A Series of Lectures by Members of the Arts and Crafts Exhibition Society, Delivered at the Fifth Exhibition of the Society in 1896*, Arts and Crafts Exhibition Society (London: Rivington, Percival & Co., 1897), 43–44; Halsey Ricardo, "Of Colour in the Architecture of Cities," 259.

46. W. R. Lethaby, "Of Beautiful Cities," in *Art and Life,* 99; Walter Crane, "Of the Decoration of Public Buildings," in ibid., 139; and Ricardo, "Of Colour in the Architecture of Cities," in ibid., 259.

47. "Patriotic Residents of Dallas Can Solve 'City Beautiful' Problem," *Dallas* 7 (December 1923): 22, 23; and Arthur L. Kramer, "Beauty in City Building," ibid. 9 (January 1930): 9, 21. Wilson, "J. Horace McFarland" (see chap. 4, n. 6), 329, 330–31.

48. Thomas Adams, "Some Town Planning Principles Restated," *American City* 12 (March 1915): 213; Nelson P. Lewis, *The Planning of the Modern City: A Review of the Principles Governing City Planning,* 2d ed. rev. (1916; New York: John Wiley & Sons, 1923), 23, 25; Hegemann and Peets, *The American Vitruvius* (see chap. 4, n. 42); John Nolen, "The Place of the Beautiful in the City Plan: Some Everyday Examples," in *Proceedings of the Fourteenth National Conference on City Planning* (Springfield, Mass., 1922), 133–47; Andrew Wright Crawford, "The Value of Art Commissions in City Planning," in ibid., 148–58. Mumford, in *Sticks and Stones,* criticizes the City Beautiful, 123–51 (quotation, 131). For the Honolulu plan, see Mumford, *City Development: Studies in Disintegration and Renewal* (New York: Harcourt, Brace & Co., 1945), 86–153. Mumford's mentor, Patrick Geddes, criticized "town planning" in the United States but also found much to admire, in *Cities in Evolution: An Introduction to the Town Planning Movement and to the Study of Civics* (1915; reprint, New York: Howard Fertig, 1968), 232–37, 248. Theodora Kimball Hubbard and Henry Vincent Hubbard, *Our Cities To-Day and To-Morrow: A Survey of Planning and Zoning Progress in the United States* (Cambridge: Harvard University Press, 1929), 5–78, 125, 135, 140, 216–17, 238, 248–51, 263–80 (quotation, 263).

49. George B. Ford, "What Makes 'The City Beautiful'?" in *Planning Problems of Town, City and Region: Papers and Discussions at the Twenty-first National Conference on City Planning* (Philadelphia: Wm. F. Fell Co., 1929), 170, 171, 172–73.

50. Harland Bartholomew and Associates, *Your Dallas of Tomorrow: Master Plan for a Greater Dallas, Report Number One: Character of the City* (Dallas: City Plan Commission, 1943), 31. A biography of Bartholomew and his place in city planning is Norman John Johnston, *Harland Bartholomew: His Comprehensive Plans and Science of Planning* (Ann Arbor: University Microfilms, 1964).

51. Christopher Tunnard, *The City of Man* (New York: Charles Scribner's Sons, 1953); Henry Hope Reed, Jr., *The Golden City* (Garden City, N.Y.: Doubleday & Co., 1959). For comments on Reed, see Burchard and Bush-Brown, *Architecture of America,* 295–96, 451, 490; and Larkin, *Art and Life in America* (see chap. 4, n. 37), 471.

52. For criticisms of planning and planners, see Edward P. Eicher and Marshall Kaplan, *The Community Builders* (Berkeley and Los Angeles: University of California Press, 1967); and Marshall Kaplan, *Urban Planning in the 1960s: A Design for Irrelevancy* (New York: Praeger Publishers, 1973; Cambridge: MIT Press, 1974), especially 85–103. A 1960s planner who had some appreciation for the City Beautiful movement was Edmund K. Faltermayer, *Redoing America: A Nationwide Report on How to Make Our Cities and Suburbs Livable* (New York: Harper & Row, 1968), 24, 25, 46, 191, 225–26. Lorraine B. Diehl, *The Late, Great Pennsylvania Station* (New York: American Heritage Press, 1985), 18–20, 26–28, 147–48. Scully, *American Architecture and Urbanism,* 142. Leonard K. Eaton, *Landscape Artist in America: The Life and Work of Jens Jensen* (Chicago: University of Chicago Press, 1964).

53. Ada Louise Huxtable, *Kicked a Building Lately?* (New York: Quadrangle Books, 1978), 3–5, 8–12, 217–21, 221–24; August Heckscher, *Alive in the City: Memoir of an Ex-Commissioner* (New York: Charles Scribner's Sons, 1974); idem, *Open Spaces* (see chap. 3, n. 30); George E. Condon, *Cleveland: The Best Kept Secret* (Garden City, N.Y.: Doubleday & Co., 1967), 352–56; Kidney, *The Architecture of Choice* (see chap. 3, n. 10); John J.-G. Blumenson, *Identifying American Architecture: A Pictorial Guide to Styles and Terms, 1600–1945* (Nashville: American Association for State and Local History, 1977); Brooklyn Institute of Arts and Sciences, *The American Renaissance, 1876–1917* (New York: Pantheon Books, 1979) (Wilson's essay is on pages 74–109). Scholarly production, in addition to works already cited, includes two articles by Michael P. McCarthy: "Chicago Business-

men and the Burnham Plan," *Journal of the Illinois State Historical Society* 63 (Autumn 1970): 228–56; and "Politics and the Parks: Chicago Businessmen and the Recreation Movement," ibid. 65 (Summer 1972): 158–72. See also Elizabeth Anne Mack Lyon, "Business Buildings in Atlanta: A Study in Growth and Form" (Ph.D. diss., Emory University, 1971). Joseph L. Arnold, "City Planning in America," in *The Urban Experience: Themes in American History*, ed. Raymond A. Mohl and James F. Richardson (Belmont, Calif.: Wadsworth Publishing Co., 1973), 14–43, is a brief, interpretive review. Joanna Schneider Zangrando, *Monumental Bridge Design in Washington, D.C., as a Reflection of American Culture, 1886 to 1932* (Ann Arbor: University Microfilms, 1974), is detailed and excellent. Among more recent articles are Ralph L. Pearson and Linda Wrigley, "Before Mayor Richard Lee: George Dudley Seymour and the City Planning Movement in New Haven, 1907–1924," *Journal of Urban History* 6 (May 1980): 297–319; John Fahey, "A. L. White, Champion of Urban Beauty," *Pacific Northwest Quarterly* 72 (October 1981): 170–79; and Shirley Leckie, "Brand Whitlock and the City Beautiful Movement in Toledo, Ohio," *Ohio History* 91 (1982): 5–36. On urban horticulture, see David F. Karnosky and Sheryl L. Karnosky, eds., *Improving the Quality of Urban Life with Plants: Proceedings of the June 21–23, 1983, International Symposium on Urban Horticulture*, New York Botanical Garden publication no. 2 (Millbrook, N.Y.: Institute of Urban Horticulture, 1985), especially the following articles: Harold B. Tukey, Jr., "An Overview of Urban Horticulture," 1–6; David R. DeWalle, "Amenities Provided by Urban Plants," 7–14; John F. Dwyer, "The Economic Values of Urban Plants," 15–27; Charles A. Lewis, "Human Dimensions of Horticulture," 35–44; and Rachel Kaplan, "Human Response to Plants and Landscapes," 45–60.

54. Statements not cited in this and subsequent notes are based on my observations. Dallas Master Plan Committee, *A Look At Past Planning for the City of Dallas* (Dallas, 1956), 7–8; Patsy Swank, "Mill Creek," *Vision* 2 (March 1979): 6; Jane Summer, "Getting to the Bottom of Town Lake," *Dallas Life: Sunday Magazine of the Dallas Morning News* 1 (14 November 1982): 10–12, 21–22, 24; and David Dillon, "City Park with a View," *DMN*, 26 Apr. 1984. *Denver Post*, 27 Feb. 1973, 28 Apr. 1976; and *Cervi's Rocky Mountain Journal* 31 (July 1972).

55. Kansas City Board of Park Commissioners, *Cowtown 1890 Becomes City Beautiful 1962: The Story of Kansas City's Parks* (Kansas City, 1962); Urban Design Advisory Board, *Designing a Great City* (Seattle: City Planning Commission, 1965), 3, 6, 7, 28; City Planning Commission, *Framework for Tomorrow: City Planning for Seattle* (Seattle, 1966) (see chap. 10, n. 45), 2–4; and Dennis Ryan, "Lay of the Land," *Planning* 49 (March 1983): 18–21. For Seattle organizations, see Barrett A. Lee et al., "Testing the Decline-of-Community Thesis: Neighborhood Organizations in Seattle, 1929 and 1979," *American Journal of Sociology* 89 (March 1984): 1161–88.

56. For Jacobs on the City Beautiful, see her *Death and Life of Great American Cities* (see intro., n. 2), 24–25. Jacobs may be correct in her claim that parks do not by themselves raise property values, a subject of much debate, but she loads her argument with a discussion of four small Philadelphia squares obviously unable to control the construction around them, 92–101. Her discussion of a "clay dog"-making beach replaced by a park lawn is poignant but it draws a false analogy between the action of waves and sun on clay deposits and the values of unplanned human activity, 446–47. For one criticism of Jacobs, see Fitch, *American Building*, 298–307. For another criticism of the City Beautiful with little practical effect on the growing interest in the movement, see Robert Goodman, *After the Planners* (New York: Simon & Schuster, 1971), 60, 98–103, 122, 130.

57. McFarland to Editor, *Jersey City Journal*, 21 Mar. 1908, box 15, McFarland Papers.

58. Goodman, *After the Planners*, illustrations on 104, 105.

59. For various problems of the Garden City and "back-to-the-land" movements, see Park Dixon Goist, "The City as Organism: Two Recent American Theories of the City" (Ph.D. diss., University of Rochester, 1967), 5; Frederick C. Howe, *The Modern City and Its Problems* (New York: Charles Scribner's Sons, 1915), 6–8; and Merwin Robert Swanson, "The American Country Life Movement, 1900–1940," (Ph.D. diss., University of Minnesota, 1972), 13–17, 25–29, 34–35. For a sympathetic treatment of Ebenezer

Howard and the Garden City idea, see Fishman, *Urban Utopias*, 23–88. For the relationship between sanitation and the City Beautiful, see Melosi, *Garbage in the Cities* (see chap. 2, n. 2), 110–13.

60. Bender and Taylor, "Culture and Architecture." For the impact of women on their communities, see Karen J. Blair, *The Clubwoman as Feminist: True Womanhood Redefined, 1868–1914* (New York: Holmes & Meier Publishers, 1980), 93–115, 119.

61. McFarland to Clinton Rogers Woodruff, 31 Dec. 1913, box 12, McFarland Papers. For a sampling of the extensive material on Washington, see ACA resolution, "Referring to the Improvement of the City of Washington and District of Columbia under Plans of the Commission Appointed by the Senate of the United States" (1904) file 2823, box 135, Olmsted Records; and American Institute of Architects et al., *An Appeal to the Enlightened Sentiment of the People of the United States for the Safeguarding of the Future Development of the Capital of the Nation* (Washington, D.C., 1916). Unfinished Washington, not historical continuity, was part of an inspiration for a 1960s effort to beautify the city, although a few of the participants in the movement were aware of their predecessors. See Lewis L. Gould, *Lady Bird Johnson and the Environment* (Lawrence: University Press of Kansas, 1988), 37–135.

62. Elements of City Beautiful plans survived in later planning schemes, a phenomenon noted as early as 1927 by Jacob L. Crane, Jr., "Errors to Avoid in City Planning," in *Official Proceedings of the Thirty-third Annual Convention Held at Dallas, Texas, November 14–18, 1927*, American Society for Municipal Improvements (St. Louis, 1928), 98.

63. Dana F. White claims the status of comprehensive planner for the senior Olmsted, and David C. Hammack claims it for Andrew Green and others. See White, "Frederick Law Olmsted, the Place Maker," in *Two Centuries of American Planning*, ed. Daniel Schaffer (London: Mansell, 1988), 87–112; and Hammack, "Comprehensive Planning before the Comprehensive Plan: A New Look at the Nineteenth-Century American City," in ibid., 139–65 (quotation, 156).

64. McFarland to Richard B. Watrous, 27 Sept. 1915, box 11; and to W. C. Reed, 4 Oct. 1921, box 8, McFarland Papers. *DMN*, 9 June 1980. David Dillon, "The Strangling of Turtle Creek," *DMN*, 8 July 1984; idem, and "A Changing Turtle Creek," *DMN*, 5 Aug. 1984. For the Kansas City Union Station, see Roy Kahn, "Tackling 'Impossible' Buildings," *Historic Preservation* 38 (May/June 1986): 42, 44. Although it concerns parks, Patricia O"Donnell's "Historic Preservation as Applied to Urban Parks," in *The Yearbook of Landscape Architecture: Historic Preservation* (New York: Van Nostrand Reinhold Co., 1983), 35, 53, deals effectively with difficult problems of changing uses, design, and restoration.

65. Draper, *San Francisco Civic Center* 59.

Note on Sources

Many secondary sources refer to the City Beautiful movement, but only a relative handful rise to the analytical level. The following review includes some of the books and articles that truly comprehend the movement. Mel Scott, in *American City Planning since 1890* (Berkeley and Los Angeles: University of California Press, 1969), first studied the origins and development of the national City Beautiful. Scott's categories are refined and extended in Jon A. Peterson, "The City Beautiful Movement: Forgotten Origins and Lost Meanings," *Journal of Urban History* 2 (August 1976): 415–34. Of the national City Beautiful figures, only Daniel H. Burnham has received full-length biographical treatment. Thomas S. Hines is a skilled and sympathetic biographer. See his *Burnham of Chicago: Architect and Planner* (New York: Oxford University Press, 1974). Charles Moore, *Daniel H. Burnham: Architect, Planner of Cities* (Boston: Houghton Mifflin, 1921; reprint, New York: Da Capo Press, 1968), remains important. The analysis of the movement in Paul Boyer, *Urban Masses and Moral Order in America: 1820–1920* (Cambridge: Harvard University Press, 1978), repays reading. Standard on the World's Columbian Exposition is David F. Burg, *Chicago's White City of 1893* (Lexington: University Press of Kentucky, 1976).

Among the archival sources necessary to this book are the J. Horace McFarland Papers, Pennsylvania State Archives, Harrisburg. The McFarland papers are essential to an understanding of events in Harrisburg and nationally, especially when supplemented by the Dock Family Papers in the Pennsylvania State Archives and the Mira Lloyd Dock Papers in the Manuscript Division, Library of Congress. Kansas City, Dallas, and national developments are illuminated by the George E. Kessler Collection, Missouri Historical Society, St. Louis, while the George B. Dealey Collection, Dallas Historical Society, throws much light on the situation in Dallas. The Washington State Chapter, American Institute of Architects Papers, and the Reginald Thomson Papers, Manuscripts Division, University of Washington

Libraries, Seattle, explain many Seattle circumstances, as does the John Charles Olmsted–Sophia White Olmsted Correspondence, Frances Loeb Library, Graduate School of Design, Harvard University. The Records of the Olmsted Associates, Inc., Manuscript Division, Library of Congress, reveal much about Seattle, Denver, and national issues. The Edward H. Bennett diaries in the office of E. H. Bennett, Jr., Chicago, are very helpful to an understanding of some aspects of Denver's civic center movement.

Other, relatively less important manuscript sources are mentioned in the notes. This book could not have been written without the many municipal records and reports available in each case-study city and without the superb collection of planning reports and related materials in the Frances Loeb Library.

Acknowledgments

Two chapters of this book are based on much the same source material as my *City Beautiful Movement in Kansas City* (Columbia: University of Missouri Press, 1964). Readers should know some of the justifications for including the chapters here. A restudy of the George E. Kessler Collection and other sources, fresh research, and a quarter-century's maturation have convinced me of the need to modify some earlier interpretations. I no longer believe that it was so important that an episodic park and boulevard crusade preceded William R. Nelson's planning publicity. It is now clear to me that Kessler shared the authorship of the pivotal 1893 park board report with the board chairman, August R. Meyer. I have recast and extended my analysis of City Beautiful proponents and opponents, and of key City Beautiful votes, to fit the critique of what I call determinism. Some of this material is evident in chapter 5, but most of it is confined to the notes for chapter 9. I have shifted my view of neoclassical architecture. The language of the earlier study has been altered, especially in chapter 5, but if a phrase, sentence, or paragraph seemed valid, it survived unchanged. I am grateful to the University of Missouri Press for relinquishing its copyright claim to the older book.

Before proceeding to other reprint acknowledgments, I wish to thank the people who helped with this book. I am grateful to those who invited me for all-too-brief visits that were anodyne for work on the East Coast. The late Lee Arney and Joe Miller of Washington, D.C., provided boon companionship and, on one occasion, a home away from home. Cathy and Dick Hotvedt of Bethesda, Maryland, and Marilynn and Jack Nussbaum of Tenafly, New Jersey, have my thanks for similar kindnesses. Mary and Lyle Dorsett opened their Boulder, Colorado, home to me during part of one stay in the Denver area. I benefited, as well, from Lyle's remarkable knowledge of the history of Denver. My several visits to Seattle were spent mostly in the home of Kathy Janes, now Mrs. Robert R. Baker, and Bill Janes. They lifted my spirits as only close friends can. The late Linda Doupé and Bob Doupé of Seattle cheerfully bore my interruptions of their routine. Discussions through the years about architecture and urban design with Tom Nelson, a good friend and Kansas City architect, have sharpened my understanding of those topics.

Several University of North Texas history department colleagues offered assistance, advice, and sympathy during the many years of preparation of this volume. Thanks beyond the usual measure go to Randolph B. Campbell, William Kamman, and Donald K. Pickens. Anyone who studies the City Beautiful movement is deeply indebted to the writings of Jon A. Peterson. I learned as much, however, from spirited discussions with Peterson and from his comments on an earlier draft of my manuscript. David Schuyler's and Paul Boyer's analyses of other drafts significantly improved the final version. Kenneth T. Jackson gave generous help at a critical time. After my wife Kitty and my own parents, my parents-in-law showed the most interest in my work. The dedication is an inadequate recognition of their involvement.

The members of the Organized Research and Faculty Development Leave committees of the University of North Texas generously aided my research through the years. A grant from the Johnson Fund of the American Philosophical Society assisted some of the early phases of my research. The sponsors of the First International Planning History Conference provided me with a berth, forcing me to reduce some inchoate thoughts to a more systematic presentation. The organizers of two of the American Planning Association's National Planning Conferences gave me the opportunity to present some material on Dallas and Seattle. I expanded the earlier Dallas presentation in a paper for an annual meeting of the Texas State Historical Association. The National Association for Olmsted Parks extended an invitation to explore the relationship between John Charles Olmsted and Seattle in a paper before one of its annual meetings. Joan E. Draper and John Zukowsky arranged for me to lecture at the Art Institute of Chicago on Edward H. Bennett's role in the development of the Denver Civic Center. The happy result for me was that I organized my thoughts on that subject.

At the Johns Hopkins University Press I am especially indebted to my editor, George F. Thompson, to his assistant, Margaret Gillespie, and to Pamela Bruton, my copy editor.

Archivists, librarians, and individuals outside the five case study cities were essential to my project. I am pleased to acknowledge the help of the staff of the Frances Loeb Library, Graduate School of Design, Harvard University, and especially the kindnesses from Christopher Hail, assistant librarian. I am grateful to James Hodgson, librarian, for permission to quote from the John Charles Olmsted–Sophia White Olmsted Correspondence housed in the Frances Loeb Library. I appreciate the assistance of the staffs of the Manuscript Division, Library of Congress; the Department of Manuscripts and University Archives, Olin Library, Cornell University; the Alumni/Lydon Library, University of Lowell; the Texas State Archives; and the Missouri Historical Society, St. Louis. Edward H. Bennett, Jr., graciously opened his father's diaries to me and generously granted permission to quote from them. The staffs of the Willis Library, University of North Texas, and the Blagg-Huey Library at Texas Woman's University, also helped. In Dallas, the staffs of the Fondren, De Golyer, and Fine Arts libraries at Southern Methodist University; the Dallas Historical Society; the Texas/Dallas History and Archives Division, J. Erik Jonsson Central Library, Dallas Public Library; and the offices of the City Secretary and the Park and Recreation Department lent assistance. Permission to use material from the George B. Dealey Collection, Dallas Historical Society, is acknowledged with gratitude.

In Denver, I received the unflagging assistance of the staffs of the Western History Department of the Denver Public Library and the Documentary Resources Department of the Colorado Historical Society. The staffs of the University of Colorado at Boulder's libraries, and of its Western Historical Collections, made available the pertinent Denver-related materials in their care. In Harrisburg, the staff of the Pennsylvania State Archives lent essential help. This would be a poorer book without the knowledge of Martha Simonetti, now retired from the archives. Other Harrisburg helpers include the staffs of the Pennsylvania State Library; the Dauphin County Historical Society, and the office of the Dauphin County Clerk. In Kansas City, the staffs of the Public Library and of its Missouri Valley Collection and the offices of the City Clerk and the Parks and Recreation Department came to my rescue. Other assistance from an earlier time is acknowledged in my Kansas City book, already mentioned. In Seattle the staffs of the University of Washington libraries, especially those of the Pacific Northwest Collection and the Manuscripts Division in the Suzzallo Library, gave generously of their time and archival skills. I am also indebted to the staffs of the Public Library and the office of the City Clerk. Most of the library, archives, and historical staffs previously mentioned assembled the photographs, which are individually acknowledged. All this outpouring of help carries no responsibility for this book. That responsibility is mine alone.

The following thanks for permission to reprint do not imply a transfer of a previously published article or book chapter to a chapter in this book, for all the works are more or less revised. Permission has been obtained from the proper persons in each instance, and is gratefully acknowledged. Portions of chapter 2 first appeared in "J. Horace McFarland and the City Beautiful Movement," *Journal of Urban History* 7 (May 1981), published by Sage Publications, Inc., as did sections in chapters 12 and 13. Parts of two chapters in books published by Mansell Publishing, Ltd., London, reappear here: "The Ideology, Aesthetics and Politics of the City Beautiful Movement," in *The Rise of Modern Urban Planning* (1980), forms the basis for chapter 4, and for a part of chapter 13; a different version of chapter 7 is "The Seattle Park System and the Ideal of the City Beautiful," in *Two Centuries of American Planning* (1988). Chapter 6 is developed from "Harrisburg's Successful City Beautiful Movement, 1900–1915," *Pennsylvania History* 47 (July 1980), and "'More

Almost than the Men': Mira Lloyd Dock and the Beautification of Harrisburg," *Pennsylvania Magazine of History and Biography* 99 (October 1975). Chapter 10 first appeared as "How Seattle Lost the Bogue Plan: Politics Versus Design," *Pacific Northwest Quarterly* 74 (October 1984). The *Journal of the West* published "A Diadem for the City Beautiful: The Development of Denver's Civic Center," in vol. 12 (April 1983), an earlier version of chapter 11. Chapter 12 is an extension of "Adapting to Growth: Dallas, Texas, and the Kessler Plan, 1908–1933," *Arizona and the West* 25 (Autumn 1983).

Index

NOTE: Italic numbers refer to pages with illustrations.

Abbey, Edwin Austin, 59
ACA. *See* American Civic Association
Adams, Thomas, 57, 58, 60, 298
Addams, Jane, 49
Adler & Sullivan, 55, 61
AIA. *See* American Institute of Architects
Akard Street, Dallas, 269
Alaska-Yukon-Pacific Exposition, Seattle, 153, 160, 167
ALCI. *See* American League for Civic Improvement
Alive in the City: Memoirs of an Ex-Commissioner (Heckscher), 300
Alki Beach, Seattle, 148, 232
Alki Point, Seattle, 148, 149, 167
Allison's Hill, Harrisburg, 128
American City, 259, 295
American Civic Association (ACA), 50, 52, 258, 260
American Institute of Architects (AIA), 285; Colorado Chapter, 173; Washington State Chapter, 160, 163, 215, 216, 221, 231
American League for Civic Improvement (ALCI), 41, 44, 285; activities of, in Dallas, 257; merger with APOAA, 41, 45, 49, 90
American Park and Outdoor Art Association (APOAA), 36–37, 38, 84, 285; and affirmation of Olmstedian ideals, 37, 50; "Experience Meeting" of, 40; founding and development of, 36–39; membership of, 40; and merger with ALCI, 41, 44, 49
American Renaissance, 1876–1917, 300
American Society for Municipal Improvements, 36
American Society of Landscape Architects, 40, 285
American Vitruvius: An Architect's Handbook of Civic Art, The (Hegemann and Peet), 298

Anti-Civic Center Association, Denver, 241–42
APOAA. *See* American Park and Outdoor Art Association.
Architectural League of America, 4, 49
Argus, Seattle, 166, 223–24
Armour, Simon B., Kansas City, 105
Arnold, Bion J., 217
Arnold, Henry, Denver, 242–44, 245
Art Commission, Denver, 174; and 1905 Report, 235; and MacMonnies Plan, 240; membership of, 174; powers of, 174; report of, on civic center, 235; report of, on smoke problem, 187; and Robinson, 188, 285; and Robert W. Speer, 176–78; and Welcome Arch, 177–78
Artist's Club, Denver, 172–73, 178–80, 235
Art Out-of-Doors, 36
Awakening of Harrisburg, The (McFarland), 52, 258–59
A-Y-P Exposition. *See* Alaska-Yukon-Pacific Exposition

Babcock, John R., Dallas, 260, 273
Bachman Lake Park, Dallas, 256
Badger, Reid, 64
Bailey, Liberty Hyde, 40, 78
Bailey Peninsula, Seattle, 149, 153, 167. *See also* Seward Park
"Ballard Bluff Park," Seattle, 161
Ballard district, Seattle, 161
Bannock Street, Denver, 240, 248
Bartholomew, Harland, 299
Bates, Dr. Mary E., Denver, 172
Bates Triangle, Denver, 249, 252
Beacon Hill Park, Seattle. *See* Jefferson Park
"Beautiful America" series, *Ladies' Home Journal*, 52

Beaux Arts. *See* Ecole des Beaux-Arts
Beman, Salon S., 55
Bender, Thomas, 12
Bennett, Edward H., Chicago, 281, 293; civic
    center plan of, 248–49, 249, 250, 251; and
    "Proctor's Bronco," 252; and solution of
    Bates triangle problem, Denver, 248, 252
Benton Boulevard, Kansas City, 210
Berkeley Lake Park, Denver, 181, 187
Birmingham, Alabama, 292
Bitter, Karl, 61
Blackwell, J. D., Seattle, 150
Blaine, Elbert F., Seattle, 149–50, 155
Blashfield, Edwin H., 61
Blumenson, John J.-G., 300
Board of Public Welfare, Kansas City, 210–11
Board of Public Works: Denver, 171, 175;
    Kansas City, 104, 106, 116, 197; Seattle,
    156–57, 163, 166
Bogue, Virgil, Seattle, 213, 217–18, 220
Bogue plans, Seattle, 213, 214, 222, 222, 223,
    225, 227–30, 230–32, 232
Bonfils, Frederick G., 123
Boston, Massachusetts, 58, 78
Boyer, Paul, 80, 282
Brace, Charles Loring, 11
Broadway, Dallas, 269
Broadway, Denver, 240
Brown, Lancelot "Capability," 18
Brunner, Arnold, 83, 90, 214–15, 288
Burling & Whitehouse, Chicago architectural
    firm, 55
Burnham, Daniel H., 3–4, 7, 34, 199, 288,
    289; Cleveland, group plan for, 91, 92–93,
    94; as director of World's Columbian
    Exposition, 54–57, 65; as McMillan Plan
    commissioner, 67–70; *Plan of Chicago*, 281–
    85, 300; San Francisco, plan for, 293
Busch, August A., 70, 268
business elite. *See* Dallas; Harrisburg; Kansas
    City

Campbell, Charles, Kansas City, 116, 123
Cannon, James S., Kansas City, 117
Capitol Park, Harrisburg, 128, 141
Cassatt, Mary, 58
Cavallo, Dominick, 80
"Central Avenue," Seattle, 221, 223
Central Improvement Association, Kansas
    City, 200–201
Central Improvement League, Dallas, 269
Central Labor Council, Seattle, 160, 217, 227
Central Park, New York, 23
Chamber of Commerce. *See under* Dallas;
    Denver; Seattle
Charities and the Commons, 285
Charlesbank, Boston, 284

charter amendments. *See under* Kansas City;
    Seattle
Chavannes, Puves de, 59
Cheesman, Walter S., Denver, 180–81
Cheesman Memorial, Denver, 181, 182, 185
Cheesman Park, Denver, 181, 187, 187, 241,
    242
Cherry Creek, Denver, 169, 175, 176, 187,
    188
Cherry Creek Boulevard, Denver. *See* Speer
    Boulevard
Chicago, 60, 66. *See also* World's Columbian
    Exposition
Chicago school, 295–96
Chicago World's Fair. *See* World's Columbian
    Exposition
Chittenden, Hiram M., Seattle, 226
CIL. *See* Civic Improvement League
CIS. *See* Civic Improvement Society
"citizen's association for the charter
    amendments," Kansas City, 116–17
City Beautiful movement, 4, 75–95, 281–305;
    advocates of, 75, 77; aesthetics of, 86–95;
    beauty as corrective in, 82, 301–2; belief in
    social control, 73, 80–81; citizen
    involvement in, 76–77, 285–86; civic
    centers in, 293–94; contributions of, 302–5;
    contributions of village improvement
    movement to, 50; and Country Life
    movement, 78; criticisms of, 285–90, 291;
    and Darwinism, 78–80, 81; decline of, 285–
    90; determinist view of, 75–77, 79; and
    efficiency, 83, 289; environmentalism of,
    73–85; experts in, 83; and Garden City
    movement, 78, 302; geographic distribution
    of, 291, 292; ideology of, 78–86; linked with
    World's Columbian Exposition, 53, 57, 61,
    62, 64–65, 70–71, 90–91; and McMillan
    Plan, 69, 303; Marxist evaluation of, 296–
    97; neoclassicism of, 87–90, 294; in New
    York City, 292–93; as planning movement,
    2; and playground movement, 81–82; as
    political movement, 1, 3; as reform
    movement, 30–32, 76–77; revival of interest
    in, 299–300; and skyscrapers, 296; as slogan,
    128; as solution to urban problems, 78–79,
    82–83; successes of, 21, 291–92; women's
    role in, 44–45, 75, 129, 135–36, 171, 302–
    3. *See also chapters on Dallas, Denver,
    Harrisburg, Kansas City, and Seattle*
City and County Building, Denver, 169, 252
City Ditch, Denver, 169
city functional, 3
City Park, Denver, 170, 178, 180, 185, 187,
    189, 304
City Park, Seattle. *See* Jefferson Park
City Park Esplanade, Denver, 181

City Plan and Improvement League (CPIL), Dallas, 260, 274. *See also* Manning, Warren H.

City Plan for Dallas, 257, 261–66, *262, 263, 264,* 268

city planning, 57, 60–65, 291. *See also chapters on Dallas, Denver, Harrisburg, Kansas City, and Seattle*

City Planning Progress in the United States: 1917, 284, 291

city practical, 2, 3, 278, 285

city scientific, 3

Civic Alliance, 40–41

Civic Center Commission, Denver, 245–47

Civic Center League, Denver, 241–42

civic centers, 92–94, 293–94; in Dallas, 265–66, 275; in Denver, 187, 234–53, *236, 239, 243, 245, 246, 247, 249, 250, 251;* in Kansas City, 202–4; in Seattle, 220–27, *222, 223, 225,* 230–32, *232*

Civic Club of Harrisburg, 44, 129, 135

Civic Federation of Denver, 171–72

Civic Improvement League (CIL), Dallas 257–58

Civic Improvement Society (CIS), Denver, 172–73

Civic Plans Investigation Committee (CPIC), Seattle, 224–26, 227

"Clean City Club," Denver, 172

Cleaner Dallas League, 257

Cleveland, Horace W. S., 9, 38

Cleveland (Ohio) Architectural Club, 61–62

Cliff Drive, Kansas City, 209

Cobb, Henry Ives, 55, 63

Codman, Henry Stuart, 33, 53

Cole, Thomas, 15

Colfax Avenue, Denver, 235

Colman Park, Seattle, 154, *164*

Colonnade of Civic Benefactors, Denver, 252, *253*

Commerce Street, Dallas, 256, 269

Commercial Club. *See* Kansas City; Seattle

Committee on Congestion of Population, 285, 286

Condon, George E., 300

Congress Park, Denver, 170, 180. *See also* Cheesman Park

Convention Hall, Kansas City, 202

Copeland, Robert Morris, 33

Copley Square, Boston, 58

Corrigan, Bernard, Kansas City, 120

Cotterill, George F., Seattle, 149, 227

Cowen Park, Seattle, 167

Cowtown 1890 Becomes City Beautiful 1962, 301

Cox, Kenyon, 61

CPIC. *See* Civic Plans Investigation Committee

CPIL. *See* City Plan and Improvement League

Craftsman, The, 94

Cravens, John K., Kansas City, 104

Crews, Nelson, Kansas City, 119

Croly, Herbert, 292

Dallas, 79, 254–78, 300–301; business elite involvement in planning in, 256–57, 272, 273, 275; chamber of commerce in, 260, 267, 268, 298; civic center in, 265–66, 275; comprehensive plan of, 261–66; *Dallas Metropolitan,* 269; development of parks and boulevards in, 256, *263, 264,* 274, 276; effectiveness of planning approach of, 257, 266–67, 275; Fair Park, 256–57; population growth of, 254, 275; and railroads, 255–56, *255;* street paving in, 255; and Trinity River flood, 254–55, 261

Dallas Metropolitan, 269

Dallas Morning News, 259–60, 265–66, 267. *See also* Dealey, George B.

Dallas Property Owners' Association (DPOA), 269–70

Dallas Union Station, 267–68, *268*

Daniel, L. O., Dallas, 260

Davis, Webster, Kansas City, 117

Dawson, James F., 218

Dealey, George B., Dallas, 258, 269, 270–72; and Dallas City Plan and Improvement League, 260; and Dallas Property Owner's Association, 269, 270; early improvement efforts of, 257–59; early life of, 257; and low-income housing, 273; and J. Horace McFarland, 257–58; relationship with George E. Kessler, 259, 265–66, 267, 273–74; support of, for Trinity levees, 261

Dealey Plaza, Dallas, 267

Death and Life of Great American Cities, The (Jacobs), 301

DeBoer, Saco Rienk, Denver, 176, 183–84, 187–88, 252–53

Denny Park, Seattle, 149

Denny regrade, Seattle, 220, 226

Denver, 168–89, 234–53; 1906 bond election in, 238; 1907 Civic Center plan of, 238–40, *239;* 1909 bond election in, 241–42; Bennett's civic center plan for, 248–52, *249, 250–51;* Board of Public Works in, 171, 175; building height limitations in, 173, 241, 301; chamber of commerce, role of, 172, 235; City Ditch, 169; civic center in, 187, 234–53, *236, 242, 243,* 252–53; and Denver Tramway, 171; development of park system of, 185, 242; early parks in, 170–73; fate of City Beautiful artifacts in, 252–53, 304–5; geographic problems of, 168–69; Kessler's plan for, 181; MacMonnies plan

Denver (cont.)
  for, 239, 240–44; mountain parks of, 184–
    85; Municipal Art League of, 172–73; park
    commission of, 171, 185; park boards of,
    242; park districts in, 174, 186; playgrounds
    in, 187; population growth in, 168;
    Robinson's plan for, 235–37, 236; women's
    efforts in, 171–73. See also Bennett, Edward
    H.; Speer, Robert W.
Denver Gas & Electric Co., 177
Denver mountain parks, 184–87
Denver Municipal Facts, 183, 242
Denver Tramway, 171
D. H. Burnham and Company, 199
Discovery Park, Seattle, 148, 154
Dock, Mira Lloyd, Harrisburg, 35, 44, 129,
    146; and Civic Club of Harrisburg, 129, 136;
    early life of, 129–30; as representative to
    International Congress of Women, 130;
    speeches of, on City Beautiful, 130–31,
    135–36; A Summer's Work Abroad, 130
Downing, Andrew Jackson, 9, 13–14, 16, 17
DPOA. See Dallas Property Owners'
    Association
Draper, Joan E., 293, 304
Dunn, Wilbur H., Kansas City, 208
Durand, Asher B., 15

East Park District, Denver, 237, 238
Eaton, Leonard K., 300
Ecole des Beaux Arts, Paris, 24, 59
Eliot, Charles, 9, 33
Eliot, Rev. Thomas L., 150
Elm Street, Dallas, 255, 269
Ervay Street, Dallas, 266
Evans, Anne, Denver, 177
Evans, John, Denver, 171
Evans, William Gray, Denver, 171

Fairmount Parkway, Philadelphia, 66, 292
Fair Park, Dallas, 256, 256–57
Federal Boulevard, Denver, 180, 187
Fillius, Jacob, Denver, 176
First National Conference on City Planning,
    288, 299. See also Olmsted, Frederick Law,
    Jr.
Flower, John S., Denver, 237–38
Ford, George B., 288, 299
Forestry and Artistic Improvement
    Association, Kansas City, 205
Franklin High School, Seattle, 163
Franklin Parkway. See Fairmount Parkway
French, Daniel Chester, 61, 63
Frink Park, Seattle, 165
Front Street, Harrisburg, 140
Fuertes, James H., 133–34, 273

Gage, Lyman H., 54
Garden and Forest, 35
Garden City movement, 78, 302
Gilbert, Cass, 287
Gill, Hiram C., Seattle, 227
Gillham, Robert, Kansas City, 116
Gillham Road, Kansas City, 203, 210
Gilpin, William, 15
Gladstone Boulevard, Kansas City, 211
Glass, William C., Kansas City, 105
Golden City, The (Reed), 299–300
Good, Jesse M., 44, 83
Gottlieb, Abram, 56
Gould, A. Warren, Seattle, 215–16, 231
Gourlay, Robert Fleming, 33
Grand Avenue Station, Kansas City, 196
Grant Park, Chicago, 281
Greek Theater, Denver, 252, 253
Green Lake, Seattle, 148, 154, 304
Greensboro, North Carolina, 291
Greensward plan of Olmsted and Vaux, 18–19
Griffin, Walter Burley, plan of Canberra, 296
Griffiths, Austin E., Seattle, 160
Grouping of Public Buildings, The (Municipal
    Art Society of Hartford), 92
Guerin, Jules, 305

Haff, Delbert J., Kansas City, 115–16, 204
Hammerslough, Louis, Kansas City, 105
Hannibal Bridge, Kansas City, 193
Harrisburg, 48, 126–46, 284; bond issues in,
    134, 136–39, 141; business elite support of
    city plan in, 132–34; city plan of, 132; fate
    of City Beautiful artifacts in, 301–4; growth
    of, 126, 139; and Harrisburg League for
    Municipal Improvements, 134–35;
    improvement campaign in, 128–39; Warren
    H. Manning in, 133–34, 139; park and
    boulevard map, 127; water filtration plant of,
    143; women's role in, 129, 135–36. See also
    Dock, Mira Lloyd; Fuertes, James H.;
    McFarland, J. Horace; Manning, Warren H.
Harrisburg League for Municipal Improvements
    (HLMI), 84, 129, 134–35. See also
    Harrisburg Municipal League
Harrisburg Municipal League, 141, 143
Harrisburg Telegraph, 131–32, 133
Harris' Ferry. See Harrisburg
Heckscher, August, 300
Hegemann, Werner, 298
Hiawatha Playfield, Seattle, 163
History of Denver (Smiley), 173
HLMI. See Harrisburg League for Municipal
    Improvements
Holden, L. E., 38–39
Holland, W. M., Dallas, 273

Holmes Square, Kansas City, 117
Home and Flowers, 44
Hopkins, Mary, 42
Horticulturalist and Journal of Rural Art and Rural Taste, The, 14
Houston and Texas Central Station, Dallas, 255, *255*, 266
Houston Street, Dallas, 267
Howe, Frederick C., 86, 184
Howe, Hoit, and Cutler, 199
Hunt, Jarvis, 199; and Dallas Union Station, 268; design for Kansas City Union Station, 199–200; and "Jarvis Hunt plan," 200; and Kansas City civic center plan, 203–4; plan of, for Main Street, Kansas City, 203; and World's Columbian Exposition, 199
Hunt, R. H., 117
Hunt, Richard Morris, 37, 55, 59, 61, 199
Huxtable, Ada Louise, 300
Hyde Park, Kansas City, 108

Identifying American Architecture (Blumenson), 300
Improvement of Towns and Cities; or, the Practical Basis of Civic Aesthetics, The (Robinson), 45, 46–47, 94
Industrial Council, Kansas City, 117, 122
Inspiration Point, Denver, 181–83, 185, 187
Interlaken Boulevard, Seattle, 165
Island Park, Harrisburg, 139

Jackson Park, Chicago, 23, 54, 56, 281
Jacobs, Jane, 301
Jefferson Park, Seattle, 154, 233
Jenny, William LeBaron, 61
Jenny & Mundie, 55
Jones, Percy R., 150, 151

Kahn, Judd, 293
Kansas City, 79, 99–125, 193–212; 1875 charter, 102–4; 1889 charter amendment, 104; 1893 park and boulevard report, 84, 100, 108; 1895 charter amendment, 112–18; 1903 park bond election, 207–8; 1905 charter, 208; 1908 charter, 208; 1910 park bond election, 208; boulevards, 110–11, 119; business elite in, 99; civic center plans for, 201, 202–4; Commercial Club in, 111, 115, 117, 122, 195, 204, 207; comparisons of, with Chicago, 102–3; Cravens law, 104; fate of City Beautiful artifacts in, 301, 304; growth of, 99; and Hannibal Bridge, 193; Municipal Improvement Association, 104–5; neighborhood improvement associations in, 119; North Terrace Park, 111, 121, 123, 209, *209*; parks and boulevards of, 100, 104,

105, *112*, *113*, *114*, 208–11; Penn Valley Park (Penn Street Ravine), 212; and railroads, 143–44; Swope Park, 118–19; Taxpayer's League, 120; Union Depot, 194, 196; Union Terminal complex removal, 194; west bluff problem, 110; West Terrace Park, 121, 123, 210. *See also* Kansas City Union Station
Kansas City Art Commission, 211
Kansas City Belt Railway Company, 196, 197. *See also* Kansas City Terminal Railway Company
Kansas City Journal, 202, 211
Kansas City Star: campaign of, for smoke abatement, 211; and civic center support, 203, 204; "good roads" campaign of, 102–3; improvement campaign techniques of, 102–3, 121–22; and parks and boulevards campaign, 102; and Taxpayer's League, 120–22; and union station, 195–96. *See also* Nelson, William R.
Kansas City Terminal Railway Company, 197, 198
Kansas City Union Station, 193, 205; 1878 Union Station, 194–95; 1903 flood, 196; charter amendment, 197–98; civic center, 201–4; Hunt's plans for, 199–200; opening of, 201, 205, 206, *207*; siting of, 198; terminal removal, 193, 194–99. *See also* Central Improvement Association
Kansas River, 99, 194, 196
Kaw River. *See* Kansas River
Kelsey, Albert, 49, 50
Kent, William, 18
Kessler, George E., *107*, 259; 1893 Kansas City park board report, 100, 108–12, 284; collaboration with George B. Dealey, 265–66, 267; collaboration with Robert W. Speer, 181; and Dallas, 260–66, *262*, *263*, 264, 269, 273–74; and Denver, 181; development of Hyde Park, 106; early life of, 100, 106–8; and Kansas City, *112*, *113*, *114*, 208–10, 211; Kansas City civic center plan of, 203–4; and playgrounds, 210, 265; removal of Pacific Avenue, Dallas, tracks, 265, 266; and John E. Surratt, 270–71
Kessler Plan Association (KPA), Dallas, 270, 271–73, 275, 276
Kidney, Walter C., *The Architecture of Choice*, 300
Kimball, Justin F., 272, 276
Kinnear park, Seattle, 149, 154
"Kipona," Reservoir Park, Harrisburg, 146
Kirkham, Guy, 78
KPA. *See* Kessler Plan Association
Kriehn, George, 39

Lake Cliff Park, Dallas, 301
Lake Union, Seattle, 148–49, 154, 159
Lake Washington, Seattle, 148, 149, 154
Lake Washington Boulevard, 284
Land of Enchantment, The, 187
Laurel Hill Association, 42–43
Leschi Park, Seattle, 154
Lewis, Nelson P., 298
Liberty Memorial, Kansas City, 204
Lighthouse Point, Seattle. *See* Discovery Park
Lincoln Park, Seattle, 162
Lindsley, Henry D., Dallas, 273
Linwood boulevard, Kansas City, 210
Little, Frank N., Seattle, 150
Lorrain, Claude, 15
Louisiana Purchase Exposition, St. Louis, 45, 49, 50
Lover's Lane, Dallas, 262
Low, Seth, 293
Low, Will H., 61
Lowell, Massachusetts, 12–13

McCall, Mrs. Louis Marion, 49
McCormick, Cyrus W., 54
McCormick, Vance C., Harrisburg, 132
McDonough, John, Denver, 130, 181–83
McFarland, J. Horace, Harrisburg, 83, 86, 87, 130, 301–2; and *The Awakening of Harrisburg,* 52, 258–59; and "Beautiful America" series, 52; and billboards, 143; "Crusade Against Ugliness," 51; and Dallas, 258, 260; and Denver, 187; as feminist, 50; and functional aesthetics, 288; and Harrisburg, 133, 136, 139–45; and Harrisburg park commission, 142; and "meddling," 145; as national spokesman for City Beautiful, 51, 129; as president of the ACA, 50–52; as president of ALCI, 49
McKim, Charles F., 58, 67, 88–89, 293
McKim, Mead & White, 58, 61
McMillan, James, 67
McMillan Commission, 67–70, 73, 151
McMillan Plan, 65, 67–70
MacMonnes, Frederick, 61–62, 240–44
MacMonnies, Mary, 58
Madison Park, Seattle, 149
Magnolia Hill, Seattle, 154, 161
Main Street, Dallas, 256, 267, 269
Manning, Warren H., 33, 36, 130, 133–34, 146, 284, 293
Manual of the Plan of Chicago (Wacker's Manual), 272
Marsalis Park, Dallas, 276
Marsh, Benjamin C., 286, 287
MDA. *See* Metropolitan Development Association

Mead, Mrs. Edwin D., 64
Metropolitan Development Association (MDA), Dallas, 269
Meyer, August R., Kansas City, 104–5, 106; 1893 Kansas City Park and boulevard report, 108–12; and American Park and Outdoor Art Association, 40; and boulevards, 110–11; early life of, 105; and parks as social control, 109; as president of Kansas City park board, 208; as president of Municipal Improvement Association, 104; as president of park board, 104–5, 106, 122–23
Meyer Boulevard, Kansas City, 210
Michigan Avenue, Chicago, 281
Mill Creek, Dallas, 265, 273, 301
Millet, Francis D., 56
Missouri-Kansas-Texas Station, Dallas, 255
Modern Civic Art, or the City Made Beautiful (Robinson), 38, 71–74, 90–91, 94
Monaco Street Parkway, Denver, 187
Montview Boulevard, Denver, 180
Moody, Walter D., 272
Mould, Jacob Wrey, 24
mountain parks system, Denver, 184–87
MPC. *See* Municipal Plans Commission
MPL. *See* Municipal Plans League
Mumford, Louis, 299, 300
Municipal Affairs, 64–65, 66, 91, 297
Municipal Art League, Denver, 172–73, 174, 234–35
Municipal Art Society, Hartford, Connecticut, 92
Municipal Art Society, New York, 37, 61, 65
Municipal Improvement Association, Kansas City, 104, 211
Municipal League, Seattle, 221, 228, 229, 231
Municipal League News, Seattle, 222
Municipal Plans Commission (MPC), Seattle, 217, 220, 221
Municipal Plans League (MPL), Seattle, 216, 217, 221, 232

National League of Improvement Associations. *See* American League for Civic Improvement
National Municipal League, 35, 285
National Playground Association of America, 50, 82, 285
Nelson, William Rockhill, Kansas City, 101; contributions of, to park and boulevard campaign, 101, 212; early life of, 100–101; and Kansas City Civic Center, 203; and *Kansas City Star,* 101–103; *See also* Kansas City Star
Nolen, John, 87, 290
North End Improvement Club, Seattle, 221
Northrup, Birdsey Grant, 43

North Terrace Park, Kansas City, 111, 121,
    123, 209
Norton, Charles D., 84

Oak Cliff, Dallas, 262, 265, 301
Ohage, Justus, 49
O.K. Creek, Kansas City, 197, 198
Olmsted, Frederick Law, Sr., 9–34, 63;
    admiration of, for English parks, 14, 16, 18;
    Boston parks of, 23, 26, 31; and Central
    Park, 11, 19, 23, 24, 25–26; consulting
    practice of, 33; contributions of, to City
    Beautiful Movement, 10, 18, 22–23, 99;
    design for Wooded Island, World's
    Columbian Exposition, 22, 23; early life of,
    10–15; economic argument of, for parks,
    29–31; *Greensward* plan of, 18–19;
    intellectual legacy of, 29–33; Jackson Park,
    Chicago, 23; in Kansas City, 109–10; and
    natural landscape preservation, 16; planning
    contributions of, 10; plan of, for Prospect
    Park, Brooklyn, 26, 27–29, 30; plan of, for
    San Francisco, 26–27, 29; "Public Parks and
    the Enlargement of Towns," 19–21; social
    utility of parks, 31–32; and South Park,
    Buffalo, 23; view of, regarding cities, 19–21,
    32; and Stanford White, 22, 23; work of, on
    Sanitary Commission, 11; and World's
    Columbian Exposition, 53–54
Olmsted, Frederick Law, Jr., 288–89; civic
    center designs, 246, 247; and Denver, 176,
    184–85, 244–45; and McMillan
    Commission, 67, 151; and mountain parks,
    185; on native trees, 185; and planning in
    Seattle, 150; speech of, at Second National
    Conference on City Planning, 39, 290
Olmsted, John C., 149, 150, 151–56, 162,
    245, 289; 1903 report of (Seattle), 153–56;
    1908 report of (Seattle), 161; 1910 report of
    (Seattle), 162–63; and APOAA, 36; class
    bias of, 155; compromise plan of, for Seattle,
    155–56; and Interlaken Boulevard, 165; and
    impressions of Seattle, 151, 164, 165–66;
    and Eugene O. Schwagerl, 149; and
    Reginald Thomson, 218–19
Olmsted Brothers, 149, 150, 213
Omaha, Nebraska, 61, 79
Open Spaces: The Life of American Cities
    (Heckscher), 300
Our City—Dallas: A Community Civics
    (Kimball), 272, 276

Pacific Avenue, Dallas, 255–56, 265–66, 268–
    69, 270, 277
Pan-American Exposition, Buffalo, 44, 90–91
Parade, The, Kansas City, 111, 210

Paris Universal Exposition of 1889, 90
Park and Cemetery and Landscape Gardening, 35
Parker, George A., 39, 78, 92, 163
Parsons, John, Denver, 178
Paseo, The, Kansas City, 111, 124, 125, 210
Patterson, John H., 78
Patterson, Thomas M., Denver, 181
Paxtang Park, Harrisburg, 128
Paxton Creek, Harrisburg, 126, 136, 144
Peabody & Sterns, 55
Peet, Elbert, 298
Pendergast, James, Kansas City, 111, 116–17,
    198–99
Pendergast, Thomas, Kansas City, 199
Pennsylvania Canal Company, 136
Penn Valley Park, Kansas City, 111, 122, 123,
    197, 208–9, 210
Phillips, Paul B., Seattle, 222–23
P-I. See Seattle Post-Intelligencer
Pioneer Monument, Denver, 240, 248, 304
Plan of Chicago (Burnham), 217, 305; analysis
    of, 281–85; building height limitations of,
    282–83; Burnham's intentions in, 282; civic
    center plans in, 282; slum housing solutions
    of, 283–84
Plan of Seattle (Bogue), 213. *See also* Bogue
    plans
playground movement, 38, 81–82, 160. *See
    also* Kessler, George E.; National Playground
    Association of America; Olmsted, John C.
Pope, Robert Anderson, 286–87
Port of Seattle, 229
Post, George B., 55, 61
Pratt, Mrs. Robert, 38
Pretyman, William, 56
Price, Sir Uvedale, 15
Proctor's Bronco, Denver, 252, 253
progressive movement, 41
Property Owners' Association, Denver, 237
Prospect Park, Brooklyn, 109

Queen Anne Hill, Seattle, 154

railroads. *See* Dallas; Kansas City; Seattle
"Rainier Heights Landslide Section," Seattle,
    154
Ravenna Improvement Club, Seattle, 166
Ravenna Park, Seattle, 153, 154, 166–67, 232
Read, Henry, Denver, 177
Real Estate Exchange, Denver, 173, 237
Reed, Henry Hope, Jr., 299–300
Reform Club, New York City, 64–65
*Report of the New York City Improvement
    Commission*, 4, 292
Repton, Humphrey, 18
Reservoir Park, Harrisburg, 128, 142

Reverchon Park, Dallas, 276
Reynders, John V. W., Harrisburg, 133
Richardson, Henry Hobson, 88
River Front Park, Harrisburg, 139, 284
Roanoke Park, Kansas City, 210
Robbins, Mary Caroline, 44
Robinson, Charles Mulford, 287–88;
    acceptance of, of city, 47, 85; and APOAA,
    40–41; and Denver, 87, 180; early life of,
    45–46; *Improvement of Towns and Cities*, 45,
    46–47, 94; *Modern Civic Art, or, The City
    Made Beautiful*, 38, 71, 84–85, 91–92, 94;
    plan of, for Denver, 235–37; plan of, for
    Denver civic center, 235–38, 237; plan of,
    for Greensboro, North Carolina, 291; plan
    of, for Raleigh, North Carolina, 87, 291
Rochester, New York, 79
Rockhill Road, Kansas City, 210
Rocky Mountain Lake, Denver, 181
Rocky Mountain News, Denver, 181
Root, John Wellborn, 53, 54, 55–56
Rosa, Salvatore, 15
Ross, Edward A., 81

Saint-Gaudens, Augustus, 56, 59, 67
Saint-Gaudens, Luis, 59, 61, 67
St. Louis World's Fair. *See* Louisiana Purchase
    Exposition
St. Paul Street, Dallas, 269
Salmon Bay, Seattle, 148
Sand Point Park, Seattle. *See* Warren G.
    Magnusson Park
San Francisco, 3–4, 26–27, 29, 293
Sanger, Charles L., Dallas, 269
Sargent, Charles S., 35
Sargent, Irene, 94–95
Sargent, John Singer, 59
Saunders, Charles W., Seattle, 157
Schmitz Park, Seattle, 148
Schuyler, David, 10
Schwab, Charles H., 54
Schwagerl, Eugene O., Seattle, 148–50
Scully, Vincent, 300
Seattle, 147–67, 213–33; 1903 park and
    boulevard plan, 153–56; 1904 charter
    amendment election, 157–60; 1906 bond
    issue, 160; 1908 bond issue, 160; 1910 bond
    issue, 216–17; Bogue plan of, 213, 222, 225,
    227–32; boulevards in, 148, 149, 232–33;
    civic center of, 230–32; Commercial Club
    of, 163, 215–16; Federation of Women's
    Clubs of, 166; neighborhood improvement
    clubs in, 150; and Olmsted Brothers, 150,
    152; Olmsted's plan for, 151–56; park board
    in, 156, 166; "park committee," 156; parks,
    149; playgrounds in, 160; population growth
    in, 147; role of chamber of commerce in,

216; Schwagerl's plan for, 148–50;
    topographical situation of, 153. *See also*
    Municipal Plans League; Olmsted, John C.;
    Thomson, Reginald H.
Seattle Argus. See Argus
Seattle Central Labor Council. *See* Central
    Labor Council
Seattle Civic Center Association, 230
Seattle Federation of Women's Clubs, 166
Seattle Park Board, 156–57
Seattle Playgrounds Association, 160
Seattle Post-Intelligencer, 157, 163
Seattle Real Estate Association, 160
Seattle Times, 226
Seattle Union Record, 230
Seward Park, Seattle, 148, 232
Shannon, Joseph B., Kansas City, 117
Shaw, Albert, 85–86
Shelley Park, Kansas City, 210
Sheridan, Lawrence V., Dallas, 269
Sherred, M. R., 133–34
Shippen, Joseph, Seattle, 150
Shuey, Edwin L., 38, 80
Simmons, Edward G., 61
"Skyscraper Bill," Denver, 241
Smiley, Jerome C., 173
Social Control (Ross), 81
Southeast Improvement Association, Kansas
    City, 205–6
South Platte River, Denver, 169
Speer, Robert W., Denver, 169–70, 170, 173–
    76, 187–89, 284; and 1903 home-rule
    charter election, 173–74; and 1904 charter
    election, 174; 1907 address to businessman's
    banquet, 180; and Art Commission, 176–77;
    as boss-broker, 175–76; and civic center,
    235, 237, 238–40, 239, 241–42, 247–48;
    collaboration with Bennett, 248–51; early
    life of, 174–75; European trip of, 184;
    purchase of Inspiration Point, 181–83; and
    "Skyscraper Bill," 241; speech to Artist's
    Club, 178–80; support of, of City Beautiful
    movement, 170, 178–80; tree planting
    campaign, 183–84
Speer Boulevard, Denver, 180, 187
Spring Valley Park, Kansas City, 209
Star. See Kansas City Star
Station Park, Kansas City, 201, 202, 204
Steffens, Lincoln, 184
Sticks and Stones (Mumford), 299
Stokes, J. G. Phelps, 93
Stone Avenue, Seattle, 218
Sullivan, Louis, 56, 63, 199, 295–96
Surratt, John E., Dallas, 270–72, 275
Susquehanna River, Harrisburg, 131
Swope, Thomas H., Kansas City, 118–19,
    121–22

Swope Park, Kansas City, 118–19, 209, 210
Syracuse Boulevard, Denver, 187

Taft, Lorenzo, 61
Tarsney Act, 68
Tate, J. Waddy, Dallas, 276
Taxpayer's League, Kansas City, 120, 121, 123
Taylor, M. Harvey, Harrisburg, 145
Terrace, The, Kansas City, 124
Texas and Pacific Railway, Dallas, 256
Texas Town and City Planning Association, 270–71
Thirty-First and Main Street Improvement Association, Kansas City, 204
Thompson, John W., Seattle, 163
Thomson, Reginald H., Seattle, 157, 163, 217–19; and Virgil Bogue, 218, 219, 226; charter amendment opposition of, 219; early life of, 217; and John C. Olmsted, 218–19
Trans-Mississippi and International Exposition of 1898, Omaha, 61
Trinity River, Dallas, 254–55, 261–62, 272, 276. See also Kessler, George E.
Tunnard, Christopher, The City of Man, 299
Turtle Creek, Dallas, 265, 300–301, 304

Ulrickson plan, Dallas, 272
Union Avenue, Kansas City, 194–99
Union Depot, Kansas City, 194, 196
Union Depot Company, Kansas City, 194–97, 200. See also Kansas City Terminal Railway Company
union station in City Beautiful ideology and aesthetics. See Dallas Union Station; Kansas City Union Station
Union Terminal Company, Dallas, 267. See also Dallas Union Station
University of Washington, Seattle, 149, 153

Van Brunt, Adriance, Kansas City, 105
Van Brunt and Howe, 55
Van Brunt Boulevard, Kansas City, 210
Van Leyen, Edward C., 40
Van Rensselaer, Mrs. Schuyler (Marianna Griswold), 35, 36, 40
Vaux, Calvert, 10, 11, 18, 24
village improvement, 41–44, 50, 65
Volunteer Park, Seattle, 149, 154, 155, 158, 159, 164
Voorhies Memorial, Denver, 252

Waring, George E., Jr., 19
Warner, John DeWitt, 91
Warren G. Magnusson Park, Seattle, 148
Washington, D.C., 37–38, 48, 50, 66–69
Washington Park, Denver, 171, 180, 304
Washington Park, Seattle, 149, 153, 164, 168
Washington Park Boulevard, Seattle, 153
Way, Eugene, Seattle, 167
Welcome Arch, Denver, 177–78
West Dallas, Dallas, 262, 265
West point, Seattle. See Discovery Park
West Seattle, 161, 162, 167
West Terrace Park, Kansas City, 121, 123, 210
Wetzel's Swamp, Harrisburg, 121, 128, 134. See also Wildwood Park
White, Stanford, 87
"White City." See World's Columbian Exposition
White Rock Lake, Dallas, 304
Whiting, Lillian, The Land of Enchantment, 187
Wildwood Park, Harrisburg, 139, 305
Wilkinson, Miss F. R., 129–30
Wilson, Richard Guy, 300
Women's Civic League, St. Paul, 44
Women's Club of Denver, 171, 172
Women's Club of Raleigh, 291
women's movement, 43, 44; in Denver, 171–73; in Harrisburg, 129–32; involvement of, in City Beautiful, 44, 57–58
Wooded Island, World's Columbian Exposition, 22, 23
Woodland Park, Seattle, 148, 149, 154, 164, 167
Woodruff, Clinton Rogers, 40–41, 49
Wood Street, Dallas, 267
Workingmen's League, Seattle, 217
World's Columbian Exposition, 48, 53–74; American quality of, 62–63; attendance figures of, 64; background of, 53; design of, 56, 57; as example of civic improvement, 48, 57; influence of, on city planning, 60–61, 62, 65, 66; and neoclassical style, 56, 58; and women's movement, 57–58
World's Fair. See World's Columbian Exposition

Young Street, Dallas, 267

Zueblin, Charles, 45, 48, 65, 70, 92

ABOUT THE AUTHOR

William H. Wilson is professor of history
at the University of North Texas.

He is the author of
The City Beautiful Movement in Kansas City,
Coming of Age: Urban America, 1915–1945, and
Railroad in the Clouds: The Alaska Railroad in the Age of Steam.

The City Beautiful Movement

Designed by Ann Walston

Composed by The Composing Room of Michigan, Inc.,
in Goudy Old Style text and display type

Printed by The Maple Press Company
on 60-lb. Glatfelter Eggshell Offset